Budget 2006

A strong and strengthening economy:

Investing in Britain's future

Economic and Fiscal Strategy Report and Financial Statement and Budget Report

March 2006

Return to an Order of the House of Commons dated 22 March 2006

Copy of Economic and Fiscal Strategy Report and Financial Statement and Budget Report – March 2006 as laid before the House of Commons by the Chancellor of the Exchequer when opening the Budget.

John Healey
Her Majesty's Treasury
22 March 2006

Ordered by the House of Commons to be printed 22 March 2006

HC 968   LONDON: The Stationery Office   £45.00

HM Treasury contacts

This report can be found on the Treasury website at:

hm-treasury.gov.uk

For general enquiries about HM Treasury and its work, contact:

Correspondence and Enquiry Unit
HM Treasury
1 Horse Guards Road
London
SW1A 2HQ

Tel: 020 7270 4558
Fax: 020 7270 4861
E-mail: public.enquiries@hm-treasury.gov.uk

This and other government documents can be found on the Internet at:

www.official-documents.co.uk

ISBN-10: 0-10-293731-1
ISBN-13: 978-0-10-293731-2

The Economic and Fiscal Strategy Report and the Financial Statement and Budget Report contain the Government's assessment of the medium-term economic and budgetary position. They set out the Government's tax and spending plans, including those for public investment, in the context of its overall approach to social, economic and environmental objectives. After approval for the purposes of Section 5 of the European Communities (Amendment) Act 1993, these reports will form the basis of submissions to the European Commission under Article 99 (ex Article 103) and Article 104 (ex Article 104c) of the Treaty establishing the European Community.

CONTENTS

Economic and Fiscal Strategy Report

OVERVIEW

The Government's economic objective is to build a strong economy and a fair society, where there is opportunity and security for all. Budget 2006, *A strong and strengthening economy: Investing in Britain's future*, presents updated assessments and forecasts of the economy and public finances, and reports on how the Government's policies are helping to deliver its long-term goals. The Budget:

- shows that the economy is stable and growing and that the Government is meeting its strict fiscal rules for the public finances;

- announces further measures to help families and children, including a commitment to increase the child element of the Child Tax Credit in line with average earnings to the end of this Parliament;

- announces that the payments into Child Trust Fund accounts at age 7 will be £250 for all children, with £500 for children from lower-income families;

- takes further steps to extend employment opportunity for all, through measures which focus help and support on those who face the greatest barriers to work;

- announces that from April 2008 every pensioner and disabled person will have free off-peak national bus travel in England;

- announces £585 million of additional resources over 2006-07 and 2007-08 to provide further support for personalised learning in schools in England;

- announces further measures to boost productivity and growth, to build on the UK's position as a leading location for inward investment, advance the science and innovation ten-year framework, and to reduce further the burden of regulation on business;

- provides £100 million to accelerate the recruitment of Police Community Support Officers;

- commits funding, in partnership with commercial sponsorship, to support the most talented British athletes to prepare for the 2012 Olympics;

- takes steps to tackle the global challenge of climate change, including reforms to vehicle excise duty and measures to encourage energy efficiency in the household and business sectors;

- introduces measures to modernise the tax system, and to tackle tax fraud and avoidance; and

- defers the inflation-based increase in main road fuel duties to 1 September 2006.

1.1 The Government's economic objective is to build a strong economy and a fair society, where there is opportunity and security for all.

1.2 The long-term decisions the Government has taken – giving independence to the Bank of England, new fiscal rules and a reduction in debt – have created a strong platform of economic stability. In recent years, the international economy has been affected by geopolitical uncertainty, rising oil prices, and large current account imbalances and shifting exchange rates between the US, Asia and Europe. In the UK, with low and stable inflation, interest rates set by the Monetary Policy Committee to meet the Government's symmetric inflation target, and fiscal policy supporting monetary policy over the cycle, the economy has grown continuously throughout this period. The UK economy is currently experiencing its longest unbroken expansion since quarterly records began, with GDP now having grown for 54 consecutive quarters.

Meeting long-term global challenges **1.3**   The global economy is undergoing a major transformation, with far-reaching and fundamental changes in technology, production and trading patterns. Faster information flows and falling transport costs are breaking geographical barriers to economic activity. The boundary between what can and cannot be traded is being steadily eroded, and the global market is encompassing ever-greater numbers of goods and services. This fast pace of change, combined with emergence of rapidly industrialising economies such as China and India and their integration into the global economy, presents new opportunities for the UK as well as new challenges. The increasing demands placed on the world's resources and environment also heightens the need to tackle the global challenge of climate change.

1.4   A more integrated global economy increases the speed and magnitude with which global shocks and imbalances can affect the UK. The UK's strong macroeconomic framework has helped to underpin increased stability compared to earlier decades, and put the UK in a strong position to resist the inflationary pressure bought by recent sustained increases in oil prices. The UK has been experiencing an unprecedented period of economic stability since 1997, with volatility at historically low levels and now the lowest in the G7. Economic stability provides the platform for building prosperity, achieving social justice with security and opportunity for all, and maintaining investment in public services. Stability allows businesses, individuals and the Government to plan more effectively for the long term, improving the quantity and quality of investment and helping to raise productivity.

1.5   The Government is committed to locking in stability and investing in the UK's future, enabling it to meet the challenges and rise to the opportunities of the global economy. To respond to these global challenges, this Budget sets out further reforms to reduce the regulatory burden on business; to create a world-class environment for scientific research and development; to improve the skills of the nation; to lock in the UK's track record of attracting high levels of inward investment; and to tackle the global challenges of climate change.

1.6   Fairness must go alongside flexibility, providing security and support for those that need it and ensuring that everyone has the opportunity to fulfil their potential. The reforms of the welfare state introduced since 1997 reflect the Government's aims of eradicating child poverty, supporting families to balance their work and family life, promoting saving, and ensuring security for all in old age. The Government is also committed to a modern and fair tax system which encourages work and saving, and ensures that everyone pays their fair share of tax. The Budget announces further measures to help support families, children and pensioners, and to promote employment opportunity for all.

1.7   This Budget describes the next steps the Government is taking to enhance its long term goals of:

- **maintaining macroeconomic stability,** ensuring the fiscal rules are met and that inflation remains low;

- **raising the sustainable rate of productivity growth,** through reforms that promote enterprise and competition, enhance flexibility and promote science, innovation and skills;

- **providing employment opportunity for all,** by promoting a flexible labour market which sustains a higher proportion of people in employment than ever before;

- **ensuring fairness,** by providing security for people when they need it, tackling child and pensioner poverty, providing opportunity for all children and young people and delivering security for all in retirement;

- **delivering world-class public services,** with extra investment alongside efficiency, reform and results; and

- **addressing environmental challenges,** such as climate change and the need for energy efficiency in response to rising oil prices.

MAINTAINING MACROECONOMIC STABILITY

1.8   The Government's long-term economic goal is to maintain macroeconomic stability, ensuring the fiscal rules are met at all times and that inflation remains low. Chapter 2 describes how the Government is working to achieve this goal and summarises prospects for the UK economy and public finances, full details of which are set out in Chapters B and C of the *Financial Statement and Budget Report (FSBR)*.

The policy 1.9   The Government's macroeconomic framework is based on the principles of
framework transparency, responsibility and accountability, and is designed to ensure lasting stability so that businesses, individuals and the Government can plan effectively for the long term. The Bank of England has operational independence to meet the Government's symmetrical inflation target. Fiscal policy is underpinned by clear objectives and two strict rules which ensure sound public finances over the medium term. The fiscal rules underpin the Government's public spending framework which facilitates long-term planning and provides departments with the flexibility and incentives they need to increase the quality of public services and deliver specified outcomes.

Economic 1.10   The UK economy is currently experiencing its longest unbroken expansion on record,
prospects with GDP now having grown for 54 consecutive quarters. The domestic stability delivered by the Government's macroeconomic framework, with volatility in the UK economy at historically low levels and the lowest in the G7, puts the UK in a strong position to respond to the global economic challenges of the next decade.

1.11   Overall economic developments since the 2005 Pre-Budget Report have been as forecast. Economic growth has gradually increased momentum through the latter stages of 2005 and into 2006. With the outturn for 2005 and the forecast for 2006 as expected at the time of the Pre-Budget Report, the UK economy remains well placed for a pick-up in growth to above trend rates later this year and into 2007, supported by the continuing domestic stability delivered by the Government's macroeconomic framework. Overall, the Budget forecast is as set out in the 2005 Pre-Budget Report. GDP is forecast to grow by 2 to $2^{1}/_{2}$ per cent in 2006, rising to above-trend rates of $2^{3}/_{4}$ to $3^{1}/_{4}$ per cent in both 2007 and 2008.

The public 1.12   The Budget 2006 projections for the public finances are broadly in line with the 2005
finances Pre-Budget Report and show that the Government is meeting its strict fiscal rules:

- the current budget shows an average surplus as a percentage of GDP over the current economic cycle, even using cautious assumptions, ensuring the Government is meeting the golden rule. Beyond the end of the current cycle, the current budget moves clearly into surplus including, by the end of the projection period, the cyclically-adjusted current budget in the cautious case; and

- public sector net debt is projected to remain low and stable over the forecast period, stabilising at a level below the 40 per cent ceiling set in the sustainable investment rule.

Table 1.1: Meeting the fiscal rules

	Outturn	Estimate	Projections				
	2004-05	2005-06	2006-07	2007-08	2008-09	2009-10	2010-11
Golden rule							
Surplus on current budget	−1.6	−0.9	−0.6	0.1	0.5	0.7	0.8
Average surplus since 1997-1998	0.2	0.1	0.0	0.0	0.1	0.1	0.2
Cyclically-adjusted surplus on current budget	−1.3	−0.3	0.4	0.7	0.7	0.7	0.8
Sustainable investment rule							
Public sector net debt[1]	35.0	36.4	37.5	38.1	38.3	38.4	38.4

Per cent of GDP

[1] Debt at end March; GDP centred on end March.

Budget policy decisions 1.13 Against this backdrop, and building on steps already taken, Budget 2006 announces further decisions to lock in stability and invest in the UK's future, including:

- a commitment to increase the child element of the Child Tax Credit in line with average earnings to the end of this Parliament;

- that the further payments into Child Trust Fund accounts at age 7 will be £250 for all children, with £500 for children from lower-income families;

- £585 million of additional resources over 2006-07 and 2007-08 to provide further support for personalised learning in schools in England;

- an increase in the stamp duty land tax threshold to £125,000, exempting an additional 40,000 home buyers each year;

- the introduction of Real Estate Investments Trusts to create greater flexibility for investors;

- measures to modernise the tax system, and to tackle tax fraud and avoidance; and

- the deferral of the inflation-based increase in main road fuel duties to 1 September 2006, in response to sustained volatility in oil prices.

1.14 Consistent with the requirements of the *Code for Fiscal Stability*, the updated public finance projections in Budget 2006 take into account the fiscal effects of these and all other firm decisions announced in the Budget. The fiscal impact of Budget policy decisions is set out in Table 1.2. Full details are provided in Chapter A of the FSBR.

1.15 An updated analysis of long-term fiscal sustainability was published alongside the 2005 Pre-Budget Report in the *2005 Long-term public finance report*, and is updated in Annex A of the Economic and Fiscal Strategy Report. Using a range of sustainability indicators, this shows that the public finances are sustainable in the longer term, and that the UK is well placed relative to many other countries to face the challenges of an ageing population.

MEETING THE PRODUCTIVITY CHALLENGE

1.16 Productivity growth, alongside high and stable levels of employment, is central to long-term economic performance. In the increasingly knowledge-driven global economy, science, innovation and creativity are important drivers of productivity growth, backed up by a highly skilled workforce and a competitive and enterprising economy. The UK has historically experienced comparatively low rates of productivity growth. However, as set out in *Productivity and the UK 6: Progress and New Evidence,* published alongside this Budget, UK performance has improved in relation to other major economies in recent years. The Government's long term goal is for the UK to continue to close the productivity gap by achieving a faster rate of growth than its main competitors.

Action so far 1.17   The Government's strategy focuses on five key drivers of productivity performance:

- **improving competition** which promotes flexible markets and increases business efficiency and consumer choice;

- **promoting enterprise,** including through reducing the regulatory burden on business, to ensure that UK firms are well-placed to respond to opportunities in a rapidly changing global market;

- **supporting science and innovation** which is central to success in the international economy, as global restructuring focuses developed economies toward knowledge-based and high value-added sectors;

- **raising UK skills** to create a more flexible and productive workforce, and to meet the long-term challenge of rising skills levels in emerging markets; and

- **encouraging investment** to increase the stock of physical capital supported by stronger, more efficient capital markets. In the global economy, attracting international capital and investment will require macroeconomic stability and a robust and efficient investment environment.

Next steps 1.18   Building on the reforms and initiatives already introduced, Budget 2006 sets out the next steps the Government is taking to strengthen the drivers of productivity growth and meet the long-term challenges of the global economy, including:

- **advancing the goals of the ten-year Science and Innovation Investment framework to maximise the impact of science funding,** including an intention to create a single health research fund of at least £1 billion per year, to simplify radically institutional research funding, to expand R&D support to mid-sized companies and introduce a package of measures to improve science teaching, raise the quality of science lessons and entitle able pupils to study three separate sciences at GCSE;

- **measures to reduce further burdens on business,** including new commitments to reduce the administrative burden of the tax system, introducing the Hampton Review's principles into law, and a review of how the experiences of large business can be taken into account in administering the tax system;

- **a comprehensive package of measures further to enhance the UK's position as a leading location for inward investment,** developing an ambitious strategy for marketing the UK;

  - **promoting London as the world's leading international centre for financial and business services,** with a new strategy to be developed and implemented by a high-level group representing the City's key interests by summer 2006;

  - **establishing a new International Business Advisory Council** comprising some of the world's foremost business people;

- a programme of organisational changes to UK Trade and Investment with the aim of a fundamental transformation of its effectiveness in marketing the UK;

- strengthening the UK's reputation as one of the world's best locations for higher education, by boosting support for international students to the UK, and establishing three new University Partnership Schemes;

- building on the Government's commitment to raise skills levels by investing in the reform of further education and training provision, and asking the Leitch Review of Skills to report specifically on how skills and employment policy can better complement each other;

- boosting access to finance to enable early-stage companies with real growth potential to bridge the equity gap and progress through to market, announcing a further £50 million in 2006-07 and £50 million in 2007-08 for the Enterprise Capital Funds scheme; and

- taking forward the Government's strategy for tackling the long-term lack of supply and responsiveness of housing and property and introducing Real Estate Investment Trusts to create greater flexibility for investors.

INCREASING EMPLOYMENT OPPORTUNITY FOR ALL

1.19   The Government's long-term goal is employment opportunity for all – the modern definition of full employment. It aims to ensure a higher proportion of people in work than ever before by 2010. To achieve this, each individual who wants and is able to work should be provided with the support to enable them to find work and develop skills. The Government is also determined to build a flexible labour market which allows the economy to respond quickly and efficiently to economic change, driven for example by shifting patterns of international production and trade.

Action so far 1.20   The Government's strategy for extending employment opportunity to all builds on the strong performance of the UK labour market over recent years. UK unemployment has fallen to 5.0 per cent, significantly below the EU average of 7.7 per cent, while the working age employment rate has reached 74.5 per cent. Chapter 4 describes the successful action the Government has already taken to increase employment opportunity, through:

- delivering employment opportunity to all, to provide everyone who is able to work with the support they need to move into work as quickly as possible;

- extending employment opportunity to those groups and regions which have faced the greatest barriers to work;

- enhancing skills and mobility, to ensure that everyone can fulfil their potential in the labour market and that business has access to the skilled workforce they need to compete in the global economy; and

- making work pay, through the National Minimum Wage and tax credits which create a system of support that provides greater rewards from work, improving incentives for individuals to participate in the labour market.

Next steps 1.21   Budget 2006 describes the further steps the Government is taking to build on this success and further strengthen the labour market, with a long-term vision for extending support to the inactive and those who face particular barriers to work. The Budget announces:

- an extension of the support offered to lone parents through ensuring that all lone parents who have claimed benefit for at least a year will be required to attend a Work Focused Interview every six months;

- a strengthened, refocused, Fortnightly Job Review for Jobseeker's Allowance claimants, from June 2006, to ensure that only those claimants who are able to demonstrate that they have undertaken their responsibilities to look for work are allowed to continue their claim;

- measures to reduce anomalies in, and further simplify, housing benefit; and to tackle fraud and error in the housing benefit system;

- in response to the Women and Work Commission report, new funding to:

  - double the number of existing Skills Coaching pilots to 16 Jobcentre Plus districts with a specific focus on helping low-skilled women return to work;

  - increase, by 50 per cent, the number of pilots delivering level 3 skills, with an additional pilot focused on women with low skills; and

  - help Sector Skills Councils in industries with skills shortages test new recruitment, training and career pathways for over 10,000 low skilled women;

- publication of *Employment Opportunity for all: analysing labour market trends in London*, alongside this Budget, examining the underlying reasons why employment rates are lower in London compared to other parts of the country, as a basis for future policy action;

- publication of the Welfare Reform Green Paper announcing national roll out of the successful Pathways to Work pilot projects by 2008 for Incapacity Benefit claimants, and consulting on replacement of the current system of incapacity benefits with a new Employment and Support Allowance;

- following the Low Pay Commission's recommendations, the adult rate of the National Minimum Wage will rise to £5.35 from October 2006.

BUILDING A FAIRER SOCIETY

1.22   The Government's long-term economic goal is to combine flexibility with fairness. Policies that ensure fairness act to minimise the short-term costs that can be associated with the changes that are needed in flexible outward-looking economies. Fairness provides security and support for those that need it and ensures that everyone has the opportunity to fulfil their potential in the global economy, now and in the future. The Government is also at the forefront of global efforts to achieve the Millennium Development Goals for global poverty, and to reduce debt in the poorest countries.

Action so far **1.23**   Chapter 5 describes the range of reforms the Government has undertaken to achieve its goals in these areas, including:

- support for families and children to lift children out of poverty and so ensure they have the opportunity to fulfil their potential;

- support for pensioners to tackle poverty and ensure security in retirement for all pensioners, with extra help for those who need it most and rewards for those who have saved modest amounts;

- steps to encourage saving, including through the introduction of the Child Trust Fund, stakeholder pensions and Individual Savings Accounts; and

- measures and reforms to improve the tax system, and to ensure that everyone pays their fair share toward extra investment in public services.

Next steps **1.24**   Building on these reforms, the Government is committed to taking the long-term decisions to promote opportunity and fairness. The Budget announces:

- that from April 2008 every pensioner and disabled person in England will have free off-peak national bus travel;

- building on progress in reducing the number of children in poverty, a commitment to increase the child element of the Child Tax Credit at least in line with average earnings until the end of the Parliament;

- measures to enable employers to support working parents with their childcare, by raising the tax and national insurance contributions exemption for employer supported childcare to £55 per week and by making available capital grants to help employers establish workplace nurseries;

- that the payments into Child Trust Fund accounts at age seven will be £250 for all children, with £500 for children from lower-income families;

- a review of policy for children and young people, supported in this Budget by £10 million over two years to promote youth engagement in their communities, sports and local media;

- an increase in the stamp duty land tax threshold to £125,000, exempting an additional 40,000 homebuyers each year;

- that the inheritance tax threshold will rise to £312,000 in 2008-09 and £325,000 in 2009-10, to continue to provide a fair and targeted system; and

- establishing this Government's largest ever consultation with the third sector, to be overseen by a cross-departmental ministerial group;

- further reforms to modernise the tax system, including investing in high capacity online filing services and a number of measures to clamp down on tax fraud and avoidance.

DELIVERING HIGH QUALITY PUBLIC SERVICES

1.25   The Government's aim is to deliver world class public services, with extra investment tied to reform and results. Investment in key public services provides the foundation on which the UK will be able to meet the long-term global economic challenges. A healthy, skilled and educated workforce, modern and reliable transport networks, and an adequate supply of affordable housing will promote productivity and flexibility, and also help to ensure opportunity and security for all, both now and in future generations. The Government's strategy is to deliver improvements in public services through sustained investment and reform to ensure that taxpayers receive value for money.

Action so far **1.26** Chapter 6 sets out the steps the Government has taken to deliver lasting improvements in the delivery of public services, including:

- **a new framework for managing public spending** that strengthens incentives for departments to plan for the long term;

- **significant extra resources for public services,** consistent with the strict fiscal rules.

- **challenging efficiency targets** for all departments, delivering over £20 billion of efficiency gains a year by 2007-08 to be recycled to front-line public services.

1.27 A decade on from the first Comprehensive Spending Review (CSR), the Government will be conducting a second CSR reporting in 2007. In preparation, this Budget announces:

- **plans for a national debate about how public services should respond to the long-term challenges facing the UK;**

- **a series of reviews that will inform the CSR** in the areas where cross-departmental collaboration and innovative solutions are required to meet these challenges;

- **further details of the next phase of the Government's value for money programme,** including progress on asset disposals and a review of opportunities for transforming service delivery across government, looking at how the channels through which services are delivered can be made more efficient and responsive to the needs of users; and

- **early spending settlements for the Department for Work and Pensions, HM Revenue and Customs, Cabinet Office and HM Treasury Group** which see their Departmental Expenditure Limits fall by five per cent per year in real terms over the CSR period, releasing over £1.8 billion in total for re-investment in front-line public services.

Next steps **1.28** The Government's long-term goal is to deliver world class public services through investment and reform, while ensuring efficiency and value for money. The Budget announcements include further measures directing resources towards the Government's priorities, including:

- £585m of additional resources over 2006-07 and 2007-08 to provide further support for personalised learning in schools in England. Further, capital investment in schools will rise from £6.4 billion in 2007-08 to £8.0 billion by 2010-11, matching today's level of private sector per pupil capital investment;

- £100m to accelerate the recruitment of Police Community Support Officers (PCSOs) together with firm spending plans for the Home Office over the CSR period which lock in the large real increases in resources since 1999, providing the long-term funding certainty needed to lead the fight against crime and terrorism and realise the benefits of police force restructuring and reform;

- a commitment of £200m of Exchequer funds to ensure elite athletes have the best chance of success in a British Olympics in 2012; and

- £800m of provision for the Special Reserve in 2006-07, set aside from within existing public spending plans, to help meet the costs of Iraq, Afghanistan and other international commitments.

PROTECTING THE ENVIRONMENT

1.29   The Government's goal is to deliver sustainable growth and a better environment, by addressing the challenges of climate change, poor air quality and environmental degradation in urban and rural areas. Sustainable development is vital to ensure a better quality of life for everyone, today and for generations to come. Economic growth is key to rising national prosperity. However, growth in the developed world, accompanied with the rapidly growing and highly populated economies of China and India, will place increasing demands on the world's resources and environment over the coming decade. Meeting this long-term challenge requires action at a local and national level, but crucially also through international cooperation.

Action so far   **1.30**   Chapter 7 describes the steps the Government has taken to deliver its environmental objectives, including:

- **tackling climate change** and reducing emissions of greenhouse gases in line with domestic as well as international targets – in particular through the Climate Change Levy and reduced VAT rates for energy saving materials;

- **improving air quality** to ensure that air pollutants are maintained below levels that could pose a risk to human health – including through support for cleaner fuels and vehicles;

- **improving waste management,** so that resources are used more efficiently and waste is re-used or recycled to deliver economic value – for example through increases in the landfill tax; and

- **protecting the UK's countryside and natural resources,** to ensure that they are sustainable economically, socially and physically – in particular by introducing the aggregates levy.

Next steps   **1.31**   The Government is committed to delivering sustainable growth, and a better environment and to tackling the global challenges of climate change. It is using a range of economic instruments to address the challenges posed by sustainable development, whilst taking into account other social and economic factors. The Pre-Budget report describes the next steps in the Government's strategy, focused on tackling the global challenge of climate change, including:

- encouraging energy efficiency in the business sector through **an increase in the climate change levy, in line with inflation, from 1 April 2007;**

- further measures to improve household energy efficiency, **including an extra 250,000 subsidised insulation measures in British homes over the next two years, funding for local authority-led publicity and incentive schemes, trialling the use of 'smart' gas and electricity meters, and a new voluntary initiative with major retailers to reduce the energy use of consumer electronics;**

- the development of a new **National Institute of Energy Technologies, in partnership with the private sector** to better leverage the substantial public sector funding of energy research;

- further support for the development of alternative energy sources, including an **additional £50 million to develop microgeneration technologies and the launch of a consultation document on the barriers to large-scale commercial deployment in the UK of carbon capture and storage;**

- further detail on the Renewable Transport Fuel Obligation to increase the use of biofuels – with the obligation set at 2.5 per cent in 2008-09 and 3.75 per cent in 2009-10, and the biofuels duty incentive maintained at 20 pence per litre in 2008-09;

- reforms to vehicle excise duty (VED) to sharpen environmental incentives including reducing the rate to zero for cars with the very lowest carbon emissions and introducing a new top band for the most polluting new cars. 50 per cent of cars will see their VED frozen or reduced;

- the deferral to 1 September 2006 of the inflation-only increase in main road fuel duties, reflecting continuing volatility in the oil market; and a similar increase of 1.25 pence per litre, also from 1 September 2006, in duty for rebated fuels, maintaining the differential with main fuel duty rates to support the Oils Strategy; and

- a freeze in air passenger duty due to the impact of volatile oil prices on the aviation industry, and funding for an international scientific conference in the UK that will look at the impact of aviation on climate change.

I.32 The Budget also reports on the Government's strategy for tackling other environmental challenges, including:

- an increase in the value of the landfill tax credit scheme to £60 million in 2006-07 with a challenge to the private and voluntary sector partners in the scheme to provide additional opportunities for young people to volunteer on environmental projects; and

- a freeze in the rate of the aggregates levy.

BUDGET MEASURES AND THEIR IMPACT ON HOUSEHOLDS

I.33 The measures introduced in this and previous Budgets support the Government's objectives of promoting enterprise, skills and science, creating employment opportunity, tackling child and pensioner poverty, and protecting the environment. Consistent with the requirements of the *Code for fiscal stability*, the updated public finance projections in Budget 2006 take into account the fiscal effects of all firm decisions announced in the Budget. The fiscal impact of Budget policy decisions is set out in Table 1.2. Full details are provided in Chapter A of the FSBR.

I.34 As a result of personal tax and benefit measures coming into effect in 2006–07, by October 2006, in real terms:[1]

- families with children will be, on average, £50 a year better off, while those in the poorest fifth of the population will be, on average, £100 a year better off;

- a single earner couple with 2 children, with earnings up to the median for full time workers – £24,000 per year – will be at least £70 a year better off; and

- a lone parent with 2 children, working 16 hours a week at the National Minimum Wage,[2] will be at least £315 per week better off.

---

[1] Compared to the 2005-06 system of taxes and benefits, indexed to 2006-07 prices.
[2] The National Minimum Wage will be £5.35 for adults from October 2006.

1.35   As a result of personal tax and benefit measures introduced since 1997, by October 2006, in real terms:[3]

- households will be, on average, £950 a year better off;

- families with children will be, on average, £1,500 a year better off;

- families with children in the poorest fifth of the population will be, on average, £3,400 a year better off.

1.36   As a result of personal tax and benefit measures introduced since 1997, in 2006-07:[3]

- pensioner households will be, on average £1,400 a year better off in real terms; and

- the poorest third of pensioner households will have gained £2,050 a year in real terms.

GOVERNMENT SPENDING AND REVENUE

1.37   Chart 1.1 presents public spending by main function. Total managed expenditure (TME) is expected to be around £552 billion in 2006-07. TME is divided into Departmental Expenditure Limits (DEL), shown in Table C13 of the FSBR, and Annually Managed Expenditure (AME), shown in Table C11 of the FSBR.

---

[3] Compared to the 1997-98 system of taxes and benefits, indexed to 2006-07 prices.

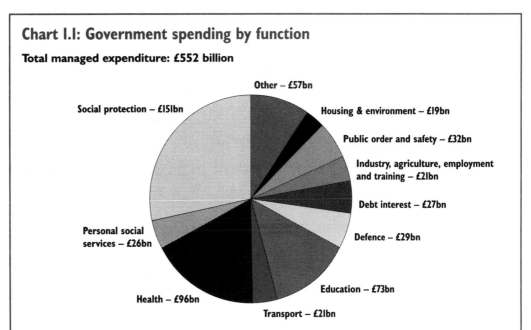

Chart 1.1: Government spending by function

Total managed expenditure: £552 billion

Other – £57bn
Social protection – £151bn
Housing & environment – £19bn
Public order and safety – £32bn
Industry, agriculture, employment and training – £21bn
Debt interest – £27bn
Defence – £29bn
Personal social services – £26bn
Education – £73bn
Health – £96bn
Transport – £21bn

Source: HM Treasury, 2006-07 near-cash projections. Spending re-classified to functions compared to previous presentations and is now using methods specified in international standards. Other expenditure includes spending on general public services; recreation, culture, media and sport; international cooperation and development; public service pensions; plus spending yet to be allocated and some accounting adjustments. Social protection includes tax credit payments in excess of an individual's tax liability, which are now counted in AME, in line with OECD guidelines. Figures may not sum to total due to rounding.

1.38 Chart 1.2 shows the different sources of government revenue. Public sector current receipts are expected to be around £516 billion in 2006-07. Table C8 of the FSBR provides a more detailed breakdown of receipts consistent with this chart.

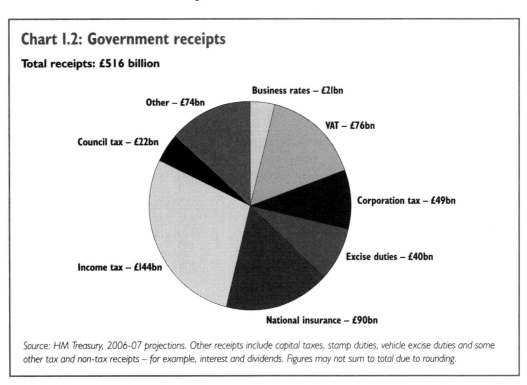

Chart 1.2: Government receipts

Total receipts: £516 billion

Business rates – £21bn
Other – £74bn
VAT – £76bn
Council tax – £22bn
Corporation tax – £49bn
Excise duties – £40bn
Income tax – £144bn
National insurance – £90bn

Source: HM Treasury, 2006-07 projections. Other receipts include capital taxes, stamp duties, vehicle excise duties and some other tax and non-tax receipts – for example, interest and dividends. Figures may not sum to total due to rounding.

Table 1.2: Budget 2006 policy decisions

		(+ve is an Exchequer yield)		£ million
	2006-07 indexed	2007-08 indexed	2008-09 indexed	2006-07 non-indexed
MEETING THE PRODUCTIVITY CHALLENGE				
1 Changes to venture capital schemes	*	−15	−15	*
2 Extending the scope of R&D tax credits	0	−15	−40	0
3 Real Estate Investment Trusts	+35	+155	+130	+35
INCREASING EMPLOYMENT OPPORTUNITY FOR ALL				
4 Work Focused Interviews for lone parents	0	−20	0	0
5 Doubling skills coaching pilots for women	−5	−5	0	−5
6 Expanding the National Employer Training Programme	−10	−10	0	−10
7 Matched funding for Sector Skill Councils	−5	−5	0	−5
BUILDING A FAIRER SOCIETY				
Supporting families and communities				
8 Income tax: indexation of starting and basic rate limits	0	0	0	−570
9 Child Tax Credit: uprating child element in line with earnings until 2009-10	0	0	−200	0
10 Employer-supported childcare	−10	−20	−25	−10
11 Inheritance tax: increase of threshold	0	0	−10	0
12 Stamp duty land tax: increase of threshold	−40	−30	−30	−40
Protecting tax revenues				
13 Financial products avoidance	+125	+135	+100	+125
14 VAT: Countering Missing Trader Fraud	+100	+500	+425	+100
15 Countering CGT avoidance	0	+40	+35	0
16 Avoidance using employment related securities	+70	+65	+45	+70
17 VAT: supplies of goods under finance agreements	*	+10	+15	*
18 Rebated oils: changes to excepted vehicles schedule	0	+10	+10	0
Duties and other tax changes				
19 Alcohol duties: freeze spirits, cider and sparkling wine, revalorise beer and wine duties	−35	−30	−30	+170
20 Tobacco duties: revalorise rates	0	0	0	+25
21 VAT: reduced rate for contraceptive products	−5	−10	−10	−5
22 Further changes to oil valuation for tax purposes	+40	+80	+80	+40
23 Changes to group relief in corporation tax	−50	−50	−50	−50
24 Film tax reliefs: expanding the scope	*	−10	−10	*
25 Stamp duty land tax: ending relief for initial transfers into unit trusts	+50	+50	+40	+50
26 Removal of income tax exemption for loaned computers	+50	+100	+150	+50
27 Aligning the inheritance tax treatment for trusts	0	+15	+15	0
PROTECTING THE ENVIRONMENT				
Environment				
28 Climate change levy: revalorise from 1 April 2007	−20	−20	−20	0
29 Climate change levy: exemption of gas used in Northern Ireland	*	*	−5	*
30 Aggregates levy: freeze	−10	−10	−10	0
31 Enhanced Capital Allowances for water efficient technologies	*	−5	−5	*
32 Increasing the landfill tax credit scheme	−10	−10	−10	−10
Transport				
33 VAT: revalorise fuel scale charges	0	0	0	+10
34 Company car tax thresholds	−10	−20	+25	−10
35 Fuel duties: revalorise rates from 1 September 2006	−275	0	0	+380

Table 1.2: Budget 2006 policy decisions

		(+ve is an Exchequer yield)		£ million
	2006-07 indexed	**2007-08 indexed**	**2008-09 indexed**	**2006-07 non-indexed**
36 Fuel duties: maintain differential for rebated oils from 1 September 2006	+40	+75	+80	+50
37 Fuel duties: maintain differential for biodiesel and bioethanol until 2008	*	0	+10	0
38 Fuel duties: maintain differential for road fuel gases	*	0	+5	*
39 Vehicle Excise Duties: enhancing environmental incentives	+5	+5	+5	+115
40 Other VED changes	0	+20	+35	+10
41 Air passenger duty: freeze	−10	−30	−30	0
OTHER POLICY DECISIONS				
42 Supporting further education reform	0	−55	0	0
43 Direct payments to schools	−270	−440	0	−270
44 Additional Police Community Support Officers	−100	0	0	−100
45 2012 Olympics: supporting elite athletes	−30	−35	0	−30
TOTAL POLICY DECISIONS	**−380**	**+415**	**+705**	**+115**
negligible				
MEMO ITEMS				
Resetting of the AME margin	−90	+200		

2 MAINTAINING MACROECONOMIC STABILITY

> The UK economy is currently experiencing its longest unbroken expansion on record, with GDP now having grown for 54 consecutive quarters. The domestic stability delivered by the Government's macroeconomic framework, with volatility in the UK economy at historically low levels and the lowest in the G7, puts the UK in a strong position to respond to the global economic challenges of the next decade.
>
> Overall economic developments since the 2005 Pre-Budget Report have been as forecast. Economic growth has gradually increased momentum through the latter stages of 2005 and into 2006. With the outturn for 2005 and the forecast for 2006 as expected at the time of the Pre-Budget Report, the UK economy remains well placed for a pick-up in growth to above trend rates later this year and into 2007, supported by the continuing domestic stability delivered by the Government's macroeconomic framework.
>
> The Budget 2006 projections for the public finances are broadly in line with the 2005 Pre-Budget Report and show that the Government is meeting its strict fiscal rules:
>
> - the current budget shows an average surplus as a percentage of GDP over the current economic cycle, even using cautious assumptions, ensuring the Government is meeting the golden rule. Beyond the end of the current cycle, the current budget moves clearly into surplus; and
>
> - public sector net debt is projected to remain low and stable over the forecast period, stabilising at a level below the 40 per cent ceiling set in the sustainable investment rule.

THE MACROECONOMIC FRAMEWORK

2.1   The UK economy is currently experiencing its longest unbroken expansion since quarterly national accounts data began, with GDP now having grown for 54 consecutive quarters. With volatility in the UK economy at historically low levels and now the lowest in the G7, the domestic stability delivered by the Government's macroeconomic framework puts the UK in a strong position to respond to the global economic challenges of the next decade.

2.2   The Government's macroeconomic framework is designed to maintain long-term economic stability. Large fluctuations in output, employment and inflation add to uncertainty for firms, consumers and the public sector, and can reduce the economy's long-term growth potential. Stability allows businesses, individuals and the Government to plan more effectively for the long term, improving the quality and quantity of investment in physical and human capital and helping to raise productivity.

2.3   The macroeconomic framework is based on the principles of transparency, responsibility and accountability.[1] The monetary policy framework seeks to ensure low and stable inflation, while fiscal policy is underpinned by clear objectives and two strict rules that ensure sound public finances over the medium term while allowing fiscal policy to support monetary policy over the economic cycle. The fiscal rules are the foundation of the Government's public spending framework, which facilitates long-term planning and provides departments with the flexibility and incentives they need to increase the quality of public services and deliver specified outcomes. These policies work together in a coherent and integrated way.

---

[1] Further details can be found in *Reforming Britain's economic and financial policy*, Balls and O'Donnell (eds.), 2002.

Monetary policy framework 2.4 Since its introduction in 1997, the monetary policy framework has consistently delivered inflation close to the Government's target. The framework is based on four key principles:

- clear and precise objectives. The primary objective of monetary policy is to deliver price stability. The adoption of a single, symmetrical inflation target ensures that outcomes below target are treated as seriously as those above, so that monetary policy also supports the Government's objective of high and stable levels of growth and employment;

- full operational independence for the Monetary Policy Committee (MPC) in setting interest rates to meet the Government's target. The Government reaffirms in Budget 2006 the target of 2 per cent for the 12-month increase in the Consumer Prices Index (CPI), which applies at all times;

- openness, transparency and accountability, which are enhanced through the publication of MPC members' voting records, prompt publication of the minutes of monthly MPC meetings, and publication of the Bank of England's quarterly Inflation Report; and

- credibility and flexibility. The MPC has discretion to decide how and when to react to events, within the constraints of the inflation target and the open letter system. If inflation deviates by more than one percentage point above or below target, the Governor of the Bank of England must explain in an open letter to the Chancellor the reasons for the deviation, the action the MPC proposes to take, the expected duration of the deviation and how the proposed action meets the remit of the MPC.

2.5 These arrangements have removed the risk that short-term political factors can influence monetary policy and ensured that interest rates are set in a forward-looking manner to meet the Government's symmetrical inflation target. The Chancellor today announces the appointment of David Blanchflower to the Bank of England's Monetary Policy Committee to succeed Stephen Nickell. This appointment will take effect on 1 June 2006.

Fiscal policy framework 2.6 The Government's fiscal policy framework is based on the five key principles set out in the *Code for fiscal stability*[2] – transparency, stability, responsibility, fairness and efficiency. The Code requires the Government to state both its objectives and the rules through which fiscal policy will be operated. The Government's fiscal policy objectives are:

- over the medium term, to ensure sound public finances and that spending and taxation impact fairly within and between generations; and

- over the short term, to support monetary policy and, in particular, to allow the automatic stabilisers to help smooth the path of the economy.

2.7 These objectives are implemented through two strict fiscal rules, against which the performance of fiscal policy can be judged. The fiscal rules are:

- the golden rule: over the economic cycle, the Government will borrow only to invest and not to fund current spending; and

- the sustainable investment rule: public sector net debt as a proportion of GDP will be held over the economic cycle at a stable and prudent level. Other things being equal, net debt will be maintained below 40 per cent of GDP over the economic cycle.

---

[2] *Code for fiscal stability*, HM Treasury, 1998.

Box 2.1: Developments in the fiscal framework

While the key steps in developing the fiscal policy framework were taken in 1997 and 1998, the framework has continued to be enhanced. In 1997, the Government set out its two fiscal rules and invited the National Audit Office (NAO) to perform the first ever audit of key assumptions underpinning the fiscal projections. In 1998, the key components of the fiscal framework and the underlying principles were brought together in the *Code for fiscal stability*. The Code set more extensive reporting requirements for governments than those set previously by the 1975 Industry Act. For example, the Code requires the publication of illustrative long-term fiscal projections, and of Pre-Budget Reports no less than three months prior to the Budget.

Developments in the fiscal framework since then have further developed the five key principles of fiscal management that were enshrined in the Code: transparency, stability, responsibility, fairness and efficiency.

The role of the NAO in ensuring that forecasts are transparent and responsible has developed since 1997. While the first audit covered five assumptions, additions in 1998 increased this to the 11 key assumptions listed in Chapter C. In 2000, the NAO were invited to conduct a three-year rolling review of the assumptions previously audited. The NAO now also audits 'spend to save' and 'spend to raise' spending packages, such as HMRC's direct tax compliance strategy audited alongside the Budget, where additional resources are specifically targeted at reducing expenditure or raising revenue. The most recent additional audit was introduced alongside the 2005 Pre-Budget Report, in which the NAO audited the Treasury's judgement that the previous economic cycle ended in 1997. In future, the NAO will be invited to audit the end date of the current and future cycles once the Treasury has made a firm judgement.

In 1999, the Government expanded the suite of fiscal indicators reported in each Budget and Pre-Budget Report, which allow for scrutiny of all aspects of fiscal policy on a consistent basis. These fiscal aggregates, including cyclically-adjusted balances, are reported in tables 2.5 and 2.6. In 2002, the Treasury started reporting on core debt, an indicator of the debt position after removing the impact of the economic cycle. In Budget 1999, the first illustrative long-term fiscal projections were published, reporting on intergenerational fairness and covering a 30-year horizon. The latest projection is in Annex A. Reporting on long-term issues was further enhanced in 2002 with the publication of the first *Long-term public finance report*. At the same time, backward-looking analysis of the Treasury's fiscal projections was enhanced with the introduction of the *End of year fiscal report*. Both reports have since been published annually alongside the Pre-Budget Report.

The IMF[a] describe the resulting UK fiscal framework as being "on the frontier of institutional development". Nevertheless, the Treasury keeps the framework under constant review to ensure it remains at the forefront of international best practice.

---

[a] IMF, Concluding Statement to the 2005 Article IV Mission to the UK.

2.8   The fiscal rules ensure sound public finances in the medium term while allowing flexibility in two key respects:

- the rules are set over the economic cycle. This allows the fiscal balances to vary between years in line with the cyclical position of the economy, permitting the automatic stabilisers to operate freely to help smooth the path of the economy in the face of variations in demand; and

- the rules work together to promote capital investment while ensuring sustainable public finances in the long term. The golden rule requires the current budget to be in balance or surplus over the cycle, allowing the Government to borrow only to fund capital spending. The sustainable investment rule ensures that borrowing is maintained at a prudent level. To meet the sustainable investment rule with confidence, net debt will be maintained below 40 per cent of GDP in each and every year of the current economic cycle.

Public spending framework   **2.9**   The fiscal rules underpin the Government's public spending framework. The golden rule states that, over the economic cycle, the Government will only borrow to invest. Departments are therefore given separate resource and capital allocations, which increases the efficiency of public spending as public investment is not crowded out by short-term current spending pressures. Departments are now given separate allocations for resource and capital spending to help ensure adherence to the rule. The sustainable investment rule sets the context for the Government's public investment targets and ensures that borrowing for investment is conducted in a responsible way.

Financial stability framework   **2.10**   A single statutory body for financial regulation, the Financial Services Authority (FSA), was set up in 1998 as part of a new tripartite structure for overseeing the UK financial system. A framework for co-operation on financial stability between the three authorities was set out in a Memorandum of Understanding in 1997. These arrangements have proven to be a robust and effective framework for responding to financial stability risks. Building on experience, the authorities have continued to develop the response frameworks for managing both financial crises and operational disruption and have published an updated version of the Memorandum, incorporating these improvements.[3]

2.11   The Standing Committee on Financial Stability, comprising the Chancellor, the Governor of the Bank of England and the Chairman of the FSA, meets monthly (at Deputies level) to discuss individual cases and developments relevant to financial stability, focusing on risks deemed to have systemic consequences. The Committee regularly reviews the key systemic risks to the UK's financial intermediaries and infrastructure and coordinates the three authorities' response and contingency plans. In the event of a crisis, it would meet at short notice and is the principal forum for agreeing policy, and, where appropriate, co-ordinating and agreeing action between the three authorities. The Memorandum of Understanding between the three authorities defines the role of the Standing Committee in both financial crisis management and in responding to operational disruptions to the financial sector.

PERFORMANCE OF THE FRAMEWORK

2.12   The frameworks for monetary policy, fiscal policy and public spending provide a coherent strategy for maintaining high and stable levels of growth and employment, and for minimising the adverse impact of external events.

---

[3] Full text available at www.hm-treasury.gov.uk.

Monetary policy **2.13** The monetary policy framework has improved the credibility of policy making and continues to deliver clear benefits. Since the new framework was introduced:

- the annual increase in inflation up to December 2003, when RPIX was used as the inflation target measure, remained close to the target value of 2¹/₂ per cent, the longest period of sustained low inflation for the last 30 years; and

- inflation expectations have remained close to target following the switch to a 2 per cent CPI target. CPI inflation has been within 1 percentage point of its target at all times since its inception in December 2003.

2.14 The monetary policy framework has given the MPC the flexibility to respond decisively to unexpected economic events over recent years. Consistent with its forward looking approach, the MPC cut interest rates by a ¹/₄ percentage point in August 2005 responding to the slackening in the pressure of demand on supply. Since then, interest rates have remained unchanged reflecting the MPC's view that monetary policy settings are consistent with inflation remaining at target.

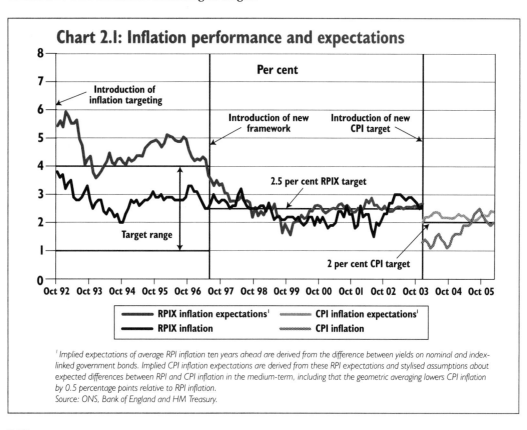

Chart 2.1: Inflation performance and expectations

Per cent

Introduction of inflation targeting

Introduction of new framework

Introduction of new CPI target

2.5 per cent RPIX target

Target range

2 per cent CPI target

Oct 92 Oct 93 Oct 94 Oct 95 Oct 96 Oct 97 Oct 98 Oct 99 Oct 00 Oct 01 Oct 02 Oct 03 Oct 04 Oct 05

RPIX inflation expectations¹   CPI inflation expectations¹
RPIX inflation   CPI inflation

¹ *Implied expectations of average RPI inflation ten years ahead are derived from the difference between yields on nominal and index-linked government bonds. Implied CPI inflation expectations are derived from these RPI expectations and stylised assumptions about expected differences between RPI and CPI inflation in the medium-term, including that the geometric averaging lowers CPI inflation by 0.5 percentage points relative to RPI inflation.*
Source: ONS, Bank of England and HM Treasury.

2.15 Low inflation expectations and a period of entrenched macroeconomic stability have helped long-term interest rates remain at historically low levels. Low long-term interest rates reduce the Government's debt interest payments, free up resources for public services and help promote investment. Over the current economic cycle, long-term spot interest rates have averaged 5 per cent compared with an average of just over 9 per cent in the previous cycle. Ten-year spot rates have fallen by 0.6 percentage points to 4.1 per cent from March 2005 to February 2006, but have remained unchanged in the United States and have fallen only slightly in the euro area. Box 2.5 describes the fall in interest rates on ultra-long bonds at the beginning of 2006 and considers some of the potential causes.

2.16 Ten-year forward rates, which abstract from cyclical influences, are around 0.8 percentage points lower than those in the United States and very slightly above those in the euro area.[4] Ten-year forward rates have fallen in the UK over the last year from 4.7 per cent in March 2005 to 4.0 per cent in February 2006. This compares with a rate of 8 per cent in April 1997 before the introduction of the new macroeconomic framework.

2.17 Alongside the UK's macroeconomic stability in recent years, the effective exchange rate has also been relatively stable, as seen in Chart 2.2. The sterling effective exchange rate remains close to levels at Budget 2004, having remained within a narrow band of just over 3 per cent of its average level over the period. Since the introduction of the euro in 1999, the volatility of sterling's effective exchange rate has been under half that of the euro and around a third that of the US dollar.

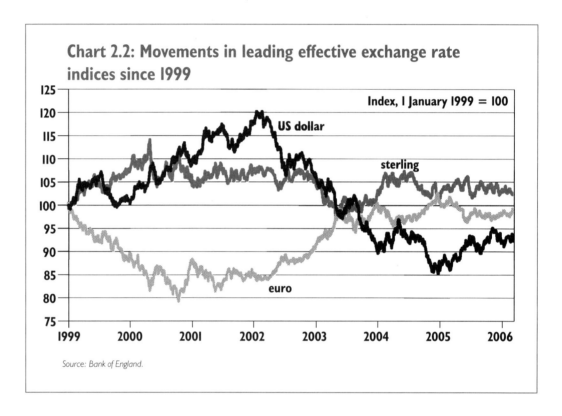

Chart 2.2: Movements in leading effective exchange rate indices since 1999

Index, 1 January 1999 = 100

Source: Bank of England.

---

[4] Ten year forward rates are market expectations, formed today, of short rates in ten years' time. They are less affected by short-term factors, such as the current cyclical position of the economy, than spot rates and are therefore a better basis for making international comparisons when cyclical conditions differ.

Box 2.2: Causes of increased stability in the UK

Since the introduction of the Government's macroeconomic framework in 1997, the UK has experienced an unprecedented period of economic stability. Both relative to the rest of the post-World War II period, and relative to other G7 countries, economic volatility in the UK is low. As the IMF stated in December 2005, "macroeconomic stability in the United Kingdom remains remarkable".[a] There has been considerable debate on the causes of increased stability, both in the UK and across the developed world.

There is strong evidence to suggest that the Government's macroeconomic framework has contributed to increased stability by creating a more certain and predictable environment for private sector decision makers:

- the credibility of monetary policy has increased since 1997. Inflation expectations have remained close to the inflation target (see Chart 2.1). Interest rate differentials between the UK and the US and Germany narrowed immediately after the announcement of the monetary policy framework in May 1997, as shown in the table, and have remained low or negative. Short-term interest rates have been low for the longest sustained period since the 1950s.

Interest rate differentials following the introduction of the new macroeconomic framework

	Differential with UK forward rates[1]				
	Day before (2 May 1997)	Day after (7 May 1997)	3 months after (6 Aug 1997)	6 months after (6 Nov 1997)	18 months after (6 Nov 1998)
US	0.7	0.1	0.1	−0.1	−0.1
Germany	0.7	0.2	0.1	0.0	0.0

[1] UK 10-year forward rates less US/German rates.

Source: Bank of England.

- the credibility of fiscal policy has increased since 1997. The Government's fiscal policy framework has restored sound public finances, and has supported monetary policy by allowing the automatic stabilisers to operate and discretionary action to be taken where appropriate (see Chart 2.6).

The extent and intensity of economic shocks could also affect stability. The UK economy has maintained stability in the face of a number of shocks with economic consequences since 1997, including: a large rise and fall in equity prices, large rises in house prices and in oil prices, wars in Afghanistan and Iraq, terrorist attacks and major economic crises in Russia and East Asia. The UK has also had to adapt to an increasingly globalised economy, with growing trade and cross border investment altering the competitive environment.

Structural changes and reforms have been taking place over many years which have also played an important role in increasing the UK economy's flexibility and resilience. They include, for example, reforms to competition policy legislation and reforms to encourage the economically inactive back to work, set out in more detail in Chapter 3 and Chapter 4.

[a] IMF, Concluding Statement to the 2005 Article IV Mission to the UK.

Fiscal policy   **2.18**   The Government has taken tough decisions on taxation and spending to restore the public finances to a sustainable position. Public sector net debt was reduced from just under 44 per cent of GDP in 1996-97 to 35.0 per cent in 2004-05. Public sector net borrowing was reduced sharply from 1997-98 on, with surpluses over 1998-99 to 2000-01 when the economy was above trend. In more recent years, net borrowing has increased, allowing fiscal policy to support monetary policy as the economy moved below trend in 2001. As Chart 2.3 shows, since 1997 the UK's public finances compare favourably with other countries.

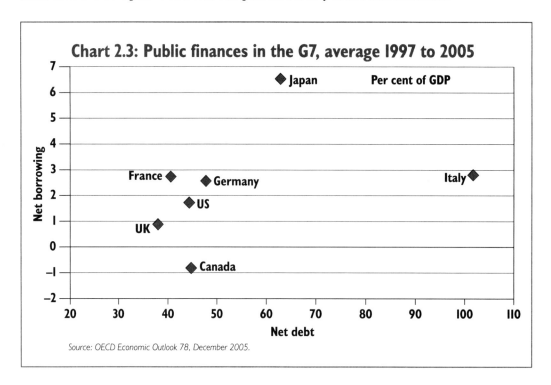

Chart 2.3: Public finances in the G7, average 1997 to 2005

Source: OECD Economic Outlook 78, December 2005.

2004 Spending   **2.19**   The 2004 Spending Review set spending plans for the years 2005-06 to 2007-08,
Review   locking in the increased investment of previous spending reviews while providing for further investment in the most crucial areas of the public services. These plans provide for:

- current spending to increase by an annual average of 2.5 per cent in real terms over 2006-07 and 2007-08;

- public sector net investment rising to $2^{1/4}$ per cent of GDP by 2007-08, compared with 0.5 per cent of GDP in 1999, to continue to address historic under-investment in the UK's infrastructure while meeting the sustainable investment rule; and

- agreed efficiency targets for all departments, delivering over £21 billion of efficiency gains a year by 2007-08 to be recycled to front-line public services.

Comprehensive   **2.20**   The overall spending limits set in Budget 2004 and confirmed in the 2004 Spending
Spending Review   Review remain sustainable and fully consistent with the fiscal rules. Building on these firm foundations, the 2007 Comprehensive Spending Review (CSR) will provide the opportunity for a fundamental and long-term review of the Government's priorities and expenditure. As outlined in more detail in Chapter 6, the CSR will take a zero-based approach to assessing the effectiveness of departments' baseline expenditure in delivering the outputs to which they are committed, and consider the further investments and reforms needed to ensure that the UK's public services are equipped to meet the global challenges of the decades ahead. The CSR will set departmental spending plans for 2008-09, 2009-10 and 2010-11, with allocations for 2007-08 held to the agreed figures already announced at the 2004 Spending Review.

RECENT ECONOMIC DEVELOPMENTS AND PROSPECTS

Recent economic developments **2.21** The UK economy was resilient in the face of a number of challenges in 2005. After strong growth at above trend rates in late 2003 and through the first half of 2004, GDP growth decelerated from mid-2004 and has since remained at below trend rates in the face of sustained higher oil prices, weak demand in the euro area, and a slowing housing market.

2.22 In previous decades, such factors would have risked being accompanied by a recession. But based on the stability provided by the government's macroeconomic framework, UK GDP has now expanded for 54 consecutive quarters. On the basis of quarterly national accounts data, this is the longest unbroken expansion since records began 50 years ago. The current economic expansion has persisted for well over twice the duration of the previous period of unbroken growth.

2.23 Overall developments since the 2005 Pre-Budget Report have been as forecast with the economy strengthening as forecast. GDP rose by 0.6 per cent in the final quarter of 2005, remaining a little below trend although slightly stronger than in the second and third quarters and significantly above growth at the start of last year. In 2005 as a whole, UK GDP is currently estimated to have risen by $1^3/_4$ per cent, the tenth consecutive year of faster growth than the euro area.

Table 2.1: Summary of world forecast

	Percentage change on a year earlier unless otherwise stated			
	Outturn	Forecasts		
	2005	2006	2007	2008
Major 7 countries [1]:				
Real GDP	$2^1/_2$	$2^1/_2$	$2^1/_2$	$2^1/_2$
Consumer price inflation [2]	$2^1/_2$	$2^1/_2$	$2^1/_4$	$2^1/_2$
Euro area:				
Real GDP	$1^1/_2$	$1^3/_4$	2	2
World GDP	$4^1/_2$	$4^1/_2$	$4^1/_2$	$4^1/_2$
World trade in goods and services	7	$7^3/_4$	7	$6^3/_4$
UK export markets [3]	$6^1/_4$	$7^1/_2$	$6^1/_2$	6

[1] G7: US, Japan, Germany, UK, France, Italy and Canada.
[2] Per cent, Q4.
[3] Other countries' imports of goods and services weighted according to their importance in UK exports.

2.24 Developments in the global economy have also been broadly as forecast in the 2005 Pre-Budget Report. World output growth in 2005 was driven by emerging Asia, particularly China, as well as by continued robust growth in the US. Oil prices have remained high since the autumn, while at the same time world growth is now estimated to have been slightly stronger than expected, largely reflecting the strength of underlying momentum in Asia.

2.25 World trade growth has also remained robust, despite having moderated compared with the four-year high reached in 2004. Asia has largely driven this growth, with the Asia-Pacific region contributing around 40 per cent to world trade growth over the past three years, in contrast to around 15 per cent from each of the US, the euro area and the rest of Europe. Asia accounts for just 15 per cent of UK export markets, whereas the euro area, which is growing more slowly, accounts for around half of the UK's export markets.

Economic **2.26**   The economy has already shown signs of gradually increasing momentum through
prospects   the latter stages of 2005 and into 2006. The Government's macroeconomic framework has
continued to deliver unprecedented stability, with inflation at target, despite the effects of
higher oil prices. The economy remains well placed to see a renewed period of above trend
growth from 2007 as factors temporarily subduing growth over the recent past abate.

2.27   Overall, the economic forecast is unchanged from the 2005 Pre-Budget Report.
Following growth of 1³/₄ per cent in 2005, UK GDP is expected to grow by between 2 and
2¹/₂ per cent this year, still slightly below trend rates, reflecting a number of temporary factors.
Private consumption growth is expected to be restrained by continued household appetite for
saving, subdued growth in labour incomes, and the residual effects of higher energy prices.
Companies are likely to remain cautious about stepping up business investment in the face
of high oil prices and high levels of gearing.

2.28   CPI inflation is expected to remain close to target, as inflation expectations remain
firmly anchored, and energy prices exert slightly more upward pressure on inflation in 2006
than expected at the time of the Pre-Budget Report.

Table 2.2: Summary of UK forecast[1]

	Outturn	Forecast		
	2005	2006	2007	2008
GDP growth (per cent)	1³/₄	2 to 2¹/₂	2³/₄ to 3¹/₄	2³/₄ to 3¹/₄
CPI inflation (per cent, Q4)	2¹/₄	2	2	2

[1] See footnote to Table B9 for explanation of forecast ranges.

2.29   With the effects of previous oil price rises on spending and the recent adjustment in
the household saving ratio receding, private consumption growth should firm a little further
in 2007 and 2008, although rising at rates well below recent peaks and below growth in the
economy as a whole. With adjustment to higher oil prices working through and corporate
fundamentals generally supportive, there should be firmer growth in investment spending as
demand accelerates in 2007. As a result, GDP growth is forecast to be above trend rates at
between 2³/₄ and 3¹/₄ per cent in both 2007 and 2008, with spare capacity being absorbed and
the output gap closing in 2008-09, unchanged from the 2005 Pre-Budget Report judgement.

2.30   The Budget 2006 forecast implies further rebalancing of GDP growth going forward,
with business investment accelerating and outpacing private consumption from the end of
2006. Private consumption growth is expected to be in line with GDP this year, but to fall
below it thereafter. Net exports are forecast to make a neutral contribution to GDP growth, in
contrast to the negative contribution in the years preceding 2005.

Risks **2.31**   The set of risks surrounding the Budget 2006 economic outlook is similar to that
surrounding the 2005 Pre-Budget Report forecast. The balance of risks has shifted a little,
with domestic risks having receded, while global uncertainties have increased somewhat.
Globalisation means that the UK economy shares increasingly in the risks affecting the world
economy and means that domestic risks are harder to differentiate.

2.32   Uncertainty continues to surround the current output gap estimate given ongoing
uncertainty as to whether the latest vintage of ONS data is correctly approximating the degree
to which the economy has been growing below trend over the recent past. To the extent that
the economy has been growing more (less) quickly than implied by existing data, then that
would mean less (more) scope for above-trend growth over the forecast horizon.

2.33 The forecast for private consumption continues to be surrounded by both upside and downside risks. Unexpected weakness of average earnings growth would tend to undermine household expenditure, although it would be at least partly offset by the boost to employment from weakening labour costs. Private consumption growth also presents potential upside risks. With increasing evidence that the housing market has undergone a smooth realignment with some modest recent firming in house prices and with consumer confidence having firmed, household spending could accelerate more sharply than envisaged.

The economic **2.34** As announced in July last year, the Treasury's judgement is that the current economic
cycle cycle began in the first half of 1997.[5] The Comptroller and Auditor General audited this judgement alongside the 2005 Pre-Budget Report and concluded that, though there were uncertainties, there are reasonable grounds to date the end date of the previous economic cycle to 1997 and that this would not reduce the extent of caution in making the fiscal projections. In the second half of 2001, the economy moved below trend with output remaining below its trend level since then. The economy is expected to return to trend in 2008-09.

Caution and the **2.35** The end date of the economic cycle is one of a number of key assumptions that
public finances underpin the public finance projections which are independently audited by the Comptroller and Auditor General to ensure that they remain reasonable and cautious. A complete list of these assumptions is set out in Chapter C of the *Financial Statement and Budget Report* and further background is provided in Box 2.1. This prudent approach to fiscal policy builds an important safety margin into the public finance projections to guard against unexpected events. It decreases the chance that, over the medium term, unforeseen economic or fiscal events will require changes in plans for taxation or spending.

2.36 For this Budget, the Comptroller and Auditor General has audited the assumption for underlying trend growth used for the purpose of projecting the public finances, which is set a $^{1}/_{4}$ percentage point below the Government's neutral view. The review concluded that over the past four years the assumption has been reasonable and cautious, though other assumptions could have been adopted that would have introduced a greater degree of caution. Looking forward, the review concluded that the assumption currently remains reasonable and cautious but recommended that, because of the uncertainties involved in estimating trend growth rates, the Treasury kept its estimate under review.

2.37 The assumption for forecasting revenue from duty on tobacco, that the illicit market share is set at least at the latest published outturn level, would normally be due for review under the three-year rolling review. However, firm data for the illicit market share is currently only available for the first year of the rolling review period so that it is not possible to reach a conclusion for the three-year period as a whole. The Comptroller and Auditor General has therefore reviewed the evidence for 2003-04, concluding that the assumption had added caution to the fiscal projections in that year, and reviewed the issues that have arisen in producing an estimate for 2004-05. The Comptroller and Auditor General recommended areas of further analysis that HM Revenue and Customs will undertake over the next year and will be invited to conduct a full review at Budget 2007.

2.38 The Comptroller and Auditor General reviewed the yield from the Budget 2003 direct taxation compliance package and found that the projections of yield were reasonable and the method adopted to make adjustments to the projections in the light of outturn evidence was a helpful one to ensure caution.

2.39 The Comptroller and Auditor General also audited the conventions on short-term interest rates and privatisation proceeds. He concluded that the interest rate assumption methodology, that three-month forward interest rates will be based on market expectations, was a reasonable one and incorporates an element of caution through the risk premium embodied in the forward rates. Over the past three years, interest rate projections had been

---

[5] *Evidence on the UK economic cycle*, HM Treasury, July 2005.

higher than outturn more often than not and so had been cautious to this extent, on the basis that higher interest rates have a negative impact on the public finances. The review concluded that the convention on privatisation proceeds had led to no systematic forecasting errors over the review period and that for the future it remains reasonable and is based on being cautious. In view of potentially large future privatisation receipts, close attention should be paid to the profile of receipts included in the fiscal projections.

Box 2.3: Follow-up to the UK Presidencies of the G7/8 and EU

In 2005, the UK used its leadership of the G7/8 and the EU to address the challenges and opportunities of globalisation. The details were set out in the 2005 Pre-Budget Report. Building on these achievements, the UK will work closely with the G7/8, the EU, International Financial Institutions and other international partnerships, including emerging market economies, to promote global prosperity and economic stability, accelerate progress towards the Millennium Development Goals (MDGs), address the challenges of structural economic reform, resist protectionist pressures and promote free and fair trade, by:

- ensuring early progress to deliver on the commitments made in 2005 to provide an extra $50 billion in aid each year, and ensuring that these commitments are transformed into concrete actions to help developing countries achieve the MDGs – including through the funding of ten-year plans to deliver free, universal primary education and health; resources to develop the capacity to trade; implementing the agreement for 100 per cent multilateral debt relief and pushing for further debt relief; launching a vaccination programme through the International Finance Facility for Immunisation; and agreeing a pilot scheme to accelerate the development of vaccines;

- strengthening the ability of EU and global institutions to respond to global challenges to economic stability – including through increasing the IMF's focus on credible, independent and persuasive surveillance and supporting the UN Secretary General in reforming the UN's institutional operations;

- promoting structural reform in the EU to build competitive, open, flexible and fair economies – by ensuring a free and open market in services and completing the single market in financial services; measurable regulatory reform, including reductions in administrative burdens and the exemption of SMEs from disproportionate rules; promoting effective competition policy; and effective monitoring of reforms to maintain momentum in the Lisbon agenda;

- securing sustainable, reliable and affordable energy sources by promoting transparent, open and competitive international energy markets – through working with the Russian G8 Presidency and G8 members to extend the principles of the recent G7 oil initiative to energy, and with EU partners to influence EU energy policy following the 2005 Hampton Court summit; and promoting investment in alternative sources of energy to support the international climate change and sustainable development agendas; and

- promoting a freer and fairer international trading system, in the face of increasing protectionist pressures – through an ambitious outcome to the Doha WTO Trade Round, which delivers substantial benefits to developing countries; enables poor countries to have the flexibility to decide their own trade reform and provides them with resources to build trade capacity; significantly increases agricultural market access; substantially reduces trade-distorting subsidies; eliminates all forms of agricultural export support; and provides greater opportunities for trade in industrial goods and services; as well as through further reform of the Common Agricultural Policy.

RECENT FISCAL TRENDS AND OUTLOOK

2.40 Budget 2006 presents the Government's annual fiscal forecast and updates the 2005 Pre-Budget Report interim projections.[6]

2.41 The Budget 2006 projections are broadly in line with the 2005 Pre-Budget Report interim projections, locking in the Government's prudent stance. As projected in the Pre-Budget Report, receipts growth has been more robust in 2005-06 than would have been anticipated against a background of slower economic growth.

Estimate for **2.42** Net taxes and national insurance contributions have strengthened through 2005-06,
2005-06 and are estimated to have grown by 7.6 per cent from the previous year, in line with the forecast in the Pre-Budget Report. Corporation tax continues to grow strongly, up 27 per cent on last year, and now estimated to be higher than at the Pre-Budget Report, boosted by strong corporate profitability, and by further growth in North Sea oil revenues. The buoyant financial services sector has also contributed to robust growth in income tax and national insurance contributions. Excise duties and VAT receipts are lower than expected, partly reflecting changes in consumers' spending patterns. Moderation in household spending has also reduced growth in consumption taxes.

2.43 The estimated 2005-06 outturn for the public sector current budget is a deficit of £11.4 billion compared with projected deficits of £10.6 billion and £5.7 billion in the 2005 Pre-Budget Report and Budget 2005 respectively. The current budget moves into surplus in 2007-08, a year earlier than expected at the time of the Pre-Budget Report. For public sector net borrowing the estimated 2005-06 outturn shows £37.1 billion, compared with £37 billion projected in the 2005 Pre-Budget Report and £31.9 billion projected in Budget 2005. While the current budget deficit in 2005-06 is £7.6 billion lower than in 2004-05, the reduction in net borrowing is more modest, reflecting the £5.0 billion increase in public sector net investment.

2.44 With economic growth having been slower over 2005, there was a notable shift in the estimated cyclically-adjusted balances in 2005-06. Cyclically-adjusted net borrowing is estimated to have fallen by around $3/4$ of a per cent of GDP to 2.4 per cent of GDP, while the cyclically-adjusted deficit on the current budget fell by 1 per cent of GDP to around $1/4$ per cent of GDP. On the basis of cautious, audited assumptions, the Government is meeting its strict fiscal rules over the economic cycle.

2.45 In making its fiscal projections, the Government distinguishes between non-discretionary factors which affect the public finances, such as changing consumption patterns affecting receipts and changes to the economic forecast, for example to GDP growth, and discretionary Budget measures. This chapter first outlines the non-discretionary changes which form the fiscal context for the Budget decisions.

Non- **2.46** As the economy returns to trend in 2008-09, stronger economic growth underpins
discretionary continued growth in receipts over the projection period, although the rate of receipts growth
changes in is set to moderate in 2006-07, in part driven by higher than forecast capital expenditure in the
receipts North Sea, changes to the pattern of oil production and changes in the impact of the Government's measure to allow North Sea firms to defer first year capital allowances. In line with the rebalancing of economic growth going forward, the forecast for corporation tax is higher than at the Pre-Budget Report, boosted by the improved profitability of non-financial corporations as well as by higher oil prices. Higher equity prices also increase the forecast for capital taxes and stamp duties. Lower growth in average earnings and changes in the composition of consumer spending act to dampen some receipts. VAT and excise duties are particularly affected by changes in spending patterns as well as by losses from Missing Trader Intra-Community (MTIC) fraud.

---

[6] The Budget 2006 fiscal projections take account of the February outturns for receipts, spending and borrowing.

Table 2.3: Public sector net borrowing compared with the 2005 Pre-Budget Report

	Estimate 2005-06	Projections				
		2006-07	2007-08	2008-09	2009-10	2010-11
2005 PBR	37.0	34	31	26	23	22
Changes since the 2005 PBR						
Economic and other forecasting effects	0.2	1½	−1	−½	1	1½
Total before discretionary measures	37.2	35	30	26	24	24
Discretionary measures	0.0	½	−½	−1	−½	0
Budget 2006	37.2	36	30	25	24	23

Note: Totals may not sum due to rounding.

Non-discretionary changes in spending **2.47** The forecast for expenditure before discretionary measures is slightly above the forecast in Pre-Budget Report. Reclassification of the BBC into the public sector increases the expenditure forecast across the projection period, but is fiscally neutral as the impact is offset by increased receipts.

BUDGET DECISIONS

2.48 The Budget is the definitive statement of the Government's desired fiscal policy settings. In making its Budget decisions the Government has considered:

- the need to ensure that, over the economic cycle, the Government will continue to meet its strict fiscal rules;

- its fiscal policy objectives, including the need to ensure sound public finances and that spending and taxation impact fairly both within and between generations; and

- how fiscal policy can best support monetary policy over the economic cycle.

2.49 Against this backdrop, and building on steps already taken, Budget 2006 announces:

- a commitment to increase the child element of the Child Tax Credit in line with average earnings to the end of this Parliament;

- further payments into Child Trust Fund accounts at age 7 of £250 for all children, with £500 for children from lower-income families;

- £585 million of additional resources over 2006-07 and 2007-08 to provide further support for personalised learning in schools in England;

- an increase in the stamp duty land tax threshold to £125,000, exempting an additional 40,000 homebuyers each year;

- the introduction of Real Estate Investments Trusts to create greater flexibility for investors;

- measures to modernise the tax system, and to tackle tax fraud and avoidance; and

- the deferral of the inflation-based increase in main road fuel duties to 1 September 2006, in response to sustained volatility in oil prices.

2.50 Table 1.2 lists the key Budget policy decisions and their impact on the public finances, including resetting the AME margin. Further details are set out in Chapter A of the *Financial Statement and Budget Report.*

MEDIUM-TERM FISCAL PROJECTIONS

2.51 Table 2.4 compares the projections for the current balance, net borrowing and net debt with those published in Budget 2005 and in the 2005 Pre-Budget Report. It includes the impact of all Budget decisions in accordance with the *Code for fiscal stability.* Further detail is provided in Chapter C of the *Financial Statement and Budget Report.*

2.52 The revised outturn for 2004-05 shows the deficit on the current budget to be £0.9 billion lower than in the 2005 Pre-Budget Report, and £2.9 billion higher compared with Budget 2005. The outturn for net borrowing in 2004-05 is £0.9 billion higher than in the Pre-Budget Report, in line with an increase of £1.7 billion in net investment, and net borrowing is £5.3 billion higher than the estimate in Budget 2005.

Table 2.4: Fiscal balances compared with Budget 2005 and the 2005 Pre-Budget Report

	Outturn[1]	Estimate[2]	Projections				
	2004-05	2005-06	2006-07	2007-08	2008-09	2009-10	2010-11
Surplus on current budget (£ billion)							
Budget 2005	−16.1	−5.7	1	4	9	12	–
Effect of revisions and forecasting changes	−3.8	−4.2	−6$^1/_2$	−6$^1/_2$	−5	−3$^1/_2$	–
Effect of discretionary changes	0.0	−0.8	2	2$^1/_2$	2$^1/_2$	2	–
2005 PBR	−19.9	−10.6	−4	0	7	11	13
Effect of revisions and forecasting changes	0.9	−0.8	−2$^1/_2$	$^1/_2$	0	−1	−1$^1/_2$
Effect of discretionary changes	0.0	0.0	−$^1/_2$	$^1/_2$	1	$^1/_2$	$^1/_2$
Budget 2006	−19.0	−11.4	−7	1	7	10	12
Net borrowing (£ billion)							
Budget 2005	34.4	31.9	29	27	24	22	–
Changes to current budget	3.8	4.9	5	4	2$^1/_2$	1$^1/_2$	–
Changes to net investment	0.6	0.1	0	0	0	0	–
2005 PBR	38.8	37.0	34	31	26	23	22
Changes to current budget	−0.9	0.8	3	−1	−$^1/_2$	$^1/_2$	1
Changes to net investment	1.7	0.6	−$^1/_2$	−$^1/_2$	−$^1/_2$	−$^1/_2$	0
Budget 2006	39.7	37.1	36	30	25	24	23
Cyclically-adjusted surplus on current budget (per cent of GDP)							
Budget 2005	−0.8	−0.3	0.1	0.3	0.6	0.8	–
2005 PBR	−1.3	−0.1	0.7	0.7	0.7	0.7	0.8
Budget 2006	−1.3	−0.3	0.4	0.7	0.7	0.7	0.8
Cyclically-adjusted net borrowing (per cent of GDP)							
Budget 2005	2.4	2.4	2.2	2.0	1.6	1.5	–
2005 PBR	2.9	2.2	1.6	1.6	1.6	1.5	1.4
Budget 2006	3.0	2.4	1.9	1.6	1.6	1.6	1.5
Net debt (per cent of GDP)							
Budget 2005	34.4	35.5	36.2	36.8	37.1	37.1	–
2005 PBR	34.7	36.5	37.4	37.9	38.2	38.2	38.2
Budget 2006	35.0	36.7	37.9	38.4	38.5	38.6	38.6

Note: Totals may not sum due to rounding.
[1] *The 2004-05 figures were estimates in Budget 2005.*
[2] *The 2005-06 figures were projections in Budget 2005.*

2.53 The estimated surplus on the current budget in 2005-06 is slightly lower than expected at the 2005 Pre-Budget Report, reflecting slightly higher expenditure. As receipts strengthen over the projection period, the current surplus rises in line with the 2005 Pre-Budget Report and Budget 2005 projections. Similarly, net borrowing is slightly higher in 2005-06, but reduces rapidly, coming back broadly into line with the projections of the 2005 Pre-Budget Report.

2.54 Table 2.4 also sets out the underlying structural position of the fiscal balances, adjusted for the impact of the economic cycle on the public finances.[7] Cyclically-adjusted, the current budget deficit and net borrowing are slightly higher in 2005-06 than projected in the Pre-Budget Report, partly because the output gap is now estimated to be slightly narrower than forecast. Over the period to 2008-09, cyclically-adjusted net borrowing remains at or below that projected in Budget 2005.

Box 2.4: Key successes of the UK fiscal framework

The UK fiscal framework was designed to address a number of challenges, discussed below. On each challenge clear progress has been made.

The first challenge was to ensure sound public finances and fairness within and between generations. Over the cycle from 1986-87 to 1997-98 the current budget was in deficit by an average of 1.9 per cent of GDP in each year, peaking at over 6 per cent in 1993-94. While the current economic cycle has not been completed, the Budget projections show that by 2008-09 the average surplus is expected to be 0.1 per cent of GDP. The largest deficit in any one year of this cycle, at 1.9 per cent of GDP, is equal to the average of the deficit over the previous economic cycle. Net debt as a percentage of GDP was 43.6 per cent in March 1997 compared with a projected 38.3 per cent at the end of the current cycle.

Current budget surplus (per cent of GDP)

Year of cycle	1	2	3	4	5	6	7	8	9	10	11	12	Average
1986-87 to 1997-98 cycle	−1.4	−0.3	1.7	1.4	0.4	−2.0	−5.6	−6.2	−4.8	−3.4	−2.8	−0.2	−1.9
1997-98 to 2008-09 cycle	−0.2	1.2	2.2	2.2	1.0	−1.2	−1.9	−1.6	−0.9[1]	−0.6[2]	0.1[2]	0.5[2]	0.1

[1] Estimate for 2005-06.
[2] Projection for 2006-07 to 2008-09.

Second, fiscal policy has supported monetary policy over the cycle. One way of demonstrating this is to compare the change in cyclically-adjusted net borrowing (the fiscal stance) with the evolution of the output gap. The economy moved above trend in the first half of 1997, and between 1996-97 and 2000-01 the fiscal stance was tightened by 4 percentage points of GDP. As the economy moved below trend in late 2001, the fiscal stance was relaxed by just under 3 percentage points of GDP between 2001-02 and 2004-05, as shown in Chart 2.6.

The third challenge in 1997 was to rebuild the public capital stock. The fiscal rules provided the framework within which an increase in public investment could take place while maintaining sound public finances. Since 1997-98 public sector net investment has increased from 0.6 per cent of GDP to an estimated 2.1 per cent in 2005-06, as illustrated in Chart 2.7. For the remainder of the cycle, public sector net investment is projected to remain at 2¼ per cent of GDP, the longest period of sustained high public investment for 26 years.

---

[7] Details of the Treasury's approach to cyclical adjustment can be found in Annex A of the 2003 *End of year fiscal report*.

ADHERING TO PRINCIPLES

2.55   Table 2.5 presents the key fiscal aggregates based on the five themes of fairness and prudence, long-term sustainability, economic impact, financing and European commitments. The table indicates that, after allowing for non-discretionary changes to receipts and spending and taking into account the Budget decisions, the Government is meeting both of its strict fiscal rules.

Table 2.5: Summary of public sector finances

	Per cent of GDP						
	Outturn	Estimate			Projections		
	2004-05	2005-06	2006-07	2007-08	2008-09	2009-10	2010-11
Fairness and prudence							
Surplus on current budget	−1.6	−0.9	−0.6	0.1	0.5	0.7	0.8
Average surplus since 1997-98	0.2	0.1	0.0	0.0	0.1	0.1	0.2
Cyclically-adjusted surplus on current budget	−1.3	−0.3	0.4	0.7	0.7	0.7	0.8
Long-term sustainability							
Public sector net debt[1]	35.0	36.4	37.5	38.1	38.3	38.4	38.4
Core debt[1]	34.3	35.2	35.4	35.5	35.7	35.9	36.0
Net worth[2]	29.0	26.0	24.8	23.3	22.9	22.9	22.8
Primary balance	−1.7	−1.3	−1.1	−0.5	−0.1	0.1	0.1
Economic impact							
Net investment	1.8	2.1	2.2	2.3	2.3	2.3	2.3
Public sector net borrowing (PSNB)	3.4	3.0	2.8	2.2	1.7	1.6	1.5
Cyclically-adjusted PSNB	3.0	2.4	1.9	1.6	1.6	1.6	1.5
Financing							
Central government net cash requirement	3.3	3.2	3.2	2.6	2.1	2.1	1.8
Public sector net cash requirement	3.3	3.0	2.9	2.4	1.8	1.8	1.5
European commitments							
Treaty deficit[3]	3.3	3.2	3.0	2.4	1.9	1.7	1.6
Cyclically-adjusted Treaty deficit[3]	2.9	2.5	2.0	1.8	1.7	1.7	1.7
Treaty debt ratio[4]	40.8	42.6	43.9	44.5	44.5	44.5	44.5
Memo: Output gap	*−0.4*	*−1.2*	*−1.4*	*−0.7*	*−0.1*	*0.0*	*0.0*

[1] *Debt at end March; GDP centred on end March.*

[2] *Estimate at end December; GDP centred on end December.*

[3] *General government net borrowing on a Maastricht basis.*

[4] *General government gross debt on a Maastricht basis.*

Golden rule   2.56   The current budget balance represents the difference between current receipts and current expenditure, including depreciation. It measures the degree to which current taxpayers meet the cost of paying for the public services they use and it is therefore an important indicator of intergenerational fairness. The current budget strengthens through the projection period, returning to surplus in 2007-08 and showing a surplus of 0.8 per cent of GDP by 2010-11.

2.57   The golden rule is set over the economic cycle to allow fiscal policy to support monetary policy in maintaining stability through the operation of the automatic stabilisers. Progress against the rule is measured by the average annual surplus on the current budget as a percentage of GDP since the cycle began.

2.58   The average surplus on the current budget since the start of the current cycle in 1997-98 is in balance or surplus in every year of the projection period. The economy is projected to return to trend in 2008-09, which means that the average annual surplus on the current budget would be 0.1 per cent of GDP. On this basis, and based on cautious assumptions, the Government is meeting the golden rule and there is a margin against the golden rule of £16 billion in this cycle, including the AME margin, the same as at the 2005 Pre-Budget Report.

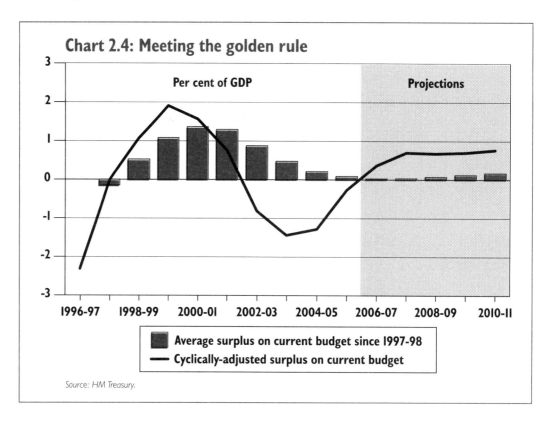

Chart 2.4: Meeting the golden rule

Source: HM Treasury.

2.59   With the economy assumed to be on trend in 2008-09, Budget projections show, based on cautious assumptions, that the average surplus on the current budget over the period 2008-09 to 2010-11 is 0.7 per cent of GDP. At this early stage and based on cautious assumptions, for example for trend growth as explained in Box C2, the Government is therefore on course to meet the golden rule after the end of this economic cycle.

Sustainable   **2.60**   The Government's primary objective for fiscal policy is to ensure sound public
investment rule   finances in the medium term. This means maintaining public sector net debt at a low and sustainable level. To meet the sustainable investment rule with confidence, net debt will be maintained below 40 per cent of GDP in each and every year of the current economic cycle.

2.61   Chart 2.5 shows, that despite output being below trend since 2001, net debt is expected to stabilise at 38.4 per cent of GDP from 2009-10. Therefore the Government meets its sustainable investment rule while continuing to borrow to fund increased long-term capital investment in public services. Chart 2.5 also illustrates projections for core debt, which excludes the estimated impact of the economic cycle on public sector net debt. Core debt rises only modestly from $35^{1/4}$ per cent in 2005-06 to 36 per cent of GDP at the end of the projection period.

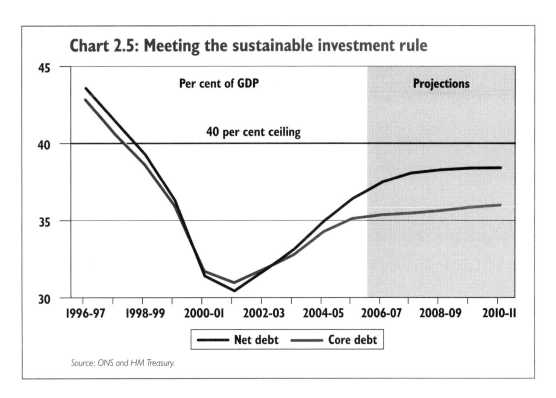

Chart 2.5: Meeting the sustainable investment rule

Source: ONS and HM Treasury.

Economic impact **2.62** While the primary objective of fiscal policy is to ensure sound public finances, fiscal policy also affects the economy and plays a role in supporting monetary policy over the cycle. The overall impact of fiscal policy on the economy can be assessed by examining changes in public sector net borrowing (PSNB). These can be broken down into changes due to the effects of the automatic stabilisers and those due to the change in the fiscal stance, as illustrated in Chart 2.6.

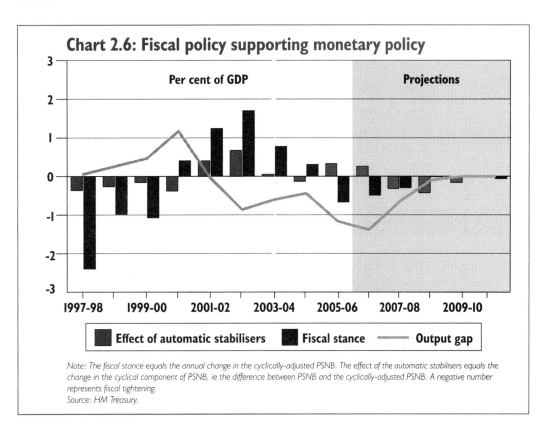

Chart 2.6: Fiscal policy supporting monetary policy

Note: The fiscal stance equals the annual change in the cyclically-adjusted PSNB. The effect of the automatic stabilisers equals the change in the cyclical component of PSNB, ie the difference between PSNB and the cyclically-adjusted PSNB. A negative number represents fiscal tightening.
Source: HM Treasury.

2.63   During the late 1990s, the fiscal stance and the automatic stabilisers tightened at a time when the economy was above trend. As the economy moved below trend in 2001, the automatic stabilisers and the fiscal stance supported the economy, with the degree of support moderating as the economy moved back towards trend in early 2004.

2.64   The overall impact of fiscal policy on the economy is made up of changes in:

- the fiscal stance – that part of the change in PSNB resulting from changes in cyclically-adjusted PSNB; and

- the automatic stabilisers – that part of the change in PSNB resulting from cyclical movements in the economy.

2.65   Between Budgets and Pre-Budget Reports, the fiscal stance can change as a result of a discretionary measure to:

- achieve a desired change in the fiscal stance; or

- accommodate or offset the impact of non-discretionary factors (non-cyclical or structural changes to tax receipts or public spending).

2.66   Table 2.6 explains how these concepts relate to the projections in the Budget. It shows the changes in both the fiscal stance and the overall fiscal impact between Budget 2005, the 2005 Pre-Budget Report and Budget 2006. There was a significant tightening in the fiscal stance between Budget 2005 and the 2005 Pre-Budget Report due to a combination of discretionary policy action and non-discretionary factors. Budget 2006 locks in this tighter fiscal stance with a modest discretionary tightening in the medium term.

Table 2.6: The overall fiscal impact[1]

	Per cent of GDP						
	Outturn[2]	Estimate[3]			Projections		
	2004-05	2005-06	2006-07	2007-08	2008-09	2009-10	2010-11
Change from Budget 2005 to the 2005 PBR							
Post Budget and PBR policy decisions	0.0	0.1	–0.1	–0.2	–0.2	–0.1	–
+							
non-discretionary factors	0.6	–0.2	–0.4	–0.2	0.1	0.2	–
=							
CHANGE IN FISCAL STANCE	0.6	–0.2	–0.6	–0.3	0.0	0.1	–
+							
automatic stabilisers	–0.2	0.6	1.0	0.6	0.2	0.0	–
=							
OVERALL FISCAL IMPACT	0.4	0.4	0.4	0.3	0.2	0.1	–
Change from the 2005 PBR to Budget 2006							
Budget measures	0.0	0.0	0.0	0.0	–0.1	0.0	0.0
+							
non-discretionary factors	0.1	0.1	0.3	0.0	0.0	0.0	0.1
=							
CHANGE IN FISCAL STANCE	0.1	0.1	0.3	–0.1	0.0	0.0	0.1
+							
automatic stabilisers	0.0	–0.1	–0.1	0.0	0.0	0.0	0.0
=							
OVERALL FISCAL IMPACT	0.1	0.0	0.2	–0.1	–0.1	0.0	0.1

[1] All the numbers represent the impact of changes on public sector net borrowing. A negative number represents fiscal tightening.

[2] The 2004-05 figures were estimates in Budget 2005.

[3] The 2005-06 figures were projections in Budget 2005.

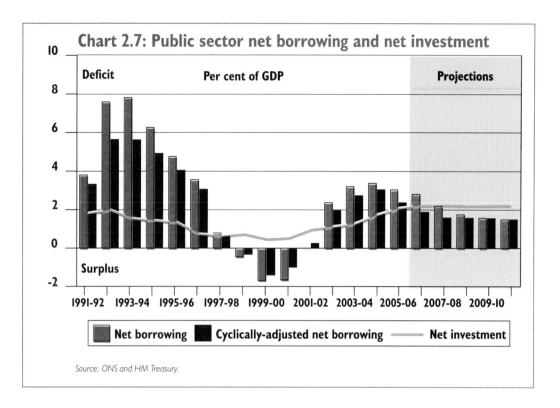

Chart 2.7: Public sector net borrowing and net investment

Source: ONS and HM Treasury.

2.67 On average since 1997-98 public sector net investment has exceeded net borrowing, reflecting the average surplus on the current budget. This is projected to continue as the Government borrows to invest in public services while continuing to meet its strict fiscal rules. Chart 2.7 shows net borrowing falling to 1.5 per cent of GDP by the end of the projection period.

Financing **2.68** The forecast for the central government net cash requirement (CGNCR) for 2005-06 is £40.6 billion, a reduction of £2.7 billion from the 2005 Pre-Budget Report forecast.

2.69 The forecast for the CGNCR for 2006-07 is £41.2 billion. The financing requirement will be met by:

- gross gilt issuance of £63.0 billion;

- an increase in the Treasury bill stock of £2.0 billion by end March 2007; and

- a £3.1 billion planned reduction in the DMO's short-term financing position by end March 2007.

2.70 Full details and a revised financing table can be found in Chapter C. Box 2.5 considers the factors underlying the recent fall in gilt yields and the Government's weighting of its gilt issuance programme towards longer maturities in the last few years. During 2006-07, the DMO will increase the amount of long-maturity and index-linked gilt issuance, with up to two-thirds of total issuance at long maturities. Further details can be found in the *Debt and Reserves Management Report 2006-07* which has been published alongside the Budget.

Box 2.5: Low yields and the Government bond market

Long-term interest rates have fallen to low levels throughout the world with inflation-adjusted interest rates on 30-year government bonds falling below 2 per cent in some countries compared with around 3½ per cent in 2001. The UK government bond, or gilt, market has experienced particularly low yields on very long-maturity gilts (30- to 50-year maturities) with inflation-adjusted interest rates reaching lows of less than ½ per cent in January 2006 compared with over 2 per cent in 2001.

The charts below illustrate how yields on both long-maturity nominal ('conventional') and index-linked gilts have fallen between May 2005 and March 2006. Yields have recovered somewhat since January.

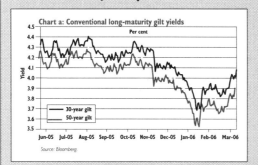

The factors underlying the recent fall in gilt yields extend well beyond the gilt market itself. Understanding the likely future duration and scale of low yields raises questions about: whether the fall in global yields is temporary or likely to be sustained, which will depend on factors including the global savings rate and global credit conditions; the macroeconomic implications of pension fund demand for long-dated and inflation-linked assets; the behaviour of pension funds and other sources of demand in the current accounting and regulatory climate; and the implications for the Government's debt management policy and plans for financing through the gilts market. The Government is keeping these factors under continuous review.

In recent years pension funds have shifted increasingly from equities into long-dated and inflation-linked bonds and this trend is likely to continue in the medium term. The Government's debt management objective is to minimise cost subject to risk. In line with this objective, the Government has weighted its gilt issuance programme increasingly towards longer maturities over the last few years (from 28 per cent of total insurance in 2003-04 to 47 per cent in 2005-06) and has extended the yield curve to 50 years during 2005-06.

Further details of the Government's financing programme for 2006-07 can be found in the *Debt and Reserves Management Report 2006-07*, which was published alongside the Budget and is available on the Treasury's website at: www.hm-treasury.gov.uk.

European **2.71**   The Government supports a prudent interpretation of the Stability and Growth Pact,
commitments as described in Box B2 and as reflected in reforms to the Pact agreed in March 2005. This takes
into account the economic cycle, the long-term sustainability of the public finances and the
important role of public investment. The public finance projections set out in Budget 2006,
which show the Government is meeting its fiscal rules over the cycle, maintaining low debt
and sustainable public finances, combined with sustainable increases in public investment,
are fully consistent with a prudent interpretation of the Pact.

Dealing with **2.72**   Forecasts for the public finances are subject to a considerable degree of uncertainty,
uncertainty in particular the fiscal balances, which represent the difference between two large aggregates.
The use of cautious assumptions audited by the NAO builds a safety margin into the public
finance projections to guard against unexpected events. The degree of caution in the
assumptions underpinning the public finance projections increases over the projection
period. For example, Box C2 explains how the Government bases its public finance
projections on a trend growth assumption that is a $1/4$ percentage point lower than its neutral
view, to accommodate potential errors arising from misjudgements about the trend rate of
growth of the economy in the medium term. This implies that the level of GDP used in the
public finance forecast is $1^1/4$ per cent below the neutral view by 2010-11.

2.73   A second important source of potential error results from misjudging the position of
the economy in relation to trend output. To minimise this risk, the robustness of the
projections is tested against an alternative scenario in which the level of trend output is
assumed to be one percentage point lower than in the central case. Chart 2.8 illustrates the
projections for this cautious case.

2.74   The Government is, on the basis of cautious, independently-audited assumptions,
meeting the golden rule in the central case. In the cautious case, Chart 2.8 shows that the
cyclically-adjusted surplus will be in balance at the end of the projection period.

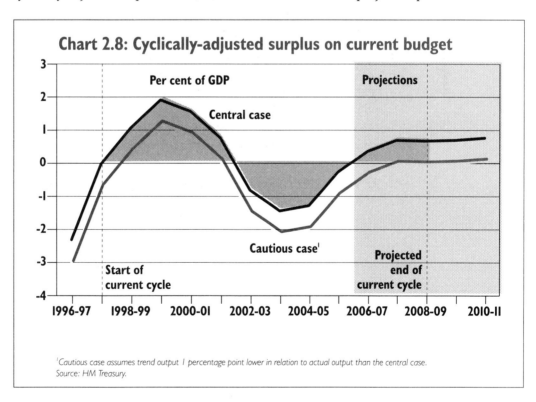

Chart 2.8: Cyclically-adjusted surplus on current budget

Cautious case assumes trend output 1 percentage point lower in relation to actual output than the central case.
Source: HM Treasury.

Box 2.6: Independence for statistics

Statistics make a crucial contribution to good government in a modern democracy: assisting in the formulation and evaluation of policies; the management of the services for which the government is responsible; encouraging and informing debate; and allowing people to judge whether government is delivering on its promises. Last November, the Chancellor announced to Parliament the Government's intention to legislate for independence in statistics. Alongside the Budget, the Government has published a consultation document outlining proposals for the further enhancement of the statistical system in the context of the planned legislation by:

* entrenching independence in legislation;

* introducing a direct reporting and accountability to Parliament, rather than through Ministers;

* placing a statutory responsibility on a new independent governing board to assess and approve all National Statistics against the code of practice, also backed by statute;

* making key appointments to the board through open and fair competition; and

* removing the statistics office from Ministerial control by establishing it as a **Non-Ministerial** department, with special funding arrangements outside the normal Spending Review process.

The Government welcomes the views of all stakeholders on the issues raised in the consultation document. Copies of the consultation document, *Independence for statistics*, can be obtained from the HM Treasury website at www.hm-treasury.gov.uk.

LONG-TERM FISCAL SUSTAINABILITY

2.75   While a key objective of fiscal policy is to ensure sound public finances over the short and medium term, the Government must also ensure that fiscal policy decisions are sustainable in the long term. Failure to do so would see financial burdens shifted to future generations, with detrimental effects on long-term growth. It would also be inconsistent with the principles of fiscal management set out in the *Code for fiscal stability*.

2.76   An analysis of long-term fiscal sustainability is presented in Annex A. The analysis shows that given the projected profile for tax revenues and transfers, current public consumption can grow at around assumed GDP growth after the medium term while meeting the Government's golden rule. Public sector net investment can also grow broadly in line with the economy without jeopardising the sustainable investment rule.

2.77   These illustrative long-term fiscal projections yield similar conclusions to those presented in the Government's 2005 *Long-term public finance report*. Using a range of sustainability indicators, and based on current policies and reasonable assumptions, the report shows that the public finances are sustainable in the longer term.

3 MEETING THE PRODUCTIVITY CHALLENGE

Productivity growth underpins strong economic performance and sustained increases in living standards. Raising productivity growth is critical to meeting the opportunities and challenges of globalisation. Budget 2006 sets out the next steps the Government is taking to strengthen the drivers of productivity growth, including:

- **advancing the goals of the ten-year Science and Innovation Investment Framework to maximise the impact of science funding,** including an intention to create a single health research fund of at least £1 billion per year, to simplify radically institutional research funding, to expand R&D support for mid-sized companies and introduce a package of measures to improve science teaching, raise the quality of science lessons and entitle able pupils to study three separate sciences at GCSE;

- **measures to reduce further burdens on business,** including new commitments to reduce the administrative burden of the tax system, introducing the Hampton Review's principles into law, and a review of how the experiences of large business can be taken into account in administering the tax system;

- **a comprehensive package of measures to enhance the UK's position as a leading location for inward investment, developing an ambitious strategy for marketing the UK:**

  - **promoting London as the world's leading international centre for financial and business services,** with a new strategy to be developed and implemented by a high-level group representing the City's key interests by summer 2006;

  - **establishing a new International Business Advisory Council** comprising some of the world's foremost business people;

  - **a programme of organisational changes to UK Trade and Investment,** with the aim of a fundamental transformation of its effectiveness in marketing the UK;

  - **strengthening the UK's reputation as one of the world's best locations for higher education,** by boosting support for international students to the UK, and establishing three new University Partnership Schemes;

- **building on the Government's commitment to raise skills levels** by investing in the reform of further education and training provision, and asking the Leitch Review of Skills to report specifically on how skills and employment services can complement each other;

- **boosting access to finance to enable early-stage companies with real growth potential to bridge the equity gap and progress through to market,** announcing a further £50 million in 2006-07 and £50 million in 2007-08 for the Enterprise Capital Funds scheme; and

- **taking forward the Government's strategy for tackling the long-term lack of supply and responsiveness of housing and property** and introducing Real Estate Investment Trusts to create greater flexibility for investors.

Globalisation and productivity 3.1 *Long-term global economic challenges and opportunities for the UK,* published alongside the 2004 Pre-Budget Report, identified the opportunities and challenges created by shifting economic activity and rapid technological change as faster information flows and falling transport costs continue to break down geographical barriers to economic activity. *Globalisation and the UK: strength and opportunity to meet the economic challenge,* published on 2 December 2005, set out the UK's existing strengths and where it needs to build on success, in order to thrive in a global environment. The latest data on international comparisons of productivity show that recently the UK has made progress in narrowing the productivity gap as set out in Box 3.1. This Budget sets out the Government's plans in these areas, particularly on science and innovation, attracting global investment to the UK, reducing the burdens on business and enhancing skills.

The UK's productivity framework and performance

The five driver framework 3.2 Alongside the Budget the Government is publishing *Productivity in the UK 6: Progress and new evidence,* which analyses the UK's recent productivity performance relative to comparator economies. It also sets out new evidence underlying the Government's five driver framework, which provides the context for the Government's strategy for raising productivity growth.

This Budget sets out reforms described in the context of the five key drivers of productivity:

- improving *competition,* vital for the adoption of innovation and increased business efficiency;

- promoting *enterprise,* by removing barriers to entrepreneurship and developing an enterprise culture;

- supporting *science and innovation,* given that increasing rewards to innovation mean that the UK's economic success will depend on its ability to create new knowledge and translate it into innovative goods and services;

- raising *skills* levels, to create a more flexible and productive workforce, which can adopt innovative technologies and enable individuals to move into new areas of work; and

- encouraging *investment,* to increase the stock of physical capital, including through stronger, more efficient capital markets.

Box 3.1: UK productivity performance

An in-depth discussion of the UK's productivity performance can be found in *Productivity in the UK 6: Progress and new evidence* published alongside Budget 2006.

In the long-run, productivity growth is the key driver of wages, profits and ultimately overall prosperity. The latest data on international comparisons of productivity shows that recently the UK has made progress in narrowing the international productivity gap. Chart a below illustrates some of this progress. Since 1995 the UK has halved the output per worker gap with France and closed the gap with Germany. Although the gap with the US remains significant, the UK is the only country in the G7 to have kept pace with the US.

Productivity performance is likely to be dampened by periods of strong employment growth. Historically, the UK has rarely experienced simultaneously strong employment and productivity growth. Since 1997 the UK has witnessed strong employment growth, with over 2.3 million more people being employed, alongside productivity growth. The UK is experiencing the longest sustained period of productivity growth and employment growth since the 1950's when records began. Chart b illustrates the UK"s recent success in combining employment and productivity growth.

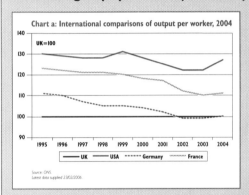

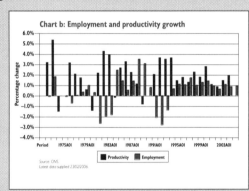

To assess progress on actual headline productivity performance and remove distortions created by cyclical factors, judgements on productivity performance should be made between on-trend points.

There is evidence that the UK has improved its trend productivity performance. Over the first half of the current economic cycle, 1997-2001, which covers the period between the first and second on-trend points in the cycle, actual productivity (trend output per hour worked) growth was 2.59 per cent per annum. This is higher than the figure of just over 2 per cent annual actual productivity growth over each of the previous two economic cycles.

European economic reform **3.3**   Strengthening economic reform in Europe is a key priority for the UK. During the UK Presidency of the EU, further steps were taken to reduce the burden of EU regulation on business, strengthen the transatlantic economic relationship and deliver greater integration in European financial services markets. Member States also submitted their first National Reform Programmes setting out the policies they intend to pursue to promote growth, employment creation and productivity[1]. The UK will continue to press for progress on this agenda. Box 3.3 later in this chapter sets out the further steps that are needed to drive up competition in the Single Market.

---

[1] *Lisbon Strategy for Jobs and Growth: UK National Reform Programme*, HM Treasury, October 2005

Productivity in the regions

3.4 The Government is also committed to strengthening economic performance across the regions, localities and countries of the UK, and to reducing the persistent gap in growth rates between the regions. The nine Regional Development Agencies (RDAs) were therefore set up to advance the shared growth priorities for each region and local area in England. The three Northern RDAs have worked together with other regional and local partners to develop the Northern Way Growth Initiative, which provides a long-term strategy for transforming the economic performance of the North.

3.5 The RDAs were asked to contribute to the development of Budget 2006 in three key areas: rationalising business support; creating links between the national and regional frameworks on innovation; and increasing private investment in economic regeneration. Budget 2006 announces measures developed with and building on the RDAs' input, set out later in this chapter, including a commitment to a radical rationalisation of the number of business support services.

Cities and regional growth

3.6 The RDAs, together with other regional and local bodies, have developed effective collaboration across city regions, in recognition of the the strong role that cities play in regional economic growth. Examples of this include the Northern Way Growth Strategy and the Regional Cities East Initiative. Through the *State of the English Cities Report*[2] and *Devolving decision making: 3 – Meeting the regional economic challenge: The importance of cities to regional growth*,[3] published alongside the Budget, the Government has been analysing the contribution that cities make to regional economic performance. High performing cities contribute to competitive regions, stimulating growth and employment, promoting excellence in surrounding areas and joining up separate business hubs to expand existing markets and create new ones. The Government's strategy for facilitating the economic growth of London so that it secures its position as a high performing city to meet the opportunities and challenges of globalisation, is set out in Box 3.2.

3.7 Given the importance of strong collaboration across regions, local areas and cities, this analysis raises a series of challenges around how the Government builds on steps already taken to devolve decision-making to the regional and local levels. In seeking to meet these challenges, the Government will conduct a review to feed into the 2007 Comprehensive Spending Review to explore the opportunities for further releasing the economic potential of English regions, cities and localities, and to more effectively respond to the ongoing challenge of tackling pockets of deprivation. *Devolving decision making: 3 – Meeting the regional economic challenge: The importance of cities to regional growth* also sets out the Government's initial assessment of the role that cities play in driving both regional and national economic growth. It explores both the current state of economic performance across English cities, and the different challenges cities face in raising this performance and in reducing disparities in outcomes for their residents.

Local Authority Business Growth Incentive Scheme

3.8 To create a direct financial incentive for local authorities to promote local business growth the Government introduced the Local Authority Business Growth Incentive (LABGI) scheme in April 2005. Local authorities receive a proportion of increases in local business rate revenues to spend on their own priorities, in addition to the grant that they have already received in the local government finance settlement. The Government announced the first year of LABGI payments in February. In England, 266 local authorities received LABGI grants for 2005-06, totalling £114 million. The Government estimates that local authorities in England and Wales could gain up to £1 billion over the three years to 2007-08.

---

[2] *State of the English Cities*, ODPM, March 2006
[3] *Devolving decision making: 3 – Meeting the regional economic challenge: The importance of cities to regional growth*, HM Treasury, DTI and ODPM, March 2006.

> ### Box 3.2: London – meeting the challenges and opportunities of globalisation
>
> London is well positioned to respond effectively to the opportunities and challenges presented by globalisation, benefiting from a long history of trading links across the world, excellent business connectivity, well developed infrastructure, and a highly skilled and flexible workforce supporting knowledge intensive economic activity. Its successful bid to host the 2012 Olympic and Paralympic Games shows the confidence in London at both a domestic and international level.
>
> To build on this historically successful foundation and advance economic success in the future, the Government, working in partnership with business and the Greater London Authority, will:
>
> - grant further strategic and delivery responsibilities to the Greater London Authority (GLA), enabling the Mayor to better match provision of public services to specific needs across the capital. The Minister for Local Government and Communities will respond to the outcome of ODPM's consultation in the spring;
>
> - bring together London's world-leading financial and business services industry in a new high-level group to develop a single coherent strategy for promoting the city's competitive advantages as a location for international finance, especially in emerging markets such as India, China and the Middle East (as described in detail later in this chapter and in *Financial Services in London: Global Opportunities and Challenges* published alongside the Budget);
>
> - set out a programme of work which will enhance the delivery of public services in the capital, improve the opportunities available to Londoners – particularly those in disadvantaged areas – and promote continued economic growth; and
>
> - publish *Employment opportunity for all: analysing labour market trends in London*, alongside this Budget, analysing the underlying reasons for low employment rates in London compared to other parts of the country, as a basis for future policy action (set out in detail in Chapter 4).

COMPETITION

3.9   Competition drives productivity by creating incentives for firms to be innovative. A competitive environment is vital to ensure UK businesses continue to thrive in the global market place. In 2004 an independent peer review described the UK competition authorities as having all the necessary powers to develop a world-class competition regime and ranked the UK regime third in the world.[4] The Government is committed to further improvements, and will commission another independent review of the comparative effectiveness of the UK competition regime with its peers in the OECD, during 2006-07.

European competition policy

Competition and the single market **3.10**   The Government's commitment to openness in trade and investment is a key driver of the UK's global competitiveness. A fully open and competitive single market would have similar benefits for the EU. Evidence suggests the creation of the single market has produced over 2.5 million jobs and delivered around £600 billion of extra prosperity for the EU over the past 10 years.[5] However, just at a time when Europe's commitment to open and liberalised

---

[4] *Peer Review of Competition Policy*, KPMG and the Department for Trade and Industry, May 2004. Available at www.dti.gov.uk.

[5] *The internal market – ten years without frontiers*, European Commission, 2003

markets needs to be stronger than ever, there is evidence of an increasingly protectionist approach emerging. The EU has seen delays in agreeing a vital package of reforms to liberalise trade in the service sector and a number of national governments have moved back towards protecting dominant companies.

3.11   The Government believes that further steps are needed to drive up competition in the Single Market, as set out in Box 3. 3

Box 3.3: Strengthening the European Single Market – levelling the playing field

The Government strongly believes that Europe must continue to strengthen and deepen the Single Market, enabling Europe's firms to compete successfully in the global marketplace, and is seeking:

- full implementation by Member States of existing market-opening legislation across the Single Market, including in the telecommunications and energy sectors;

- swift agreement by Member States and the European Parliament on an ambitious and liberalising Directive to remove barriers to trade in services; and

- rapid action by the European Commission and Member States to tackle the barriers to competition identified by the Commission's sector inquiries into competition in the EU's gas and electricity markets and in financial services.

In addition, the Government welcomes the European Commission's pledge to examine any undue interference by national governments in the process of cross-border corporate restructuring in Europe. The Government also welcomes the proposals to improve competition set out in the Commission's recent Energy Green Paper, including measures which take forward the interim findings of the gas and electricity sector inquiry.

Satisfactory action in all of these areas will be essential to drive up competition in the Single Market. If this is not achieved, the Government believes there should be further work to consider the effectiveness of competition policy enforcement in the EU, including through further independent investigations into sectors where competition is not develping as it should. The Government will continue to raise these issues with the Commission and other Member States.

Energy 3.12   Promoting competitive and secure energy markets in the UK, and beyond, are core Government goals. The UK's well-regulated energy sector has delivered secure supplies at low prices for much of the past nine years. However, more recently global oil price increases have fed through to higher gas prices, while domestic gas production from the UK Continental Shelf is declining faster than expected. This has led to a tight supply situation and higher prices in the UK gas market this winter.

3.13   The 2005 Pre-Budget Report noted that the independent energy regulator – the Office of Gas and Electricity Markets (Ofgem) – and the Government were working to ensure the effective operation of the UK energy market. This included Ofgem action to maximise the use of Liquefied Natural Gas (LNG) facilities and a request from the Government for the European Commission to investigate the operation of the gas interconnector (during the period when gas prices were high in the late autumn the gas interconnector to the continent was under-utilised, despite the price premium on the UK side). As a result, during the winter, LNG import capacity has been used to the fullest possible extent and the flow of gas through the interconnector has risen to the levels forecast by National Grid. Nonetheless questions remain about the operation of the interconnector and the Government is urging the European Commission to complete its investigation, in particular into whether there are any barriers to the free movement of gas. As set out in Box 3.3, speeding up liberalisation of EU energy markets is a key priority for the Government. This reaffirms the importance of fully liberalised energy markets across the EU to deliver sustainable, competitive and secure energy.

Energy review 3.14   The Government recognises the importance of energy in supporting sustainable growth, as well as meeting our environmental aims (described in Chapter 7). Work is going on across Government to identify how we can meet our long-term energy needs while achieving our goals on security of supply and climate change, particularly through the comprehensive review of UK energy policy announced last November by the Prime Minister. The review will make policy recommendations to the Prime Minister and the Secretary of State for Trade and Industry in summer 2006. Building on the recommendations of the Energy Review, the Government will identify how competitive markets can best be enabled to meet the future energy challenges the UK faces.

Competition in specific markets

Payment systems 3.15   Innovation, price inefficiency, access and governance are key issues in improving competition in payment systems. The Government therefore welcomes the progress made in the Payment Systems Task Force's work on governance across all payment schemes and looks forward to detailed proposals that ensure that payment systems are run in the interests of users and the wider economy. The Government remains committed to legislating if there has not been a significant improvement in competition by the end of the Task Force's four-year lifespan.

Spectrum use 3.16   Radio spectrum is a vital resource for communications and other services, and the public sector uses over a third of the entire spectrum for defence, aeronautical, maritime, scientific and emergency services. In December 2005, Professor Martin Cave published an independent audit of spectrum holdings in the public sector.[6] The Government agrees with the audit that there is scope for more efficient management in the majority of public sector spectrum.

3.17   The Government has today **published detailed plans for the implementation of changes to public sector spectrum, in response to the audit's recommendations.**[7] This will create new opportunities for public bodies to make more effective use of their spectrum holdings, by enabling and encouraging trading and increased sharing with other users.

3.18   To support this, Ofcom has agreed to take forward work on defining the spectrum rights of public bodies. Departments will outline specific proposals for the release or sharing of spectrum by the end of 2006, and the Government will produce a spectrum strategy in March 2007. This will examine current spectrum use and forecast future requirements. Spectrum charges will also be more consistently applied across the public sector to provide stronger incentives for efficiency, and Ofcom plans to introduce pricing in aeronautical and maritime radar spectrum from 2008.

---

[6] *Independent Audit of Spectrum Holdings Final Report*, December 2005

[7] *Independent Audit of Major Spectrum Holdings: Government Response and Action Plan*, Cabinet Official Committee on UK Spectrum Strategy (UKSSC), March 2006

Creating competition with public procurement

3.19 The purchase of goods and services by the public sector – public procurement – accounts for a significant proportion of public expenditure, and of demand for goods and services in the economy. In some markets the public sector is likely to be by far the largest buyer, and in a position to affect competition through its purchasing behaviour.

Better public procurement **3.20** Good progress continues to be made on improving value for money through better public procurement. The Government is ahead of schedule in meeting its targets with £2.3 billion of savings having already been made across central civil government. Further improvement is supported by new simplified procurement regulations accompanied by Office of Government Commerce (OGC) guidance on e-auctions, framework agreements, competitive dialogue and the scope to take account of environmental and social issues.

SME procurement **3.21** The (OGC) and the Small Business Service's national Small and Medium Enterprise (SME) procurement programme has continued to make improvements. Data gathered from 95 local authorities indicates that SMEs have a 59 per cent share (in terms of value) of local authority procurement against 51 per cent SME share of turnover in the UK economy. Achievements since the progress report of December 2005 include:[8]

- the imminent launch of the national portal to advertise low value public sector contracts;

- 800 procurers and more than 3,000 SMEs have been trained (including those from the Third Sector) through a nationwide training programme; and

- an investigation into the public sector's use of third-party accreditation services. Recommendations will be published in spring 2006.

Small Business Research Initiative **3.22** The Small Business Research Initiative (SBRI) is monitoring departmental compliance with the mandatory target to procure at least 2.5 per cent of their extra-mural R&D from small firms. The Government comfortably exceeded its target in 2004-05 and 10.6 per cent of the £2.5 billion of extra-mural R&D expenditure in participating Government departments went to SMEs.

Procurement in major government markets **3.23** As part of the Kelly programme to increase competition and capacity in major government markets, proposals for better strategic management of waste management resulting from a comprehensive survey of all local authorities in England will be published in spring 2006.[9] In addition, the Public Sector Construction Clients' Forum, chaired by Sir Christopher Kelly, has begun work to implement better planning of public sector demand for construction in relation to the capacity of the industry; developing improved whole-life value for money construction procurement performance measurement; and embedding Achieving Excellence in Construction best practice. An in-depth analysis of the impact of construction on the UK, particularly in London and the Southeast, is due in summer 2006.

---

[8] http://www.supplyinggovernment.gov.uk/pdf/SBS_progress_rep_Dec_05.pdf
[9] See *Increasing competition and improving long-term capacity planning the Government market place*, Office of Government Commerce, December 2003.

ENTERPRISE

3.24   In an increasingly open, competitive, global economy, a vibrant and thriving environment for entrepreneurial activity is critical in ensuring that the UK can respond flexibly to new challenges. Total early stage entrepreneurial activity in the UK is the third highest rate of the G7 economies behind the US and Canada.[10] *Productivity in the UK 6: Progress and new evidence* sets out the latest evidence on the contribution of enterprise to productivity growth.

3.25   The Government is committed to improving the UK business environment and tackling barriers to business growth to allow the UK to enhance its competitive position in the global economy. The Government's strategy has focused on five areas: regulatory reform; modernising and simplifying the business tax system; improving access to finance for small business; improving business support services, with a focus on businesses with high growth potential; and promoting an enterprise culture including encouraging enterprise in disadvantaged areas.

Leading regulatory reform

3.26   Effective and well-focused regulation can play a vital role in correcting market failures, promoting fairness and increasing competition. However, inefficient and over-burdensome regulation can impose a significant cost on business without improving regulatory outcomes. The Government has pursued a programme of reform to deliver better regulation:

- reducing the administrative burdens upon business of understanding regulations and complying with them, including the costs of paperwork, undergoing inspection and complying with enforcement activity;

- examining the existing stock of regulation to ensure that outdated and outmoded regulations, and those encouraging practices that are not risk-based, are removed from the statute book;

- ensuring that there is a clear rationale to new regulations, that the benefits outweigh the costs and that alternatives to regulation are not feasible; and

- pursuing an agenda of regulatory reform in Europe.

Delivering better regulation

3.27   The Government believes that the costs to businesses of administering regulations should be as low as possible without jeopardising regulatory outcomes. Following the publication at Budget 2005 of Philip Hampton's report[11] on reducing administrative burdens, and the Better Regulation Task Force (BRTF) report[12] on reducing the administrative cost of regulations on business, the Government launched a Better Regulation Action Plan in May 2005. Progress is shown in Box 3.4.

---

[10] Global Entrepreneurship Monitor 2005

[11] *Reducing administrative burdens: effective inspection and enforcement*, Budget 2005

[12] *Less is More: Reducing Burdens, Improving Outcomes*, Better Regulation Task Force, March 2005

Regulatory 3.28   To support the Plan and to strengthen the regulatory scrutiny of all new regulatory
scrutiny proposals that impose a significant cost upon business, the Prime Minister's Panel on
Regulatory Accountability (PRA) has been holding departments to account for their
regulatory performance since it was established in 2004. To support the PRA in holding
departments and regulators to account, and to drive delivery of the Government's ambitious
plans for regulatory reform, the Better Regulation Executive (BRE) was established in May
2005 in the Cabinet Office. The Better Regulation Commission (BRC) was also launched on 1
January 2006 and sits alongside the BRE, providing independent, business-focused advice to
the Government about its overall regulatory performance. Under the new Chair, Rick
Haythornthwaite, former Chief Executive Officer of Invensys Plc, the BRC plays a crucial role
in holding departments to account for their plans to reduce regulatory burdens on business.

Box 3.4 Implementing the Better Regulation Action Plan

In May 2005, the Government published an Action Plan, which set out the timetable for
implementing the wide-ranging reforms to the UK's regulatory framework that were
announced at Budget 2005. The Government has met the milestones set out in that plan
and remains on track to deliver these fundamental reforms in full by 2009. Already the
Government has:

- introduced the Legislative and Regulatory Reform Bill to Parliament, which will
  reinforce the principles of risk-based regulatory enforcement as the heart of
  regulatory practice. It will make the removal of complex or outdated regulation,
  and the reform of regulatory structures, simpler and quicker;

- published today a draft Code of Practice, which will entrench the Hampton
  Review's principles in law if the Bill receives Royal Assent;

- following the recommendation of Sir David Arculus and the BRTF, been
  undertaking a project to measure the administrative burden of regulation, with
  departments due to present their simplification plans to the Prime Minister's
  Panel for Regulatory Accountability before the end of the year;

- made progress merging regulatory bodies, with the Horticultural Marketing
  Inspectorate and Defra Investigations Service being merged into the Rural
  Payments Agency by 1 April, DTI Companies Investigation Branch being merged
  into the Insolvency Service on 3 April, and work to merge the Adventures Activity
  Licensing Authority and the Engineering Inspectorate into the Health and Safety
  Executive (HSE) to be completed in the near future;

- announced a Local Better Regulation Office to minimise local regulatory burdens
  on business and work in partnership with local authorities and the national
  regulators to deliver a risk-based approach to business inspection and
  enforcement; and

- started a BRE-led review of regulatory penalty regimes, under Professor Richard
  Macrory. It aims to make penalty systems more consistent across regulatory
  bodies, ensuring that they reflect the impact of the offence, with tougher penalties
  for businesses that persistently break the rules.

3.29 The 'Hampton enforcement principles' set out in the Hampton Review are that:

- regulators, and the regulatory system as a whole, should use comprehensive risk assessment to concentrate resources on the areas that need them most;

- regulators should be accountable for the efficiency and effectiveness of their activities, while remaining independent in the decisions they take;

- no inspection should take place without a reason;

- businesses should not have to give unnecessary information, nor give the same piece of information twice;

- the few businesses that persistently break regulations should be identified quickly;

- regulators should provide authoritative, accessible advice easily and cheaply; and

- regulators should recognise that a key element of their activity will be to allow, or even encourage, economic progress and only to intervene when there is a clear case for protection.

Hampton Code of **3.30** The Legislative and Regulatory Reform Bill, currently before the House of Commons,
Practice contains powers to enable the Hampton enforcement principles to be established in UK law through a statutory Code of Practice. It is the Government's intention that these principles should apply at the point where regulators make their policies, rules, codes, and guidance. The Government also intends to ensure that regulators give businesses easy access to complaints procedures. The BRE and BRC will scrutinise regulators' compliance with the Code, and the Local Better Regulation Office (LBRO) will scrutinise local authorities' compliance with the Code as part of their wider role in devising a performance management and prioritisation scheme for local enforcement. **The Government today announces that it intends to use powers in the Bill to introduce a statutory Code of Practice, and the Cabinet Office is today publishing an initial draft.**[13] If the Bill receives Royal Assent, the Code of Practice will be subject to a statutory consultation period.

Reducing **3.31** Following the recommendation of the BRTF to adopt an approach first used in the
burdens on Netherlands, the Government has been carrying out work to measure the total administrative
business burden on business of complying with government regulations. The baseline methodology will draw on the lessons from the best practice in the Netherlands. This work is currently ongoing and in the course of the next few months, each department will publish detailed targets for the reduction of these burdens. Alongside this, Government departments are being asked to draw up 'simplification plans,' which will outline measures being taken by departments to implement the Hampton review, and remove outdated or outmoded regulations. Examples of initiatives already making a difference to businesses, which are being considered for possible future adoption, include removing 50 per cent of HSE's forms; up to 30 per cent savings in routine planned inspections in the retail sector; and £150 million savings, particularly for small and medium-sized enterprises (SMEs), in reducing the burden of regulatory compliance when trading internationally. Stakeholder views on simplification plans are welcome and many departments have published their plans in draft. Additional suggestions for simplification can be made through the Government's simplification portal.[14]

---

[13] http://www.cabinetoffice.gov.uk/
[14] http://www.betterregulation.gov.uk

3.32   Departments must present their simplification plans to the Prime Minister's PRA over the coming months. The Government will then set stretching but achievable targets for reducing each department's administrative burden over time. **In areas where the administrative burden of regulation appears relatively high compared to international comparators, the Government will set particularly demanding targets.** In areas where the UK is already ahead of other countries, as a result of an active and ongoing simplification programme, the target will reflect progress already made. One such area, although not regulation, is the administrative burden imposed on business by the tax system where targets have been set, and are described later in this chapter.

Local Better **3.33**   A key concern for business identified by the Hampton Review was lack of consistency **Regulation Office** and coordination in local authority regulatory services. To address this concern the Government announced in the 2005 Pre-Budget Report the establishment of the Local Better Regulation Office (LBRO). The LBRO will be responsible for minimising local regulatory burdens on business and working with local authorities and national regulators to deliver a risk-based approach to business inspection and enforcement while maintaining a high level of public protection. A vision statement was published in January 2006 and HM Treasury, DTI and the BRE are now working together to deliver the LBRO. Further details will be published towards the end of 2006 and a draft Bill published as soon as possible in 2007.

3.34   In addition, the Office of Fair Trading (OFT) is working to incorporate some of the smaller regulators and strengthen its relations with Trading Standards to deliver better local regulation.

Consumer Credit **3.35**   Today, following discussion with industry and consumer groups, the Financial Services Authority (FSA) and the OFT are publishing a joint statement of intent in order to strengthen their policy coordination, streamline their separate contact with firms, and improve their consumer communications. The intention is to reduce duplication for firms dealing with both bodies. A more detailed action plan will be published by the end of April.

3.36   The Hampton report asked the Government to consider passing the consumer credit functions of the OFT to the FSA. UK regulation of mortgages and consumer credit is undergoing a period of extensive change, with the introduction of FSA mortgage regulation from 31 October 2004, the Consumer Credit Bill currently before Parliament and European Commission proposals for a new Consumer Credit Directive. Following consultation with a range stakeholders, and in the light of the ongoing changes mentioned above, the Government does not propose additional reforms of the consumer credit regime at this time. It may look again at the regulation of consumer credit, including lending secured on land, when these changes have taken effect.

Haulage Industry **3.37**   The findings from the Burns Inquiry into fuel costs, foreign competition and freight taxes have informed the Government's work to ensure that foreign, as well as domestic, hauliers operating in the UK comply consistently with UK road safety regulations. At the 2005 Pre-Budget Report, the Government announced a programme of investment in 'weigh-in-motion' sensors, to allow better targeting of enforcement activities on non-compliant hauliers, and a pilot will be underway in the next few months. Fairer enforcement for hauliers of all nationalities will be further strengthened by the enabling provisions contained in the Road Safety Bill. The Government is also currently consulting on proposals to simplify the operator licensing regime, to reduce hauliers' administrative costs and allow them greater flexibility.

Davidson Review **3.38**   The 2005 Pre-Budget Report announced that the Government had asked Neil Davidson QC to conduct a review of the UK's implementation of EU legislation, due to report by the end of 2006. **Neil Davidson QC is today writing to government departments with guidance on how to screen the stock of their legislation that derived from the EU for**

potential 'over-implementation'. This information will be used when drawing up their simplification plans. Alongside the PRA, the Review will scrutinise the plans and suggest further proposals relating to how EU legislation has been implemented for inclusion. The Review launched a Call to Evidence on 3 March, inviting business, voluntary groups and other stakeholders to submit evidence of over-implementation, including goldplating, double banking and 'regulatory creep', which will run until 25 May.[15] As well as submissions of evidence, the Review is drawing on international comparisons to identify further high-risk areas of over-implementation.

Regulation of **3.39**   At the 2005 Pre-Budget Report, the Government announced a ten-point action plan
financial services of reforms to wholesale and retail financial markets, which reflected the greatest concerns of businesses in relation to the burden of financial services regulation. An update on progress on the plan is described in Box 3.5.

Box 3.5: Progress on reforming the regulation of financial services

Substantial progress has been made on the ten point plan announced at the 2005 Pre-Budget Report for further modernising the regulation of financial services:

- **reviewing the "controllers regime" in Part XII of Financial Services and Markets Act (FSMA)** a consultation launched today proposes wide ranging deregulatory reforms;[a]

- **broadening exemptions for employers:** a consultation launched today proposes more freedoms for employers to advise employees on work-related financial services;[a]

- **introducing a Regulatory Reform Order:** the Government is considering responses to this consultation, including additional proposals for further deregulation;

- **improving consumer credit regulation:** the Financial Services Authority FSA and the OFT have today published a joint commitment to strengthen their policy coordination, streamline their contact with firms, and improve their consumer communications;

- **conducting a value for money review into the FSA:** the Government has discussed what should be covered with industry and consumers and will launch the review soon;

- **reviewing the effectiveness of mortgage and general insurance regulation:** the FSA is assessing how far the intended outcomes for consumers are being met;

- **enhancing consumer education and understanding of financial services:** the FSA is devoting more resources and implementing the national strategy for financial capability, including in schools and workplaces, in partnership with other stakeholders;

- **introducing simplification plans and quantified burden reduction targets:** the FSA and HM Treasury will publish regulatory simplification plans in the near future;

- industry has asked for work on **reviewing the Financial Promotion Order and the financial promotion restriction in FSMA** and **reviewing the Regulated Activities Order** to start after the EU Markets in Financial Instruments Directive has been implemented.

---

[a] http://www.hm-treasury.gov.uk/Consultations_and_Legislation/consult_index.cfm

---

[15] www.cabinetoffice.gov.uk/regulation/davidson_review/

Regulatory reform in Europe

3.40   The Government placed regulatory reform at the centre of its presidency of the EU. In the second half of 2005, the UK Presidency worked closely with the Commission and the other 24 members states and achieved significant progress on this agenda including:

- agreement to simplify over 1400 existing rules and regulations;

- withdrawal of 68 proposed EU regulations;

- a commitment to test the competitiveness impact of all new EU regulations in impact assessments; and

- a commitment for administrative burdens to be measured in all EU proposals.

3.41   The Government recognises that significant challenges remain if the EU and its Member States are to have an appropriate regulatory environment that will enable Europe to compete in the global economy while protecting other legitimate policy objectives. At their December 2005 meeting, EU finance ministers welcomed proposals tabled by the UK presidency in collaboration with the incoming Austrian and Finnish Presidencies that set out the next steps on the European better regulation agenda in 2006 and beyond.[16] This stressed the importance of all EU Member States and institutions implementing the agreed measures to improve both the stock and flow of regulation. The Government will continue to prioritise the integration of the methodology for measuring administrative burdens into the regulatory simplification programme; greater focus on improving the EU's approach to implementation and enforcement; and strengthened stakeholder consultation, including business input to the process of regulatory design.

3.42   During the UK presidency the Commission also committed to examine systematically new EU proposals to ensure that the needs of SMEs are properly prioritised. Research consistently shows that small businesses suffer disproportionately from poor regulation. Greater consideration will now be given to measures including exemptions, longer transition periods, reduced fees, and simplified reporting requirements. In consultation with business groups, the Small Business Services will lead efforts within the UK to identify regulations for which measures to reduce the regulatory burden for SMEs would be appropriate and will work with the Commission to deliver these proposals.

Modernising and simplifying tax administration

Modernising the tax system for small businesses **3.43**   HMRC has today published *Progress towards a new relationship: How HMRC is working to make life easier for business* - the third in a series of reports on how the department is delivering improvements to SMEs' experience of the tax system. The paper provides an update on the extensive package of work that HMRC are undertaking to make it cheaper, quicker and easier for small business to comply with their obligations.

3.44   The paper sets out the conclusions of research carried out by KPMG into the administrative burdens of the tax system. The research has found that the UK tax system imposes burdens of 0.41 per cent of GDP, or 1.1 per cent of tax take. This compares well with the results in the Netherlands (0.82 per cent of GDP) and Denmark (0.57 per cent of GDP), the only other countries that have so far carried out a similar exercise, and confirms the recent findings of a National Audit Office report[17]. Nevertheless, the Government is determined to reduce burdens further, while continuing to collect and repay the right amount of tax and credits.

---

[16] *Advancing Better Regulation in Europe* –- a joint UK, Austrian and Finnish Presidency discussion paper, December 2005

[17] *Corporation Tax: Companies managed by HM Revenue and Customs' Area offices*, National Audit Office, 13 January 2006 http://www.nao.org.uk/

Reducing the administrative burdens of tax   **3.45**   The KPMG research has shown that 85 obligations relating to dealing with forms and returns impose 85 per cent of total costs, but that there is a large 'tail' of another 2607 obligations that, although they only apply to a small number of businesses, collectively can cause irritation and contribute to an impression that the tax system is complex and difficult to understand. HMRC will tackle both aspects of the burden on business. To reduce the impact of the most costly burdens, HMRC will:

- reduce the administrative burdens on business of dealing with HMRC forms and returns by at least 10 per cent over 5 years; and

- reduce the administrative burden on business of dealing with HMRC's audits and inspections, by 10 per cent over three years and at least 15 per cent over five years.

Administrative Burdens Advisory Board   **3.46**   To deal with the remaining 'tail' HMRC is launching a new business-led Administrative Burdens Advisory Board that will be independently chaired by Teresa Graham, non-executive director of four businesses and Deputy Chair of the Better Regulation Commission. The Board will use the KMPG research to identify the areas of future work HMRC should focus on, proposing and developing reforms to the way the tax system is administered that will make a noticeable difference to businesses.

Review of HMRC links with business   **3.47**   The 2001 Review of Links with Business led to the establishment of the Business Tax Forum to foster a stronger relationship and greater understanding between large businesses and the former Inland Revenue. To build on that work, the Chancellor has asked Sir David Varney to work with business representatives to identify opportunities to further improve the extent to which the views and experiences of large business are taken into account in the administration of the tax system.

Deregulating tax administration   **3.48**   The Government is committed to simplifying and updating tax administration for all taxpayers. This Budget announces that the Government will:

- simplify and clarify the stamp duty land tax treatment of a range of transactions, including commercial leases, transfers of partnership interests and the reallocation of assets within settlements;

- undertake a radical reform of the excise duty deferment guarantee system, in light of consultation responses from business. Subject to further consultation on the details, HMRC plan to introduce the new system during 2006-07 delivering considerable cost savings for compliant businesses;

- repeal or simplify over 40 provisions in alcohol legislation which are obsolete or over-burdensome, and simplify or clarify a number of provisions in the Tobacco Products Duties Regulations; and

- simplify administrative aspects of amusement machine licence duty, easing financial and compliance burdens for licence holders.

3.49   This programme of work will continue, and further discussion with industry is planned during 2006 to identify other provisions that can be repealed or simplified. This will allow further reductions in compliance costs and allow process and regulation to fit better with trade practice.

Compliance cost reviews **3.50**   As part of the Government's continuing commitment to review regulations after they are implemented, HMRC has introduced a rolling programme of compliance cost reviews. These aim to confirm whether estimates of compliance costs and savings included in Regulatory Impact Assessments were reasonable. HMRC will publish the results for their programme for 2005-06 shortly and feed directly into future improvements to the impact assessment process.

Supporting small businesses

3.51   As set out in *Devolving decision making: 2*, the Government believes that support to help businesses start up and grow should be regionally led, in order to address local and regional enterprise challenges.[18] Responsibility for co-ordination of Business Link services has therefore been devolved to RDAs since March 2005. There is concern at all levels that the proliferation of business support schemes has created a complex picture making it difficult and time consuming for businesses to access relevant support. **The Government will work with RDAs and other local and national bodies to reduce the number of business support services from around 3,000 now, to no more than 100 by 2010.**

High growth SME coaching **3.52**   Increasing the number and performance of high growth SMEs in the UK is central to improving our levels of productivity. Building on the current services available via Business Link, all nine RDAs are rolling out **a structured programme of intensive coaching and assistance for high growth SMEs** on a phased basis from April this year. Subject to the outcome of a robust evaluation at the end of the first year, the support programme will be scaled up in every region in the coming years.

Promoting creativity **3.53**   UK businesses have a strong tradition of applying creative and innovative approaches to maintain a competitive edge. Increasing competition in international markets is demanding even higher quality products and services from businesses, and the application of creativity and design can be a key route to building competitive advantage through the distinctiveness and value added of goods and services. The Government has been taking forward the recommendations made to the public sector by the Cox Review in response to these emerging global challenges.[19]

3.54   The Government intends to extend additional support through the R&D tax credit system, as recommended by the Cox Review, subject to the outcome of state aids discussions with the European Commission, as described in further detail later in this Chapter. The Government is encouraging the RDAs to build on the progress since the Cox Review in making the Design Council's Design for Business programme available, including a number of pilot initiatives already underway. In addition, a feasibility study for a London creativity and innovation hub, at the centre of a wider network of creativity and innovation centres has been launched and is being overseen by a high-level group of leading figures from design, the arts and business led by Sir George Cox.

---

[18] *Devolving decision making: 2 – meeting the regional economic challenge*, HM Treasury, March 2004
[19] *Cox Review of Creativity in Business – building on the UK's strengths*, December 2004, www.hm-treasury.gov.uk

Access to finance   **3.55**   Availability of appropriate sources of finance is crucial for businesses seeking to invest and grow. Following on from *Bridging the finance gap*, the Government is committed to tackling market failures in the supply of risk capital and improving access to finance for small businesses.[20] In July 2005 Government invited bids from experienced fund managers to run the first pathfinder Enterprise Capital Funds (ECFs). ECFs will invest a mixture of public and private capital in early-stage companies with real growth potential, with up to £2 million per company. **The first two Enterprise Capital Funds have now been selected**, subject to contract. One of the funds focuses on sustainable technologies and the other fund supports high technology firms. The Government will finalise the full list of the first pathfinder ECFs in the coming months.

3.56   The success of the first stage of the ECFs pathfinder in attracting the private sector to work with Government to bridge the equity gap has led the Government to **decide to continue with the pathfinder, with a further £50 million in 2006-07 and £50 million in 2007-08.**

3.57   In Budget 2004 the Government introduced a two-year increase to the rate of income tax relief for investments in Venture Capital Trusts (VCTs). This provided the intended stimulus to VCT fundraising, which reached a record £520 million in 2004-05. **The Government today announces a new 30 per cent rate of income tax relief for investments in VCTs from 6 April 2006.** This is an increase from the original 20 per cent rate and will help ensure that the VCT industry has a solid foundation for stable fundraising and continued growth.

3.58   This new rate of income tax relief is introduced as part of a package of changes to VCTs, the Enterprise Investment Scheme (EIS) and the Corporate Venturing Scheme. These changes will renew the schemes' focus on providing incentives for long-term investments in small companies facing the most severe barriers to accessing equity finance. These measures will be introduced from 6 April 2006 and include:

- **a refocusing of the 'gross assets test' to £7 million immediately before investment and £8 million afterwards,** to focus on the companies most in need of improved access to finance;

- in response to industry representations, **an increase to the minimum holding period for new shares in VCTs to five years** to incentivise more stable, longer-term investments; and

- **a doubling of the annual EIS investment limit eligible for income tax relief to £400,000,** to incentivise greater investment in growth companies.

Small Firms Loan   **3.59**   The newly enhanced Small Firms Loan Guarantee (SFLG), launched on 1 December
Guarantee   2005, is focused on those businesses that face the greatest difficulty in accessing debt finance. The administrative processes underlying SFLG have been streamlined, making it easier for lenders to administer loans and enabling them to provide quicker decisions to their customers. The changes, in response to the recommendations made by the Graham Review, are also encouraging lenders to be more innovative in their use of SFLG. **The Small Business Service is working to accredit a number of additional lenders to operate SFLG, thus ensuring that it is accessible to all sections of the small business community.**

---

[20] *Bridging the finance gap: next steps in improving access to growth capital for small businesses*, HM Treasury and SBS, December 2003

Tax-motivated incorporation   **3.60**   The 2005 Pre-Budget Report announced a package of measures simplifying corporation tax through a single small companies' rate and enhanced support for small business investment. The Government will continue to examine further simplification of business taxation and will bring forward proposals for discussion with business and other representatives that are consistent with fairness between businesses, irrespective of their legal form; simplicity for compliant businesses; support for businesses in their aspirations to grow; and maintaining the attractiveness of the UK as a business location. It will also consult on action to tackle those who undermine competitive business by disguising employment through managed service company schemes. Chapter 5 sets out these next steps.

Alignment of income tax and NICs   **3.61**   The Government has received representations to build on previous work aligning the income tax and national insurance systems with the objective of reducing burdens on employers, especially smaller employers. Chapter 5 sets out action on this issue.

First year capital allowances   **3.62**   The Government also announced in the 2005 Pre-Budget Report an extension to first year capital allowances available to small businesses investing in plant and machinery. For expenditure in the year from April 2006, the first year capital allowance for small businesses will be set at an increased rate of 50 per cent. This measure will assist small businesses' cashflow and provide enhanced support for new investment.

VAT   **3.63**   From 1 April 2006 the Government will increase the VAT registration threshold in line with inflation from £60,000 to £61,000, thereby keeping around 2,000 businesses out of the VAT system and maintaining the highest threshold in Europe.

3.64   The 2005 Pre-Budget Report announced that, to help small businesses with cashflow difficulties and reduce administrative burdens, the turnover threshold up to which businesses are able to take advantage of the Annual Accounting Scheme would be increased from £660,000 to £1,350,000. This change will take effect from 1 April 2006. The Government also wrote to the European Commission last December for derogation to increase the Cash Accounting Scheme threshold to the same level.

3.65   Following an informal consultation on possible changes to the VAT Bad Debt Relief scheme, the Government did not identify any immediate changes that would be simple for business to operate without unacceptable risk of fraud. HMRC will continue to work with businesses affected by customer insolvency, and consider ways in which businesses in these circumstances could be further supported.

Enterprise in disadvantaged areas

Local Enterprise Growth Initiative   **3.66**   Budget 2005 announced a Local Enterprise Growth Initiative (LEGI) to provide flexible, devolved investment in some of the most deprived areas to support locally developed and owned proposals to stimulate economic activity and productivity through enterprise. The first round of LEGI has allocated £126 million over three years to transform and stimulate deprived areas, on the basis that the successful bids demonstrated clear plans to create sustainable change in the region, making them more attractive places for businesses to start up and grow. A national advisory panel, which included senior private sector representatives, recommended that 10 applications, from 15 local authorities, should receive full multi-year funding from 2006-07 under LEGI. LEGI funding has been awarded to proposals from Bradford; St Helens; Croydon; Ashfield, Mansfield and Bolsover; Derwentside, Easington, Sedgefield and Wear Valley; Great Yarmouth; South Tyneside; Coventry; Hastings, and Barking & Dagenham.

3.67   The next round for local authorities to apply for funding is now underway for projects starting in 2007-08, and central and local government are working together to ensure that lessons from the first round are learned. A national event will be held in the coming months to enable bidding authorities to discuss their proposals and applications for the second round with representatives from the LEGI National Advisory Panel and successful applicants from the first round, ahead of the closure date for applications in the autumn. In addition, the Government will consider targeted support for future rounds for Local Authorities with the least capacity to bid, including those in this group shortlisted by the Government Offices in the regions for the first round.

Creating an enterprise culture

Enterprise Education   **3.68**   Enterprise culture encourages positive attitudes towards entrepreneurship and risk. A more enterprising culture can only be achieved through widespread engagement by individuals and organisations across the UK. This must begin with helping young people develop the enterprise skills and aspirations necessary to start up and grow their own business, or to bring a more innovative approach to the workplace. The Government will take a number of new steps to ensure that young people in the UK continue to experience the world of enterprise including:

- creating a Schools Enterprise Education Network (SEEN) as part of the £60 million roll out of enterprise education to all pupils at key stage 4;

- creating 23 enterprise summer school pathfinders to be delivered by Young Enterprise to 1000 pupils across the UK in summer 2006; and

- launching a US enterprise scholarship scheme for UK university students in 2006. This scheme is for students who have excelled in engineering, science and technology and will be administered by the National Council for Graduate Entrepreneurship and the Ewing Marion Kaufmann foundation in the US.

Enterprise Education through LEGI   **3.69**   A number of successful LEGI bidders (Bradford; St Helens; Croydon; Ashfield, Mansfield and Bolsover; Great Yarmouth; Coventry; Hastings; Barking and Dagenham) will focus on delivering enterprise education to children in primary school and early secondary school to influence attitudes and behaviour on entrepreneurship. These bids include:

- an improved enterprise education programme for young people in schools;

- better opportunities for involvement in extra-curricular enterprise activities and entrepreneurial programmes for the young; and

- enhanced personal development through more targeted coaching and mentoring in order to create a more 'can do' entrepreneurial attitude amongst young people.

Women and enterprise   **3.70**   The Government recognises the high potential of women's enterprise to contribute to economic growth in the UK and is keen to emulate the success of the US, where the number of women-owned businesses continues to grow at twice the rate of all US firms. Progress has been made on increasing levels of female entrepreneurship, with total entrepreneurial activity for women in the UK rising from 3.3 per cent to 3.9 per cent between 2002 and 2004 but huge opportunities for development remain. In recognition of this potential, RDAs from five regions will be establishing Women's Enterprise Units, subject to contract, to pilot different approaches to supporting the start-up and growth of female-owned businesses.

3.71   The 2005 Pre-Budget Report announced that the Government is establishing a Task Force on Women's Enterprise to drive implementation of specific steps to increase levels of women's business ownership in the UK. The Government is currently recruiting a chairperson to lead the Task Force, which will play a key role in the evaluation of the Women's Enterprise Units, helping to ensure that best practice identified is shared across all nine English regions.

SCIENCE AND INNOVATION

3.72   Innovation is a key catalyst for productivity growth. New ideas drive enterprise, create new products and markets, and improve efficiency, delivering benefits to firms, customers and society. In July 2004 the Government published the *Science and Innovation Framework 2004-14* which set out the Government's framework for securing its long-term vision for UK science and innovation, together with the ambition that public and private investment in R&D should reach 2.5 per cent of GDP by 2014. The first annual report published in July 2005[21] found that good progress had been made on key indicators for implementing the framework. The UK science base is retaining its strong position, second only to the US in global scientific excellence as measured by citations, and remains the most productive among G8 nations. The annual report also identified some key challenges, notably on further increasing levels of business investment in R&D, and making more rapid progress on improving science, engineering, technology and mathematics skills.

Maximising the impact of science funding

3.73   The Government is investing an additional £1 billion in science and innovation over the period of the 2004 Spending Review, in support of the objectives set out in the ten-year framework. Together with the commitments made in previous Spending Reviews, this amounts to an unprecedented increase in public funding: by 2007-08 total UK science spending will be £5.4 billion representing an average annual growth of 5.8 per cent in real terms in the 2004 Spending Review period. If the impact of additional public investment in science on the economy is to be maximised, it is essential to ensure that the right structures are in place to deliver the benefits of this investment. *Science and Innovation Investment Framework 2004-2014: Next Steps*[22] published today, takes forward policy to ensure that this is the case.

Impact of science on innovation   **3.74**   The Government is keen to create a more effective science and innovation system, which maximises the impact of public investment in science on business innovation, and provides greater incentives for businesses to collaborate with the science base to meet the challenges of globalisation. **The Technology Strategy Board will now have a wider remit to stimulate business innovation in those areas which offer the greatest scope for boosting UK growth and productivity, and plans for it to operate at arms length from central Government are being developed.** The Government is also taking forward a new strategy to better market the UK science base to business and attract foreign R&D investment, set out later in this chapter. The Government is also seeking views on how the UK can best support higher-risk, high-impact research in novel fields of scientific enquiry; how national and regional policies can work together more effectively to increase innovation and business-university collaboration in the regions; and on how, building on the Lambert Review, a wider spectrum of business-university interaction can be encouraged, spreading best practice across different regions and sectors.

Research Councils   **3.75**   In order to increase the responsiveness of the science base to the needs of the economy and enhance the UK's capacity to conduct internationally excellent science, the Government believes that there is scope for reviewing the effectiveness of the Research Councils' existing structures and operations. **The Government is inviting views on whether a Large Facilities Research Council should be created to improve the strategic management of public investment in large research facilities such as telescopes, light sources and space programmes. The Government is also inviting views on whether the funding arrangements for the physical sciences should be simplified in the wake of these changes, and what further measures could be taken by Research Councils to improve their effectiveness.**

---

[21] *Science and Innovation Investment Framework Annual Report 2005*, HM Treasury/DTI/DfES July 2005 available at: http://www.ost.gov.uk/policy/sifreview05.pdf

[22] *Science and Innovation Investment Framework 2004-2014: next steps*, HM Treasury, March 2006

University research   **3.76**   In order to maintain the UK's world-class university system, the Government is keen to ensure that excellent research of all types is rewarded, including user-focused, and interdisciplinary research. It also wants to ensure that institutions continue to have the freedom to set strategic priorities for research, undertake blue skies research and respond quickly to emerging priorities and new fields of enquiry. The Government is strongly committed to the dual support system and to rewarding research excellence, but recognises some of the burdens imposed by the existing Research Assessment Exercise (RAE). The Government's firm presumption is that after the 2008 RAE the system for assessing research quality and allocating 'quality-related' (QR) funding from the DfES will be mainly metrics-based. **In May 2006, the Government will launch a consultation on its preferred option for a metrics-based system for assessing research quality and allocating QR funding, publishing results in time for the 2006 Pre-Budget Report.** The Government is aware that preparations for the 2008 RAE are well underway. It is therefore the Government's presumption that the 2008 RAE should go ahead, incorporating a shadow metrics exercise alongside the traditional panel-based peer review system. However, if an alternative system is agreed and widely supported, and a clear majority of UK universities were to favour an earlier move to a simpler system, the Government would be willing to consider that.

World-class health research   **3.77**   The Government believes that there is scope for creating more effective structures to support world-class health research in the UK, aligning research priorities more closely with wider health objectives, and providing a more coherent approach for translating the results of research into economic benefit. Research budgets in the Office of Science and Technology are already ring fenced. Following the reforms to the medical research environment announced in the 2005 Pre-Budget Report, together with the willingness of the biomedical industry to significantly grow R&D investment in the UK by up to £1 billion a year in the medium to long-term, **the Government is today announcing its intention to ring fence the Department of Health's R&D budget and that the Secretaries of State for Health and Trade and Industry will create a single, jointly held health research fund of at least £1 billion per year.** The Government will invite a leading independent individual to advise on the best institutional arrangements to deliver a more coherent framework for health R&D under this new structure. A consultation will be launched shortly in order to report on options to the Government in time for the 2006 Pre-Budget Report.

Improving the supply of scientists   **3.78**   A strong supply of highly qualified STEM graduates is essential to underpin the Government's long-term objectives for science and innovation, and a key factor in making the UK an attractive location for business investment in R&D. The *Science and Innovation Investment Framework 2004-2014* outlined the Government's ambition to create an education and training environment that delivers the best in science teaching and learning at every stage. Despite the progress in taking forward the framework, the Government is concerned that progress towards meeting its ambitions is relatively slow in some areas and that there is scope for further action to improve the quality of STEM education and increase the supply of STEM skills. **Budget 2006 announces new ambitions, including to:**

- achieve year on year increases in the number of young people taking A levels in physics, chemistry and mathematics so that by 2014 entries to A level physics are 35,000 (currently 24,200); chemistry A level entries are 37,000 (currently 33,300); and mathematics A level entries are 56,000 (currently 46,168);

- continually improve the number of pupils getting at least level 6 at the end of Key Stage 3 (11-14 year olds);

- continually improve the number of pupils achieving A*-B and A*-C grades in two science GCSEs; and

- step up recruitment, retraining and retention of physics, chemistry and mathematics specialist teachers so that by 2014 25 per cent of science teachers have a physics specialism, 31 per cent of science teachers have a chemistry specialism and the increase in the number of mathematics teachers enables 95 per cent of mathematics lessons in schools to be delivered by a mathematics specialist (compared with 88 per cent currently).

3.79   To meet these ambitions the Government announces a package of measures to improve the skills of science teachers, the quality of science lessons and increase progression to A level sciences including new commitments to:

- make science a priority in schools by including science in the School Accountability Framework;

- entitle, from 2008, all pupils achieving at least level 6 at Key Stage 3 to study three separate science GCSEs to increase progression to and attainment at A level science;

- continue the drive to recruit science graduates into teaching via Employment Based Routes with new incentives to providers of £1,000 per recruit to attract more physics and chemistry teachers; and

- develop and pilot a continuing professional development programme leading to an accredited diploma to give existing science teachers without a physics and chemistry specialism the deep subject knowledge they need to teach these subjects effectively.

Business Research and Development

R&D tax credits   **3.80**   The Government remains committed to improving the experience of companies claiming the R&D tax credit. In *Supporting growth in innovation: next steps for the R&D tax credit,* published in December 2005, the Government announced that HMRC would set up dedicated R&D units to handle all SME claims for tax credits. It is envisaged that these units will be fully operational across the country before the end of the year. At the same time, a statement of practice will be published presenting the standard of service and support that SMEs can expect from the new units. These changes should ensure that all R&D performing companies can receive the full value from R&D tax credits.

3.81   At present, only companies with up to 250 employees can qualify for higher relief under R&D tax credits. Following discussions with business, the Government has noted evidence of lower levels of innovation among companies with 250-500 employees.[23] In the light of the recommendations of the Cox Review, the Government wishes to better support R&D investment in growing firms. The Government therefore intends to extend additional R&D tax credit support to companies with 250-500 employees, subject to the outcome of state aids discussions with the European Commission.

---

[23] Based on *Creativity and Design Study for the DTI using the Community Innovation Survey,* Haskel, Cereda, Crespi & Crisuolo 2005. Further details available at www.dti.gov.uk.

Gowers Review of Intellectual Property **3.82** At the 2005 Pre-Budget Report, the Chancellor asked Andrew Gowers to lead an independent review to examine the UK's intellectual property (IP) framework. The review will examine how the IP regime functions in the digital age and consider the challenges that rapid technological change pose for the system The review will undertake a rigorous analysis of the IP system in the UK and will provide practical policy recommendations. The review is committed to consulting widely, and to this end, a formal Call for Evidence was published on 23 February 2006. Andrew Gowers will report to the Chancellor, the Secretary of State for Trade and Industry and the Secretary of State for Culture, Media and Sport in autumn 2006.

SKILLS

3.83 The quantity and quality of skilled labour in an economy is a key driver of economic performance and productivity growth. As well as contributing to productivity, a highly skilled workforce also enables firms to update working practices and products faster, making the economy more flexible and competitive. Despite improvements over the last few years, the UK still has a large stock of workers with low or no skills, including poor basic literacy and numeracy. This stock of low skills directly accounts for some of the productivity gap between the UK and peer economies, as well as wider impacts on social welfare. *Productivity in the UK 6: Progress and new evidence* published alongside the Budget sets out the latest evidence on the contribution of skills to productivity.

Leitch Review of Skills **3.84** Alongside the 2005 Pre-Budget Report, Lord Leitch, the former chief executive of Zurich Financial Services and the chairman of the National Employment Panel, published *Skills in the UK: The long-term challenge* detailing the interim findings of his independent review of the UK's long-term skills needs. It highlighted that, though skills levels have improved the UK must urgently raise skills levels further and set itself a greater ambition to have a world-class skills base by 2020. The next phase of the Leitch Review will build on this analysis and address:

- the skills profile that the UK should aim to achieve in 2020 to support the needs of the economy and society over the longer-term;

- the appropriate balance of responsibility between Government, employers and individuals for the action required to meet this level of change; and

- the policy framework required to support this.

3.85 The Review will report its conclusions and recommendations to the Government in 2006.

Skills and employment **3.86** *Skills in the UK: The long-term challenge* not only emphasised the importance of skills for UK productivity and competitiveness, but also their importance in preparing the economy and individuals for the challenges of globalisation. Changing patterns of production and employment across the world put a greater premium on economic flexibility. Skills are vital to achieve this flexibility, allowing individuals to adapt and move into new jobs or across economic sectors, increasing their security in the labour market, as businesses compete for opportunities in an increasingly global market for goods and services.

3.87   In this environment, skills will become increasingly important for the individual – supporting moves into and progression within work, reducing the risk of unemployment or inactivity and increasing family income and security. For the Government, skills policy will be key to promoting a flexible labour market and to ensuring that work pays, to support individuals as they move between jobs, between sectors of the economy or from benefits into work so that we create a high skills economy. The forthcoming white paper on further education (as described later in this chapter) will set out further measures being taken to better align skills and employment policies. Within the framework of reform set out in the White Paper, the Chancellor has also asked Lord Leitch, in the final phase of his review on skills, to report specifically on how skills and employment services can complement each other even more effectively in supporting labour market flexibility, better employment outcomes and greater progression to productive and sustainable jobs for those with skill needs. Chapter 4 sets out the latest development in the New Deal for skills and specific measures the Government is taking in response to the recent Women and Work Commission report.[24]

3.88   Since September 2002 the Government has been testing the effectiveness of a radical new policy approach aimed at stimulating the demand for work-based training for low-skilled employees. So far these Employer Training Pilots have benefited over 29,000 employers and 240,000 employees. All evaluations of the pilot have shown high levels of satisfaction among learners and employers, relatively high completion rates and learners and employers identifying skill and work performance gains. Final evaluation is expected to be published by May 2006. As announced in Budget 2005, a national programme, Train to Gain, based on lessons learned from the pilots will begin to roll-out from April 2006. It will create a step-change in participation of workplace training among the low-skilled, when the programme is operating at full capacity, it is forecast to benefit 50,000 employers and 350,000 employees each year. By 2009-10 it is forecast that Train to Gain will have contributed over 500,000 first, full Level 2 achievements towards the Adult Skills PSA target.

Young people   **3.89**   The Government has introduced a number of measures to encourage all young people to take part in some form of education or training up to the age of 19. However despite this and other progress in recent years, the UK ranks among the lower performing OECD countries in terms of post-16 participation. The *14-19 Education and Skills White Paper*, published in February 2005 set out the next steps the Government will take to tackle this problem. An implementation plan, setting out in detail how these changes will be put into effect was published in December 2005.[25]

3.90   From April 2006 new Learning Agreements will be piloted in eight areas of the country. These will be aimed at 16 and 17 year olds who are in work but not receiving accredited training, to improve training options. Building on the existing statutory right to paid time off to train or study for this group, the pilots will test the effectiveness of formal learning agreement, financial incentives and wage compensation in encouraging greater involvement in training by young people and their employers.

Further   **3.91**   High quality training, responsive to the needs of employers and individuals is **education reform**   essential for meeting the Government's ambitions for skills. To ensure that further education colleges and training providers in England are ready for more stretching ambitions, the Government is setting out a far-reaching programme of reform. The details of this reform programme will be contained in a White Paper to be published on 27 March. Box 3.8 sets out the key themes of the reform programme.

---

[24] *Shaping a fairer future*, Women and Work Commission, 2006.

[25] *14-19 Education and Skills: Implementation Plan*, Department for Education and Skills, 2005.

Box 3.8: Further Education Reform White Paper

The reforms in the forthcoming White Paper will address the system for further education and training provision for 14-19 year olds and adults. The key themes cover:

- **Mission and Specialisation:** putting the economic mission of the sector at the heart of its role, with new support and incentives for colleges and training providers to develop their own areas of specialist excellence.

- **Meeting Employer and Learner Needs:** putting real purchasing power in the hands of the customer – learners and employers and more government support for those that need it.

- **Raising Quality, Achieving Excellence:** new performance indicators, emphasising employability; tougher measures to address poor performance; lighter touch regulation on high-performing providers; and support for a more highly-skilled FE workforce.

- **Funding and Organisation:** provider competitions will be used to expand participation or remove poor quality provision.

- **A New Relationship with Colleges and Providers:** the Learning and Skills Council (LSC) will streamline its operations, working more strategically with colleges, at regional level to support Regional Economic Strategies, and at local level, to deliver 14-19 reforms.

Higher education **3.92** At the 2005 Pre-Budget Report, the Government announced measures to help the Higher Education sector benefit from the opportunities of globalisation, and ensure the UK retains its reputation as one of the most attractive places for students to study abroad. The Government is today announcing further reforms, set out later in this Chapter.

INVESTMENT

3.93 The accumulation of physical capital through investment is an important determinant of an economy's productivity performance. Physical capital stock is closely correlated with productivity performance, as it directly influences how much a unit of labour can produce. Total investment in fixed capital in the UK economy, incorporating investment by businesses and government, and investment in housing, has been low relative to comparable economies over long periods of the UK's post-war history. This has had significant impacts on the productivity of the business sector, on the nature of the UK's housing stock and housing market, and on the quality of public services.

3.94 The Government's macroeconomic reforms have provided an environment of low and stable interest rates and a flexible labour market. These reforms help to provide a certain and rewarding environment for businesses to invest for the future. However, measured rates of UK business investment as a percentage of GDP have not yet caught up with rates in Germany, France and the US. Business investment data are prone to relatively large revisions and, as discussed in Chapter B of the *Financial Statement and Budget Report*, the ONS has recently published details of improvements to the way in which computer software is measured, suggesting that firms' own account in-house software investment has been significantly underestimated in the UK. The UK has a strong record in attracting foreign inward investment but will increasingly face further challenges from emerging markets stimulated by their rapid integration into the financial markets.

The UK as a competitive centre for global investment

Strategy for promoting the UK

3.95 In *Long-term global economic challenges and opportunities for the UK,* published alongside the 2004 Pre-Budget Report and *Globalisation and the UK: strength and opportunity to meet the economic challenge,* published on 2 December 2005, the Government has set out how the UK is well-placed to meet the challenges and opportunities of globalisation, and especially the rise of China and India. The UK has many strengths, including the stability of its macroeconomic framework, its openness to competition and trade and the strength of its science base. Building on its strengths, an ambitious strategy for marketing the UK economy internationally, led at the most senior levels of Government, is vital to securing an effective response to globalisation.

3.96 Before the summer, the Government will publish a new five year strategy for a step-change in the Government's drive to market the strengths of the UK economy internationally. This will have a number of themes, including a particular focus on high-growth countries of strategic importance such as India and China, and a focus on innovative and R&D intensive sectors.

3.97 The five year strategy will form the basis of a partnership between all Government departments and agencies, RDAs, devolved administrations, and numerous private sector bodies active in this field. Responsibility for co-ordinating and driving this strategy across Government lies with UK Trade & Investment (UKTI). It will embrace UKTI's twin roles of trade development and inward investment, both of which are vital.

UK Trade and Investment

3.98 In order to deliver this new strategy, UKTI will undertake a programme of organisational change, under the leadership of its new chief executive, Andrew Cahn, with the clear aim of a fundamental transformation in its effectiveness in marketing the UK. Details of this programme will be published alongside the strategy.

3.99 The overall goal is to ensure that within UKTI there is the capability and sense of mission to deliver the Government's objective that the UK should be a key location of choice for many more high value-added international businesses, including from high-growth countries of strategic importance such as India and China, with:

- an entrepreneurial culture of recognised professional marketing excellence throughout the organisation;

- more strategic use of resources internationally, redeploying savings into front-line activities; and

- a clearer role for UKTI in co-ordinating the UK's international marketing drive overall.

3.100 As a first step towards implementing its strategy, UKTI will build on the findings of the Asia Task Force. Recognising the strategic importance of high growth markets such as India and China, UKTI will allocate further resources to increasing trade activities between the UK and these emerging markets.

3.101 The strategy will also build on the UK's strengths in scientific discovery, to attract knowledge intensive businesses to the UK. At the outset, UKTI will implement an international R&D strategy with funding of £9 million, in partnership with the academic and business communities, to attract more business research and development to the UK, and to promote Britain's innovative firms abroad. UKTI will spearhead this effort across Government, deploying a new cadre of technology specialists with expertise in key technology sectors.

Financial services **3.102** The Government is also committed to doing more to promote London as a centre for financial and business services. As set out in *Financial Services in London: Global Opportunities and Challenges*, published alongside the Budget, London starts from a strong position. London is the location for 70 per cent of the global secondary bond market; over 40 per cent of the derivatives market; over 30 per cent of world foreign exchange business; over 40 per cent of cross-border equities trading and, 20 per cent of cross-border bank lending. It is the world's most competitive financial centre with: a proportionate regulatory regime for its wholesale financial markets that is widely regarded as the best in the world; a tradition of openness that allows UK companies to attract the most talented individuals to London; a central location between the US and Asian time zones; and the use of English as the main language of international finance and English law as the law of choice for international contracts.

3.103 London is the world's leading international financial centre, and the Government's objective is for it to be even more successful in an integrated global economy. Recognising the opportunity that emerging markets such as China and India present and the strength of international competition from other financial centres, **key stakeholders in London's financial sector are joining forces with the Government to promote London as the world's leading international financial centre. Leading London markets and financial sector industry bodies have endorsed plans to set up a high-level group to agree before the summer a strategy to consolidate London's position.** The group will also include representatives of HM Treasury; the Corporation of London and the Lord Mayor; International Financial Services London; and the Mayor for London.

Education exports **3.104** Higher education is an increasingly international market. Traditional barriers are falling as international collaboration increases. There are real benefits to these changes, for example, allowing researchers better access to global networks. The UK is at the forefront of developments – only the USA has a larger share of the international market for overseas students. This market is worth over £3 billion to the economy each year. However, competition is increasing as existing providers raise their performance and new entrants join the market. At the 2005 Pre-Budget Report, the Government announced measures to help the Higher Education sector benefit from the opportunities of globalisation, and ensure the UK retains its reputation as one of the most attractive places for students to study abroad. On 7 March, the Home Office announced proposals for redesigning the migration system, providing a more efficient, transparent and objective application process for those coming to the UK for work or study.[26] Students who obtain degrees from UK universities will get extra points within the new system, making it easier for them to work here on a long-term basis. Building on this progress the Government will:

- **implement early, from 1 May 2006, the announcement made in the 2005 Pre-Budget Report to allow all international students on completion of a post-graduate degree, or an undergraduate degree in a shortage sector, to work in the UK for up to 12 months, benefiting up to 50,000 students;**

- **establish three new University Partnerships Schemes** to enhance long-term sustainable links between UK universities and centres of excellence in India, Russia and South Africa through academic exchanges, scholarships and research collaboration in science and technology; and

- **lead more high-level education trade missions** to help universities and businesses open new markets and expand existing ones.

---

[26] *A Points-Based System: Making Migration Work for Britain*, Home Office, 2006

Building a future strategy
 3.105 The Government is committed to working closely with and listening to business leaders, to ensure the UK has the flexible and supportive environment it needs to attract business investment in a global environment. As the next stage in this ongoing dialogue, the Government has established an International Business Advisory Council for the UK. The council will advise the Chancellor of the Exchequer over the next three years on how to respond to the challenges and opportunities of globalisation. Membership details of the new council are set out in Box 3.9.

Box 3.9: International Business Advisory Council

The Government has established a new International Business Advisory Council for the UK comprising some of the world's leading business people. The council will advise the Chancellor of the Exchequer over the next three years on how to respond to the challenges and opportunities of globalisation to ensure the UK continues to be one of the top locations for international companies' high value-added activity. The first members of the Council are renowned internationally for their expertise and have first-hand experience of global business across a range of sectors and regions:

Bernard Arnault, Chairman and CEO, LVMH;

Lord Browne, Group Chief Executive, BP;

Bill Gates, Chairman and Chief Software Architect, Microsoft Corporation;

Dr Jean-Pierre Garnier, CEO, GlaxoSmithKline;

Sir Ka-shing Li, Chairman of the Board, Hutchison Whampoa Ltd;

Sir Terry Leahy, CEO, Tesco;

Sir John Rose, CEO, Rolls Royce;

Robert Rubin, Director and Chairman of the Executive Committee, Citigroup Inc;

Lee Scott, President and CEO, Wal-Mart;

Ratan Tata, Chairman, Tata Group;

Meg Whitman, President and CEO, eBay; and

James Wolfensohn, Special Envoy for Disengagement and Former President of the World Bank.

Investing in housing and property

Investing in housing supply
 3.106 A stable and responsive housing market is essential for the UK's future economic and social success. *The Government's Response to Kate Barker's Review of Housing Supply*, published alongside the 2005 Pre-Budget Report, set out how achieving the Government's aim of improving affordability for future generations of homebuyers requires housing supply to become much more responsive to demand. Current projections suggest that to improve affordability, new housing supply in England will need to increase over the next decade to at least 200,000 net additions per year. The Government's response to the Barker Review therefore set out a comprehensive package of proposals to help deliver investment in the infrastructure necessary to support housing growth, and to reform the mechanisms, particularly planning, by which new housing and infrastructure are delivered.

3.107 This drive to increase housing supply has delivered an upward trend in new housebuilding, with new housing completions in England reaching 160,000 in 2005 – the highest level since 1990. However, the Government is determined to see faster progress and will bring forward further measures to increase and speed the delivery of new, sustainable, housing. This includes the publication in the summer of a new Planning Policy Statement for Housing (PPS3), to ensure that local and regional plans prepare and release more land in response to demand.

Infrastructure   **3.108** To ensure that appropriate infrastructure will be provided to support housing and population growth, the Government has announced a cross-cutting review into supporting housing growth to inform the 2007 Comprehensive Spending Review (reviews informing the CSR are listed in full in Chapter 6). The review will examine the different infrastructure costs of housing growth in different spatial forms and locations, explore the wider costs and benefits of different spatial forms of growth and assess the mechanisms for planning and delivering housing growth-related infrastructure provision. The review will run over the course of 2006 and will engage with stakeholders along the way.

Planning gain-   **3.109** To help finance this infrastructure to support growth and ensure that local
supplement communities directly share in the benefits that growth brings, the Government consulted on a proposed Planning-gain Supplement (PGS) alongside the wider response to the Barker review of housing supply. The consultation, which closed on 27 February 2006, directly engaged a wide range of stakeholders across the UK. The Government is considering responses to the consultation and discussions with stakeholders will continue. Further announcements on PGS implementation will be made by the end of the year.

3.110 In developing policy and considering responses to the consultation, the Government will continue to assess PGS, and the proposed revised scope of planning obligations (s106 agreements), against the following objectives:

- to finance additional investment in the local and strategic infrastructure necessary to support growth, while preserving incentives to develop;

- to help local communities to better share the benefits of growth and manage its impacts;

- to provide a fairer, more efficient and more transparent means of capturing a modest portion of land value uplift; and

- to create a flexible value capture system that responds to market conditions and does not inappropriately distort decisions between different types of development.

3.111 **To maintain critical links to local delivery, the Government will ensure that a significant majority of PGS revenues are retained for infrastructure priorities within the local authority area where the revenues derived.** PGS revenues would be separate from the local government funding settlement to serve as an incentive to support growth. Hypothecating PGS revenues would provide certainty that planning gains created locally would directly benefit local communities. The remaining PGS revenues would be dedicated to strategic infrastructure of regional importance to help unlock development land.

Derelict land tax credit 3.112   The Barker Review also recommended that the contaminated land tax credit should be extended to long-term derelict land, provided that it would encourage genuine new investment. It is unclear how this can be done in a cost-effective way and without encouraging dereliction or subsidising development that would have taken place anyway. However, the Government remains committed to redeveloping brownfield land through a range of policy levers and will continue to examine the potential for tax measures to bring forward land that would not otherwise be developed.

Business premises renovation allowance 3.113   The Government is committed to introducing a business premises renovation allowance scheme, to provide 100 per cent capital allowances for the costs of bringing empty business properties in disadvantaged areas back into use. The scheme will be introduced as soon as state aids approval is received.

Social housing sinking funds 3.114   In the 2005 Pre-Budget Report, the Government announced that the Finance Bill would include legislation to provide relief from the 40 per cent trust rate of tax for sinking funds of registered social housing landlords. This will be extended to service charges and sinking funds in other types of social housing.

Shared equity 3.115   The Government intends to help extend home ownership to another 1 million over the next five years, taking the UK towards the Government's aspiration of 75 per cent home ownership. As part of this strategy, Government will be directly assisting over 100,000 households that could not otherwise afford a home of their own with subsidised shared-equity products, including a joint shared-equity scheme operated in partnership with lenders. **The Government is today establishing a Shared Equity Task Force to consider the scope for shared equity products to assist more households into homeownership.** It will work with the finance industry, house builders, local authorities, housing associations, and others to determine whether there are market or state failures holding back the development of affordable shared-equity products for the 'intermediate' housing sector.

3.116   Investment in social housing has almost doubled since 1997, but the Government made clear at the Pre-Budget Report that the supply of social housing needs to rise further and would be a priority in the Comprehensive Spending Review. The Government will pilot an extra homes scheme to invest in bringing sites back into use and build more social housing for rent, potentially reducing Housing Benefit costs.

Real Estate Investment Trusts 3.117   The Government will legislate in the 2006 Finance Bill to create Real Estate Investment Trusts (UK-REITs). As set out in the 2005 Pre-Budget Report, the Government's objective for the UK-REIT regime is to improve the efficiency of both the commercial and residential property investment markets by providing liquid and publicly available investment vehicles. This reform was recommended by the Barker Review and will encourage increased institutional and professional investment to support the growth of new housing, as well as the Government's wider objectives for raising productivity.

3.118   Following consultation on draft legislation released in December 2005, the Government is able to announce the following significant changes:

- to provide greater flexibility for companies to operate within the regime, **a reduction in the required distribution rate to 90 per cent of net profits;**

- in line with industry's response, **a reduction of the interest cover test to 1.25 on a pre-capital allowances basis;** and

- to enable companies to operate the 10 per cent shareholding limit effectively without preventing normal market activity, HMRC will set out in guidance mechanisms through which companies can operate the limit through their Articles of Association, in accordance with the listing rules of the Financial Services Authority.

3.119 To meet the Government's objectives for UK-REIT legislation to be introduced at no overall cost to the Exchequer, **a conversion charge will be levied on companies electing to join the new regime at a rate of 2 per cent of the gross market value of investment properties.** The Government believes that this package of measures, along with a number of further technical amendments, will enable the successful launch of Real Estate Investment Trusts from 1 January 2007 and lead to a better functioning and more efficient UK property investment market.

Barker Review of Land Use Planning   **3.120** The Government is committed to further reform of the planning system of England. At the 2005 Pre-Budget Report, the Chancellor and the Deputy Prime Minister asked Kate Barker to conduct a review of land use planning. The purpose of the review will be to consider how, in the context of the opportunities and challenges of globalisation, and building on the reforms already put in place in England, planning policy and procedures can better deliver economic growth and prosperity alongside other sustainable development goals. The review will focus on the town and country planning system, but will, where appropriate, consider wider aspects of land use regulation, for example other development consent regimes and the relationship with Regional Economic Strategies. Where appropriate, the review will take account of the emerging findings of related studies, including the Eddington Study of transport, the Government's Energy Review and the Lyons Inquiry on the future role and function of local government. Though the focus of the review is on the economy, where improvements to achieve wider environmental and social objectives are identified these will be considered. An interim report will be published in summer 2006.

Public investment and infrastructure

3.121 The performance of the public sector asset base is crucial for the delivery of public services, such as health and education. Government investment in public infrastructure also underpins private sector activity, contributing to productivity growth and labour market flexibility. The approach to capital being taken in the Comprehensive Spending Review 2007 is set out in more detail in Chapter 6.

Eddington Study   **3.122** Transport plays a vital role in equipping the UK to respond to the opportunities and challenges of globalisation, through attracting and maintaining investment in the UK and supporting international trade. It also supports the efficient and flexible functioning of the economy, playing a significant role in the operation of labour markets and facilitating the movement of goods and services. Sir Rod Eddington has been asked to advise on the long-term impact of transport decisions on the UK's productivity, stability and growth. The Eddington Study, which will report to the Chancellor and Secretary of State for Transport in mid-2006, is continuing its comprehensive analysis of the links between the transport system and the UK economy, within the context of the Government's objectives for sustainable development.

Haulage industry   **3.123** In response to the Burns Inquiry into fuel costs, foreign competition and freight taxes, the Government invited the main haulage industry associations to participate in a joint task group at the 2005 Pre-Budget Report. The task group is making good progress in analysing the competitive position of the industry, and its findings will inform future decisions on how to ensure that haulage continues to fulfil its important role in the UK economy. The task group is due to conclude its work in the early summer.

National road pricing

3.124   Congestion delays and the resulting uncertainty in journey times impose a significant cost on business and private motorists. The Government's strategy to tackle congestion includes increased investment in the road network and public transport, and better management of the road network. A well-designed system of national road pricing could deliver substantial benefits, with the potential to reduce congestion by up to a half.

3.125   The Government has announced that it will make funding available from the Transport Innovation Fund (TIF) to support forward-looking local authorities that are considering introducing road pricing as part of a package of transport measures in their areas. As well as helping to tackle congestion in places where it is already a significant problem, the implementation of local road pricing schemes would help to inform future decisions on the potential to move towards a national system of road pricing. The design of any national scheme would need to be considered in the context of meeting the Government's environmental objectives (described in detail in Chapter 7).

Box 3.10: Globalisation and product and capital market flexibility – report on progress

In an increasingly integrated global economy, flexibility is fundamental to ensure that the UK economy can meet the changes and capture the benefits that globalisation can bring. Flexible product, capital and labour markets allow more efficient allocation of resources and clearer price signals, promoting competition and encouraging innovation – critical to enable firms to respond rapidly to changing market conditions. *Globalisation and the UK: strength and opportunity to meet the economic challenge*, published alongside the 2005 Pre-Budget Report, set out the core domestic challenges the Government intends to respond to, to ensure the UK has the flexibility needed to respond to globalisation:

Skills – so the workforce has the flexibility to adapt to changes in technology and new opportunities offered by globalisation. The UK has made substantial real terms investment in education linked to reforms. To make further progress the UK needs to tackle gaps in basic and intermediate skills and ensure training is more responsive to changing economic needs. The Further Education White Paper, published next week, will set out the first part of the Government's response and the Leitch Review, published later this year, will set out the long-term challenge for skills attainment.

Science and innovation – so the economy has the capacity to expand in knowledge-based industries. The Science and Innovation Framework sets out a target to raise R&D to 2.5 per cent of GDP backed by new investment; to make further progress the UK needs to build more R&D intensive firms, including through FDI, and improve research links with business. The Budget takes forward reforms in all of these areas including extending innovation support to medium sized companies through the R&D tax credit system.

Reducing regulatory burdens to reduce unnecessary costs to business. The Government has established a far-reaching regulatory reform strategy. The Budget sets out further steps including implementing the Hampton Review's risk-based approach to reducing the burdens on business and new commitments from HMRC to reduce the administrative burden of the tax system.

Planning to ensure the planning system promotes sustainable development and employment. Reforms already implemented include a simplified planning structure. To make further progress the UK needs to ensure the planning system is flexible and responsive to changing economic needs. The Budget sets out further progress on implementing the Barker review of housing supply. Kate Barker's second review into the wider planning system will be published later this year.

Transport infrastructure needs to facilitate sustainable economic growth by providing effective and efficient global connectivity for business. The Budget confirms that the Government is continuing to invest to address historic under-investment in transport. Looking forward the Eddington Transport Study is analysing the long-term impact of transport on growth and employment.

This Budget also sets out a wider strategy to promote the UK's long-term strengths in the global economy including a high-level industry group to coordinate the marketing of London as the world's leading financial centre, a new International Business Advisory Council to advise Government on how to ensure the UK remains one of the world's key contenders as a location and further measures to promote UK Higher Education as a global destination of choice for students to study abroad.

4 INCREASING EMPLOYMENT OPPORTUNITY FOR ALL

The Government's long-term goal is employment opportunity for all - the modern definition of full employment. Delivering this requires that everyone should be provided with the support they need to enable them to find employment and develop skills. This chapter describes the further steps the Government is taking towards its aim of employment opportunity for all, including:

- **an extension of the support offered to lone parents** through ensuring that all lone parents who have claimed benefit for at least a year will be required to attend a Work Focused Interview at least every six months;

- **a strengthened, refocused, Fortnightly Job Review for Jobseeker's Allowance claimants, from June 2006,** to ensure that only those claimants who are able to demonstrate that they have undertaken their responsibilities to look for work are allowed to continue their claim;

- **measures to reduce anomalies in, and further simplify, housing benefit; and to tackle fraud and error in the housing benefit system;**

- **in response to the Women and Work Commission report, new funding to:**

  - **double the number of existing Skills Coaching pilots to 16 Jobcentre Plus districts** with a specific focus on helping low-skilled women return to work;

  - **increase, by 50 per cent, the number of pilots delivering level 3 skills,** with an additional pilot focused on women with low skills; and

  - **help Sector Skills Councils in industries with skills shortages test new recruitment, training and career pathways** for over 10,000 low skilled women;

- publication of *Employment opportunity for all: analysing labour market trends in London*, alongside this Budget, examining the underlying reasons why employment rates are lower in London compared to other parts of the country, as a basis for future policy action;

- publication of the Welfare Reform Green Paper announcing national roll out of the successful Pathways to Work pilot projects by 2008 for Incapacity Benefit claimants, and consulting on replacement of the current system of incapacity benefits with a new Employment and Support Allowance; and

- following the Low Pay Commission recommendations, **the adult rate of the National Minimum Wage will rise to £5.35 from October 2006.**

4.1 The Government has set a long-term goal of employment opportunity for all - the modern definition of full employment. This is reflected in the aspiration to achieve an employment rate equivalent to 80 per cent of the working age population. The strong labour market performance of recent years, the success of the New Deal and the creation of Jobcentre Plus, have all helped contribute towards the achievement of this objective, with the most significant improvements being demonstrated by the previously most disadvantaged groups and regions.

4.2   This Budget sets out steps to build on this strong performance, increasing flexibility and reducing inactivity still further, and doing more to help those groups in society which face particular barriers to work. The Government believes that everyone who is able to and wants to work should have the opportunity to do so, and should be given appropriate support. Alongside this sits a responsibility on the part of individuals to take steps to improve their chances of moving from welfare to work. The Government has set out its proposals for further extending rights and responsibilities to create a fair and efficient welfare system in a Welfare Reform Green Paper.[1]

Labour market **4.3**   The UK labour market has performed strongly in recent years, as Chart 4.1 shows. The
strength number of people in employment totalled 28.8 million in the three months to January 2006 while the working-age employment rate has reached 74.5 per cent. Since 1971, UK employment has increased by 16.8 per cent with over half of this rise occurring since 1997. This translates into an average annual employment growth rate of 1.1 per cent over the last 8 years, compared with an average of 0.5 per cent per year over the last 35 years. While both male and female employment levels have risen over the past 8 years, female employment growth has been particularly strong, and is now at almost record highs in terms of both the level (13.25 million) and the working age employment rate (69.8 per cent).

4.4   UK unemployment, meanwhile, has fallen, on the conventional International Labour Organisation (ILO) definition, to 5.0 per cent; down from 7.2 per cent in 1997 and around the lowest rate in 30 years. The UK unemployment rate is significantly below the EU 15 average of 7.7 per cent.

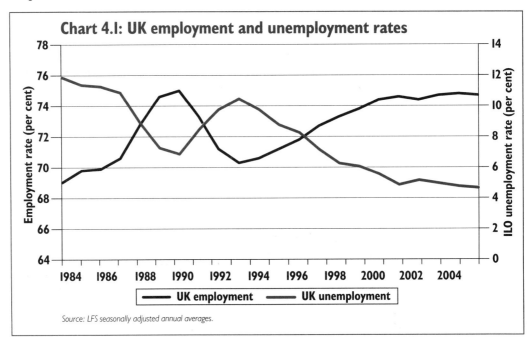

Chart 4.1: UK employment and unemployment rates

Source: LFS seasonally adjusted annual averages.

4.5   The significant improvements in labour market performance have also been reflected in falling caseloads in working age benefits. As Chart 4.2 shows, the number of people claiming Jobseeker's Allowance (JSA) has fallen dramatically, from 1,619,600 in 1997 to 919,700 in January 2006. The claimant count has now remained below 1 million for 50 consecutive months – the longest period since the mid 1970s.

---

[1] *A new deal for welfare: empowering people to work,* DWP, January 2006.

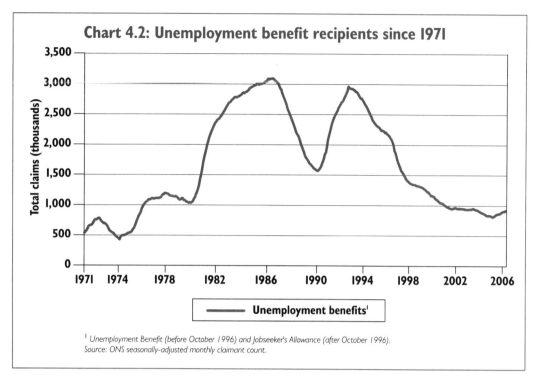

Chart 4.2: Unemployment benefit recipients since 1971

Unemployment benefits[1]

[1] Unemployment Benefit (before October 1996) and Jobseeker's Allowance (after October 1996).
Source: ONS seasonally-adjusted monthly claimant count.

4.6 As well as a reduction in unemployment, the improving employment rate of recent years has been accompanied by a decrease in the total number of people claiming working age benefits. The number of lone parents claiming Income Support (IS) – over 1 million in 1997 – is now below 800,000. Furthermore, and for the first time since 1979, the number of people claiming incapacity benefits[2] has now started to fall, after more than trebling between 1979 and 1997. In total, there are now 900,000 fewer people of working age out of work and claiming benefits than was the case in 1997. As Chart 4.3 shows, in 1997, 5.18 million people were claiming JSA, lone parent IS or incapacity benefits. By 2005, this had fallen by 17 per cent, to 4.28 million.

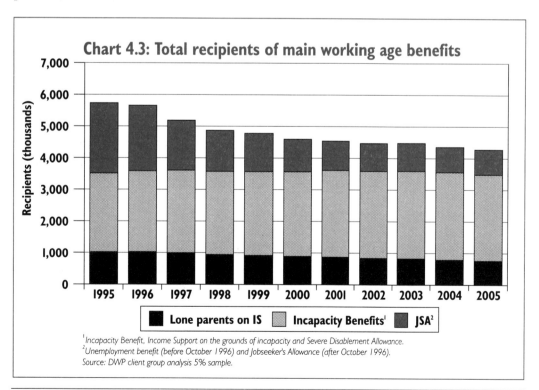

Chart 4.3: Total recipients of main working age benefits

Lone parents on IS   Incapacity Benefits[1]   JSA[2]

[1] Incapacity Benefit, Income Support on the grounds of incapacity and Severe Disablement Allowance.
[2] Unemployment benefit (before October 1996) and Jobseeker's Allowance (after October 1996).
Source: DWP client group analysis 5% sample.

[2] The current system of incapacity benefits includes: Incapacity Benefit, Income Support on the grounds of incapacity, and Severe Disablement Allowance.

DELIVERING EMPLOYMENT OPPORTUNITY TO ALL

The New Deal 4.7 With the establishment of the New Deal, the number of unemployed young people claiming JSA for more than 6 months has fallen to 53,800. This compares with 163,300 in 1997, and has occurred despite the number of 18-24 year olds increasing by nearly half a million (meaning that the proportion of this age group claiming JSA for more than 6 months has fallen from 4 per cent to 1 per cent). The number of adults and young people making long-term claims for unemployment benefits has fallen by two thirds over this same period (see Chart 4.4).

4.8 The New Deal has been fundamental to the success of the Government's labour market policies. It provides support from Personal Advisers, followed by - for JSA claimants - mandatory full time training or subsidised employment to ensure that no claimant can remain indefinitely on benefit. In the 8 years since its inception, the New Deal has, in total, helped over 1.7 million people into work, including 646,410 young people, 251,490 unemployed adults and 423,290 lone parents.

4.9 Independent evaluations have repeatedly highlighted the New Deal's success and cost effectiveness. The National Institute of Economic and Social Research (NIESR) concluded in 2000 that, without the New Deal for young people (NDYP), the level of long-term unemployment would have been twice as high, and that the economy as a whole is richer by £500 million as a result of NDYP.[3] More recent studies show that NDYP has significantly boosted exit rates from unemployment in all regions;[4] that overall youth unemployment has been reduced by between 30,000 and 40,000;[5] and that young men are now 20 per cent more likely to find work as a result of the NDYP.[6,7]

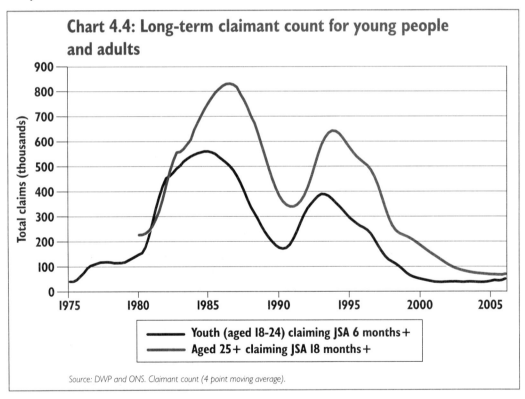

Chart 4.4: Long-term claimant count for young people and adults

Source: DWP and ONS. Claimant count (4 point moving average).

---

[3] *The New Deal for young people: implications for employment and the public finances*, NIESR, December 2000.

[4] *How well has the New Deal for young people worked in the UK?* McVicar and Podivinsky, Northern Ireland Research Centre, April 2003.

[5] *New Deal for young people: evaluation of unemployment flows*, D. Wilkinson, Policy Studies Institute, 2003.

[6] *Evaluating the employment impact of a mandatory jobsearch program*, Blundell R, Costa Dias M, Meghair C, Van Reenen J, in *Journal of the European Economic Association*, June 2004.

[7] *Active labour market policies and the British New Deal for unemployed youth in context*, Van Reenen J, in *Seeking a premier league economy*, Blundell R, Card D, and Freeman R (eds), University of Chicago Press, June 2004.

Flexibility and fairness 4.10 In an increasingly open and integrated global environment, increased prosperity depends on a flexible and outward looking economy which can respond effectively to changing circumstances, and which provides help and support to people to find employment and develop the skills they need to adapt to new technologies and new types of work. The degree of flexibility in the labour market determines the speed and efficiency with which individuals, firms and markets are able to respond to shocks. The more flexible an economy, the better able it is to accommodate shifts, and the lower the cost of change is in terms of lost output and jobs. The Government's labour market policies are committed to advancing flexibility and fairness together, ensuring that everyone in society has the support they need to achieve their full potential in a modern, dynamic economy. Box 4.1 summarises the trends and progress in UK labour market flexibility since 1997.

Box 4.1: Labour Market flexibility – report on progress

Labour market flexibility is crucial to ensure that the UK can adapt to change and thrive in a globally competitive environment. A flexible and efficient labour market has the ability to adjust to changing economic conditions in a way that maintains high levels of output and employment, minimising the cost of adjustment and maintaining economic stability. The UK Government continues to enhance flexibility through the introduction of a variety of policies to increase wage flexibility, reduce inactivity and help those groups in society which face particular barriers to work. Key measures introduced since 1997 include:

Developing skills: reforming the 14-19 curriculum to deliver a high quality vocational education route that equips all pupils with basic skills and gives opportunities to progress to higher skill levels; ambitious targets for 50 per cent of young people to participate in Higher Education by 2010; placing employers needs and priorities at the heart of the training system; rolling out the National Employer Training Programme (Train-to-Gain) across England in 2006; testing ways to increase the effectiveness of different work and skills support services for local communities and employers through the 'Fair Cities' projects. The Government will also publish tomorrow a White Paper on Further Education Reform, setting out how the sector can better provide the skills required for economic growth.

Enhancing wage flexibility: Government evidence to the Pay Review Bodies now considers whether local recruitment and retention issues for each sector should influence pay and has successfully promoted change where appropriate. Civil Service departments are exploring the potential benefits of greater local pay differentiation in the context of recruitment from local labour markets as part of their pay and workforce strategies and their pay remit business cases.

Improving labour market opportunities: the Welfare Reform Green Paper sets out proposals for widening labour market participation and providing genuine employment opportunity for all by developing a more positive and activist system of incapacity benefits; rolling out the successful Pathways to Work pilots to the whole country by 2008; enhancing employment programme support and flexible working opportunities for older workers; and further supporting lone parents. This Budget announces funding to take forward proposals in the Green Paper on more frequent work-focused interviews for lone parents.

Promoting geographic mobility and economic migration: structural reform and administrative improvements to ensure that Housing Benefit does not constrain the ability of the unemployed to find or take up work; and developing a flexible points-based system to ensure that the UK attracts the skills needed for the economy. This Budget announces further measures to reduce anomalies in, and further simplify, the housing benefit system.

4.11 The improving trends in employment and unemployment, shown in Chart 4.1, have been evident not only at a national level, but also among those areas and groups which have traditionally been the most disadvantaged in labour market terms. Employment rates have risen in every region since 1997, as Chart 4.5 shows, with the larger increases having generally been evident in the regions with the lower initial employment rates.

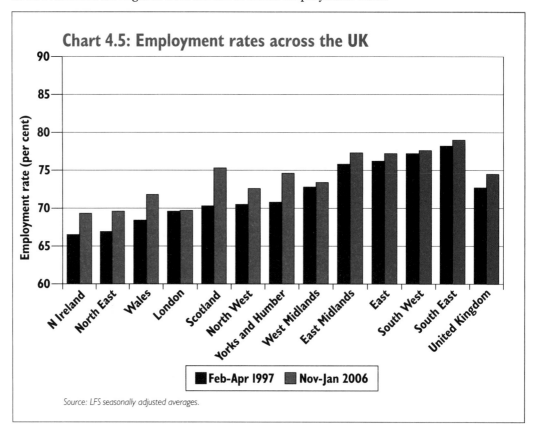

Chart 4.5: Employment rates across the UK

Source: LFS seasonally adjusted averages.

London **4.12** In the 2005 Pre-Budget Report, the Government noted that, at that time, London was the UK region with the lowest employment rate, and the only region where the employment rate was not higher than in 1997. *Employment opportunity for all: analysing labour market trends in London,* published alongside the Budget to inform future policy, examines the various factors that may lie behind low employment rates in London. The document builds on the findings of, and the subsequent cross-government efforts in response to, the *London Project Report* published in 2004.[8] The challenge is to combine London's economic, social, and cultural vibrancy with opportunity for all, harnessing the capital's strengths for its resident population and taking full advantage of unique opportunities arising from the successful bid to host the Olympic and Paralympic Games in 2012.

---

[8] *The London Project Report*, Prime Minister's Strategy Unit, Cabinet Office, July 2004

EXTENDING EMPLOYMENT OPPORTUNITY TO ALL

A new deal for welfare: empowering people to work

4.13   The Department for Work and Pensions' (DWP) Five Year Strategy[9], published in February 2005, set out a long-term aspiration of achieving and sustaining an employment rate equivalent to 80 per cent of the working age population. The DWP Green Paper, *A new deal for welfare: empowering people to work*, published in January 2006, outlines a wide ranging set of proposals to move towards this long-term goal by ensuring that all sections of the population can benefit fully from growth in employment and the economy.

4.14   The Green Paper focuses in particular on tackling inactivity and raising employment among people with a health condition or disability, among lone parents and among older people of working age. The proposals also envisage close engagement with partners in the private and third sector organisations, to find the best means of supporting and encouraging people into work.

People with a health condition or disability

4.15   Of the nearly 5.9 million people of working age with a health condition or disability, only around half are in employment. Ensuring that many more are able to take up the opportunity to work is central to achieving the Government's long-term aspiration of an employment rate equivalent to 80 per cent of the working age population. This will require the reduction and removal of the barriers that can prevent individuals in this group from finding, remaining and progressing in work.

4.16   During the 1980s and early 1990s, the welfare system did little to support people with a health condition or disability back to work. As a result, many people drifted into long-term benefit receipt, notwithstanding the fact that as many as 90 per cent of people expect to get back to work when they start a claim for incapacity benefits. As a consequence, the number of incapacity benefit claimants in the UK more than trebled between the early 1980s and mid 1990s, despite ongoing improvements in general health and life expectancy.

4.17   Since 1997, the Government has reformed the support offered to people with a health condition or disability, providing tailored help and support to make possible a return to work. Incapacity benefit claimants now receive active encouragement and support via a variety of means to plan their return to work, including:

- Jobcentre Plus ensures that incapacity benefit claimants have access to early and ongoing work focused advice;

- the New Deal helps disabled people to identify and move into employment. By November 2005, the New Deal for disabled people (NDDP) had helped over 100,000 disabled people into work;

- the Working Tax Credit and National Minimum Wage help to ensure that work pays; and

- the Government is tackling discrimination against disabled people and improving their opportunities to participate in society, as discussed in Chapter 5.

---

[9] *Opportunity and security throughout life*, DWP, February 2005

4.18   These reforms have begun to change the attitudes and expectations of incapacity benefit claimants. The longstanding rising trend in the number of claimants has now stopped, and the caseload is beginning to fall. Annual inflows to the benefits have fallen by a third since the mid 1990s, and the total number of claimants of incapacity benefits in August 2005 was 2.77 million, over 55,000 lower than August 2004. At the same time the average duration of claims for incapacity benefits has increased, as has the proportion of claimants citing mental health conditions as the primary cause of their incapacity. Notwithstanding recent and considerable success, there is still more to be done.

4.19   People with a mental health condition face a particular risk of social exclusion, including low employment rates and over representation among the homeless and offenders. Public agencies, including the NHS and criminal justice system, do not always work as effectively as they could with people with a mental health condition. Too many are excluded from the world of work when, with the proper support, it should be possible for them to find or remain in work (implying benefits in turn, to their health). To inform the 2007 Comprehensive Spending Review, the Government will therefore review the policies needed to improve mental health outcomes and employment.

Pathways to   **4.20**   The Government's Pathways to Work pilots are providing additional support to help
Work   incapacity benefit claimants return to work. The pilots are testing a new framework that combines ongoing mandatory contact with highly skilled Personal Advisers at Jobcentre Plus, and high quality employment, health and financial support. The OECD has described Pathways to Work as a considerable success,[10] and this success is demonstrated by such evidence as:

- an increase of around 8 percentage points in the off-flow from incapacity benefits after six months of a claim (Chart 4.6);[11]

- by October 2005, there had been over 21,000 job entries through the Pathways to Work pilots;

- following the initial Work Focused Interview (WFI), over 20 per cent of claimants have taken up elements of the Choices package,[12] with over 8,000 referrals to the new Condition Management Programmes; and

- nearly 10 per cent of participants in the pilots are longer-term claimants who were not required to participate in the programme, but volunteered to take part after hearing about the support on offer. In February 2005, the Government extended a mandatory WFI regime to some existing claimants, alongside a new Job Preparation Premium of £20 per week to encourage steps towards finding work.

4.21   As outlined in the Welfare Reform Green Paper, Pathways to Work will be rolled out across the country by 2008. This will ensure that all new incapacity benefit claimants can take advantage of the support that Pathways offers, complementing the introduction of a new Employment and Support Allowance.

---

[10] *Economic Survey of the United Kingdom,* OECD, 2005

[11] The off-flow rates presented are produced from the Working Age Statistical Database (WASD). WASD does not include a proportion of short-term incapacity benefits claims; therefore the off-flows presented will be lower than actual rates. However, trends over time will be consistent.

[12] The Choices package is a range of provision aimed at improving labour market readiness and opportunities. This includes NDDP and the Condition Management Programmes.

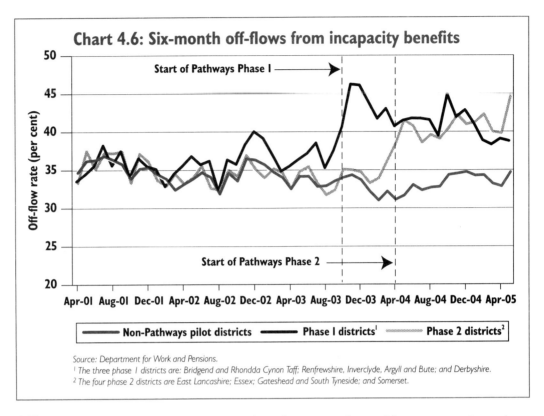

Chart 4.6: Six-month off-flows from incapacity benefits

Source: Department for Work and Pensions.
[1] The three phase 1 districts are: Bridgend and Rhondda Cynon Taff; Renfrewshire, Inverclyde, Argyll and Bute; and Derbyshire.
[2] The four phase 2 districts are East Lancashire; Essex; Gateshead and South Tyneside; and Somerset.

Incapacity **4.22** The current system of incapacity benefits is complex and has perverse incentives.
Benefit Reform Over a third of claimants come from other benefits, receiving (often higher) incapacity benefits before satisfying the main medical test. The system also does little to re-engage claimants with the labour market, tending to focus on what a person is unable to do rather than on what their capabilities are.

4.23 To address this, the Welfare Reform Green Paper proposes a new, simplified Employment and Support Allowance. This new benefit will replace the current incapacity benefits system from 2008. It builds on the successful Pathways to Work model, and strengthens the right and responsibilities agenda.

4.24 Alongside introduction of the new benefit, the Green Paper also proposes:

- steps to improve workplace health;

- improving the Gateway onto the benefit – the Personal Capability Assessment – to ensure that it focuses on assessing people's capability for work rather than their entitlement to benefits;

- supporting GPs and primary care teams in the key role they play in helping people back into work; and

- reforming Statutory Sick Pay, to simplify it and ensure that it helps people stay in work.

Contestability 4.25   Private sector and third sector organisations can bring a distinctive approach to service delivery, based on their specialist knowledge, experience and skills. Since 2000, the Government has been systematically testing the impact of opening up the design and delivery of labour market support to competition. Thirteen Employment Zones have been providing support to unemployed adults, young people who have already been through the New Deal, and lone parents. These sectors have also made a key contribution to the delivery of the New Deal for disabled people job broking service, Action Teams and Working Neighbourhood pilots.

4.26   The third sector is already playing an important role in delivering public services, but has the potential to contribute even more. The Government will continue to identify ways of working with the private and third sectors in the delivery of a wider range of programmes. The Green Paper announced that the roll out of Pathways to Work to the remaining two-thirds of the country will be delivered primarily by the private and third sectors, and that the Government would explore ways of engaging a wider array of local partners, combining strategies and pooling resources in local efforts to reduce unemployment and inactivity.

Lone Parents

4.27   Helping lone parents move into, remain in, and progress in work, is one of the key elements in achieving the Government's commitment to halve child poverty by 2010 and eradicate it by 2020 (set out in more detail in Chapter 5). Between the mid 1970s and the late 1990s, the lone parent population almost doubled in size and the distribution of work across households polarised. As a result, the proportion of children in workless households increased nearly three-fold. Of the 1.76 million children currently in workless households, nearly 70 per cent live in a household headed by a lone parent.[13] The Government accordingly set the challenging target of achieving a 70 per cent lone parent employment rate by 2010. It is estimated that meeting this target would lift at least a further 200,000 children out of poverty.

4.28   Considerable progress in raising the lone parent employment rate has already been made, as Chart 4.7 shows. The lone parent population has risen by 255,000 since 1997, to nearly 1.8 million in Spring 2005. Employment among this group has, however, risen even more strongly over this period, with an increase of 318,000 taking the number of lone parents in employment to over 1 million. More lone parents are now in work than not, and the employment rate of 56.6 per cent in spring 2005 represented an increase of over 11 percentage points[14] since 1997. In addition, the number of lone parents claiming Income Support has fallen by almost a quarter of a million since 1997.[15]

4.29   Key to this success has been a package of initiatives and reforms to support lone parents into work including: increased work focused advice through Jobcentre Plus to ensure that lone parents are aware of the opportunities available to them; the New Deal for lone parents (NDLP); and policies to make work pay. Evaluation evidence suggests that the support introduced since 1997 has been a significant reason for the rising employment rate, with Government policies accounting for about half of the gains.[16] Further independent evaluation suggests that participating in NDLP doubles an individual's chances of finding employment, relative to that of non-participants.[17] Since 1998, almost 659,000 lone parents have joined NDLP, of whom over 420,000 have been helped into work.[18]

[13] LFS Autumn 2005.

[14] LFS Spring data.

[15] August 2005.

[16] *Welfare Reform and Lone Parents Employment in the UK*, CMPO working paper no 72, Gregg and Harkness, 2003

[17] *New Deal for Lone Parents: Second synthesis Report of the National Evaluation*, DWP, June 2003

[18] NDLP starts to November 2005; NDLP jobs to August 2005.

4.30   Despite the gains that have been made in the lone parent employment rate and the extra support that is now available, the 70 per cent lone parent employment rate target remains challenging. Further progress is essential in order to continue to reduce the number of workless households and eradicate child poverty. The Welfare Reform Green Paper sets out proposals to provide further support to enable lone parents to work. The Government believes that lone parents, in return, have a responsibility to make a serious effort to return to work, especially once their youngest child goes to secondary school. The proposals include:

- holding more frequent Work Focused Interviews (WFIs) and piloting more intensive support during the first year of a claim; and

- piloting a new premium – the Work Related Activity Premium – so that lone parents are better off if they take serious steps towards preparing for work.

4.31   WFIs with skilled Personal Advisers ensure that lone parents are fully informed of the help and support available to them. Independent evaluation[19] shows that take up of NDLP rises by more than 14 percentage points among lone parents attending a WFI. Since October 2005, lone parents who have been claiming income support for 12 months or more, and who have a youngest child aged 14 years or over, are required to attend an interview once every 3 months to help them prepare for the transition to work when their child reaches 16. **This Budget announces that, from April 2007, six-monthly work focused interviews will be rolled out to all lone parents who have been on benefit for at least a year and whose youngest child is under 14.** This means that all lone parents will benefit from a WFI at least every six months.

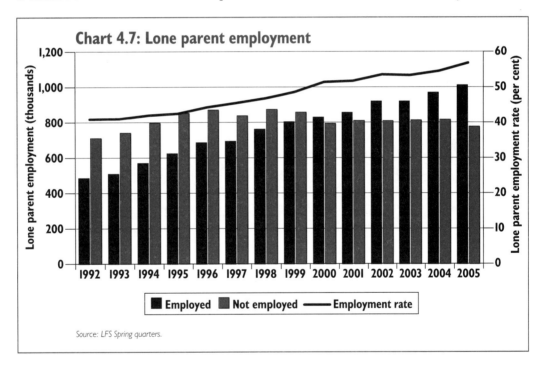

Chart 4.7: Lone parent employment

Source: LFS Spring quarters.

New Deal Plus   **4.32**   Lone parents remain less likely to participate in the labour market than partnered
for lone parents   parents with children of the same age. In order to reduce further the barriers to work faced by lone parents, the DWP Five Year Strategy announced that all current lone parent initiatives would be brought together in a coherent package and to deliver a step change in support for lone parents on benefits. The New Deal Plus for lone parents (NDLP+) pilots were launched at the end of April 2005 in five Jobcentre Plus areas.[20]

---

[19] *Integrated findings from the evaluation of the first 18 months of work-focused interviews*, Insite Consulting (DWP evaluation series, w184), March 2004.

[20] Leicestershire; Bradford; London SE; North London; and Dudley and Sandwell.

4.33   The NDLP+ pilots combine the provision of good quality and affordable childcare with work focused support, and strong financial incentives to both look for and to stay in work. The package includes the In-Work Credit and Work Search Premium payments, and Extended Childcare support. Based on positive feedback from both Personal Advisers and lone parents, the Government announced in the Pre-Budget Report 2005 that it would:

- extend the support offered through the NDLP+ pilots in the existing five locations for a further two years, to 2008; and

- extend the NDLP+ pilots to two further districts in Scotland and Wales from October 2006.[21]

Retention   **4.34**   While the probability of lone parents leaving work has fallen from 14 per cent in 1992 to around 10 per cent in 2003, lone parents are still more likely to leave their job than non-lone parents and single childless women.[22] The Government is committed to reducing the risk of lone parents alternating between work and benefits. As announced in the 2005 Pre-Budget Report the Government will explore ways to incentivise Personal Advisers to continue to support lone parents when in work, to ensure they are helped into sustainable employment.

4.35   Lone parents can already contact Jobcentre Plus for advice on the full range of support that is available to them, including help with housing costs, tax credits and childcare. The Green Paper proposes to explore new ways of increasing the support that Jobcentre Plus can give to lone parents who are moving into work, or who are already in work.

4.36   A number of in-work support measures are being piloted in NDLP+ and Working Neighbourhoods pilot areas. These include: the In-Work Emergency Fund to overcome barriers that might otherwise make it difficult to remain in work during the first 60 days in employment; Personal Adviser support during the first two months of employment; a Flexible Discretionary Fund; and specific retention payments. Employment Zone contractors, meanwhile, offer flexible in-work assistance to customers who require assistance.

4.37   Since October 2003, the Government has also been testing a new strategy, the Employment Retention and Advancement (ERA) pilots, for people in low-paid employment or who have moved into work from benefits. Alongside financial incentives to encourage retention in work, ERA is testing the effectiveness of continued support, for up to 33 months, from a dedicated Advancement Support Adviser. Preliminary evidence on the pilots will be available towards the end of 2006.

4.38   The In Work Credit (IWC), which covers almost 50 per cent of lone parents who have been on benefit for over a year, is a £40 a week payment for lone parents who have been on Income Support for more than 12 months, for their first 12 months back in work. The credit was first piloted in April 2004, and subsequently extended in October 2005 to a further six areas[23] in the South East of England, covering an extra 84,000 lone parents.

---

[21] Edinburgh, Lothian and Borders in Scotland; the former Cardiff and Vale sites within the enlarged South East Wales district: http://www.dwp.gov.uk/mediacentre/pressreleases/2006/feb/emp025-080206.asp

[22] *Lone Parents cycling between work and benefits*, DWP Research report 217, September 2004.

[23] Surrey and Sussex; Essex; Kent; Berkshire, Buckinghamshire and Oxfordshire; Bedfordshire and Hertfordshire; and Hampshire and the Isle of Wight.

Partners

4.39   Between the 1970s and the 1990s, there was a shift away from single earning households as the working age employment rate of women increased from 56 per cent to 66 per cent, and that of men decreased from 92 per cent to 80 per cent. Work also became polarised between 'work rich' double earner households and 'work poor' workless households, contributing to higher levels of child poverty and social exclusion. To meet the Government's goals of extending employment opportunity to all and tackling child and pensioner poverty, it is important that work-focused support is provided to every adult in a household who is without work.

4.40   Mandatory WFIs were introduced for partners of benefit claimants in April 2004. The New Deal for partners (NDP) includes assistance with job search, advice on training and skills, and the identification and provision of support for registered childcare, offering similar levels of support to NDLP. The Government recognises that the costs of looking for work may act as a discincentive to non-working partners in single earner families. From October 2005, a work search premium of £20 per week became available in six pilot areas with high levels of worklessness to those in a family in receipt of the Working Tax Credit who are not working, and who agree to join the enhanced NDP and search actively for a job. Since April 2004, over 72,000 WFIs have been attended, and more than 3,600 job entries have been recorded by partners of benefit claimants who have either attended a WFI or joined NDP.

Unemployed people (Jobseeker's Allowance claimants)

4.41   For the majority of jobseekers, unemployment is a short-term, transitionary state; nearly 80 per cent move off benefit within 6 months. JSA makes financial support conditional on taking the necessary steps to move back into work as quickly as possible. The intervention regime supports, monitors and enforces independent jobseeking for short-term claimants; the New Deal is reserved for the small minority who fail to find work quickly. As Chart 4.2 showed, as well as reductions in long-term unemployment, the regime has contributed to a fall in the claimant count from 1,619,600 in 1997 to 919,700 in February 2006.

4.42   In order to maximise the impact of the JSA intervention regime in bearing down on unemployment, Jobcentre Plus Personal Advisers need to ensure that jobseekers move off benefit as quickly as possible. It is critical, therefore, that advisers have the opportunities and the tools they need to set agreements on jobseeking activity, offer support, monitor agreed activity, and enforce activity where necessary. Frequent face-to-face interventions are key to this, and the Government has already taken steps to increase their frequency. All claimants who reach three months of unemployment now have to participate in a series of weekly signings. For the small proportion of adults who reach six months of unemployment, Jobseeker Mandatory Activity pilots will be introduced in twelve areas from April 2006, with mandatory participation in a three-day work course and three additional follow-up interviews.

Fortnightly Job   **4.43**   The Fortnightly Job Review (FJR) is the focal point of the JSA intervention regime: the
Review   point at which advisers are able to ensure that individuals are carrying out their responsibilities to look for work. The FJR checks that claimants continue to be available for, and are actively seeking, work. Nearly 2 million FJRs are carried out every month. The effectiveness of these interventions in increasing independent jobsearch activity and ensuring that only those who are eligible remain on benefit, is critical for maintaining flows off the benefit and maintaining downward pressure on the claimant count. From June 2006, the Government will therefore introduce a strengthened, refocused, Fortnightly Job Review, the primary function of which will be to ensure that only those claimants who are able to

demonstrate that they have undertaken their responsibilities to look for work are allowed to continue to claim JSA. Personal Advisers will be able to direct claimants towards further support where necessary, and will have effective powers to sanction those who are unable to demonstrate that they have undertaken sufficient jobsearch.

Women and Work Commission

4.44   The Women and Work Commission (WWC), set up in September 2004 to consider how to close the gender pay gap and opportunities gap within a generation, reported at the end of February.[24] The Government welcomes the broad range of the Commission's recommendations and values the ambition of closing the pay gap within a generation. In response to *Shaping a Fairer Future*, the Government today announces a package of measures to enhance lifelong learning opportunities for women in training and work, described further in Box 4.2.

Box 4.2: Supporting Women and Work

The Government has already done much to improve the rights of working mothers and work-life balance (set out in more detail in Chapter 5). The National Minimum Wage will increase to £5.35 this October and around 70 per cent of the beneficiaries will be women. The New Deal employment programmes have helped many women into work, and the Government has taken steps to extend the support available. As announced in 2005 Pre-Budget Report, new private and third sector led employment teams will deliver outreach support for people who are neither in work nor on benefit, especially the non-working partners of people in low income families, in groups which face particular barriers to employment. Ethnic minority outreach projects are committed to reaching customers who do not usually access existing provision, using voluntary and community sector organisations to identify and support them. The London Development Agency (LDA) and the East Midlands Development Agency (EMDA) will also be running pilots to better understand the particular barriers that women returners face.

Progress in helping more women move into work has been reflected in an increase in the employment rate of women from 67 per cent in 1997 to nearly 70 per cent today. Nevertheless, over 1 million women who are currently not working would like to work, and nearly 15 per cent of the 5.1 million women working part-time would like to increase their hours.[a] The aspiration of an employment rate equivalent to 80 per cent of the working age population will only be reached if more women are helped into work, and both the economy and individuals will be richer if the skills of women not currently working can be harnessed.

The Government recognises the scale of the challenge and is committed to helping more women into work. This Budget therefore announces, in response to the Women and Work Commission's report:

- doubling the number of existing Skills Coaching pilots to 16 Jobcentre Plus districts with a specific focus on helping low-skilled women return to work;
- increasing, by 50 per cent, the number of pilots delivering level 3 skills and focusing an additional pilot on women with low skills; and
- funding for Sector Skills Councils, matched by employers in industries with skills shortages, to develop new ways of recruiting and training low skilled women, benefiting over 10,000 women.

---

[a] LFS 2005.

---

[24] *Shaping a Fairer Future*, Women and Work Commission, February 2006.

Ethnic Minorities

4.45 The gap between the employment rate of ethnic minorities and the employment rate overall has narrowed by around 1 percentage point betwen 2003 and 2005,[25] as Chart 4.8 shows. The overall ethnic minority employment rate now stands and 59 percent. New Deals, Employment Zones, Action Teams, Ethnic Minority Outreach, the Flexible Fund and Specialist Employment Advisers have together helped over 213,000 ethnic minority people find work. As reported in the 2005 Pre-Budget Report, however, while some ethnic minority groups are doing relatively well in the labour market, some are facing distinct disadvantages. These disadvantages may be caused by barriers to succeeding in education or accessing employment opportunities, or sometimes through job discrimination.

4.46 In 2003, and in response to a Cabinet Office report *Ethnic Minorities in the Labour Market,* the Government established a Ministerial Ethnic Minority Employment Task Force to take forward a cross-government strategy to overcome the barriers faced in education, employment and discrimination. The Task Force has made good progress and the majority of the original Cabinet Office recommendations have been implemented. Nevertheless, and as Chart 4.8 shows, employment progress for some ethnic minority groups has still been slow.

Enterprising People, Enterprising Places **4.47** In Budget 2005, the Government therefore agreed to implement the main recommendations of the report by the National Employment Panel (NEP), *Enterprising People, Enterprising Places,* incorporating them into the overall cross-government strategy. In the 12 months since publication, the Government has made strong progress towards implementing the main recommendations of the report, as outlined in Box 4.3.

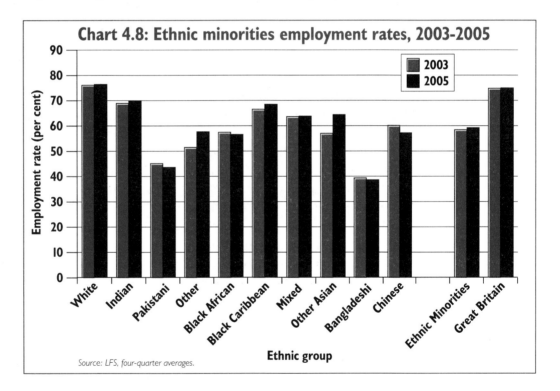

Chart 4.8: Ethnic minorities employment rates, 2003-2005

Source: LFS, four-quarter averages.

---

[25] Spring four-quarter average.

4.48   In the 2005 Pre-Budget Report, the Government introduced two further measures based on the NEP's recommendations: new private and third sector led employment teams to deliver outreach support for people who are neither in work nor on benefit based in areas of disadvantage and high ethnic minority populations; and a new Commission of private sector business leaders who will be asked to advise on helping to tackle race discrimination in employment. The Commission will report to the Chancellor in early 2007.

4.49   Another key recommendation of the NEP was to introduce new partnerships for employment and skills delivery in the UK's major cities, led by new Workforce Investment Boards, to better co-ordinate efforts to tackle the employment problems of the most disadvantaged groups, including some ethnic minority groups. The Welfare Reform Green Paper announced the intention to pilot new partnerships between Jobcentre Plus, Local Authorities, Learning and Skills Councils, employers, the third sector and other partners to deliver employment and skills support in UK cities. The NEP recommendations on Employment and Skills frameworks will be incorporated into these pilots.

Box 4.3: Update on NEP recommendations

The 2005 National Employment Panel report *Enterprising People, Enterprising Places* set out measures to improve employment and business growth for ethnic and faith minority groups. The report recommended a focus on 5 main cities where two thirds of the UK's ethnic minority population live (London, Birmingham, Manchester, Bradford and Leicester).

The main measures recommended by the NEP included: new Centres of Vocational Excellence (CoVEs) for Entrepreneurship as part of the overall support for ethnic minority enterprise; Workforce Investment Boards to oversee new integrated employment and skills frameworks; and ensuring outreach support is targeted specifically at those who are not in work, not on benefit and may have been traditionally excluded from the labour market.

The NEP also called for improved leadership on race and diversity within the public and private sector to end discriminatory practices and promote equality. Its recommendations included creating a high level commission of business leaders to advise on tackling discrimination and greater incorporation of race equality into procurement.

In the 12 months since the report was published, the Government has:

- been developing two new pilot Centres of Vocational Excellence (CoVEs) for Entrepreneurship in London and Birmingham;

- set aside resources for additional outreach to partners of benefit claimants in the five designated cities, beginning in 2007;

- given Regional Development Agencies responsibility for assessing the needs of ethnic minority businesses within their Regional Economic Strategies;

- proposed piloting new flexible and integrated local arrangements that will incorporate the NEP's recommendation that employer-involved partnerships co-ordinate employment and skills support for disadvantaged groups;

- announced the intention to invite business leaders to join a Commission to advise, by Budget 2007, on increasing ethnic minority employment in the private sector; and

- worked across four central departments to develop an approach to public procurement that provides greater assurance that race equality conditions are being met, and that procurement is helping the Government meet its wider objectives on race equality.

Extending Working Lives

4.50 The Government is committed to ensuring that everyone who wishes to extend their working life should have the opportunity to do so. Evidence suggests that remaining in work can increase social inclusion and improve health; it also enhances the ability to save for retirement, helping address the impacts of demographic change. Raising employment among older people of working age will be a key element in realising the Government's long-term aspiration of an employment rate equivalent to 80 per cent of the working age population.

4.51 The Government has improved the back to work support available to older people through Jobcentre Plus and the New Deal for people aged 50 and over, which is estimated to have supported around 150,000 job starts. The Welfare Reform Green Paper proposes that employment support for jobseekers aged over 50 should be aligned with that for younger age groups. DWP also signalled the intention to work with employers to extend flexible working opportunities to older workers. Facilitating this, in October 2006 (subject to Parliamentary approval), and in line with the European Employment Directive, the Government will introduce legislation that outlaws age discrimination in employment and vocational training. The financial incentive to work, meanwhile, has been enhanced through the Working Tax Credit, which includes additional support for people over 50. The increase in the UK female state pension age from 60 years to 65 years between 2010 and 2020 is expected to lead to significant growth in female labour-market participation rates.

4.52 These measures have, in the context of a strong and stable economy, delivered impressive results. Since May 1997, the employment rate of people aged between 50 and State Pension Age has increased from less than 65 per cent to over 70 per cent. Furthermore, there are now nearly 1.1 million people over State Pension Age in employment.

HOUSING BENEFIT REFORM

Housing Benefit   **4.53**   The structure and effective delivery of Housing Benefit are important factors in promoting labour mobility and participation. The Government has initiated a comprehensive reform programme to address the complexity of the current system, and this has already led to considerable improvements in delivery. In the second quarter of 2002/03, for example, local authorities took an average of 57 days to process new claims. This had improved to 46 days in 2004/05 and, by the second quarter of 2005/06, to 36 days. The latest data show that the 60 worst performing authorities now take an average of 59 days to process new claims; a reduction of 48 days since 2002/03. The Government has also introduced regulations, effective since 6 March, that consolidate more than 200 sets of amending regulations to the Housing Benefit (General) Regulations 1987 and the Council Tax (General) Regulations 1992. This will make it much easier for administrators and advisers to understand and apply the correct legislation.

4.54 The Government will continue its drive to simplify the administration of Housing Benefit by introducing **a package of measures aimed at reducing anomalies in, and further simplifying, the system, including:**

- **applying regulations more equally to customers and their partners; and**

- **implementing regulations that clarify the treatment of owner-occupiers and former owner-occupiers and their partners.**

4.55   The Government will also continue to promote home ownership and the greater involvement of private sector providers in offering shared ownership opportunities. Bringing arrangements into line with those where ownership is shared with a social sector landlord, **the Government will enable tenants to receive Housing Benefit on the rental portion of a shared ownership arrangement where the tenancy is granted by an organisation other than a Housing Association or Housing Authority.**

Local Housing   **4.56**   The Government is also making progress with structural reform of Housing Benefit.
Allowances   The flat-rate Local Housing Allowance (LHA) was first introduced in 9 pilot areas between November 2003 and February 2004, and in a further 9 areas from April 2005. The LHA provides a simpler, more transparent way of calculating payments and, through payment to the recipient rather than the landlord, helps to promote personal financial responsibility and ease the transition to work. Early evidence from the pilots is promising and, building on this evidence, the Government is currently consulting on proposals for a scheme suitable for rolling out across the country.

Tackling fraud   **4.57**   Spending on Housing Benefit has been rising in real terms since 2000-01. There have
and error   been a number of reasons for this, including above inflation increases in private sector rents. While ensuring that tenants continue to receive an appropriate level of benefit, the Government will take steps to maintain overall Housing Benefit spending at a more stable level, building on progress to date in reducing fraud. The Government will take forward a number of measures to reduce fraud and error, including:

- as announced in the 2005 Pre-Budget Report, **providing funding to ensure that all local authorities can take steps to reduce housing benefit fraud and error by reviewing or visiting at least 50 per cent of their claimants each year, in line with best practice;**

- introducing **new methods of identifying predictable changes of circumstances that would affect a claim, and taking early action to prevent overpayments; and**

- providing **new IT links between the Housing Benefit Matching Service and local authorities to speed up the transmission of data.**

MAKING WORK PAY

4.58   The Government believes that work is the best route out of poverty and is committed to making work pay by improving incentives to participate and progress in the labour market. Through the Working Tax Credit and the National Minimum Wage, the Government has boosted in-work incomes, improving financial incentives to work and tackling poverty among working people.

The National   **4.59**   The National Minimum Wage guarantees a fair minimum income from work. Since
Minimum Wage   October 2005, the adult rate has been £5.05 an hour. In February 2005, the Low Pay Commission recommended that the rate should rise to £5.35 from October 2006, subject to a review to check that this remained appropriate in the light of economic circumstances. It has now reviewed the most recent evidence on the labour market and economy, and confirmed that the rate should rise as planned. It has also made other recommendations, including that the rate for 16-17 year olds, first introduced in October 2004 at £3 per hour, should rise to £3.30. The Government has accepted this, and its full response was set out in a statement on 20 March.

The Working Tax **4.60** The Working Tax Credit provides financial support on top of earnings for households
Credit with low incomes. By December 2005, 2.2 million working families and over 250,000
low-income working households without children were benefiting from the Working Tax
Credit. Tax credits have reduced the burden of tax for low-income households and for workers
with a disability.

4.61 The 2005 Pre-Budget Report set out a series of improvements to the Tax Credits
system, based on lessons learned from the first two years of its operation. These measures will
mean that there will be greater certainty for claimants, while maintaining the flexibility to
respond to changes in income and circumstances. In particular, the disregard for increases in
earnings will rise from £2,500 to £25,000. Financial support for childcare is discussed in more
detail in Chapter 5.

Tackling the **4.62** The unemployment trap occurs when those without work find the difference between
unemployment in-work and out-of-work incomes too small to provide an incentive to enter the labour
trap market. Table 4.1 shows that, since the introduction of the National Minimum Wage in April
1999, the Government has increased the minimum income that people can expect when
moving into work, thereby reducing the unemployment trap.

Table 4.1: Weekly Minimum Income Guarantees (MIGs)

	April 1999	October 2006	Percentage increase real terms[2]
Family[1] with one child, full-time work	£182	£268	23%
Family[1] with one child, part-time work	£136	£210	29%
Single person, 25 or over, full-time work	£113	£175	30%
Couple, no children, 25 or over, full-time work	£117	£206	48%
Single disabled person in full-time work	£139	£218	31%
Single disabled person in part-time work	£109	£160	23%

Assumes single earner household, the prevailing rate of NMW and that the family is eligible for Family Credit/Disability Working Allowance or Working
Tax Credit/Child Tax Credit.
Full-time work is assumed to be 35 hours. Part-time work is assumed to be 16 hours.
[1]Applies to lone parent families and couples with children alike.
[2]RPI growth is taken from HM Treasury's economic forecasts.

Tackling the **4.63** The poverty trap occurs when those in work have limited incentives to move up the
poverty trap earnings ladder because it may leave them little better off. Marginal deduction rates (MDRs)
measure the extent of the poverty trap by showing how much of each additional pound of
gross earnings is lost through higher taxes and withdrawn benefits or tax credits.

4.64 The Government's reforms are ensuring that workers have improved incentives to
progress in work. Table 4.2 shows that, as a result of these reforms, around half a million fewer
low-income households now face MDRs in excess of 70 per cent than in April 1997. The
increase in the number of households facing MDRs of between 60 and 70 per cent is primarily
due to the introduction of tax credits, which have extended financial support so that far more
families benefit.

Table 4.2: The effect of the Government's reforms on high marginal deduction rates

Marginal deduction rate[1]	Before Budget 1998	2006-07 system of tax and benefits
Over 100 per cent	5,000	0
Over 90 per cent	130,000	35,000
Over 80 per cent	300,000	170,000
Over 70 per cent	740,000	240,000
Over 60 per cent	760,000	1,730,000

[1] Marginal deduction rates are for heads of working households in receipt of income-related benefits or tax credits where at least one person works 16 hours or more a week, and the head of the household is not a disabled person.

Note: Figures are cumulative. Before Budget 1998 based on 1997-98 estimated caseload and take-up rates; the 2006-07 system of tax and benefits is based on 2004-05 caseload and take-up rates.

FUNDING FOR WELFARE TO WORK

4.65   The Welfare to Work programme is delivered by DWP. The programme was originally funded from the Windfall Tax on the excess profits of the privatised utilities. Since 2003-04, Welfare to Work has increasingly been funded from within DWP's own resources, as the Windfall Tax receipts are exhausted. The DWP Annual Report sets out expenditure plans and outturn information.

Table 4.3: Allocation of the Windfall Tax

£ million	1997-98	1998-99	1999-00	2000-01	2001-02	2002-03	2003-04[2]	2004-05[3]	2005-06[3]	TOTAL
Spending by programme[1]										
New Deal for young people[4]	50	200	310	300	240	260	170	0	0	1,530
New Deal for 25 plus	0	10	90	110	200	210	150	0	0	770
New Deal for over 50s	0	0	5	20	10	10	10	0	0	60
New Deal for lone parents	0	20	40	40	40	80	60	0	0	280
New Deal for disabled people[5]	0	5	20	10	10	30	30	0	0	100
New Deal for partners	0	0	5	10	10	10	10	0	0	40
Childcare[6]	0	20	10	5	0	0	0	0	0	35
University for Industry[7]	0	5	0	0	0	0	0	0	0	5
Workforce development[8]	0	0	0	0	0	40	50	150	80	320
ONE pilots[9]	0	0	0	5	5	0	0	0	0	10
Action Teams	0	0	0	10	40	50	50	0	0	150
Enterprise development	0	0	0	10	20	10	0	0	0	40
Modernising the Employment Service	0	0	0	40	0	0	0	0	0	40
Total Resource Expenditure	50	260	480	560	570	700	530	150	80	3,380
Capital Expenditure[10]	90	270	260	750	450	0	0	0	0	1,820
Windfall Tax receipts	2,600	2,600								5,200

[1] In year figures rounded to the nearest £10 million, (except where expenditure is less than £5 million). Constituent elements may not sum to totals because of rounding.

[2] Windfall Tax expenditure on welfare to work programmes is reduced from 2003-04 onwards as Windfall Tax resources are exhausted. Remaining in-year expenditure will be topped up with general Government revenues.

[3] Figures are provisional for the years from 2004-05 to 2005-06.

[4] Includes funding for the Innovation Fund.

[5] Includes £10 million in 1999-2000, an element of the November 1998 announcements on welfare reform.

[6] Includes £30 million for out-of-school childcare. The costs of the 1997 Budget improvements in childcare through Family Credit are included from April 1998 to October 1999, after which the measure was incorporated within the Working Families' Tax Credit.

[7] Start up and development costs. Other costs of the University for Industry are funded from within Departmental Expenditure Limits.

[8] Includes £219 million funding for Employer Training Pilots.

[9] Funding for repeat interviews. Other funding is from the Invest to Save budget.

[10] Includes capital spending on renewal of school infrastructure, to help raise standards.

5 BUILDING A FAIRER SOCIETY

The Government is committed to promoting fairness alongside flexibility and enterprise, to ensure that everyone can take advantage of opportunities to fulfil their potential. The Government's reforms of the welfare state reflect its aims of eradicating child poverty, supporting families to balance their work and family lives, promoting saving and ensuring security for all in old age. The Government is also committed to a modern and fair tax system that ensures that everyone pays their fair share of tax. This Budget sets out the next steps the Government is taking to support these aims, including:

- announcing that **from April 2008 every pensioner and disabled person will have free off-peak bus travel in England;**

- building on progress in reducing the number of children in poverty, **a commitment to increase the child element of the Child Tax Credit at least in line with average earnings until the end of this Parliament;**

- enabling employers to support working parents with their childcare, by **raising the tax and national insurance contributions exemption for employer-supported childcare to £55 per week** and by making available **capital grants to help employers establish workplace nurseries;**

- **announcing that the payments into Child Trust Fund accounts at age seven will be £250 for all children, with £500 for children from lower-income families;**

- launching a review of policy for children and young people, supported **in this Budget by £10 million over two years to promote youth engagement in their communities, sports and local media;**

- **increasing the stamp duty land tax threshold to £125,000**, exempting an additional 40,000 homebuyers each year;

- **announcing that the inheritance tax threshold will rise to £312,000 in 2008-09 and £325,000 in 2009-10,** to continue to provide a fair and targeted system;

- **establishing this Government's largest ever consultation with the third sector,** to be overseen by a cross-departmental ministerial group; and

- further reforms to **modernise the tax system,** (including investing in high capacity online filing services), and a number of measures to clamp down on **tax fraud and avoidance.**

5.1 The Government's aim is to promote a fair and inclusive society in which everyone shares in rising national prosperity and no one is held back from achieving their potential by disadvantage or lack of opportunity. The Government is committed to advancing fairness and flexibility together, so that all people, at all stages of life, can benefit from the UK's modern and dynamic economy.

SUPPORT FOR FAMILIES AND CHILDREN

5.2 The Government believes that every child, irrespective of background or circumstances, deserves the best start in life. To achieve this, since 1997, the Government's strategy has been to reform financial support for families with children, help parents into work and provide better public services for children and their families.

Eradicating child poverty

5.3   In the 1980s and early 1990s, the number of children growing up in poor households more than doubled, so that the UK had the highest rate of relative child poverty in the EU. The Government has therefore made tackling child poverty one of its key priorities and, in 1999, committed to eradicating child poverty in a generation.

Progress to date **5.4**   The Government has made significant progress across all of its child poverty measures. Since 1996-97, the Government has more than halved the number of children living in absolute poverty, lifting 1.8 million children out of absolute poverty before housing costs (BHC) and 2.4 million children after housing costs (AHC), by 2004-05. Absolute poverty is measured against a household income threshold that rises in line with inflation, so these reductions demonstrate the extent to which incomes of the poorest families are rising in real terms. Recent evidence shows that there have also been significant falls in the number of children living in material deprivation poverty. As incomes of the poorest families have risen, they have been able to spend more on their children's needs[1] and there are fewer families unable to afford key items such as new shoes and winter coats.[2]

Public Service **5.5**   The Government set itself an ambitious Public Service Agreement (PSA) target to
Agreement reduce child poverty on a relative low-income measure by a quarter between 1998-99 and 2004-05. The relative measure of poverty is the European standard and captures the extent to which incomes of the poorest families are keeping pace with the rising incomes of the population, so is the most challenging measure of child poverty. Outturn data for 2004-5, released on 9 March, shows that 700,000 children had been lifted out of relative poverty since 1998-99 on both a BHC and an AHC basis.[3] This represents a fall of 23 per cent and 17 per cent respectively. This decisively reverses the long-running trend, from the late 1970s to mid 1990s, of rising relative low-income poverty. While these reductions represent strong improvement, they are less than the Government's ambition.

Halving child **5.6**   The Government is firmly committed to eradicating child poverty by 2020. HM
poverty Treasury and the Department for Work and Pensions share a target to halve child poverty between 1998-99 and 2010-11 on both a relative low-income and material deprivation basis.[4] The *Child Poverty Review*,[5] published alongside the 2004 Spending Review, set out the Government's strategy to reach the 2010 target. **Budget 2006 announces that the Government will continue to increase the child element of the Child Tax Credit at least in line with earnings until the end of this Parliament.** This will provide a solid foundation for meeting the target to halve child poverty. In line with the Government's view that work is the best route out of poverty, Chapter 4 sets out further measures to help lone parents move into and stay in work.

Child poverty **5.7**   In February the Greater London Authority and the Association of London
in London Government launched the London Child Poverty Commission to investigate the reasons behind high child poverty levels in the capital and to identify policy solutions. The Government warmly welcomes the launch of the Commission and looks forward to considering the proposals it develops.

---

[1] *That's where the money goes*, Gregg, Waldfogel and Washbrook, 2005.

[2] *Families and children study*, Department for Work and Pensions (DWP), 2005.

[3] *Households Below Average Income: an analysis of the income distribution 1994-5–2004-5*, DWP, 2006.

[4] Now that data is available on material deprivation, the Government will analyse that and other information and set a baseline and threshold for the material deprivation measure later in 2006.

[5] *Child Poverty Review*, HM Treasury, July 2004.

Box 5.1: Trends in child poverty

The fall in the number of children living in relative poverty since 1997 followed a period where child poverty in the UK rose significantly and was the highest in the EU. The chart below shows how, since 1997, the UK's reduction in child poverty has been the largest in Europe and the UK has more than halved the child poverty gap with the EU-15, where the rate of child poverty has remained stable overall. All this has been achieved against a background of strong economic growth in the UK, with median incomes growing by an average of 2.4 per cent in real terms each year.

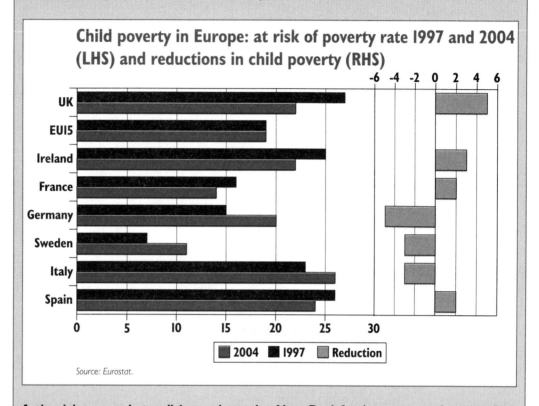

Child poverty in Europe: at risk of poverty rate 1997 and 2004 (LHS) and reductions in child poverty (RHS)

Source: Eurostat.

Active labour market policies such as the New Deal for lone parents have made a significant impact and helped reduce the number of children in workless households by more than 350,000. Reforms to the tax and benefit system – to provide financial support for families and to make work pay – have also contributed. If the Government had simply indexed the 1997 tax and benefit system to prices, there would be over 1.5 million more children in poverty than is currently the case.

Financial support for families with children

5.8   Radical reform of the provision of financial support for families has been a key driver of the fall in the number of children in poverty. The Government's reforms have been underpinned by two principal objectives: support for all families with children and greatest support for those who need it most. This is delivered primarily through a combination of Child Tax Credit (CTC) and Child Benefit.

Increased support for families   **5.9**   Tax credits are reaching far more low- and moderate-income families than any previous system of income-related financial support, benefiting around six million families and ten million children. New figures published in March 2006 showed that in the first year of new tax credits (2003-04), 79 per cent of eligible families were claiming CTC, while the proportion of the money claimed was even higher, at 87 per cent. Some 89 per cent of low income working families claimed tax credits in 2003-04, a higher level of take-up than for Working Families' Tax Credit (WFTC) and significantly higher than for Family Credit, as shown in Chart 5.1 below. In their first year of operation, take-up was 65 and 57 per cent for WFTC and Family Credit respectively.

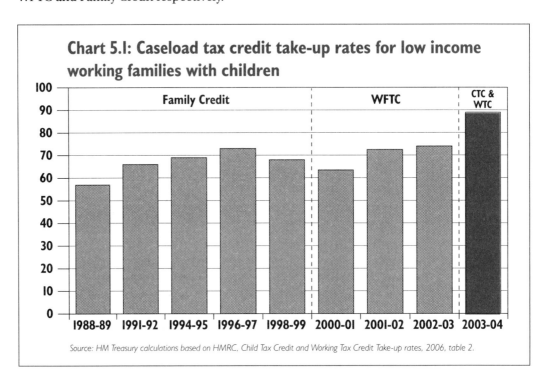

Chart 5.1: Caseload tax credit take-up rates for low income working families with children

Source: HM Treasury calculations based on HMRC, Child Tax Credit and Working Tax Credit Take-up rates, 2006, table 2.

5.10   The Pre-Budget Report announced that **from April 2006 the child element of CTC will increase by £75 to £1,765 a year.** This represents a total increase of £320 since its introduction in April 2003. As a result of the Government's continuing programme of reform, by this April a family with two young children and a full-time earner on £15,800, half male mean earnings, will receive over £105 per week in CTC and Child Benefit, more than double the equivalent support in 1997-98. Table 5.1 shows the levels of support that CTC and Child Benefit will provide for families from April 2006. In addition, CTC ensures that families are supported both in and out of work and therefore acts as a secure income bridge as parents move into employment.

Table 5.1: Minimum annual levels of support for families from April 2006

Annual family income	up to £14,155	up to £50,000	all families
Per cent of families	*29*	*81*	*100*
1 child	£3,220	£1,455	£910
2 children	£5,595	£2,065	£1,520
3 children	£7,970	£2,675	£2,130

Making families better off   **5.11**   Chart 5.2 shows the impact of the Government's measures to support families since 1997. It shows that all families have benefited but the greatest benefit has gone to families with low to middle incomes. For example, families with two children and an income in the range £10,000 to £20,000 are on average over £70 a week better off.

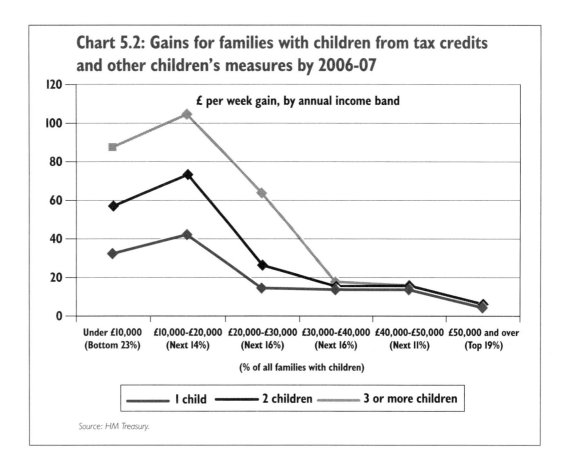

Chart 5.2: Gains for families with children from tax credits and other children's measures by 2006-07

£ per week gain, by annual income band

Under £10,000 (Bottom 23%) · £10,000-£20,000 (Next 14%) · £20,000-£30,000 (Next 16%) · £30,000-£40,000 (Next 16%) · £40,000-£50,000 (Next 11%) · £50,000 and over (Top 19%)

(% of all families with children)

1 child — 2 children — 3 or more children

Source: HM Treasury.

5.12   As a result of the Government's reforms to the personal tax and benefit system and the National Minimum Wage, by October 2006 and in real terms:

- families with children will be on average £1,500 a year better off, while those in the poorest fifth of the population will be on average £3,400 a year better off;

- a single-earner family on half male mean earnings with two children will be £3,950 a year better off; and

- a single-earner family on male mean earnings with two children will be £235 a year better off.

5.13   Tax credits are the central component of the Government's programme of financial ...y in the support for families. The Government has carefully monitored the operation of the tax credit .redit system system during its first two years and in May 2005 announced that HM Revenue and Customs (HMRC) would improve the administration and communication of the system. Many of the measures announced as part of this improvement have already taken effect and others will do so shortly. For example, a new award notice and simplified guidance notes will be introduced in April 2006.

5.14   The Pre-Budget Report announced a further series of steps to give greater certainty to claimants while maintaining the flexibility to respond to changes. In particular, the income disregard was increased from £2,500 to £25,000. There are also new responsibilities for claimants to tell HMRC about changes in their circumstances promptly. In February the Government announced extra help for claimants, with more generous additional payments to people who may be caused financial hardship as a result of paying back overpaid tax credits. HMRC are now working – in partnership with the voluntary sector – to ensure that the implementation of these measures fully reflects the needs of claimants.

Support for children and young people

5.15   The *Child Poverty Review* and *Every Child Matters*[6] set the broad policy framework for supporting children and young people. In *Support for parents: the best start for children*, published at the Pre-Budget Report, HM Treasury and the Department for Education and Skills identified further steps to be taken to improve outcomes for children and young people. To take these conclusions forward, **this Budget launches a policy review of children and young people to inform the 2007 Comprehensive Spending Review.**

Box 5.2: Children and young people review

Building on *Support for Parents: the best start for children*, the policy review for children and young people will consider:

- the role of universal services in providing access to protective and preventative support, risk assessment and referral;

- how to deliver effective early intervention by targeted and specialist services before problems become acute;

- how to sustain the impact of intervention to prevent children and young people with complex needs repeatedly moving in and out of contact with services; and

- how rights and responsibilities for individuals, families and communities can be integrated into services to improve the lives of children and young people.

Under the umbrella of the children and young people review, there will be three sub-reviews, considering:

- how services can provide greater support to families with disabled children to improve their life chances;

- what strategy should be adopted over the next ten years to deliver a step change in youth services and support for young people; and

- how services for families and children at risk of becoming locked into a cycle of low achievement, high harm and high cost can be reformed to deliver better outcomes.

---

[6] *Every Child Matters*, HM Government, September 2003.

Budget-holding lead professionals **5.16** A key element of delivering better integrated services around the needs of children and families is the concept of the lead professional. This role can be enhanced by making the lead professional a single account holder, with a budget to commission services directly from providers. The Pre-Budget Report announced a series of Single Account Holder pathfinders and the Government can now announce **the expansion of the Single Account Holder pilot, so that 12-15 local authorities are able to trial the budget-holding role.**

Young people **5.17** The Government believes that young people should be given more choice and influence over services and facilities that are available to them. The Youth Opportunity Fund and Youth Capital Fund will provide for the improvement of facilities and allow young people to establish their own small-scale projects, for example renting space in a community centre to organise events and activities, establishing a neighbourhood council or youth cafe, or running sports leagues and tournaments. The Pre-Budget Report announced additional funding of £53 million over 2006-07 and 2007-08 to extend both Funds, bringing the total available over two years to £115 million. This will mean an average local authority receiving £500,000 over 2006-07 and 2007-08. **Budget 2006 announces an additional £2 million to fund a national competition in 2006-07 to recognise and reward innovative projects run by young people, for young people, from the two Funds.** The competition is intended to encourage, highlight and reward projects that are particularly innovative in their design and planning.

5.18 A total of £2 million over two years is being made available to the Football Foundation to fund programmes for young people that will involve football clubs working in partnership with local police forces and community groups. Similar projects, like Midnight Football, have proved successful in reducing crime and anti-social behaviour.

5.19 Budget 2006 also announces a total of £6 million over two years to fund opportunities for disadvantaged young people to develop new skills in a range of media and promote young people's involvement in producing programmes for television and radio.

Childcare and work-life balance

5.20 Flexible, affordable and high-quality childcare provision is an important element of the Government's strategy to both provide support to families and eradicate child poverty. *Choice for parents, the best start for children: a ten year strategy for childcare,* published alongside the 2004 Pre-Budget Report, set out the Government's long-term vision for childcare and early years services.

Choice and flexibility **5.21** The Government is committed to ensuring that parents have greater choice and flexibility in balancing work and family life. Legislation is now being considered by Parliament to extend paid maternity leave from six to nine months from April 2007, and the Government has an aim of 12 months paid maternity leave by the end of the Parliament. The Government will continue to examine the case for extending the right to request flexible working to parents of older children in the future. In addition, **from April 2006 the flat rate of Statutory Maternity, Paternity and Adoption Pay and Maternity Allowance will be increased to £108.85 a week.**

Availability of childcare and early years services **5.22** The Childcare Bill now before Parliament places new duties on local authorities to improve outcomes for young children and to secure a sufficient supply of childcare to meet the needs of working families. Offering integrated services for young children and their families is a key component of the ten year strategy and the Government is committed to developing a nationwide network of 3,500 Sure Start Children's Centres by 2010. Some 700 of these have been established so far. Budget 2006 announces **new capital grants to help small- and medium-sized employers establish workplace nurseries.** Some £8 million for this will be made available in each of 2006-7 and 2007-8.

Affordability for families 5.23 The Government wants childcare to be affordable, as well as high-quality, flexible and appropriate to parents' needs. As announced in the 2004 Pre-Budget Report, to help improve affordability, from April 2005 the eligible cost limit of the childcare element of the Working Tax Credit (WTC) was increased to £300 a week (£175 for one child) and **from April 2006, the maximum proportion of costs that can be claimed will be increased to 80 per cent.** The Government continues to believe that WTC is the most effective way of delivering support for low- to moderate-income families. To engage employers and help working families with childcare costs, the Government offers an income tax and national insurance contributions exemption for good quality formal childcare contracted by the employer or paid for with childcare vouchers provided by the employer. To enhance this support, Budget 2006 announces that from April 2006 **the value of the exemption will be increased from £50 to £55 per week.**

High-quality provision 5.24 To ensure that childcare is of high quality, the Government is working with the Children's Workforce Development Council, the Training and Development Agency for Schools and other experts to draw up draft professional standards for a new graduate level Early Years Professional status. A prospectus outlining these standards and the different routes for achieving this status will be published in the summer. To ensure that the costs of reforming the childcare workforce are not passed on to parents, the Government has created the Transformation Fund, worth £250 million a year over 2006 to 2008. This funding will enable childcare providers to employ more staff at graduate level and train more childcare workers to achieve higher qualifications.

SUPPORTING YOUNG PEOPLE

5.25 The Government is committed to ensuring that all young people reach the age of 19 equipped to enter higher education or skilled employment and has an aim to raise participation in education and training from 75 per cent to at least 90 per cent at age 17 by 2015.

Review of financial support for 16-19s 5.26 The Government has a vision of a single, coherent system of financial support for 16-19 year olds that is focused on encouraging and supporting all young people to participate and achieve in education and training. Young people are engaged in a range of different activities and the system should respond to their individual circumstances, with simplified administration and improved accessibility. Chapter 3 sets out steps the Government is taking to reform further education colleges and training providers.

5.27 Budget 2005 announced important changes to the financial support offered to young people. **From April this year, entitlement to Child Benefit, Child Tax Credit and Income Support will be extended to 19 year olds** completing a course of non-advanced education or unwaged training that they started before their nineteenth birthday, until they reach age 20 or the end of their course. In addition, **entitlement to Child Benefit and Child Tax Credit will also be extended to unwaged trainees** on work-based learning programmes arranged by the Government from April 2006. These reforms will improve the financial support available to these learners and, with the extension of Education Maintenance Allowance in England, deliver parity in financial support for education and unwaged training.

Engaging the most disadvantaged young people 5.28 At any one time in the UK, around 150,000 16-17 year olds are not in education, employment or training. The Government has an ambition to ensure that no teenager faces long-term unemployment or inactivity and so will **from April 2006 introduce pilot Activity Agreements and an Activity Allowance targeted on the most disadvantaged 16 to 17 year olds.** This will extend conditional financial support to this group, setting a clear expectation that young people will progress into learning. It will also offer them the financial support and opportunity to progress to learning. The introduction of these measures in April represents a significant milestone for the review of financial support for 16-19 year olds. The Government is, however, determined to make further progress and will be seeking the views of stakeholders to inform the next phase of the review in the coming months.

FAIRNESS FOR DISABLED PEOPLE

5.29   The Government is committed to improving the rights of, and opportunities for, disabled people, to ensure that everyone has the opportunity to lead an independent and fulfilling life. The Disability Rights Commission, established by the Government in 2000, continues to work to create a society where all disabled people can participate fully as equal citizens. The Disability Discrimination Act (DDA), extended in 2005, now offers improved protection to more people. Under the DDA, from December 2006 all public sector organisations will have a statutory duty to promote equality of opportunity for disabled people. The Government is also improving support to help more disabled people move into employment. The Welfare Reform Green Paper,[7] described in Chapter 4, sets out a package of reforms.

Improving the **5.30**   The Government's report, *Improving the life chances of disabled people*,[8] set out a
life chances of 20-year strategy for supporting disabled people in four key areas. Government departments
disabled people are collectively driving forward the strategy through the Office for Disability Issues, launched in December 2005. The first annual report on progress will be published this summer. Also in 2006, a Task Force for Independent Living will be created to provide expert advice to Government and a national forum will be established to ensure that individuals and disability organisations are involved on an ongoing basis.

Individual **5.31**   Thirteen local authorities have been selected to run individual budget pilots, from
budgets spring 2006, which aim to improve the ability of disabled people and older people to live independently. These bring together funding streams across government departments and give individuals control over the support that they need, offering the budget in the form of cash, public services, or a combination of the two.

PROMOTING SAVING, ASSET OWNERSHIP AND INCLUSION

5.32   The Government seeks to support saving and asset ownership for all, from childhood, through working life and into retirement, using the right combination of financial education, support through the tax and benefit system and the effective use of public spending. In aggregate, household sector net wealth is now higher than ever before, having grown by around 60 per cent in real terms since 1997.

Promoting saving and asset ownership for all

Child Trust Fund **5.33**   The Child Trust Fund was introduced in April 2005. The scheme promotes saving and financial education and will ensure that in future all children have a financial asset at age 18, regardless of family background. Under the scheme, all children born on or after 1 September 2002 receive £250 to be invested in a long-term savings and investment account, and children from lower-income families receive £500. In the first year alone, nearly 1.5 million accounts have been opened and there are now over 110 official providers and distributors of Child Trust Funds.

5.34   In response to the consultation launched in the 2004 Pre-Budget Report, the Government can announce that **the payments into Child Trust Fund accounts at age seven will be £250 for all children, with children from lower-income families receiving £500.** The payments will be made on a similar basis to the initial endowments. As announced in Budget 2005, the Government continues to consult on whether further payments should be made into Child Trust Fund accounts at secondary school age.

---

[7] *A New Deal for Welfare: Empowering people to work,* DWP, January 2006.

[8] *Improving the life chances of disabled people,* Prime Minister's Strategy Unit, January 2005.

5.35   The Child Trust Fund and age-related payments will bring financial education in schools to life. The Government is working with financial education bodies and the devolved administrations to identify appropriate opportunities for learning and is **exploring a focused Schools Money Week, with tailored Child Trust Fund supporting materials** to link with children's learning through the school curriculum.

Individual Savings Accounts

5.36   Individual Savings Accounts (ISAs) have proved extremely popular. Over 16 million people – more than one in three adults – have an ISA, with nearly £190 billion subscribed since their launch in 1999. The Government remains committed to ISAs. ISA and Personal Equity Plan (PEP) savings are supported by an estimated £1.8 billion a year in tax relief. As announced in Budget 2005, **higher annual investment limits of £7,000, with a maximum of £3,000 in cash, will be extended until at least April 2010.** To build on the recent extension of the list of qualifying investments for ISAs to include all FSA-authorised retail investment schemes, **UK Real Estate Investment Trusts will, on their introduction, become qualifying investments for ISAs, PEPs and Child Trust Funds.**

Matching and the Saving Gateway

5.37   In addition to tax relief, the Government is exploring the use of matching to promote saving among those who do not usually save. Matching provides a simple, transparent and equitable framework of incentives for those on lower incomes. The second Saving Gateway pilot, which was launched in spring 2005, is testing the effect of alternative match rates and monthly contribution limits, an initial endowment and a range of financial education support for savers.

5.38   Around 22,000 Saving Gateway accounts are open and saving levels in all pilot areas are encouraging. Early findings from the interim evaluation show that so far nearly all participants have saved into their accounts and nearly half have contributed the maximum allowable each month. The evidence suggests that participants are overwhelmingly positive about the scheme and the matched payments they receive on their savings, and that participants intend to save regularly into their accounts. A report on the interim evaluation of the pilot will be published later this year.[9]

Stakeholder savings and investment products

5.39   Following the Sandler Review of the retail savings industry, the Government introduced in April 2005 a new range of simple, low cost, risk-controlled 'Stakeholder' savings and investment products.[10] There are two products designed to meet short and medium-term saving needs and to meet long-term saving needs there is a Child Trust Fund and revised Stakeholder pension. A campaign to raise awareness of the features and benefits of these products was launched in September 2005.

Capital limits in benefits

5.40   The Government is committed to ensuring that the benefit system encourages households, particularly those on lower incomes, to save appropriately. As announced in Budget 2004 and Budget 2005, **from April 2006 the lower and upper capital limits for Income Support, Jobseeker's Allowance, Housing Benefit and Council Tax Benefit are being raised to £6,000 and £16,000 respectively.**

---

[9] An independent evaluation of the second Saving Gateway pilot is being conducted by MORI and the Institute for Fiscal Studies.

[10] *Medium and Long-Term Retail Savings in the UK: A Review*, Ron Sandler, July 2002.

Promoting financial capability and inclusion

Financial **5.41**   Many consumers are far from confident in the decisions they make about their
capability finances and in response to this, the Financial Services Authority (FSA) has developed a
National Strategy for Financial Capability.[11] The Government will play a full and active part in
the delivery of the National Strategy and **will host, jointly with the FSA, a financial capability
conference in the summer.** The FSA has also commissioned a financial capability survey to
show the level of capability within the general UK population and will report on this shortly.
In the Pre-Budget Report, the Government announced that it would embed financial
capability more explicitly in the school curriculum by including it in the new functional
mathematics component of GCSE maths. An important element of the National Strategy will
be the provision of support, training and resources to teachers until financial education is
incorporated into the curriculum.

Financial **5.42**   Access to mainstream financial services can be restricted for many people on low
inclusion incomes. *Promoting financial inclusion* outlined the Government's strategy to tackle financial
exclusion, including the establishment of a Financial Inclusion Taskforce to oversee progress
and a Financial Inclusion Fund of £120 million to support initiatives to tackle financial
exclusion.[12] **£20 million of the Financial Inclusion Fund will now be made available for
broader financial inclusion objectives,** including stimulating demand for mainstream
financial services.

Access to **5.43**   Lack of access to banking services imposes costs on those who can least afford them.
banking In December 2004, the banks and the Government agreed to work together towards a goal of
halving the number of adults in households without a bank account and of making significant
progress within two years. The Financial Inclusion Taskforce was asked to monitor progress
towards the goal. In its first annual report, the Taskforce concludes that steady progress has
been made towards the goal but also encourages the banks to continue to address the
difficulties faced in opening a bank account. In addition, the Taskforce wants to work with the
Government, the banks and others to increase demand for banking services among those that
remain unbanked.

Access to **5.44**   Many low-income households rely on credit products with interest rates of over 100
affordable credit per cent. The Financial Inclusion Fund is being used to establish a 'growth fund' of £36 million
to support third sector lenders providing alternative affordable credit and successful bidders
to this fund will be announced in June. To give flexibility to better serve low-income groups,
**the maximum rate of interest that credit unions can charge on loans will be increased from
1 per cent a month to 2 per cent a month.** This change will be implemented as soon as
possible.

5.45   The Government has also consulted on extending Community Investment Tax Relief
to the personal lending activities of community development finance institutions. Responses
to the consultation indicated support for an extension and highlighted a range of practical
issues that need to be addressed. As announced in the Pre-Budget Report, the Government
will continue to consider the case for, and practicalities of, this extension. In order to reduce
some of the increased risk and cost associated with lending to vulnerable groups, the
Government **will implement, by December 2006, a scheme where, under certain
circumstances, lenders can apply for repayment of arrears through deduction from
benefits,** where normal repayment arrangements have broken down.

---

[11] *Building Financial Capability in the UK*, Financial Services Authority, May 2004.

[12] *Promoting financial inclusion*, HM Treasury, December 2004.

5.46 The Social Fund provides a safety net of grants and interest free loans for the most vulnerable in times of need. As announced in Pre-Budget Report 2004, **reforms to the Budgeting Loans scheme that amount to an increase of funding of £210m over the three years to 2008-09 will take effect from April 2006.** This will improve access to Budgeting Loans by changing the way existing debt is counted, reducing the normal repayment rate, introducing a simple method to calculate how much an applicant can borrow and increasing the capital limits to enable applicants to save appropriately. The treatment of capital in Community Care Grants is not changing at present and Crisis Loans do not have a capital limit.

Access to money advice **5.47** Credit is a useful tool for managing expenditure for most people but some have difficulty managing their borrowing and become over-indebted. The Government recognises that face-to-face money advice is an effective mechanism for tackling problem debt and is currently undertaking a competition to support increased provision, based on £45 million from the Financial Inclusion Fund. Bids for this element of the Fund have been received and successful bidders will be announced shortly. In addition, the Government has awarded £6 million to organisations across England and Wales to pilot debt advice outreach.

FAIRNESS FOR PENSIONERS

5.48 A fair society guarantees security in old age and ensures that pensioners can share in rising national prosperity, while making sure that older people are able to play a full and active role in society. The Government is committed to tackling pensioner poverty and rewarding saving, and to enabling people to meet their retirement income aspirations in an ageing society.

Fairness for today's pensioners

Support for all pensioners **5.49** The Government's strategy for pensioners is based on progressive universalism, providing support for all and more for those who need it most, through both financial support and access to services. The foundations upon which the Government provides support for all pensioners are the basic and additional state pensions. Beyond this the Government has:

- guaranteed that the April increase in the basic state pension will be in line with the Retail Prices Index for the previous September or 2.5 per cent, (whichever is higher), meaning that from April 2006 the basic state pension will rise to £84.25 for single pensioners and £134.75 for couples.

- announced the continuation of Winter Fuel Payments of £200 for households with someone aged 60 or over, rising to £300 for households with someone aged 80 or over, for the duration of this Parliament;

- introduced free television licences for the over 75s, and free prescriptions and eye tests for those aged 60 and over; and

- ensured that those entering hospital receive their full entitlement to Basic State Pension and some other benefits for the duration of their stay.

Free nationwide bus travel **5.50**   Budget 2005 announced free off-peak local area bus travel for those aged over 60, and all disabled people, in England from April 2006. Building on this and recognising the importance of public transport for older people and the role access to transport has to play in tackling social exclusion and maintaining well-being, **this Budget announces free off-peak bus travel for all pensioners and all disabled people, in England from April 2008,** at a cost of up to £250 million a year. The Government will consult with local authorities and other interested parties on the best framework for delivering this entitlement.

Support for the poorest pensioners **5.51**   Pension Credit is key to providing more support for those pensioners who need it most. Since its launch in October 2003 over 2.7 million pensioner households have benefited from Pension Credit's guarantee element and/or reward for savings. 2.1 million pensioner households are receiving the element that guarantees a minimum income, a take-up level achieved a year ahead of target, while Savings Credit rewards 1.9 million pensioner households who saved for their retirement. From April 2006 the guarantee element of Pension Credit will rise to £114.05 for single pensioners and £174.05 for couples and from April 2006 the savings reward will rise to a maximum of £17.88 a week for single pensioners and £23.58 for couples.

5.52   Concentrating resources on the poorest pensioners has ensured that between 1996-97 and 2004-05 over one million pensioner households were lifted out of relative low-income poverty and 2.1 million pensioner households have been lifted out of absolute low-income poverty. Half a million pensioner households were lifted out of relative low income since the introduction of Pension Credit. As Chart 5.3 below shows, during periods of substantial economic growth the poorest pensioners have tended to see their incomes fall below those of the general population – between 1984 and 1990 the risk of a pensioner household being poor rose from 14 per cent to 40 per cent. As a result of the Government's reforms to support for the poorest pensioners the risk of a pensioner household being poor has fallen to 16 per cent – and, apart from 1984, it is for the first time since 1960 that a pensioner is no more likely to be poor than the population as a whole.

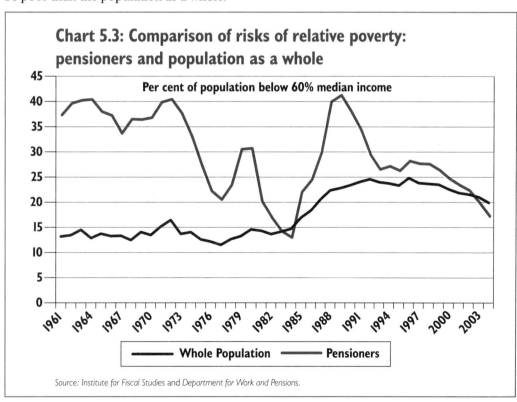

Chart 5.3: Comparison of risks of relative poverty: pensioners and population as a whole

Per cent of population below 60% median income

Whole Population ———— Pensioners

Source: Institute for Fiscal Studies and Department for Work and Pensions.

Warm Front **5.53**   The Pre-Budget Report announced further help for the poorest pensioners, through an increase in funding for the Warm Front programme. This enables households in receipt of Pension Credit, who do not currently have central heating, to have it installed free of charge. Energy suppliers have also agreed to provide free cavity and loft insulation for Pension Credit households who need it and pensioner households not in receipt of Pension Credit will be able to access the same service at a £300 discount.

Support for **5.54**   The Government is committed to supporting pensioners who pay income tax.
pensioners who Increases in the age-related tax allowances will mean that in 2006-07 no one aged 65 or over
pay tax need pay tax on an income of up to £140 a week. This will mean that 45 per cent of pensioners pay no tax on their income.

Effects of **5.55**   As a result of measures implemented since 1997, the Government is spending around
measures to £11 billion a year more in real terms on pensioners. This is around £7.5 billion a year more
support than if the basic state pension had simply been linked to earnings over the same period. This
pensioners approach has focused support on those who need it most. If the extra £11 billion had been spent on raising the basic state pension, the poorest third of pensioners would on average be £33 a week worse off than they are now. As a result of tax and benefit measures the Government has introduced, the poorest third of pensioner households will be on average £2,050 a year, or around £39 a week, better off. Chart 5.4 shows the distributional impact of the Government's measures to support pensioners.

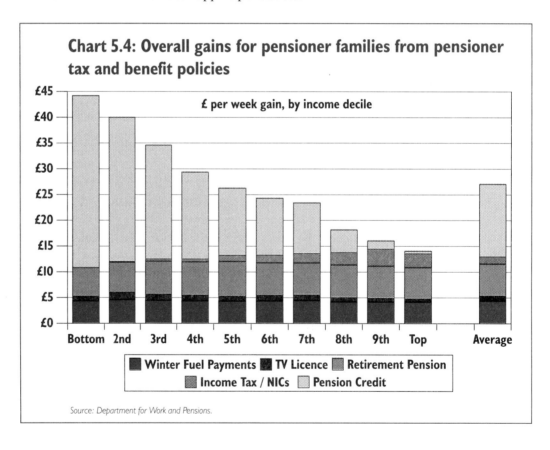

Chart 5.4: Overall gains for pensioner families from pensioner tax and benefit policies

Source: Department for Work and Pensions.

Fairness for tomorrow's pensioners

Pensions **5.56** The Government's 2002 Pensions Green Paper[13] established the Pensions
Commission Commission to examine the regime for private pensions and long-term saving and to
consider whether the current level of compulsion within the UK pensions and retirement
system is appropriate. The Commission's interim report was published in October 2004,[14] and
a final report was published on 30 November 2005.[15]

5.57 The Government has welcomed the broad framework of the Commission's report and
has set out the five principles on which its response will be based: the pension system must
promote personal responsibility; it must be fair; it must be affordable; it must be simple; and
it must be sustainable. The Government has said that the principle of affordability will be
central. There will be no relaxation in fiscal discipline and the long-term sustainability of the
public finances will not be put at risk. In preparation for the publication of a White Paper in
Spring 2006, the Government has engaged in a major consultation exercise, and convened
public debates in six cities across the UK in March 2006 to mark National Pensions Day.

Information **5.58** Empowering individuals to make informed choices about working and saving for
retirement is fundamental to ensuring that future pensioners receive the income in
retirement that they expect. During 2004-5, as part of the Government's informed choice
strategy, 6.8 million automatically generated state pension forecasts and 2.6 million
combined state and private pensions forecasts, were issued.

Security **5.59** The establishment of the Pension Protection Fund in April 2005 ensures that, for the
first time in the UK, members of defined benefit pension schemes will receive a meaningful
proportion of their expected pension income if their pension scheme is in deficit when the
sponsoring employer becomes insolvent. The establishment of a proactive Pension Regulator
further improves the security of occupational schemes, while its risk based approach to
regulation minimises burdens on schemes which are appropriately funded and run.

Simplification **5.60** **Pensions tax simplification sweeps away the numerous existing tax regimes and
replaces them from 6 April 2006 ('A-day') with a single universal regime for tax-privileged
pensions saving.** The new regime will provide individuals with greater flexibility and choice
over their retirement savings and will benefit both employers and pension providers through
increased flexibility and reduced administration costs. A small package of supplementary
measures providing additional flexibility for schemes and individuals, clarifying aspects of
the new rules and smoothing the transition from old to new regime, is being introduced in
this year's Finance Bill. The Government will keep all aspects of the pensions tax
simplification regime under review and will where necessary take action to tackle any abuse
of the flexibilities offered by the new regime.

5.61 The longstanding position of successive Governments is that pension assets should
be converted into a secure income in retirement by age 75. For most people an annuity or
scheme pension is the best means by which they can do this. The new pension rules
introduce an additional option for achieving this – an alternatively secured pension (ASP). As
the Government made clear during the development of the new pension tax provisions, ASPs
are specifically designed for those who have a principled religious objection to annuitisation.
It has become clear, however, that some advisors are intending to use the ASP provisions for
a much wider purpose to enable individuals to pass on tax-privileged retirement savings to
their dependants rather than to provide a pension in retirement.

---

[13] *Simplicity, security and choice: Working and saving for retirement*, Department for Work and Pensions, HM Treasury and
Inland Revenue, December 2002.

[14] *Pensions: challenges and choices*, Pensions Commission, October 2004.

[15] *A new pension settlement for the twenty-first century*, Pensions Commission, November 2005.

5.62   In order to prevent this, the Government is examining how best to restrict ASPs to their original limited purpose. Following consultation, **legislation in Finance Bill 2006 will prevent ASPs being used to avoid inheritance tax by ensuring that appropriate inheritance tax charges apply.** The current inheritance tax position for all other pension schemes will also be confirmed in the Finance Bill.

SUPPORTING CHARITIES, COMMUNITIES AND GIVING

5.63   The Government recognises the vital role played by a vibrant third sector in our society, from bringing people together through voluntary action and advocacy, building social capital and strengthening communities, to the delivery of public services. That is why the Government has introduced such a wide range of support for the sector both through the tax system and new policy initiatives targeted on developing capacity. Building on these measures and going forward into the next phase of this relationship, the government now wants to ensure that the third sector is fully consulted and recognised through the Comprehensive Spending Review process.[16]

Third sector **5.64**   This Budget announces that **HM Treasury will undertake a review into the future role**
review **of the third sector in social and economic regeneration.** The review, overseen by a cross-departmental ministerial group, will take a cross-cutting approach to the long-term priorities for the sector, in the context of the future challenges that our society now faces. Campbell Robb, Director of Public Policy at the National Council for Voluntary Organisations, will play a leading advisory role in the review. In its first phase, the review will be informed by the largest consultation ever undertaken with the third sector, seeking views from a wide range of organisations. It will be launched at a conference in May and then taken to every region by the ministerial group. The results will feed into the Comprehensive Spending Review, as set out in Chapter 6, with initial conclusions available at the time of the Pre-Budget Report.

5.65   This Budget announces that working with the Active Communities Directorate in the Home Office, the DTI's Social Enterprise Unit and the HMRC Charities unit, **an Office of Charity and Third Sector Finance will be established in HM Treasury,** linking the work of HM Treasury across the range of third sector issues to provide strategic coordinated engagement. A third sector advisory panel will be established to advise the Office on third sector issues. The advisory panel will include young volunteers, representatives of third sector umbrella bodies and members of different faith communities and will report to the Chancellor.

Volunteering **5.66**   The Year of the Volunteer 2005 successfully promoted active community participation across the country. Going forward, the Government will work with third sector and corporate partners to embed the achievements of the year, maximising participation of all age groups from a diverse range of backgrounds, as well as **encouraging corporate community involvement through a responsible business conference later this year.**

Youth action and **5.67**   The Russell Commission reported at Budget 2005 and set out recommendations to
engagement deliver a step change in the quality, quantity and diversity of young people's volunteering.[17] Budget 2005 announced public investment of up to £100 million, including a fund available to match contributions from business. This Budget announces that **over £10 million has been raised from 19 new corporate supporters**[18] and the seven Founding Partner companies.[19]

---

[16] The role of the third sector in delivering public services is detailed in Chapter 6.

[17] *A national framework for youth action and engagement,* Russell Commission, March 2005.

[18] GCap, Edge, Premier League, BT, Emap, The Vodafone UK Foundation, HSBC, BAA Communities Trust, ARK, RWE npower, Channel 4, Diageo, HBOS Foundation, Sainsbury's, Barclays, flextech television, JPMorgan*foundations,* Jack Petchey Foundation and Norwich Union General Insurance.

[19] T-Mobile, ITV, KPMG, MTV, Tesco, Sky and The Hunter Foundation pledged the first £3.5 million at the Pre-Budget Report.

5.68   A new independent charity, to be led by Rod Aldridge as chair and Terry Ryall as chief executive, has been established to take forward the recommendations of the Russell Commission. Board members of the new charity have been appointed and will be responsible for commissioning a series of taster, part-time and full-time volunteering opportunities for one million new volunteers over the next five years. A board of young people, V20, will advise the new charity, which will be formally launched in May. The first wave of opportunities will then be commissioned. **The Budget announces that, based on young people's priorities for action, these will include sport,**[20] **the arts, media and the environment.** Additional private sector support will be generated for environmental volunteering schemes by focusing the over £10 million increase in the value of the landfill tax credit scheme on such projects, as set out in Chapter 7.

Invest to Save   **5.69**   The Invest to Save Budget (ISB)[21] was launched following the 1998 Comprehensive Spending Review to create a 'venture capital fund' for public sector delivery with an emphasis on innovation and partnership working. Since it was created in 1998, the ISB has funded some 463 projects worth nearly £450 million. Of this, approximately £97 million has been allocated to projects relating to the third sector.

5.70   The eighth annual ISB bidding round has now been completed. The Government is today **announcing the allocation of £31 million from the ISB to fund 30 innovative projects** dedicated to delivering cash releasing efficiencies, improving energy efficiency and increasing access to arts and culture. The ISB continues to promote partnerships involving the third sector, with 12 of the successful partnership bids, totalling some £12.4 million, being sector-led. The Government can now also **announce a ninth bidding round for the ISB for 2007,** focused on the third sector's role in building fairer communities and delivering public services.

Memorial to   **5.71**   There will be **a permanent memorial to those who lost their lives in the London**
victims of 7 July   **bombings on 7 July 2005.** The Chancellor has already announced that the Government will make a contribution to the costs of any memorial chosen by the victims' families. The total Government contribution will depend on the level of donations that may be given in support of an appropriate memorial but the Budget confirms that up to £1 million will be available to underwrite the costs.

Terrorism Relief   **5.72**   This Budget confirms that **the Government will support with an initial endowment**
Fund   **of £1 million the creation of a new charitable Terrorism Relief Fund** to provide rapid relief to victims of terrorism at home and abroad.

Charitable giving   **5.73**   The Government continues to find ways to support the use of the tax reliefs for giving. HM Revenue and Customs has set up a Charities unit to provide an integrated service for charities and their donors, with improved web-based guidance and dedicated expert support.

5.74   The Home Office funded Payroll Giving Grant Scheme continues to increase the numbers of small- and medium-sized businesses offering Payroll Giving schemes. In January 2006, HM Treasury hosted the launch of the Quality Mark Award, recognising employers who achieve minimum employee participation rates in their schemes. Over 700 employers have received awards since the launch. The Government is keen to encourage greater use of tax reliefs for giving and wants to ensure these are used for the purposes intended – this chapter also announces measures to preserve the integrity of charitable reliefs.

---

[20] 47 per cent of young people's volunteering takes places in sport, Home Office Citizenship Survey 2003.

[21] For more information see www.isb.gov.uk.

5.75   In recognition of the importance of places of worship and memorials for local communities, the Government will **extend the period for which funding will be available for the listed places of worship and memorials VAT refund schemes for three further years until 2010-11.** Both schemes will now also cover the VAT costs incurred on professional fees and include fixtures and fittings for listed places of worship, such as bells, pews, clocks and organs.

Unclaimed assets   **5.76**   Following the announcement in the Pre-Budget Report, the banking industry has set in train work to develop a scheme to enable unclaimed assets to be reinvested in society. The Government continues to be clear that such a scheme should be introduced, on a basis consistent with retaining the rights of owners to reclaim assets at any time and with this in mind it is continuing to assess the legal and accounting issues involved. The industry's steering group will consider issues of reuniting, definition and operation and distribution. The Government welcomes this and the industry's commitment, building on existing work in this area, to launch a comprehensive new exercise to reunite owners and assets prior to such a scheme being launched.

5.77   Looking ahead, the industry will continue to work to establish a scheme that allows genuinely unclaimed assets to be reinvested in the community in a sustainable way and through a coordinated delivery mechanism, with a focus on youth services and encouraging more active community engagement among young people, and on financial education and exclusion. The industry will work in consultation with the Government and other key stakeholders, including voluntary and community sector organisations and social enterprises.

DELIVERING A MODERN AND FAIR TAX SYSTEM

5.78   A modern and fair tax system encourages work and saving, keeps pace with developments in business practices and the global economy and provides the foundation for building world-class public services. In order to ensure the tax system meets these objectives, the Government will continue to develop a modern tax administration to support taxpayers, modernise tax policies to keep pace with a changing world and ensure that the tax system does not provide unfair advantages for the non-compliant.

Modernising tax administration

5.79   Since the creation of HM Revenue and Customs (HMRC), the Government has introduced the short tax return, continued the successful withdrawal of payment via employer for tax credits and introduced a new online direct debit system for electronic VAT returns. Further simplification of tax administration to provide better support for compliant taxpayers remains a priority. Improved use of information and technology is enabling better risk assessment so that compliance work can be better targeted, thereby reducing audit and inspection burdens for the vast majority of compliant businesses and taxpayers. This work proceeds alongside simplification measures announced in Chapter 3.

Review of HMRC   **5.80**   In 2005 the Government launched a review of HMRC powers and safeguards, to **powers**   develop a more integrated framework of law and practice to underpin the new department.[22] A further consultation document will be issued shortly. The specific areas it will consider for HMRC include how to intervene more quickly and with less cost for the compliant while tackling non-compliance more effectively, and how to develop a more responsive penalty framework.

---

[22] *HM Revenue and Customs and the Taxpayer: Modernising Powers, Deterrents and Safeguards,* HMRC, March 2005.

Carter Review of **5.81**   Lord Carter's review of the use of HMRC's online services is published today. He has
Online Services   concluded that well-designed online filing services can bring benefits to taxpayers and the
Government. The Government agrees with his aspirational goal of universal electronic
delivery of HMRC tax returns from businesses and IT-literate individuals by 2012. It accepts
his recommendations, which are summarised in Box 5.3. They are expected to deliver
recurring benefits of over £175 million per year for businesses and taxpayers, and secure
benefits of £84 million per year for the Government.

Box 5.3: Carter Review of online services

In July 2005, the Government asked Lord Carter of Coles to advise on measures to increase
the use of HMRC's key online services, in order to ensure sustainable and efficient service
delivery for taxpayers, while continuing to support compliance. The review consulted with
stakeholders to consider measures to deliver the Government's aim of maximising the use
of online services for a number of taxes. Lord Carter recommends that HMRC should
continue to invest in its online infrastructure and supporting systems to deliver robust,
high capacity services, which should be rigorously tested. Subject to these services being
in place, his other key recommendations are to:

- require businesses to file their VAT returns, company tax returns and pay as you
  earn in-year forms (the P45 and P46) online, in phases from April 2008;

- introduce new filing deadlines for income tax self assessment returns, of 30
  September for paper forms, and 30 November for online returns, from 2008;

- promote online filing by tax agents and better-quality data by withdrawing
  computer-generated paper 'substitute' self assessment returns in 2008; and

- remove perceived barriers to early filing of self assessment and company tax
  returns by linking the period that HMRC has to query a return to the date it is
  filed.

HMRC will work with businesses, taxpayers, software developers, agents and other
intermediaries on the implementation of these changes.

Aligning company **5.82**   HMRC and Companies House have also been consulting on aligning the dates for
filing dates   filing corporation tax returns and delivering accounts to Companies House. The consultation
closed on 3 March 2006 having achieved a high level of engagement, with over 100 written
responses received. Emerging findings indicate that there is a real opportunity to secure
deregulatory gains for smaller companies. The Government will continue discussions with
interested parties over the coming months on how best to achieve this without imposing
unrealistic obligations on large companies.

Modernising the tax system

5.83   The Government believes that the tax system should ensure fairness between all
taxpayers and support the Government's wider economic and social objectives. This Budget
announces changes to the tax system to ensure that it remains modern and relevant in a
changing world.

Tax-motivated incorporation

5.84 In the Pre-Budget Report the Government responded to increased tax-motivated incorporation by simplifying the corporation tax system with a new single small companies' rate of 19 per cent. It also announced that it would continue to review the tax and national insurance contributions (NICs) systems. Responses to the Pre-Budget Report indicated that business generally welcomed the single small companies' rate but wanted the Government to go further in simplifying the corporate tax system.

5.85 Since the Pre-Budget Report, further evidence has emerged that employment income is being disguised as dividends in order to take advantage of the small companies' tax rate, often encouraged by promoters of mass-marketed managed service company schemes. There is also evidence of some agencies, contractors and employers requiring workers to use corporate structures, thereby denying them employment rights as well as avoiding paying their fair share of tax and NICs.

5.86 The Government believes that all individuals and businesses must pay their fair share of NICs and tax, irrespective of legal form. **It will continue to review the tax and NICs systems to ensure that this is the case and will bring forward proposals for discussion** that are consistent with simplicity for compliant businesses, support for businesses in their aspirations to grow and maintaining the attractiveness of the UK as a business location. As the first stage of this review the Government will **consult on action to tackle disguised employment through managed service company schemes.**

Alignment of income tax and NICs

5.87 There is a case for building on previous work to align, for low paid workers, income tax and national insurance systems, in order to improve outcomes for the low paid and to reduce burdens on employers, especially smaller employers. While recognising that aligning two very different systems with very different purposes presents difficult challenges, the Government will **conduct a review in time for consultation after the Pre-Budget Report.**

Meeting global challenges

5.88 The Government is determined to maintain the overall competitiveness of the UK business tax system and will continue its constructive dialogue with business on international tax issues. The Government **will introduce a small extension to the group relief legislation for companies** which will, in some very limited circumstances, allow a UK company to claim relief for otherwise unrelievable foreign losses incurred in the European Economic Area.

5.89 The Government will continue to defend the tax system robustly against legal challenges under EU law.

Film tax reform

5.90 New and more generous tax incentives for the production of culturally British films were announced at the Pre-Budget Report. Final details of the new scheme are published today and the new regime will come into effect from 1 April 2006, subject to final state aids approval. **This Budget also announces that the minimum UK spend threshold will be set at 25 per cent, to allow a wider range of films to qualify.**

Capital allowances for cars

5.91 The Government today publishes a consultation document, *Modernising tax relief for business expenditure on cars.* This gives further consideration to modernising the capital allowance regime for business cars, including the existing 'expensive cars' rules. The proposed package would reduce compliance costs, while also creating a further incentive for business to purchase cleaner cars, bringing the regime in line with other vehicle taxes, such as vehicle excise duty and company car tax.

Leasing reform

5.92 The Government has welcomed the ongoing constructive relationship with industry over the past two years on reforms to the taxation of leased plant and machinery. **The new regime will take effect from 1 April 2006** and final details are announced today.

Shari'a finance **5.93** Building on the success of the measures introduced in 2005 and arising out of ongoing consultation with industry, the Government will introduce measures enabling Shari'a compliant business finance by ensuring that:

- wakala (agency), diminishing musharaka (partnership finance) and ijara wa'iqtina (hire purchase) will be taxed similarly to their conventional equivalents; and

- the existing stamp duty land tax reliefs for alternative property finance products will be extended to all entities, including companies.

General insurance **5.94** The Government will consult with industry about the need for and scope of changes to the rules dealing with general insurers' reserves for future claims by policyholders.

Life insurance **5.95** The Government will issue a consultation document shortly that will examine options for simplifying certain aspects of the taxation of life insurance companies. In addition, legislation will be introduced to establish the 2005 apportionment rules in primary legislation and to remove unintended tax charges where there is a business transfer, including a demutualisation.

North Sea oil tax **5.96** The Government recognises the importance of a positive climate for investment and of maximising economic recovery of the UK's oil and gas reserves. To support these objectives, the Government has given a commitment to no further increases in North Sea taxation for the lifetime of this Parliament. Discussions have also begun with the oil and gas industry to gather views on the current structure of the North Sea fiscal regime, in particular on issues that impact the stability of the regime as the basin continues to mature. These discussions are expected to continue until early autumn.

5.97 Building on the announcement in the Pre-Budget Report regarding changes to non-arm's length valuation of oil, the Government will make changes to the nomination scheme and to the rules for allocating oil lifted from terminals. This will take effect from 1 July 2006 and will ensure that the existing tax regime remains robust.

International Accounting Standards **5.98** The Government will continue to work with business to identify issues arising from the implementation of International Accounting Standards and will continue to monitor the impact on the corporate tax base.

Stamp duty land tax **5.99** Budget 2005 doubled the residential starting threshold for stamp duty on property to £120,000 to help first-time buyers and those on low incomes. Budget 2006 increases the starting threshold to £125,000 with effect from 23 March 2006, exempting an additional 40,000 homebuyers each year from stamp duty. Over 50 per cent of first-time and over 45 per cent of all buyers will not pay stamp duty. The threshold in 2,000 Enterprise Areas will remain at the higher level of £150,000.

Inheritance tax **5.100** At Budget 2005, the Government announced that the inheritance tax threshold would rise to £285,000 in 2006-07 and £300,000 in 2007-08. To continue to provide a fair and targeted system the Government can now announce that the threshold will rise to £312,000 in 2008-09 and £325,000 in 2009-10.

Unit trust seeding relief **5.101** The Budget today announces the ending of stamp duty land tax relief for the initial transfer of property to trustees of a unit trust scheme. This will remove a distortion in the tax system and prevent unit trusts being used to avoid stamp duty land tax.

Tax regime for trusts **5.102** Trusts have a positive role to play in assisting people to manage their affairs. Measures introduced by the Government in recent years have recognised this while continuing to ensure that trusts are not used to achieve an unfair tax advantage. As part of this ongoing package of reforms, the Government has announced that **the inheritance tax exemptions which presently apply to some types of trust will only be available in certain prescribed circumstances.** Where this is not the case, inheritance tax charges will apply in the same way as for all other trusts, preventing these trusts from being used to shelter wealth from inheritance tax. The new rules will take effect from today but there will be transitional arrangements for existing trusts.

5.103 The Government is also continuing to implement rules to make the system of trust taxation less burdensome for those not using trusts to gain an unfair tax advantage. The Government has today announced that it will **build on its previous reforms by doubling the standard rate band for trusts to £1,000,** reducing the tax bill for 66,000 trusts and meaning that a total of 30,000 trusts no longer have to submit a self assessment return every year. This will apply from 6 April 2006.

Residence and domicile **5.104** The Government is continuing to review the residence and domicile rules as they affect the taxation of individuals and in taking the review forward will proceed on the basis of evidence and in keeping with its principles.

Accrued income scheme **5.105** Following consultation on proposals to simplify the accrued income scheme and exempt more small investors, the Government will be publishing draft legislation for consultation over the summer.

Employer-provided equipment **5.106** Many employees have benefited from the tax exemption to get a computer into their homes, but the Government now wishes to focus support on groups with the poorest access to technology, to meet the goals set out in the Digital Strategy. As a result, the Govenment has decided to **remove the current tax exemptions for employer-provided computer equipment, from 6 April 2006.** The tax exemption for mobile phones is also **being refocused to ensure it delivers on its objectives.**

VAT **5.107** In 1984, a VAT-free threshold on imports of small commercial consignments from outside the EU was introduced at a level of £18, as an administrative relief. The Government is aware that this provision is currently being exploited and the relief now costs the Exchequer around £85 million per year. If the relief continues to be exploited by businesses using offshore locations, the Government will consider changes to prevent this type of behaviour.

5.108 The Government will in Finance Bill 2006 **implement the rewrite of the complex 'option-to-tax' legislation** to make it clearer and easier to use, following a consultation issued at the Pre-Budget Report. Following a consultation on certain VAT arrangements concerning land and property,[23] the Government has decided to make no changes in this area.

VAT on contraception **5.109** To support its strategy to improve sexual health, **the Government will reduce the rate** of VAT chargeable on contraceptive products to 5 per cent.

---

[23] *VAT: Disapplication of the option to tax,* HM Customs & Excise, March 2004. A summary of responses is published today.

Alcohol duty   **5.110**   The Government remains committed to creating a fairer balance of taxation on different alcoholic drinks. In order to continue these efforts, Budget 2006 announces the following duty changes, which will take effect from midnight on 26 March 2006:

- **spirits duties are again frozen,** for the ninth successive Budget, meaning that the total tax on a standard bottle of spirits will be £1.51 lower than if duty had risen in line with inflation since 1997;

- **duties on beer and wine will increase in line with inflation,** adding 1 penny to a pint of beer and 4 pence to a standard 75 centilitre bottle of wine; and

- **duty on sparkling wine and cider will be frozen.**

Tobacco duty   **5.111**   Smoking remains the greatest cause of preventable illness and premature death in the UK. Maintaining high levels of tax helps to reduce overall tobacco consumption. Budget 2006 announces that from 6pm on Budget day **tobacco duties will increase in line with inflation, adding 9 pence to the price of a packet of cigarettes.**

Gambling   **5.112**   Building on announcements on gambling taxation at the Pre-Budget Report, the Government today details **changes to amusement machine licence duty (AMLD) rates and categories.** Measures to simplify some aspects of the administration of AMLD will be introduced later in the year.

5.113   The Government has decided to defer announcements on the taxation of remote gaming until the tax regime is implemented in Budget 2007, so that the tax system can reflect detailed regulations for the sector being developed by the Gambling Commission. Following the conclusion of a periodic review, the Government has decided to continue the VAT registration scheme for racehorse owners.

International   **5.114**   International travellers may currently bring certain goods (excluding cigarettes, wine, **shopping**   spirits and perfume) for personal use into the UK from outside the EU, up to a limit of £145, without paying tax or duty. To support travellers' freedom to shop outside the EU and following action taken by the Government at Budget 2005, the Commission has now issued a proposal to increase the limit to £340. The Government has written to the EU Presidency suggesting that the limit be raised to £1,000 by 2011.

Protecting tax revenues

5.115   The Government recognises that most taxpayers comply with their tax obligations. However, tax fraud and avoidance distort markets and add no value to the UK economy. They are also unfair on the majority who do pay their fair share and can undermine the funding of public services. The Government's approach to tackling non-compliance will continue to ensure actions are effectively tailored to the needs and behaviours of different taxpayers.

Tackling tax   **5.116**   The Government will continue to tackle avoidance using legislation and litigation, **avoidance**   while ensuring that the competitiveness of the UK is maintained. In recent Budgets, the Government has built on this approach and introduced: disclosure rules to allow HMRC to take rapid, focused action; targeted anti-avoidance measures based on purposive tests; and legislation with effect from the date of announcement, as a proportionate response to those who seek to avoid paying their fair share.

5.117   After closing down a series of ever more complex and contrived schemes designed to avoid income tax and national insurance contributions on remuneration and bonuses, the Government announced in the 2004 Pre-Budget Report that it would counter any schemes of this type that were developed in the future, where necessary with effect from the date of that announcement. Despite this, a minority of employers are continuing to enter into schemes that use employment-related securities and which frustrate the Government's intention to prevent tax avoidance. Having considered the risks to the Exchequer, the Government has decided to close down a number of schemes with effect from 2 December 2004, so that those using these schemes will not succeed in obtaining an unfair advantage over the majority of employers and employees who do pay their fair share of tax and NICs.

5.118   Budget 2004 introduced a disclosure regime that has enabled the Government to respond to avoidance more swiftly and in a more targeted fashion. The Pre-Budget Report announced changes to this regime to ensure that it continues to function as intended. Following discussions with stakeholders, the Government can announce that:

- the direct tax 'filters' will be replaced with 'hallmarks', in line with the system used for VAT; and

- individuals and small- and medium-sized businesses will be excluded from the requirement to make disclosures of in-house schemes.

5.119   The Government will introduce further measures which will:

- close down a number of avoidance schemes which use financial products;

- prevent charitable reliefs being exploited for tax avoidance purposes, to preserve the integrity of the reliefs and protect the reputation of charities;

- close a loophole in the controlled foreign companies legislation;

- combat VAT avoidance involving face-value vouchers, such as phonecards; and

- prevent avoidance of capital gains tax by schemes exploiting the 'bed and breakfasting' identification rules.

VAT fraud   **5.120**   Missing Trader Intra-Community (MTIC) fraud is an EU-wide, criminal attack on the VAT system. In order to strengthen further the Government's strategy to combat VAT fraud, the Government announced in January that it had written to the European Commission for a derogation to introduce a change of accounting procedure on certain goods. Finance Bill 2006 will include an enabling clause for the introduction of this change.

5.121   In addition, the Government will introduce legislation to support HMRC in intensifying its operational activities in relation to MTIC fraud, including:

- making explicit HMRC's powers to evidence the inspection of goods; and

- directing individual businesses to maintain relevant records.

Tackling VAT   **5.122**   HMRC will consult informally on a new requirement for businesses to declare the
losses   suitability of a proposed partial exemption special method before HMRC gives approval for its use. This will speed up the approval process and further strengthen the partial exemption regime. Subject to this consultation, this will be introduced from April 2007.

5.123   The Government will make changes to the VAT treatment of goods supplied under finance agreements. These will remove a loophole that allows finance companies to account for VAT on less than the full proceeds they receive in relation to the goods sold in certain circumstances.

Tackling tobacco **5.124** Since its launch in March 2000, the Tackling Tobacco Smuggling Strategy has
smuggling successfuly cut the illicit market share of cigarettes by a quarter and protected almost
£6 billion in revenue. But smugglers are constantly changing their tactics and the
Government needs to anticipate and adapt to new threats and challenges. Building on the
measures announced in the Pre-Budget Report, and to clamp down further on smuggling, the
Government today publishes a paper setting out how it is reinforcing its strategy.

5.125 Alongside HMRC's operational strategy, the Government has strengthened its agreements
with tobacco manufacturers in line with the announcement in the Pre-Budget Report and will
introduce legislation to ensure tobacco manufacturers control their supply chains effectively,
with penalties of up to £5 million for those who fail to do so. A new communications strategy aims
to raise awareness among smokers of the risks of smuggled products, especially counterfeit.

Oils fraud **5.126** The Government today announces an increase in duty of 1.25 pence per litre for
rebated oils, maintaining the differential between main and rebated duty rates and
supporting the oils strategy to prevent fraud. The Government also today publishes details of
changes to the categories of vehicles eligible to use rebated oil. HMRC will continue to
consult with industry over the next few months on ways to deter fraud in the aviation turbine
fuel sector and will subsequently consult with the marine fuels sectors.

Identity fraud **5.127** Identity fraud poses a serious threat to the private and public sector, including the tax
and the tax system. The Government, working with the financial services industry, is taking a range of
system new measures to counter this threat, for example developing the work of public-private
groups such as the Home Office-led Identity Fraud Steering Committee.

5.128 New industry guidance to be published shortly will strengthen the system of identity
checks while reducing the inconvenience for the consumer. HMRC will carry out an
assessment of the typical profile of frauds committed against it, to assist banks in identifying
suspect payments and accounts, enabling them to make timely Suspicious Activity Reports to
the National Criminal Intelligence Service (NCIS). HMRC will contact any firms that have
been party to these frauds.

5.129 In December 2005, both the public e-portal for internet applications to tax credits
and the DWP e-portal were closed due to new evidence that they had been used to make
fraudulent claims. Following checks to ensure that safeguards against fraud are sufficiently
robust, the DWP e-portal for applications to tax credits will be reopened in April. Other
aspects of the internet service will be opened later, once HMRC have developed extra security
measures and can be sure that the risk of fraud is minimised.

TACKLING GLOBAL POVERTY

5.130 2005 was a vital year for international development. The UN Millennium
Development Goals (MDGs) and global poverty were at the heart of the UK Presidencies of
the G7/8 and EU. The key challenge now is to ensure that the commitments made in 2005 are
translated into concrete action to accelerate progress towards the MDGs.

Aid – delivering **5.131** The aid commitments made by the EU and the G8 in 2005 are important steps
commitments towards helping the poorest countries achieve the MDGs. However, more needs to be done
both to deliver and to bring forward these commitments, which is why the Government
supports the use of innovative financing instruments including the International Finance
Facility (IFF). This works by frontloading donors' existing long-term aid commitments
through bond issuances on the international capital markets, to deliver immediately the
additional and predictable funding needed to achieve the MDGs.

5.132   In September 2005, the UK launched the pilot International Finance Facility for Immunisation (IFFIm), in partnership with France, Italy, Spain and Sweden and alongside contributions from the Bill & Melinda Gates Foundation. In December 2005, Norway announced that it would contribute to the Facility and in March 2006 Brazil also committed to contribute. The IFFIm will use the frontloading principles of the IFF to provide $4 billion over ten years to support the efforts of the Global Alliance for Vaccines and Immunisation to tackle preventable diseases in the poorest countries all over the world. The IFFIm will demonstrate the technical feasibility of the IFF and the clear economic benefits of frontloading resources. At the Innovating Financing Mechanisms Conference in Paris in February 2006, France and the UK agreed to jointly establish a working group to consider the implementation of an IFF, partly funded by an air ticket levy. The UK will hypothecate part of its existing levy (air passenger duty) to this purpose.

Box 5.4: 2005 – Progress in 2005 for international development

Meeting the MDGs requires a fully-funded, comprehensive plan to eliminate poverty and put countries on a sustainable path to growth and eventual graduation from aid. 2005 saw significant progress on establishing such a plan:

- EU development and Finance Ministers agreed to reach the long-standing UN target of spending 0.7 per cent of national income on aid by 2015. Combined with the financing commitments agreed by the G8 this is expected to lead to an additional $50 billion a year in development aid by 2010 compared with 2004, of which $25 billion will be for Africa;

- the multilateral debt relief proposal was agreed by G8 Finance Ministers in June 2005 and then endorsed at the annual meetings of the World Bank and IMF in September. In January 2006 the Multilateral Debt Relief Initiative was implemented by the IMF;

- in September 2005 the International Finance Facility for Immunisation was launched. By frontloading $4 billion over 10 years through the IFFIm mechanism, an estimated additional five million children's lives could be saved in the years to 2015; and

- at the Sixth World Trade Organisation Ministerial Conference in Hong Kong, agreement was reached to end all agricultural export subsidies by 2013. While progress was disappointing, it was agreed for all developed countries to grant duty-free and quota-free market access to Least Developed Countries on 97 per cent of tariff lines by 2008.

Aid effectiveness   **5.133**   The G8 has agreed to focus aid on low-income countries that are committed to growth and poverty reduction, to democratic, accountable and transparent government and to sound public financial management – while acknowledging that aid is also important to respond to humanitarian crises and countries affected by or at risk of conflict. The UK and other donors will be monitored on commitments made in the OECD Development Assistance Committee's Paris Declaration on aid effectiveness. The Government remains committed to the principles of country ownership of policy, as set out in *Partnerships for poverty reduction: rethinking conditionality,*[24] Aid effectiveness and the particular challenges posed by fragile states are themes that the Government is exploring though the third White Paper on International Development. The Chancellor will also be considering these issues as a member of the UN Secretary General's 'High Level Panel of System Wide Coherence'. The Panel will develop recommendations over the following six months to improve the efficiency and effectiveness of the UN's development, humanitarian and environmental operations.

---

[24] *Partnerships for poverty reduction: rethinking conditionality,* Department for International Development (DfID),

Debt relief **5.134**   The UK believes that no poor countries should have to choose between servicing their debt obligations and making the necessary investments in health, education and infrastructure necessary to meet the MDGs. The Government has been at the forefront of international efforts to cancel the debts of the most heavily indebted poor countries (HIPCs). This culminated in securing G8 agreement in June 2005 for 100 per cent cancellation of the debts owed by the HIPCs to the major international institutions. This Multilateral Debt Relief Initiative (MDRI), which will cover the cancellation of debts owed to the IMF and the concessional lending arms of the World Bank and African Development Bank, has already been implemented at the IMF. In January 2006, irrevocable debt relief from the IMF worth around $3.3 billion became effective for 19 countries.[25] Implementation of the MDRI by the World Bank and African Development Bank is expected later this year. When fully implemented the MDRI will provide $50 billion in debt relief for the 38 HIPCs.

5.135   The UK attaches great importance to extending multilateral debt relief to all of the poorest countries, not just those countries deemed eligible under the HIPC Initiative. The UK will therefore continue to pay its share of the debt service owed to the World Bank and African Development Bank by other low-income countries that meet criteria for ensuring that the debt service savings are used for poverty-reduction. The UK urges other donor countries to agree to deeper debt relief for all low-income countries.

Nigeria debt **5.136**   The debt deal agreed through the Paris Club saw Nigeria's debt reduced by $30 billion, **relief** freeing up at least an additional $1 billion a year for Nigeria to spend on poverty reduction, helping to employ an extra 120,000 teachers and put 3.5 million children into school. The proposal was made by the Nigerian government, based on their wish to use their additional oil reserves in this way, and in support of their own economic reforms and development strategy. The UK was pleased to support the Nigerian Government in reaching an agreement with the Paris Club. The UK alone wrote down £4.5 billion of debt, and in exchange the Export Credit Guarantee Department received into its balance sheet a payment of £1.7 billion, providing debt relief to Nigeria of £2.8 billion. The debt was written off in two tranches in 2005 and 2006.

5.137   Because of the way the deal is structured, instead of being spread over several years, the OECD's Official Development Assistance (ODA) figures will score all the debt relief in 2005 and 2006. This will result in a short-term increase in the figures as reported by the OECD Development Assistance Committee (DAC) that does not reflect the underlying trend path of ODA, or the fact that the benefit to Nigeria is spread over several years. The Government will consider whether there is a more appropriate way to report Nigerian debt relief over several years to enable more accurate monitoring of trends in ODA to meet the targets committed to in 2005.

Universal free **5.138**   Education is one of the best investments that a person or country can make – not just for **primary** economic growth but also for wider societal reasons. Investment in education contributes not **education** only to the MDGs on education and gender equality but also to MDGs on child mortality and combating disease. The Education for All Fast Track Initiative (FTI) exists as a platform for channelling donor funding for education to those countries with fully developed plans for universal primary education. At Gleneagles in July 2005, the G8 countries committed that every FTI-endorsed country should have sufficient resources to implement their education plans and in 2006 the UK will work to ensure that donors come together to make sure that this commitment is fulfilled.

---

[25] Further information at www.imf.org

5.139 User fees for education are sometimes as much as a quarter of the annual income of households in poor countries and are the single biggest barrier to increasing enrolment across sub-Saharan Africa. As outlined in *From commitment to action: education*,[26] the UK stands ready to assist countries that wish to eliminate user fees and make services free at the point of delivery. The UK will work to ensure that extra revenues committed in 2005 are transformed into concrete actions to provide long term predictable financing for universal free education. This requires the abolition of user fees for education but this alone is not enough. The bulk of finance is needed for teacher training, school buildings, school materials and targeted programmes to get girls and other disadvantaged groups into school.

5.140 The UK will also work to underline the importance of developing countries drawing up ambitious long term education plans. In order to do this, donors need to provide both assistance in drawing up ten-year plans and the assurance that they will finance their implementation. In the coming months the Government will work towards this end. The overall goal must be ten-year, comprehensive, ambitious, country-owned and fully financed plans to achieve all the MDGs by 2015.

Universal and free health services **5.141** Healthy populations are key to growth and poverty reduction. To underpin progress against all of the MDGs, donors need to support countries that wish to invest in strengthening health systems and making them responsive to poor people. As outlined in *From commitment to action: health*,[27] the UK stands ready to assist countries that wish to eliminate user fees and make services free at the point of delivery. The UK is also taking significant action on prevention and treatment for diseases that primarily affect poor countries and is working with the G8 to develop an Advance Market Commitment (AMC). At the February G8 meeting in Moscow it was agreed that Ministers would consider a specific proposal at their next meeting. The Gleneagles G8 communiqué also committed countries to supporting as close as possible to universal access to HIV treatment by 2010, through mechanisms such as the Global Fund for AIDS, TB and malaria.

Box 5.5: Advanced market commitments (AMCs)

The UK is exploring the use of AMCs to stimulate the research and development of vaccines against diseases like malaria, HIV/AIDS, TB and pneumococcus, which kill millions in developing countries each year. At present the resources invested in finding vaccines against these diseases – especially by the private sector – are minimal when compared to the scale of the challenge because markets for vaccines in developing countries are too small to justify the huge investment required to bring an effective vaccine to the point of sale.

An AMC works by creating a market where one is currently missing. Rich countries underwrite a market for vaccines, subject to them meeting pre-defined standards of efficacy against a particular disease and subject to demand from developing countries. When the vaccine is in demand from developing countries, rich countries fulfil their commitment to buy, thereby ensuring that it is widely accessible. The UK is also a strong supporter of direct funding for research efforts being undertaken around the world, such as the Global HIV Vaccine Enterprise.

---

[26] *From commitment to action: education*, DFID and HM Treasury, November 2005.
[27] *From commitment to action: health*, DfID and HM Treasury, November 2005.

Trade **5.142**   A fairer international trading system is key to development, poverty reduction and global growth. With the opportunity for all countries to benefit from what could be at least an extra $300 billion in world growth every year, the EU, US and other key WTO players must seize the opportunity to secure a new trade deal by the end of 2006. The Sixth World Trade Organisation Ministerial Conference took place in Hong Kong, China in December 2005 as part of the Doha Development Round. Agreement was reached to end all agricultural export subsidies by 2013. All developed countries will now grant duty-free and quota-free market access for at least 97 per cent of products originating from Least Developed Countries by 2008. However, progress made was disappointing and did not meet the UK's level of ambition.

5.143   Nevertheless there is basis for concerted effort to achieve the comprehensive deal to conclude the Doha Round. The UK Government continues to work with fellow EU and WTO Member States towards an ambitious and pro-development conclusion to the Doha Round, that would: substantially increase market access for developing countries; substantially reduce all trade-distorting domestic support; and provide effective special and differential treatment to enable developing countries to capture the gains from trade. All WTO members need to maintain committment to the Round so that we can deliver on the promises of Doha without lowering the level of ambition.

5.144   The need for a fairer global trading system was a key message of the UK Presidency reflected in the communiqués of the G7 Finance Ministers in June, the G8 Heads of State at Gleneagles in July 2005 and G7 Finance Ministers in December 2005. In the latter meeting a commitment was made to grant additional support for trade capacity building to help Least Developed Countries, particularly in Africa. G7 Finance Ministers stated that expenditure on aid for trade is expected to increase to $4 billion, including through enhancing the Integrated Framework. In the context of their shared commitment to double aid for Africa by 2010, agreement was reached to give priority to the infrastructure necessary to allow countries to take advantage of the improved opportunities to trade. The UK will contribute funds to an aid for trade fund that will help build in developing countries the infrastructure and capacity for them to trade with the world.

Peacekeeping **5.145**   Peace is the first condition for successful development. The Government will **and** continue to support African-led peacekeeping operations and work to strengthen the African **humanitarian** Standby Force. Since September 2003, the UK has committed £32 million to the African Union **assistance** Mission in Darfur and provided over £92 million in humanitarian assistance. The Government has also provided £56 million to support peacebuilding and conflict prevention in the Democratic Republic of Congo and has provided the largest bilateral contribution, £22 million, toward the organisation of free and fair elections. The Government has set aside £12 million towards the new Peacebuliding Fund that will be established at the UN.

5.146   The UK is leading ongoing work with the international community to improve the international response to humanitarian disasters. The Government is the leading donor, providing £40 million each year, to the reformed UN Central Emergency Revolving Fund. The UK provided over £180 million to countries affected by the tsunami in the Indian Ocean and also responded quickly to other disasters such as the earthquake in Kashmir, contributing £58 million to the immediate relief effort and a further £70 million to longer-term reconstruction. The UK is at the forefront of the international response to the famine in the horn of Africa and has committed £35.9 million to the immediate relief effort in the worst affected countries. In addition, the Government will provide £70 million to tackle the underlying causes of the persistent food crises affecting the region and elsewhere in Africa.

Reconstruction in Iraq   **5.147**   The UK has worked alongside the Transitional Government of Iraq and its international partners to support reconstruction in Iraq. This work will continue with the new Iraqi Government to support the implementation of the December 2005 Stand-By Arrangement IMF programme. The UK and Iraq signed a bilateral debt agreement in January 2006, implementing the November 2004 Paris Club deal, which agreed to write off 80 per cent of Iraq's debt in three tranches. Upon signing, the UK retroactively cancelled 60 per cent of Iraq's £1.12 billion debt to the UK. The final 20 per cent tranche of debt cancellation will be implemented, as per the terms of the Paris Club deal, once Iraq has successfully followed three years of substantive IMF Programmes.

Terrorist financing   **5.148**   The Government will publish, later in 2006, a comprehensive progress report on countering money laundering and terrorist financing. This will set out the Government's strategy for the next five years to consolidate the UK's money laundering framework, based on the principles of effectiveness, proportionality and engagement with industry.

6 DELIVERING HIGH QUALITY PUBLIC SERVICES

> The Government's aim is to deliver world-class public services through sustained investment matched by far-reaching reform. The 2004 Spending Review set outcome-focussed targets and spending plans to 2007-08 that built on the sustained increases in resources delivered in previous Spending Reviews.
>
> The Government will be conducting a second Comprehensive Spending Review (CSR) reporting in 2007. A decade on from the first CSR, the review will assess what further investments and reforms are needed to equip the UK to respond to the global challenges of the decade ahead. In preparation for the CSR, this Budget announces:
>
> - plans for a national debate about how public services should respond to the long-term challenges facing the UK;
>
> - a series of reviews that will inform the CSR in the areas where cross-departmental collaboration and innovative solutions are required to meet these challenges;
>
> - further details of the next phase of the Government's value for money programme, including progress on asset disposals and a review of opportunities for transforming service delivery across government, looking at how the channels through which services are delivered can be made more efficient and responsive to the needs of users; and
>
> - early spending settlements for the Department for Work and Pensions, HM Revenue and Customs, Cabinet Office and HM Treasury Group which see their Departmental Expenditure Limits fall by five per cent per year in real terms over the CSR period, releasing over £1.8 billion in total for re-investment in front-line public services.
>
> The Budget outlines further measures directing resources towards the Government's priorities, including:
>
> - £585 million of additional resources over 2006-07 and 2007-08 to provide further support for personalised learning in schools in England. Further, capital investment in schools will rise from £6.4 billion in 2007-08 to £8.0 billion by 2010-11, matching today's level of private sector per pupil capital investment;
>
> - £100 million to accelerate the recruitment of Police Community Support Officers (PCSOs) together with firm spending plans for the Home Office over the CSR period which lock in the large real increases in resources since 1999, providing the long-term funding certainty needed to lead the fight against crime and terrorism and realise the benefits of police force restructuring and reform;
>
> - a commitment of £200 million to ensure elite athletes have the best chance of success in a British Olympics in 2012; and
>
> - £800 million of provision for the Special Reserve in 2006-07, set aside from within existing public spending plans, to help meet the costs of Iraq, Afghanistan and other international commitments.

6.1 The Government's aim is to deliver world-class public services through sustained investment matched by far-reaching reform. High-quality education and training, a modern and reliable transport network, an effective criminal justice system and a modern health service provide the essential foundations for a flexible economy and a fair society, equipped to respond to the global challenges ahead.

6.2 The 1998 Comprehensive Spending Review (CSR) set the Government's priorities for the long-term: sustainable growth and employment; fairness and opportunity; modern and effective public services; and a secure and fair world. To lay the foundations for achieving these goals, the 1998 CSR put in place a modernised public spending and performance management framework that supports the prudent and efficient planning of expenditure over the medium to long term. The 1998 CSR involved the most fundamental and in-depth examination of public spending ever attempted, enabling resources to be re-focussed on the incoming Government's priorities in health, education and transport. Subsequent spending reviews in 2000, 2002 and 2004 delivered further increases in resources for these areas, made possible by stable and sustainable economic growth with falling debt interest payments and low unemployment, as illustrated in Chart 6.1.

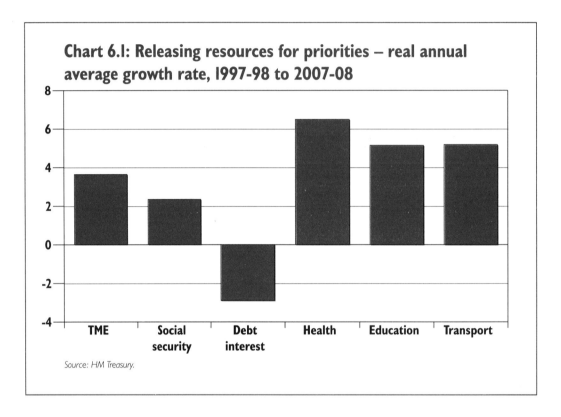

Chart 6.1: Releasing resources for priorities – real annual average growth rate, 1997-98 to 2007-08

Source: HM Treasury.

6.3 This investment has been matched by steps to ensure value for money and reform the delivery of public services, making the most of increased spending and fulfilling the Government's obligation to taxpayers to employ resources efficiently and effectively. Reforms to public services have strengthened accountability and improved outcomes for society, including higher standards, reduced inequalities and greater user satisfaction.

2007 Comprehensive Spending Review

6.4 A decade on from the first CSR, the Government will be conducting a second Comprehensive Spending Review in 2007, which will set departmental spending plans and priorities for the years 2008-09, 2009-10 and 2010-11. In the context of a rapidly changing world the 2007 CSR provides an appropriate opportunity for a fundamental review of the balance and pattern of public expenditure, taking stock of what investments and reforms have delivered to date and identifying what further steps are needed to meet the challenges and opportunities of the decade ahead. To lay the groundwork for the CSR, the Government is taking forward a programme of work over the next year involving:

- an examination of the key long-term trends and challenges that will shape the next decade – including demographic and socio-economic change, globalisation, technological change, global insecurity and climate and environmental change;

- detailed studies of key areas where cross-cutting, innovative policy responses are required to meet these long-term challenges;

- an ambitious and far-reaching value for money programme to release the resources needed to address the challenges, involving both further development of the efficiency areas developed in the Gershon Review, and a set of zero-based reviews of departments' baseline expenditure to assess its effectiveness in delivering the Government's long-term objectives; and

- a more strategic approach to asset management and investment decisions, ensuring the UK is equipped with the infrastructure needed to support both public service delivery and the productivity and flexibility of the wider economy.

MEETING THE LONG-TERM CHALLENGES

6.5   The UK will only succeed in the modern global economy if the Government plans for the long term. The 2007 CSR will therefore be informed by a detailed assessment of the long-term trends and challenges that will shape public services over the next decade, including:

- demographic and socio-economic change, such as the rapid increase in the old age dependency ratio as the 'baby boom' generation reaches retirement age;

- the intensification of cross-border economic competition as the balance of international economic activity shifts toward rapidly growing emerging markets such as China and India;

- the acceleration in the pace of innovation and technological diffusion and a continued increase in the knowledge-intensity of goods and services;

- continued global uncertainty and poverty, with ongoing threats of international terrorism and global conflict; and

- increasing pressures on our natural resources and global climate from rapid economic and population growth in the developing world and sustained demand for fossil fuels in advanced economies.

Reviews **6.6**   These long-term challenges have fundamental and far-reaching implications for
informing the public services that require innovative policy responses, co-ordination of activity across
CSR departmental boundaries and sustained investment in key areas. The CSR will therefore be informed by the analysis and conclusions of a series of detailed reviews on specific cross-cutting issues.

6.7 To respond to demographic and socio-economic change and continue making progress on social exclusion:

- **this Budget launches a joint HM Treasury and Department for Education and Skills policy review of children and young people to secure further** improvement in outcomes. Under the umbrella of this review, sub-reviews will focus on support for families with disabled children, youth services, and services for families at risk of becoming locked into a cycle of low achievement (further details in Chapter 5);

- **this Budget announces a review of the policies needed to improve mental health outcomes and employment,** recognising that too many people are excluded from the world of work when, with the proper support, it should be possible for them to find or remain in work benefiting their health and the wider economy (further details are set out in Chapter 4); and

- as announced at the Pre-Budget Report and described in Chapter 3, the Government is conducting a cross-cutting review to ensure that appropriate infrastructure will be provided to support housing and population growth.

6.8 To equip the UK economy for future challenges, including the changing global economy and technological innovation:

- the Eddington Transport Study is reviewing the long-term impact of transport decisions on economic productivity, stability and growth, as described in Chapter 3;

- the Leitch Review of Skills will set out the skills profile that the UK should aim to achieve in 2020 in order to maximise productivity and growth over the long-term, as described in Chapter 3;

- as set out in *Devolved Decision Making 3: The Economics of Cities*, published alongside Budget 2006, **the Government will review the effectiveness of sub-national interventions on economic development and the regeneration and renewal of deprived neighbourhoods;** and

- building on the recommendations of Kate Barker's independent review of housing supply, 2005 Pre-Budget Report announced a review of how planning policy can better deliver economic growth and prosperity alongside other sustainable development goals (further details are set out in Chapter 3).

6.9 Whilst the UK has faced a variety of terrorist threats in the past, the global reach, capability and sophistication of international terrorist groups places the current threat on a scale not previously encountered. More broadly, global security in the decade ahead will be shaped by a range of factors, including international responses to poverty, future conflict, areas of instability and organised crime. **As part of its response to these challenges, the Government will review the delivery of its counter-terrorism and security strategies to inform the CSR.**

6.10 In order to respond to the challenges presented by environmental change, the Government is reviewing:

- the economics of climate change, led by Sir Nicholas Stern (further details are set out in Chapter 7); and

- the future UK energy policy and the UK's progress against the medium and long-term Energy White Paper goals (further details are set out in Chapters 3 and 7).

6.11   The Government alone cannot meet these challenges: citizens, communities, businesses and non-governmental organisations will all play a vital role in shaping the the future of UK society. To inform the CSR and develop a shared understanding of how the country must respond to the challenges of the decade ahead:

- as set out in Box 6.1, **this Budget announces plans for a national debate about how public services should respond to these challenges;**

- **this Budget announces a review of the third sector's future role in social and economic regeneration,** involving the largest consultation with the third sector ever conducted by the Government (further details are set out in Chapter 5); and

- the CSR will be informed by Sir Michael Lyons' Inquiry into the funding, role and function of local government.

Box 6.1: A national debate to inform the Comprehensive Spending Review

The Government carried out its first Comprehensive Spending Review in 1998, designed to ensure that existing spending was properly focused on its priorities and delivering maximum value for money.

Since then, the Government has built on the platform of a stable economy and sound public finances to deliver a sustained increase in public spending, meaning that by 2007-08, compared to 1996-97:

- spending on the NHS will be around 90 per cent higher in real terms;

- spending on schools in England will be over 65 per cent higher in real terms; and

- spending on transport will be over 60 per cent higher in real terms.

With the 2007 Comprehensive Spending Review coming a decade after the first CSR, the Government sees it as an opportunity to do a fundamental review of the balance and pattern of public expenditure, take stock of what investments and reforms have delivered to date and identify what further steps are needed to meet the challenges decade ahead, which include, for example:

- by 2017, there are expected to be nearly 2.3 million more people over the age of 65 in the UK, including a 32 per cent increase in those aged over 85;

- by 2017, China and India will have nearly doubled their share of wold income and are likely to be bigger than the UK, French and German economies combined; and

- global temperatures are predicted by the Inter-Governmental Panel on Climate Change to rise by at least 1–2 degrees by the end of the century and the change could be as much as 5.8 degrees if carbon emissions continue to increase.

The Government believes it is critical that its response to these challenges and its priorities for public spending and the reform of the public services are informed by:

- a broad expert consensus about the nature of the long-term trends and challenges facing the UK;

- a wide cross-section of views about how to meet those challenges and what it means for the priorities for spending and public services over the coming decade; and

- consultation with front line professionals and the third sector.

The Budget therefore announces that the Government plans to initiate a national debate on the future priorities for public spending and public services, to inform the CSR.

ENSURING VALUE FOR MONEY

6.12   To ensure that historic increases in investment are translated into better outcomes across public services, the Government has taken a series of steps to drive improvements in delivery and value for money:

- the 1998 CSR saw the introduction of the first systematic, transparent, outcome-based performance management system for public services, in the form of the Public Service Agreements (PSAs) framework. It also set for the first time fixed, three-year budgets for all departments separated into resource and capital, removing the previous bias against investment and supporting the efficient planning of expenditure over the medium term;

- the Spending Reviews in 2000 and 2002 saw the improvement of the PSA framework and targets, including formal monitoring of PSA delivery, together with the introduction of selected value for money targets; and

- the 2004 Spending Review represented the first systematic attempt to drive operational efficiencies across the public sector through the Gershon Review, which focused on key processes that are common across government business and bringing the worst performing business units up to the level of the best.

Efficiency 6.13   The 2004 Spending Review set out the Government's ambition of achieving over £20 billion worth of annual efficiencies by the end of 2007-08 for re-investing in front line services, in line with the recommendations of the Gershon Review. As a recent National Audit Office report[1] recognised, this efficiency programme is the first to look at the efficiency of the public sector as a whole. Unlike previous attempts, it requires departments to demonstrate reforms have at least maintained the quality of public services. It provides a more structured and potentially more transparent model for delivery and accountability. Although the first full year of the programme is not yet complete, departments and local authorities have reported provisional annual efficiency gains totaling £6.4 billion by the end of December 2005. These include:

- the Ministry of Defence has made £511 million worth of efficiency gains, including gains from better contract negotiations and in procurement reform;

- the Department for Work and Pensions has made around £300 million worth of efficiency gains, for example through rationalisation of the benefit network, IT improvements and procurement efficiencies; and

- the Department for Environment, Food and Rural Affairs has made £141 million worth of efficiency gains as a result of better contract management and improved e-transactions.

6.14   Time lags mean that there could already be further gains achieved beyond what has been reported. These provisional gains will be subject to further verification, with the Government committed to continuing to report on progress against efficiency targets openly and transparently, including through Departments' Autumn Performance Reports and annual Departmental Reports.

---

[1] *Progress in Improving Government Efficiency*, NAO, February 2006.

Box 6.2: Delivering the Gershon efficiency programme

The efficiency gains of £6.4 billion reported by the end of December 2005 have been achieved through improvements across the public sector. In addition to the initiatives previously reported in the Budget and Pre-Budget Reports, further departmental efficiency examples include:

- The **Department for the Environment, Food and Rural Affairs** has supported Local Authorities in delivering savings in the procurement and contract management of environmental services and waste management. £54 million was achhieved in 2004-05; £143 million is forecast for 2005-06 and £299 million is expected by March 2008.

- Within the **Ministry of Defence (MOD),** the negotiation of a new engine contract for the Tornado will save £136 million over the next 5 years. Regional Rehabilitation Units in the MOD are getting more medically-downgraded staff Fit for Task more quickly by reducing times spent waiting for appointments, treatment and rehabilitation for orthopaedic injuries. From April 2005 to September 2005, a total of 450,000 man deployable days were gained achieving over £44 million worth of efficiency gains.

- The **Department for Work and Pensions** is delivering efficiencies in the Jobcentre Plus and in the Pension Service. Jobcentre Plus will reduce its management and support overhead from 13 per cent to between 7 and 8 per cent by March 2008, so that it focuses a higher proportion of its resources on front line staff directly helping customers. This will lead to a reduction of 4,300 posts. Innovative processes, joining up services and a focus on performance management has led to the Pension Service delivering better customer service with over 5,000 (27 per cent) less staff. In addition, significant levels of improvement in customer service targets for State Pension, Pension Credit and State Pension Forecasts have been achieved, including time taken to clear applications and targets for answering the telephone.

- The **Department of Health** has reported improved productivity in the NHS from lower levels of staff sickness and reduced use of agency staff in 2004-05. This has meant that around £60 million has been saved for investment in better patient care.

Lyons Relocation 6.15   The 2004 Spending Review announced that the Government plans to relocate 20,000 public sector posts out of London and the South East. As at the end of December 2005, 6,640 posts had been relocated, due to rise to 7,800 by April 2006. Recent moves include over 50 Valuation Office Agency Posts to Plymouth and Halifax. Posts have been relocated to every nation and region in the UK including:

- over 1,800 to Yorkshire and the Humber including over 200 to Sheffield;

- over 1,500 to the North West including 480 to Liverpool;

- over 1,400 to Wales including 500 to Wrexham; and

- over 550 to the North East including 450 to Newcastle .

Workforce **6.16** The 2004 Spending Review set out plans for a gross reduction of 84,150 Civil Service
Reduction and military posts in administrative and support functions by 2007-08, with 13,550
reallocated to frontline service, resulting in a net reduction of 70,600 posts. The 2005 Pre-
Budget Report reported that a gross reduction of over 31,000 civil service posts had been
achieved by the end of September 2005. An additional 9,300 posts had been removed by the
end of December 2005, taking the total gross reduction to over 40,000 by that date. Table 6.1
shows the details of the progress made. The Government is on course to achieve significant
reductions in posts as set out by Sir Peter Gershon.[2]

Table 6.1: Workforce reduction across departments

Department	Reductions	Reallocations to front line roles	Total reduction
Department for Work and Pensions	14,698	5,594	20,292
Ministry of Defence	8,560	0	8,560
HM Revenue & Customs	3,671	1,560	5,231
Other departments	6,308	0	6,308
Total	33,237	7,154	40,391

Public Sector Pay **6.17** The Government is continuing its commitment to ensure that public sector pay is
targeted towards delivering and administering high quality public services. Given that it
accounts for around a quarter of all public spending, controlling pay is also essential in
delivering value for money and keeping inflationary pressures in check. In November the
Chancellor of the Exchequer wrote to the public sector pay review bodies emphasising the
need to ensure pay settlements are based on the achievement of the Government's inflation
target of two per cent.

6.18 The 2005 Pre-Budget Report announced the establishment of the new Public Sector
Pay Committee (PSPC) – the Pay Gateway. The PSPC has met on several occasions since then
to discuss specific workforce issues and has made good progress in strengthening the
consistency and quality of the information base used to underpin pay decisions. The PSPC
will set common objectives for pay across Government and will ensure that both pay awards
and pay systems across the public sector are evidence based, represent value for money and
are financially sustainable over the long run.

6.19 The PSPC will review progress on local pay. The terms of reference in remit letters to
the Pay Review Bodies (PRBs) require them to have regard to regional/local labour markets
and their effects on recruitment and retention. Departments responsible for workforces
covered by PRBs are required to provide robust evidence on local and regional recruitment
and retention issues and make clear to PRBs how they expect pay to reflect these different
markets. In addition, civil service remit guidance instructs Departments to fully consider
local pay.

---

[2] *Releasing Resources to the Front Line, an independent review of public sector efficiency,* Sir Peter Gershon, July 2004.

Value for money in the Comprehensive Spending Review

6.20   The 2007 CSR marks the next stage of development in the Government's programme for delivering better value for money in public services. To continue to improve front-line service delivery and release the resources needed to respond to the long-term challenges, the CSR will go beyond the ambition set in the 2004 Spending Review efficiency programme by:

- deepening the government-wide efficiency programme in the operational areas established by the Gershon Review, with greater engagement of front-line professionals to identify opportunities for service improvements;

- taking a radical look at the way that government spends money on programmes and policies ten years on from the first CSR, through a set of zero-based reviews of departments' baseline expenditure;

- reviewing the opportunities for transforming service delivery across government, looking at how the channels through which services are delivered can be made more efficient and responsive to the needs of users; and

- delivering a step-change in the management of the public sector asset base, taking forward the recommendations of the Lyons Review of asset management.

6.21   The Government is developing an ambitious efficiency programme for the CSR period building on the foundations laid in the 2004 Spending Review. Further progress is possible on all of the strands of work that make up the existing programme as the lessons of best practice on efficiency spread across Whitehall and the wider public sector. In particular, significant gains are still to be made through the extension of current work on collaboration in procurement and the shared provision of corporate services to government departments and the wider public sector. There is also scope to learn from best practice in redesigning working practices to substantially increase the productive use of the time of front-line staff.

6.22   Alongside this work on improving operations and processes, departments are also taking forward a set of zero-based reviews of their baseline expenditure to assess its effectiveness in delivering the Government's long-term objectives. Whereas past spending reviews have traditionally focussed on allocating incremental increases in expenditure, the process of setting new long-term objectives in the CSR provides an important opportunity – with many past objectives achieved and supporting programmes and spending potentially available for reallocation – for a more fundamental review of the balance and pattern of expenditure within and across departments. The aim of these zero-based reviews is to renew each department's baseline expenditure to reflect changing priorities ten years on from the first CSR.

6.23   This Budget announces early CSR spending settlements for the Department for Work and Pensions, HM Revenue and Customs, HM Treasury and the Cabinet Office which embed ongoing efficiency savings into their medium-term expenditure plans and lay the foundation for a spending review focused on meeting the challenges of the decade ahead. Box 6.3 sets out details of these settlements.

Box 6.3: Embedding efficiency in departmental expenditure planning

This Budget announces that the Department for Work and Pensions, HM Revenue and Customs, HM Treasury and the Cabinet Office have already agreed to deliver ambitious value for money reforms over the CSR period, enabling them to continue improving services within Departmental Expenditure Limits (DEL) that will fall by 5 per cent in real terms per year in 2008-09, 2009-10 and 2010-11. These early settlements embed efficiency savings into their medium-term expenditure planning and release £1.8 billion in total over the three years of the CSR period for reallocation to front-line services. **To meet the transitional costs of transforming these departments, the Government is setting aside a modernisation fund of over £800 million.**

Department for Work & Pensions

The 2004 Spending Review announced plans for DWP to modernise and streamline the delivery of its services by 2007-08 while its Departmental Expenditure Limit for 2006-07 and 2007-08 was held constant in nominal terms at 2005-06 levels, representing a real terms cut. To date, this modernisation programme has enabled DWP to reduce its workforce by 14,698 posts and redeploy 5,594 posts to customer facing roles, while still maintaining employment at historically high levels. Going forward into the CSR, DWP will make further progress in improving the efficient delivery of its services to the public, including by:

- redesigning and simplifying business processes;
- implementing a channels strategy to improve the customer experience and reduce waste; and
- consolidating delivery and support functions to generate economies of scale.

HM Revenue and Customs

The 2004 Spending Review announced that the Inland Revenue and HM Customs and Excise would merge, releasing resources, providing a one-stop service to businesses and allowing tax flows to be managed more effectively. Since its establishment HMRC has generated efficiency savings of £75 million in 2005-06 and headcount reductions of 3,653 full-time posts. Building on this success, over the CSR period HMRC has committed to a programme of service transformation that will further increase efficiency and place customers at the heart of what they do, including by:

- supporting customers to get it right first time;
- simplifying business processes and implementing more flexible ways of working; and
- improving risk targeting to increase compliance.

HM Treasury and the Cabinet Office

Both HM Treasury Group and the Cabinet Office have initiated ambitious change programmes aimed at transforming their organisations, improving their strategic focus and enhancing the service provided at the centre of government. This will involve comprehensive, zero-based reviews of their activities and services, including identifying opportunities for the rationalisation and sharing of services.

Transforming **6.24**   This Budget also announces that the Chancellor has asked Sir David Varney,
service delivery Executive Chairman of HMRC and former CEO of O₂, to advise him on the opportunities for
transforming the delivery of public services. Drawing on the Government's recent strategy
paper on service transformation, *Transformational Government, Enabled by Technology*,[3] the
review will look at how the channels through which services are delivered can be made more
efficient and responsive to the needs of citizens and businesses, for example by:

- exploiting the full potential of electronic service delivery, including by making wider use of online provision to make services more accessible to the public;

- raising the quality of service provided by call centres, learning from private sector experience in simplifying processes for call handling, improving support to front-line staff and rationalising the number of call centre sites;

- identifying the opportunities for more efficient and innovative use of local office networks, building on the success of many local authorities in basing service provision around the concept of "one-stop shop" local offices that provide a wide range of services from a single site; and

- exploring the scope to improve processes for handling identity.

Public investment

6.25   The 1998 CSR established public investment as a long-term priority, recognising its
crucial contribution to both public service delivery and the productivity and flexibility of the
wider economy. Since then, subsequent Spending Reviews have addressed the legacy of
under-investment in the nation's public infrastructure, increasing public sector net
investment from just 0.5 per cent of GDP in 1999 to a planned level of 2¼ per cent by the end
of the 2004 Spending Review period. This substantial growth in public investment has been
underpinned by the reforms to the budgetary and fiscal framework, including separate
capital and resource budgets, that safeguard long-run capital investment.

6.26   Together with private investment, public sector investment is delivering
improvements to capital assets across the public sector:

- the NHS is undertaking the biggest hospital building programme in history, with 57 new hospital schemes open since 1997, and another 31 under construction;

- 20,000 schools have benefited from building improvements, and the Government has committed to providing twenty-first century facilities for all secondary pupils and rebuilding or refurbishing half of all primary schools; and

- significant improvements have been achieved in the quality of the strategic road network.

---

[3] *Transformational Government, Enabled by Technology,* Cabinet Office, November 2005.

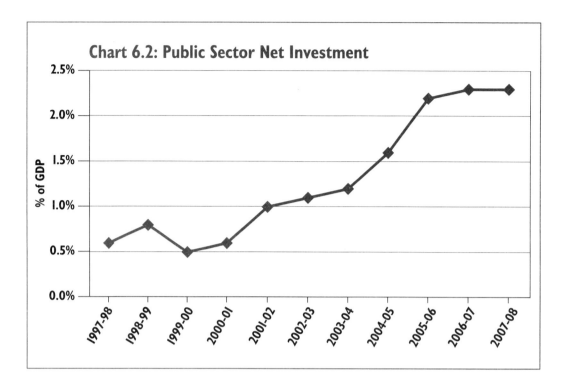

Chart 6.2: Public Sector Net Investment

Capital in the CSR 6.27 Building on the recommendations of the Lyons Review of Asset Management, the 2007 CSR will place a particular focus on the condition and management of the underlying asset stock as a basis for looking at investment decisions across the public sector. This will ensure that departments are realising the maximum value from the assets they hold by:

- disposing of assets that are no longer required for service delivery;

- improving the management and utilisation of assets retained in the public sector; and

- basing future investment decisions on a more complete assessment of the condition and performance of the existing asset base.

Asset disposals 6.28 The disposal of surplus assets and the full exploitation of under-utilised assets are crucial to ensuring the efficient use of public sector resources. The 2007 CSR will continue to drive forward the Government's objective of realising £30 billion of asset disposals by 2010. With asset disposals of £6.3 billion in 2004-05, the Government is on track to meet this objective, with strong progress made across government:

- the Ministry of Defence has sold over £250 million of assets in the last year and is conducting a strategic programme of estate rationalisation including: the merger and co-location of Royal Navy, Royal Air Force and Army bases; reviews of defence training sites, Royal Marines bases and defence airfields; and relocation and consolidation of defence estates in Greater London on to a number of core sites;

- the Department for Transport will, by 2008, dispose of around £185 million of land and property;

- the Home Office and its frontline partners are expecting to sell assets worth over £125 million during 2005-06. The Metropolitan Police have launched a programme to reconfigure their estate over the next decade, supporting wider policing initiatives and reflecting changing technology;

- the Department of Health has concluded a landmark deal with the Office of the Deputy Prime Minister to transfer a portfolio of former NHS hospital sites to English Partnerships, for an affordable housing initiative. The 96 sites, with land totalling 1,600 hectares and a gross book value of over £700 million, are expected to generate up to £1 billion in private sector investment by 2010; and

- the Department for Constitutional Affairs is taking forward an extensive plan to rationalise land and buildings held by the Court Service.

6.29   Building on this progress, departments will, as part of the 2007 CSR, set out plans that demonstrate how the Government will meet its ambition of realising £30 billion of asset disposals by 2010. In line with its commitment to retain only those assets which are required to meet its public service objectives, the Government will:

- complete the sale of Westinghouse for approximately £3 billion;

- look to realise value from our stake in Urenco;

- move ahead with the sale of the Tote;

- consider selling part of its stake in British Energy after completion of the Energy Review; and

- as described in Chapter 3, bring forward specific proposals for the sale or sharing of public sector spectrum by the end of 2006. Departments will also set targets for spectrum release in the CSR, supported by the publication of a strategy document early next year examining current spectrum use and forecasting future requirements.

Asset 6.30   Recognising that the efficient management of the £766 billion public sector asset
management stock is crucial for effective public service delivery, the 2007 CSR will build on the recommendations of the Lyons Review of Asset Management in 2004 by focussing on effective asset management as the basis for new investment decisions:

- a joint ODPM and HMT taskforce will work to improve the release of surplus public sector land for housing, aiming to identify an estimated 3,000 hectares of land that has the potential for development or redevelopment;

- to reinforce the effective management of assets across the public sector and to complement the approach being taken by central departments, ODPM are leading work to explore opportunities for strengthening asset management by local authorities – delivering improved outcomes for local communities through more efficient use of public assets and realising greater potential for disposal of surplus local assets; and

- in order to improve incentives for effective asset management, HM Treasury will consult departments on possible changes to the budgeting rules for impairments in order to remove any unnecessary barriers to asset disposal.

A zero-based **6.31** Since the 1998 CSR, significant strides have been made to address the backlogs in
approach to investment across the public sector. To ensure that new investment is focused where it will be
capital most effective and in the areas where it is needed to meet the long-term challenges, the 2007
CSR will introduce a more strategic approach to capital budgeting by:

- **updating the National Asset Register, as part of a comprehensive survey of
  the condition and performance of the public service asset base,** together with
  an assessment of what the sustained increases in investment have achieved at
  a sectoral level;

- introducing a more zero-based approach to setting capital baselines and capital
  budgets, to fully realise the benefits of separate capital and resource budgets; and

- requiring departments to prepare asset management strategies that build on
  the principles of asset management identified in the Lyons Review.

REFORMING THE DELIVERY OF PUBLIC SERVICES

6.32 Recognising that increased resources alone are not enough to transform the
performance of public services, the Government has established an ambitious programme of
reform designed to raise standards of service, reduce inequalities and increase user
satisfaction. Strengthening accountability, as part of an overall framework for devolved
decision making, is key to this reform agenda to ensure that public services are responsive to
the needs and preferences of individuals and communities. The successful implementation
of this ambitious reform programme is driven by the Government, frontline professionals,
communities and individuals, including through:

- *setting clear goals and establishing national standards,* to raise performance
  and increase accountability;

- *increasing frontline flexibility and capability,* giving front-line professionals
  greater operational autonomy and support to provide services that are
  personalised to users' needs;

- *promoting community and citizen engagement* – including in the design,
  delivery and governance of public services – to increase local responsiveness
  and accountability; and

- *empowering users,* to create personalised services which meet individual
  needs and preferences, including by exercising choice.

Clear goals and **6.33** Outcome-oriented targets and incentives for achievement, backed up by high quality
national regulation and inspection regimes, are the key approaches that the Government has used to
standards improve performance and enforce minimum standards across public services. Since their
introduction in the 1998 CSR, Public Service Agreements (PSAs) have been central to this
approach, setting national goals with unprecedented levels of transparency and focusing
energy and resource on the highest national priorities at a time when past investment in
public services has been low and capacity was weak. The 2004 Spending Review signalled an
evolution in the relationship between central government, local government, regional
organisations and the frontline, with a rationalisation of targets and an increased focus on
clearly measurable outcomes to enable greater freedom for providers to decide upon the
most effective method of delivery. Resulting improvements in performance, increased
capacity and the availability of transparent data provide impetus for a more devolved
approach and the 2007 CSR provides an opportunity to further progress this agenda.

Frontline flexibility and capability **6.34**   The Government recognises that public service professionals, operating within a framework of clear goals and national standards, need the flexibility to apply their first-hand knowledge and expertise to raise standards and deliver personalised services that are responsive to individual needs. In parallel with reforms designed to increase frontline flexibility, the Government has also taken steps to increase the capability of frontline professionals, and introduced measures designed to stimulate the spread of best practice through organisational collaborations and informal networks of professionals. Examples include:

- The Government has earmarked £220m in 2006-07 and £565m in 2007-08 within the core schools funding settlement to support personalisation and tailored support. This will enable intensive support for those who have fallen behind and will be focused on local authorities with the largest numbers of under-achieving and deprived children. This funding will support provision for catch-up classes and greater stretch for gifted and talented pupils; and

- Practice-Based Commissioning in the NHS, where GP practices will be able to directly commission care and services tailored to the specific needs of their patients. This should lead to local innovation resulting in higher quality services for patients and will mean that patients can benefit from a greater variety of services from a larger number of providers in settings that are closer to home or more convenient for them.

Community and citizen engagement **6.35**   Outcome-focused goals and national standards work best as part of an overall framework of devolution and local accountability, enabling communities and citizens to have a greater say in the design, delivery and governance of their local services. Therefore, the Government has been increasing opportunities for community engagement, for example through:

- Tenant Management Organisations (TMOs), where council tenants in England have a statutory right to manage collectively the council-owned housing in their area. TMOs may take on the running of council services such as organising repairs and maintenance, making sure buildings are kept clean and tidy, letting vacant homes and collecting rents and service charges. Currently, around 250 groups of tenants now manage 85,000 homes, with a further 30 groups currently in development;

- the national neighbourhood policing programme, where neighbourhood teams are developing innovative approaches to community engagement based on local needs. These range from regular neighbourhood panels and open meetings to surveys, door knocking and focused problem-solving events; and

- as part of national debate on the CSR set out in Box 6.1, the Government will be looking to identify further opportunities to increase public and user engagement as a driver for improving public service delivery.

Empowering users **6.36** Improving public service outcomes, in health, education and elsewhere, is as dependent on the actions of users themselves as on the work of public service professionals. In recognition of this, the Government is committed to providing users with new mechanisms to influence service design and delivery, so that services are more personalised to their diverse needs and preferences. For example:

- in social care, the Government is piloting Individual Budgets for older and disabled people to give service users greater control and choice over their support. Service users eligible for Individual Budgets will be allocated a transparent sum or 'budget' based on the resources that would typically have been spent on that individual. Using this nominal 'budget' the service user can then select a package of services more tailored to their specific needs; and

- the Department of Health is giving NHS patients greater choice over when, where and how they are treated, and increasingly over what treatment they receive. Since January 2006 patients have been offered the choice of at least four hospitals and a booked appointment when they need a referral for elective care. By 2008 choice will widen even further, with patients able to choose any healthcare provider that meets NHS standards and can provide care within the price the NHS is prepared to pay.

Increasing Personalisation **6.37** A number of the long term trends and challenges that will shape public services over the next decade are likely to drive an increased need for, and provide opportunities to deliver, more responsive public services. Increasing user expectations of public services, the needs of an increasingly diverse population and the necessity to equip all individuals to compete in a globalising world will require us to move further away from "one size fits all" and towards public services which deliver for each individual. At the same time technological progress is opening up new opportunities to personalise public services, including new ways to access services and more scope to tailor delivery to individuals' needs. However, technology alone is insufficient. The capacity and capability of both frontline professionals and users of services themselves to work together to secure better more responsive services are also crucial. In the CSR, the Government will examine how to achieve more personalised services.

Inspection Reform **6.38** Budget 2005 outlined the Government's strategy for inspection reform, building on the policy outlined in July 2003.[4] Significant progress has already been made, with legislation to establish the first of the new inspectorates in the areas of justice, community safety and custody and children's services, education and learning already before Parliament. The structural mergers of the inspectorates will in themselves encourage better joint working between inspection functions that focus on similar service areas and service users. In addition, the new inspection bodies being created will adopt common legal powers and duties that will better facilitate the sharing of information and allow for further coordination and alignment of inspection schedules. The reforms will also give inspectorates the duty to challenge proposals made by other inspectorates that may represent an unreasonable burden on inspected bodies. These new powers will make real the Government's ambition that inspection activity be rationalised.

6.39 These reforms will lead to a reduction in overall inspection activity, giving the best performers as much freedom as possible, ensuring appropriate and swift action to tackle poor performance and driving improvement across public services. As a result, the Government is working with public service inspectorates to assess more fully the scope for reducing inspectorate expenditure by around a third over the medium term as overall inspectorate activity is reformed, rationalised and ultimately reduced.

---

[4] *Inspecting for Improvement: developing a customer focused approach*, Office of Public Sector Reform, July 2003.

Regional Funding Allocations

6.40 In July 2005 the Government published indicative regional funding allocations across the inter-related areas of transport, housing and economic development to enable regions to better align their strategies and enhance their input into public spending decisions that affect the regions. Each region has now submitted advice to the Government on their priorities within these allocations. The advice sets out for the first time a clear list of regional transport priorities within the indicative allocations, demonstrates widespread agreement within each region on strategic priorities, and succeeds in strengthening the alignment between Regional Economic and Spatial Strategies. The Government is now considering the advice provided by the regions and will set out in due course how it will be utilised and developed upon in the Comprehensive Spending Review process.

6.41 Budget 2005 announced new measures to strengthen devolution, performance management and accountability in the Regional Development Agencies (RDAs). The first of these, an independent assessment conducted by the National Audit Office and based on the Initial Performance Assessment (IPA) of the London Development Agency (LDA) has been introduced for the RDAs on a rolling basis during 2005-06. Initial findings from the IPA exercise will be available towards the end of summer and will inform the Government's wider assessment of subnational performance ahead of the Comprehensive Spending Review 2007.

Review of Government Offices

6.42 The Review of Government Offices (GOs) published alongside this Budget will provide an enhanced opportunity for the significant decentralisation and devolution of Government activity. It proposes a smaller, more strategic role for the GOs:

- transforming the way central Government focuses on places, by working with local and regional partners to determine priorities and stretch performance;

- translating Departmental policies into operational delivery, by providing focussed policy and performance feedback to departments about regional delivery challenges and solutions in delivering Public Service Agreements (PSAs); and

- supporting and challenging regional strategies to improve their quality and consistency.

6.43 To meet the challenge of this new role the Review finds that the GO network must make a transformational change refocusing more clearly on priority outcomes and seizing the opportunity to streamline activity by, inter alia, reducing overall staff by at least 33 per cent.

The Third Sector

6.44 The third sector, encompassing voluntary and community organisations, charities, social enterprises, co-operatives and mutuals, has a key role to play in identifying more effective ways of engaging citizens and delivering more innovative, responsive and personalised services.[5] Both the *Welfare Reform Green Paper* and the *Out of Hospital Care White Paper* highlighted the potential for the sector to play an even greater role, and the Government will outline next steps to build capacity and promote third sector involvement in public services through three forthcoming documents:

- the Government's response to the Public Accounts Committee (PAC) report *Working with the Voluntary Sector;*[6]

- the publication of a comprehensive cross-government action plan for achieving a step-change in the level of public services delivered by the third sector (co-ordinated by the Home Office); and

- the Government's action plan for social enterprise, led by DTI.

---

[5] The wider role of the third sector is discussed in Chapter 5.
[6] 32nd Report, 2005-06 session – HC 717.

6.45   As a further step towards supporting the third sector **this Budget announces the participation of Cumbria, Portsmouth, Tower Hamlets and Dorset Councils as local area pathfinders** who have committed to explore ways in which the third sector can add value to the delivery of local services. The pathfinders' approaches will be shared with other councils through key national partners.

6.46   The Government is also committed to supporting the development of the sector's infrastructure and capacity through the Capacity Builders programme and the Futurebuilders Fund which has now made 110 investments totalling £37.2 million since summer 2004. Revised funding guidance *'Improving financial relationships with the third sector'* will also be published in the spring – including new guidance on best practice in funding full costs and clarification of the clawback rule which covers the conditions that are placed on grants provided for the acquisition or improvement of assets.

6.47   The Government wants to ensure that the third sector is consulted and recognised throughout the CSR process. As well as the long-term policy review on the future role of the third sector in social and economic regeneration, the Government will run a series of evidence-based workshops examining best practice in third sector delivery of public services, including in health, education, employment and crime.

Local   **6.48**   Co-ordinated action at a local level offers an opportunity to bring many of these
government themes together to deliver both national priorities, embodied in PSAs, and local priorities. Consideration of the strategic role of local government, and the relationship between local authorities and their partners, are key to this. Sir Michael Lyons is examining these issues as part of his Inquiry into Local Government and is due to publish a paper on the role and function of local government later in the spring.

6.49   Local Area Agreements (LAAs), first introduced in April 2005 for 20 upper and single tier authorities, play a key role in improving the delivery of both national and local public service outcomes, by offering authorities the chance to pool a wide range of area-based funding streams in a single payment and performance framework, encouraging a coherent dialogue between central and local government and its partners, communities, individual users and the voluntary and community sector. The outcome of the Review of Government Offices (GOs) offers a crucial opportunity to build on the GOs' strategic role in the development, negotiation and ongoing management of LAAs.

6.50   LAAs will be extended in 2006-07 to a further 66 authorities, due to be signed off by Ministers shortly. From 2007-08, when all upper or single tier authorities will have the opportunity to negotiate an LAA, some area-based funding streams will be automatically pooled within LAAs, to increase the efficiency of the performance monitoring arrangements at both a central Government and local level.

6.51   In the context of the Local Government White Paper, due to be published in June, and the CSR, the Government will be considering how other area-based funding streams could be included in LAAs to further improve the efficiency and delivery of outcomes across public services.

DELIVERING BETTER OUTCOMES ACROSS PUBLIC SERVICES

Education **6.52**   The 2004 Spending Review provided for education spending in England to increase by an annual average of 4.4 per cent in real terms, building on sustained high levels of investment in education since 1997. Across the system and at all levels there have been substantial improvements in attainment, with, for example, 2005 GCSE results showing the biggest year on year increase for a decade, and 56.3 per cent of pupils now achieving five or more grades A*-C. However, there remain significant gaps in attainment by socio-economic background, ethnicity, and gender – this year over 60 per cent of girls achieved five or more grades A*-C at GCSE, but only around 50 per cent of boys reached this standard.

6.53   Personalisation – tailoring teaching and wider support to the needs of individual pupils – is key to tackling these gaps. Research clearly suggests that tailored teaching – whether in a traditional whole class setting or for smaller groups or individuals – can have a strong positive impact on attainment. Wider activities beyond the curriculum can also boost aspirations and attainment. The Government is committed to build on the available evidence base by ensuring that schools and teachers have access to the best possible information about how to implement effective personalisation. **The Secretary of State for Education has therefore asked Christine Gilbert, Chief Executive of Tower Hamlets local authority, to lead a Review to ensure that personalised learning is a reality in every classroom and set out a vision for how teaching and learning should develop between now and 2020.** The review will report back to the Secretary of State for Education by the end of the year.

The long-term **6.54**   Closing gaps in attainment and ensuring that all children reach their potential is a **challenge** long-term challenge, but one that it is essential to meet if the UK is to prosper in an increasingly competitive global economy.

6.55   Higher levels of resource and capital per pupil in the maintained sector, rising from £2,500 in 1997 to £5,000 in 2005-06, are allowing an increasing number of state schools to offer a wider range of individual attention and support. However, the higher overall level of resources in the independent sector – an average of £8,000 per pupil in private sector day schools in 2005-06 – means that a minority of pupils still benefit from a greater depth and breadth of support than is available to many in the state sector.

6.56   The Government's long-term ambition is for all pupils to have access to the same level of support and opportunities that are currently available to pupils in the independent sector. The Government will therefore aim – over time, and adjusting for inflation – to increase funding per pupil towards today's private sector day school levels. As a first step towards this long-term goal, the Government will match today's levels of private sector per pupil capital investment[7] by the end of the CSR. **Budget 2006 therefore announces that school capital investment will rise from £6.4 billion in 2007-08 to £8.0 billion by 2010-11.** This unprecedented level of investment will support the Government's commitment to transform the schools estate by providing 21st century facilities for all secondary school pupils through Building Schools for the Future, and by rebuilding and refurbishing at least half of all primary schools through the primary schools capital programme first announced in Budget 2005.

6.57   As the Government moves towards this long-term ambition, it will continue to support effective personalisation by providing resources targeted according to need, to enable intensive support for those who need it most. Effective personalisation also requires a

---

[7] Estimated at £975 per pupil in 2005-06, excluding spend specifically on boarding accommodation.

highly skilled teaching workforce and a high quality school environment which gives teachers the flexibility to teach in different ways. There is also an important role for extended services and activities in providing all pupils with the opportunities to reach their full potential.

Resources for personalisation
6.58   The Government has already earmarked £220 million in 2006-07 and £565 million in 2007-08 within the core schools funding settlement to support personalisation and tailored support. This will enable intensive support for those who have fallen behind and will be focused on local authorities with the largest numbers of underachieving and deprived children. **Budget 2006 announces additional resources of £220 million in 2006-07 and £365 million in 2007-08 to provide further support for personalisation in schools in England.** In recognition of the important role that personalisation can play in closing gaps in attainment, a significant proportion of this funding will be targeted towards schools with low prior attainment and high levels of deprivation. This funding will go directly to schools through a reformed and more targeted School Standards Grant (SSG) – increasing direct payments for an average primary school from £31,000 in 2005-06 to a total of £39,500 in 2006-07 and £44,000 in 2007-08, and for an average secondary school from £98,000 in 2005-06 to a total of £150,000 in 2006-07 and £190,000 in 2007-08. Payments to the largest secondary schools in the most challenging circumstances through the reformed SSG and the former Leadership Incentive Grant[8] will rise to over £500,000 in 2007-08, compared to £267,000 in 2005-06.

6.59   Schools will be able to use this funding to support increased personalisation by, for example, improving the skills and knowledge of their teaching staff, and by supporting access to extended activities for pupils who may otherwise not benefit from the full range of opportunities that extended schools can offer.

6.60   Budget 2006 also announces the following specific measures to support schools in providing more personalised teaching and learning:

- The Government's ambition is to create an education and training environment that delivers the best in science teaching and learning at every stage.[9] **Budget 2006 announces funding for a nationwide pilot of 250 after school science clubs for small groups of Key Stage 3 pupils with interest and potential in science, to offer an engaging and intellectually stretching programme of science to supplement the school's science curriculum.**

- Budget 2005 announced £50 million over the next two years for schools in deprived areas to provide home access to Information and Communication Technology (ICT) for pupils with the greatest need. Schools are increasingly providing online resources to support their pupils learning and **Budget 2006 therefore announces additional revenue funding of £10 million over the next two years to ensure that pupils benefiting from this scheme have access to the internet.**

Schools workforce
6.61   Delivering effective personalisation requires a high quality and highly skilled teaching workforce. The Training and Development Agency for schools is reviewing the framework of professional standards for classroom teachers, and has recently completed consultation on a draft revised set of professional standards. The new standards, which strengthen the requirements for teachers to develop the skills they need to effectively deliver personalised learning, will be available to schools from September 2006.

---

[8] Now incorporated in School Development Grant.

[9] *The Science and Innovation Investment Framework 2004-2014,* HM Treasury, DTI and DfES 2004.

Quality school **6.62**   Investment in schools buildings is essential to provide high quality learning
environments environments that give teachers the flexibility they need to deliver personalised learning.
Budget 2005 announced additional funding of £150 million in 2008-09 and £500 million in
2009-10 to support a 15-year programme to equip primary schools to deliver personalised
learning and play a lead role at the heart of their communities. DfES and HM Treasury have
recently published a consultation document seeking views on the Government's proposed
approach to delivering this investment. The document invites stakeholders to comment on a
number of key issues, including how capital investment can most effectively support primary
schools in contributing to the Every Child Matters agenda by increasingly delivering
integrated services for children.[10]

Health **6.63**   The Government is half-way through a ten-year NHS improvement programme, a
programme based upon major investment coupled with service reform. Since 1997 this
Government has delivered a record increase in investment in the NHS. By 2007-8 spending
will have risen to £92 billion compared with £33 billion in 1996-97. Funding for health
services has increased by 7 per cent per annum on average in real terms since 2002. With
these levels of funding, the NHS should be able to plan for and achieve financial balance
every year. However, while most NHS bodies are living within their budget, a minority of
organisations have built up significant deficits. The Government is taking urgent action to
address this, and turnaround specialists have been appointed to help improve financial
management in organisations with the biggest problems.

6.64   In line with the government's commitment, by 2007-08 the UK is likely to be spending
at least the European average share of GDP on health. Record levels of investment have
enabled us to make significant progress on improving services:

- there are 27,000 more doctors and 79,000 more nurses since 1997 and the
  biggest NHS hospital building programme in history;

- the government set itself a target to ensure that the maximum wait from GP
  referral to hospital treatment is no more than 18 weeks by 2008. In 1997 people
  waited over 18 months to see a specialist. Now few patients wait over six
  months, with the average wait being nine weeks;

- over 98 per cent of those attending accident and emergency units are now
  seen within 4 hours which is up from 80 per cent in 2001-02; and

- heart disease and cancer have been significantly reduced and 99 per cent of
  people with suspected cancers are seen by a specialist within 2 weeks of an
  urgent GP referral.

6.65   Alongside record levels of investment in the NHS the Government has introduced far-
reaching service reform to improve services for patients and increase patient choice including:

- NHS Foundation Trusts, a new type of NHS trust in England, which have been
  created to devolve decision-making from central government to local
  organisations and communities. Local people and staff directly elect
  representatives to serve on the Board of Governors;

- payment by results, which more closely links payment to activity. It means
  that hospitals will be funded in a consistent way for the work which they do.
  As payment will follow patients it will also ensure that services offered will
  more closely reflect patients' needs; and

---

[10] *Every Child Matters: Primary capital programme*, DfES, March 2005

- patient choice, which will mean NHS services becoming more personalised and tailored to individual needs. Patients now have the right to choose from at least 4 to 5 different healthcare providers.

Security **6.66**   A priority of the CSR will be to examine the UK's future security requirements. **The Government will therefore conduct a review of its counter-terrorism and security strategies.** This review will look at existing governance structures and consider the case for a single security budget.

6.67   Between 1997-98 and 2007-08, spending by the Home Office on crime, justice, security and communities will have risen by 75 per cent in real terms. To lock in this increased funding, **Budget 2006 announces as part of the CSR an early spending settlement for the Home Office which maintains the Home Office's 2007-08 Departmental Expenditure Limit in real terms over the years 2008-09, 2009-10 and 2010-11.** In the context of continued global uncertainty and security challenges at home, this funding agreement provides the Home Office with the long-term certainty needed to lead the fight against crime and terrorism. This settlement guarantees that the Home Office will be able to retain the efficiency gains from its ambitious value for money programme, including police force reform and restructuring, for reinvestment to deliver further improvements in front-line policing. Further, the Home Office will be able to continue ambitious reform programmes of the immigration and offender management systems.

6.68   The first responsibility of a government is to protect its citizens and ensure their security. The 2005 Pre-Budget Report announced significant further resources for the fight against terrorism, including an additional £85 million to advance the ongoing expansion of the security and intelligence agencies and extending the availability of the Counter-Terrorism Pool beyond 2005-06. **This Budget announces the allocation of £42.5 million to the Home Office from the Pool to help fund emerging counter-terrorism priorities in 2006-07 and 2007-08.**

Special Reserve **6.69**   International peace support operations continue to play a key role in global stability. The United Kingdom's continued engagement in these operations, either through direct contribution of military or civilian personnel or through the work of international organisations, is an important component in achieving our foreign, defence and development policy objectives. The Government provided £980 million for the Special Reserve in 2005-06 as a prudent measure to ensure the necessary funding for our continuing international commitments. **Budget 2006 announces £800 million of provision for the Special Reserve in 2006-07, set aside from within existing public spending plans, to help meet the costs of Iraq, Afghanistan and other international commitments and further allocates £200 million from the Reserves in 2006-07 to support ongoing peacekeeping activity across the world through the Global Conflict Prevention Pool.**

6.70   Our armed forces are committed to continuous modernization to ensure their effectiveness in a rapidly changing world. **This Budget announces a further £100 million funding for the Ministry of Defence in 2006-07 to support the ongoing programme through which our forces are reshaping themselves for the future security environment.**

Neighbourhood policing **6.71**   The 2004 Spending Review provided funding for the recruitment of Police Community Support Officers (PCSOs) to support the nationwide roll-out of neighbourhood policing by 2008. By September 2005 there were 6,324 PCSOs in England and Wales, an increase of 53 per cent since September 2004. In 2005, the Home Secretary announced funding through the Neighbourhood Policing Fund of £88 million in 2006-07 and £340 million in 2007-08 for further PCSO recruitment to complete the delivery of neighbourhood policing in every area. **This Budget now provides a further £100 million to bring PCSO recruitment to 16,000 by April 2007, so that every area will have neighbourhood policing by that date, a year ahead of previous plans.** This will also fund development of a new service to publish local crime and police performance data on a regular basis, building on the current review of crime statistics.

Olympics and Sport

6.72 In July 2005, the International Olympic Committee (IOC) announced that London had been awarded the 2012 Olympic and Paralympic Games. The Government believes that the Olympics is a great opportunity to showcase our best British athletes and that the Games provide opportunities and benefits for sport that are can be shared across all of the UK.

6.73 The Government wants to ensure that Team GB inspire, motivate and have the best chance of success in a British Olympics. **In continuing partnership with the Lottery the Government has decided to provide funding of £200 million for elite athletes, including paralympic athletes, for the next seven years, helping them to achieve their medal ambitions.** This is an addition to £300 million that has already been committed from the National Lottery and will fully fund the elite athlete programme in the run up to the 2008 Olympics in Beijing. However, the Government wants to see commercial sponsorship play a role in supporting elite athletes. The Department for Culture, Media and Sport and UK Sport will bring forward proposals in the Pre-Budget Report to lever in an additional £100 million of commercial sponsorship.

6.74 To encourage elite sportsmen and women to put something back into grassroots sport and inspire young people to take up sport, **this Budget announces £2 million will be made available over two years from 2006-07 to fund an extension of the successful Sporting Champions Scheme.** Because today's children and young people will play a huge part in London 2012, there will also be **£6 million over two years from 2006-07 to fund School Sport Festivals; and a further £7 million in 2006-07 for the National Sports Foundation and their 2012 Kids programme** which will fund projects including those developed and chosen by young people.

7 PROTECTING THE ENVIRONMENT

The Government is committed to delivering a strong economy based not just on high and stable levels of growth and employment but also on high standards of environmental care. This Budget sets out the next stage in the Government's strategy for tackling the global challenge of climate change including:

- encouraging energy efficiency in the business sector through **an increase in the climate change levy, in line with inflation, from 1 April 2007**;

- further measures to improve household energy efficiency, **including an extra 250,000 installations of subsidised insulation in British homes over the next two years, funding for local authority-led publicity and incentive schemes, trialling the use of 'smart' energy meters, and a new voluntary initiative with major retailers to reduce the energy use of consumer electronics**;

- the development of a **new National Institute of Energy Technologies, in partnership with the private sector**, to better leverage the substantial public sector funding of energy research;

- further support for the development of alternative energy sources, including an **additional £50 million to develop microgeneration technologies and the launch of a consultation document on the barriers to large-scale commercial deployment in the UK of carbon capture and storage**;

- **further detail on the Renewable Transport Fuel Obligation to increase the use of biofuels** – with the obligation set at 2.5 per cent in 2008-09 and 3.75 per cent in 2009-10, **and the biofuels duty incentive maintained at 20 pence per litre in 2008-09**;

- **reforms to vehicle excise duty (VED) to sharpen environmental incentives** including reducing the rate to zero for cars with the very lowest carbon emissions and introducing a new top band for the most polluting new cars. 50 per cent of cars will see their VED frozen or reduced; and

- **the deferral to 1 September 2006 of the inflation-only increase in main road fuel duties, reflecting continuing volatility in the oil market; and the same increase of 1.25 pence per litre, also from 1 September 2006, in duty for rebated fuels,** maintaining the differential with main fuel duty rates to support the Oils Strategy.

The Budget also reports on the Government's strategy for tackling other environmental challenges, including:

- **an increase in the value of the landfill tax credit scheme to £60 million in 2006-07** with a challenge to the private and voluntary sector partners in the scheme to provide additional opportunities for young people to volunteer on environmental projects; and

- **a freeze in the rate of the aggregates levy.**

Sustainable development 7.1 The Government is committed to delivering strong, stable and sustainable economic growth. To achieve this aim – for current and succeeding generations – it is crucial to take care of the natural environment and the resources on which economic activity depends. Economic growth need not be at the expense of the environment. Instead it must be based on the principles sustainable development: integrating economic prosperity with environmental protection and social equity.

7.2 Modern patterns of production and consumption are putting greater pressure on the environment and greater demand on the world's natural resources. Managing this increasing pressure has been identified in the Government's Comprehensive Spending Review (CSR 2007) as one of the principal long-term challenges facing the UK. Analysis being undertaken as part of the CSR work will provide valuable evidence to inform future action.

7.3 There are a number of environmental challenges facing the UK:

- *tackling climate change*, and reducing emissions of greenhouse gases to minimise their environmental costs;

- *improving air quality*, to ensure that air pollutants are maintained below levels that could pose a risk to human health;

- *improving waste management*, by increasing the efficiency of resource use and enabling waste to be reused or recycled to deliver economic value; and

- *protecting the countryside and natural resources*, to ensure they are sustainable economically, socially and physically.

7.4 Many environmental challenges are global and so can only be effectively tackled through co-ordinated international action. For example, the UK accounts for only 2 per cent of global carbon dioxide emissions, and this figure is expected to fall further to 1.5 per cent by 2020. Aspects of air and water quality are also an international problem, requiring multilateral intervention to ensure that the health and environmental impacts of pollution are minimised. The UK is therefore working with both developed and developing economies to reduce emissions of pollutants in a coordinated way and to encourage the development of sustainable technologies, and patterns of production to achieve this.

7.5 At the same time, however, domestic action is also needed to enable the UK to meet these environmental challenges. The Government believes that this can be done in a way that actively supports increased productivity and growth. Key to this is improving the flexibility of businesses and individuals to respond to changing circumstances. This can be achieved through both short-term policy measures and longer-term innovation and technological change. For example, improving energy efficiency is often an effective way for companies and households to reduce both emissions and energy costs, while the development of environmental technologies can not only help to enhance energy, waste and water efficiency but may also enable UK firms to gain competitive advantage.

Government intervention 7.6 Every section of society – business, individuals and government – has a role to play in helping to meet the UK's climate change and other environmental goals. For its part, the Government recognises that it is required to take action where market failure prevents long-term economic and environmental consequences from being taken into account in decision making. A key aim of government intervention is to encourage behavioural change across all sectors, particularly with regard to the use of energy, waste and water. Investment to increase efficiency in these areas is often a cost-effective option for businesses and households, but short-term cost considerations and market failures can create barriers to the take up of more efficient alternatives. Intervention can correct these market failures, ensuring the implementation of the 'Polluter Pays' principle in which environmental costs are fully internalised in economic decisions.

Principled   **7.7**   The Government set out its framework for intervention to meet environmental
approach   objectives in its *Statement of Intent on Environmental Taxation* in 1997 and the Treasury paper, *Tax and the Environment,* published in 2002. In the 2005 Pre-Budget Report the Government reiterated the criteria that need to be considered when deciding whether government intervention is needed and, if so, what the action should be:

- the decision to take action must be evidence-based;

- any intervention to tackle environmental challenges must take place at the appropriate level;

- action to protect the environment must take account of wider economic and social objectives;

- action on the environment must be part of a long-term strategy;

- the right instrument must be chosen to meet each particular objective; and

- where tax is used, it will aim to shift the burden of tax from 'goods' to 'bads'.

7.8   Within this framework, the Government has taken significant action to address environmental challenges since 1997. A key feature of the Government's approach has been the use of a variety of different policy instruments to correct market failures and deliver behavioural change. These instruments include: information schemes, voluntary mechanisms, regulation, spending programmes, economic instruments and tradable permit schemes.

7.9   Within this range of measures, fiscal instruments have a role to play. In particular, tax can be an effective way to implement the 'Polluter Pays' principle. Fiscal instruments can also provide a strong signalling effect and be a way to correct specific market failures in particular sectors. Public spending can also have an important effect in catalysing behavioural change but in some cases risks subsidising activity that would happen anyway. Where these alternatives are not available, regulation can offer an effective means to improve environmental standards, especially where price signals by themselves are too weak to achieve the behavioural changes needed to safeguard natural resources efficiently. However, it is essential that such regulation offers businesses the clarity, scope and lead times needed to respond flexibly and innovate to meet new environmental standards.

Progress to date

7.10   Using this framework and these approaches, the Government has made significant progress in tackling climate change. UK greenhouse gas emissions fell by about 14.5 per cent between 1990 and 2004. The UK is therefore on track to meet its Kyoto commitment to reduce greenhouse gas emissions by an average of 12.5 per cent compared with 1990 levels over the years 2008 to 2012. Carbon dioxide emissions, which accounted for 85 per cent of UK greenhouse gas emissions in 2004, also fell between 1990 and 2002, while the economy grew by around 35 per cent – showing that reductions in emissions can be achieved alongside economic growth. Carbon dioxide emissions increased between 2002 and 2004, largely due to increases in emissions from power generation resulting from changes in the relative prices of gas and coal, but the downward trend is projected to resume in future years.

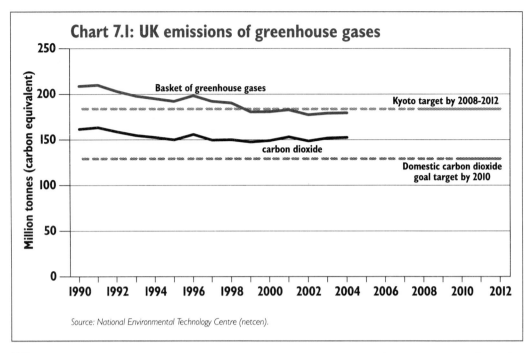

Chart 7.1: UK emissions of greenhouse gases

Source: National Environmental Technology Centre (netcen).

7.11 Against a backdrop of increasing economic activity, the Government's wider environmental policy has also delivered significant results:

- fuel duty and vehicle tax incentives have contributed to significant reductions in the key pollutants affecting air quality. Between 1997 and 2003, nitrous oxides emissions were reduced by 22 per cent, sulphur dioxide emissions were reduced by 41 per cent and particulates (PM10) were reduced by 30 per cent;

- increasing the standard rate of landfill tax has contributed to a sharp fall in the volume of waste disposed to landfill, down 28 per cent between 1997 and 2005;

- the introduction of the aggregates levy has resulted in an increase in the production of recycled aggregate in England by over 3 million tonnes between 2001 and 2003; and

- in 2004, 70 per cent of English rivers were of good biological quality and 62 per cent were of good chemical quality, compared to 60 per cent and 43 per cent respectively in 1990.

TACKLING THE GLOBAL CHALLENGE OF CLIMATE CHANGE

7.12 Climate change is the most pressing environmental issue the world faces. Global atmospheric temperatures have risen by about 0.7 degrees celsius over the last 100 years, with the majority of this rise occurring since the 1970s. Depending on the amount of greenhouse gases emitted and the sensitivity of the climate system, the Intergovernmental Panel on Climate Change (IPCC) predicts that global average temperatures could rise by between 1.4 and 5.8 degrees celsius by the end of the century. If climate change is not tackled, the consequences could be extremely damaging for the world economy. The IPCC estimates that the global economic costs of an increase in average global temperature of 2.5 degrees celsius could be between 1.5 and 2 per cent of global GDP per year.

Review of the economics of climate change   **7.13**   To tackle climate change effectively, the Government believes that the evidence base must continue to be improved. That is why the Government has set up a review to examine the global economics of climate change led by Sir Nicholas Stern, Head of the Government Economic Service and Adviser to the Government on the economics of climate change and development. The Review – which is due to report to the Prime Minister and Chancellor of the Exchequer in autumn 2006 – will enhance understanding of the consequences of climate change in both developed and developing countries. It will also assess how this analysis applies to the specific case of the UK, in the context of its existing climate change goals.

Box 7.1: Review of the economics of climate change

Sir Nicholas Stern outlined the conclusions of the review so far at a lecture to the Oxford Institute of Economic Policy, on 31 January 2006, including that:

- the problem is complex. Unlike other environmental problems, such as city smog or water pollution, climate change is global in both its cause and its effects. The long time horizons also mean that the effects are not immediately tangible;

- there is a serious risk of adverse consequences. Some risks, if they were to be realised, could be irreversible and accelerate the process of global warming – for example, the release of greenhouse gases from thawing permafrost. These impacts may justify more extensive action now to avoid the risk of such events occurring;

- the most severe impacts of climate change are likely to be felt in some of the poorest countries with the smallest margins for adjustment. Millions are at risk of being pushed back into poverty, of facing hunger and being forced to migrate;

- the current pathway of emissions is unsustainable in terms of its consequences for climate change. Urgent action is necessary to move economies onto low-carbon growth pathways, including the development and deployment of low-carbon technologies; and

- climate change requires an international response based on a shared understanding of the implications. Effective action requires both leadership from the world's richest nations, and the involvement of the fast-growing developing countries.

Tackling climate change through international action

7.14   Climate change and energy are global issues with global consequences. So national action to tackle climate change needs to take place as part of a concerted international effort. The UN Framework Convention on Climate Change and the Kyoto Protocol together provide a multilateral context for this action and ensure that progress towards reducing greenhouse gas emissions can be made in a cost-effective way without undermining national competitiveness.

Gleneagles agreement   **7.15**   To drive forward multilateral action, the Government championed climate change through its G8 and EU presidencies during 2005 and will continue to take the lead internationally on this issue. Significant steps were taken at the Gleneagles Summit in July 2005 where G8 leaders agreed to a range of actions and principles for tackling climate change, as set out in the Gleneagles Communiqué and Plan of Action. The G8 leaders formally recognised that climate change is a serious and long-term challenge, caused by human activity, which demands an urgent response. They also committed to work together on a range of global energy issues. In addition, the G8 acknowledged the importance of engaging with developing countries to ensure that they can also meet their energy needs in a sustainable way. Indeed, the leaders of a number of fast-growing economies – China, India, Brazil, South Africa and Mexico – also attended the G8 Summit and set out their own statement on the importance of international cooperation to tackle climate change. They agreed to join G8 countries in taking forward a Dialogue on Climate Change, Clean Energy and Sustainable Development and the first meeting of the Dialogue took place on 1 November 2005. Mexico has offered to host the next meeting in 2006.

World Bank Energy Investment Framework 7.16   The World Bank is playing a key role in supporting both the Gleneagles Dialogue and the Plan of Action by working with the Regional Development Banks to develop a framework for energy investment in developing countries. **At the World Bank meeting in April, the UK will propose a $20 billion target for leveraging public and private investment into alternative sources of energy, energy efficiency and adaption to climate change in developing countries.** The International Energy Agency is also developing its work on energy efficiency, power generation and alternative energy strategies. These international institutions will play a key role, alongside efforts by the UK and other donors, in helping the poorest and most vulnerable countries plan for the effects of climate change.

EU ETS 7.17   The UK Government set up the first national economy-wide emissions trading scheme, then helped lead implementation of the first international carbon-trading mechanism, the EU Emissions Trading Scheme (EU ETS). The EU ETS sets a limit on carbon emissions for 12,000 installations in major industrial sectors across the 25 EU Member States, including over 1,000 sites in the UK. Phase One of the EU ETS began in January 2005 and will deliver significant carbon savings in an effective way – helping Member States to move towards their Kyoto emissions reduction targets. These targets will have to be met during Phase Two of EU ETS (2008-2012).

7.18   Building on the experience so far of Phase One, a public consultation on Phase Two of the EU ETS was held during summer 2005 and the UK's draft National Allocation Plan will be published shortly. Given that the EU represents around a quarter of total global emissions, a well-designed trading scheme can be a cost-effective instrument to reduce emissions. That is why the UK is working with other EU Member States to secure agreement on a robust scheme that extends beyond 2012. **The Chancellor has written today to EU Finance Ministers to highlight the economic case for extending and strengthening the EU ETS beyond 2012 as the core of a global carbon market.**

Tackling climate change through domestic action

7.19   The UK has also led international efforts to tackle climate change through domestic action. Several important measures have been put in place since 1997 – including the climate change levy and climate change agreements, the Renewables Obligation, fuel duty differentials and reforms to vehicle excise duty and company car tax, as well as regulatory and spending programmes. These have helped to tackle climate change while enabling the UK economy to maintain strong levels of growth. Further domestic action to tackle climate change needs to continue to support economic growth, and take account of future energy market conditions which may be more difficult than in the recent past. This reinforces the importance of encouraging energy efficiency and exploring the potential of low-carbon technologies.

Climate Change Programme Review 7.20   The Government is shortly to publish the Climate Change Programme Review (CCPR). The CCPR will assess the performance of the Government's Climate Change Programme to date and set out how the UK can move towards a 20 per cent reduction in carbon emissions by 2010, as part of an effort to reduce carbon emissions by around 60 per cent by 2050. Alongside this, the Government is also reviewing its energy policy through the Energy Review (discussed in more detail in Chapter 3).

Reducing emissions in the energy supply sector

7.21 As set out in Chapter 3, the Government recognises the importance of energy policy in supporting sustainable growth. One of the energy policy goals of the 2003 Energy White Paper was to put the UK on a path to a reduction of 60 per cent in carbon emissions against their 1990 level by about 2050. The current Energy Review will assess progress towards that goal. How the UK's demand for energy changes, and the ways the UK will meet that demand, will profoundly influence the future profile of the country's carbon emissions. It is important to take steps now to encourage and incentivise UK energy users to adopt behaviours that help put the UK on the appropriate path.

Research and   **7.22** The Government believes that the UK has the capacity to be a world leader in energy
Development technologies. In January 2006, the Government launched the Energy Research Partnership, which is designed to give strategic direction to UK energy research, development, demonstration and deployment. The Energy Research Partnership, under the joint chairmanship of Paul Golby, Chief Executive of E.On UK and Sir David King, the Government's Chief Scientific Adviser, is today committing itself to raising substantial sums of private investment to develop a new National Institute for Energy Technologies. This will bring a new level of focus, ambition and industrial collaboration to the UK's work in the field of energy science and engineering, particularly in relation to energy sources and technologies that reduce carbon emissions and contribute to the security of energy supply. The objective of the institution will be to build on existing funding structures in order to better leverage the already substantial funding for energy research in the public research base.

7.23 The new National Institute will be a 50:50 public-private partnership. The Energy Research Partnership has committed to raising substantial sums of private investment, sufficient for the Institute to have critical mass, and BP, EDF Energy, E.On and Shell have already announced their intention to be involved. The intention is that the private sector investment would be matched (up to a pre-determined limit) by public science and technology investment, building on the Research Councils' growing energy programmes – a model that has proved to be extremely effective with other large-scale research and development projects. The intention is to establish a virtual institute with a 'design life' of a finite period, probably a decade, with clear objectives specified over that time, and a strong public-private governance structure. Funding would be allocated competitively, using existing facilities where possible, but also building strong national and international linkages.

7.24 As set out in more detail in Chapter 3, the Budget announces that one of the first new Enterprise Capital Funds (venture capital funds run by the private sector using a mix of public and private funding) will provide early-stage funding for companies developing sustainable technologies. The fund will be able to invest a total of up to £30 million and will help bring forward innovative technologies that reduce natural resource use, improve energy efficiency, waste or pollution management.

Carbon capture   **7.25** Carbon abatement technologies, which enable fossil fuels to be used with
and storage substantially reduced carbon emissions, could make an important contribution to meeting the Government's energy policy objectives both domestically and globally. In particular, carbon capture and storage (CCS) is an innovative process by which the carbon in fossil fuels is captured as carbon dioxide and committed to long-term storage in geological formations. It is likely to be a critical technology in global carbon reduction strategies, particularly for countries with fast-growing economies and rapidly growing fossil fuel consumption. To advance the understanding of CCS, the Government is launching a consultation document on the barriers to wide-scale commercial deployment of CCS in the UK and the potential role of economic incentives in addressing those barriers.

7.26   In the 2005 Pre-Budget Report, the Government also announced that it intended to work collaboratively with Norway on the issues surrounding the costs of, and barriers to, CCS. A memorandum of understanding was signed by the Energy Minister, Malcolm Wicks, and the Norwegian Energy Minister, Odd Roger Enoksen, in November 2005. As part of this initiative a North Sea Basin Task Force was established, made up of public and private organisations from the North Sea rim, with the aim of developing common principles on the regulation and management of carbon dioxide storage under the North Sea. The inaugural meeting of the Task Force was recently held in Oslo. **Since the Pre-Budget Report, discussions between the British and Norwegian Governments, and key industry players, have revealed that the UK and Norway are facing similar decisions about the commercial deployment of CCS. Further discussions will take place later this year to share information on the feasibility and costs of CCS.**

Renewable energy   **7.27**   In January 2000 the Government announced a target for renewable sources to supply 10 per cent of UK electricity by 2010, subject to the costs being acceptable to the consumer. The key policy mechanism to meet this target is the Renewables Obligation which requires all licensed electricity suppliers to supply a specific and growing proportion of their electricity from certified renewable sources. The amount of energy coming from renewable sources is growing quickly and in 2004 3.6 per cent of electricity was generated from renewable sources, enough to power around 2.5 million households. The Energy Review is examining the costs and benefits of all forms of power generation including the case for further support for renewable energy sources.

Biomass   **7.28**   The burning of biomass, excluding energy from waste, currently makes a small contribution to the UK's energy balance – about 1.5 per cent of electricity and 1 per cent of heat. The Biomass Taskforce, led by Sir Ben Gill, was established in October 2004 with the aim of assisting the Government and the biomass industry to optimise the contribution of biomass energy to renewable energy targets, to sustainable farming and forestry, and to rural economy objectives. The Taskforce reported at the end of October 2005 and the Government has committed to publishing its full response by the end of April 2006.

Microgeneration   **7.29**   Microgeneration technologies, such as solar heating and micro-wind, have the potential to contribute towards both improved energy security and lower carbon emissions. In order to stimulate demand for these new technologies, the Government has already committed £30 million over the next three years to fund microgeneration installations and introduced reduced rates of VAT to encourage their adoption by individuals. DTI will publish a Microgeneration Strategy next week which will set out how the Government intends to address the various barriers preventing widespread take-up of these technologies through measures such as ensuring microgenerators are rewarded for exports of electricity, and working with planning authorities and the construction industry to develop positive approaches. **Budget 2006 announces a further £50 million for DTI's Low Carbon Buildings Programme with the aim of encouraging manufacture at higher scale leading to lower costs. This will help fund the installation of microgeneration technologies in a range of buildings including schools, social and local authority housing, businesses and public buildings.**

Energy Services Summit   **7.30**   The development of an energy services market could improve energy efficiency across all sectors of the economy and optimise benefits to consumers in the long term. Supplying energy on an energy services basis helps shift the focus of producers and consumers from the supply of units of energy to the supply of the overall services for which energy is used. It therefore offers the potential for reducing demand and carbon emissions. HM Treasury hosted a seminar in January 2006 to explore how Government and the business community can encourage the development of energy services markets in the UK. Following the seminar, an independent industry group will develop proposals on energy services and demand reduction which will feed into the Energy Review.

Reducing emissions in the business sector

Climate change levy

7.31   The climate change levy (CCL), introduced in 2001, seeks to encourage businesses to improve the efficiency with which they use energy. Improving energy efficiency is an effective way to lower emissions of carbon dioxide, and can also help businesses reduce their energy costs. To support competitiveness, the introduction of the CCL was accompanied by a 0.3 percentage point cut in employer national insurance contributions (NICs), which has led to a net reduction in tax liability for business. The full impact of the CCL, and also the other measures introduced as part of the CCL package, is summarised in Box 7.2 and set out in more detail in a separate report published today.

7.32   The CCL has had a significant impact on business energy demand which, in turn, has helped improve energy efficiency and reduce emissions. An independent evaluation by Cambridge Econometrics published alongside Budget 2005 concluded that the levy would deliver cumulative savings to 2005 of 16.5 million tonnes of carbon (MtC). By 2010, it is estimated that the levy will be saving around 3.5 MtC a year – well above the estimates made at its introduction. It is also estimated that by 2010 CCL will reduce energy demand in the economy as a whole by 2.9 per cent a year – and in the commercial and public sector by nearly 15 per cent a year – compared with the levy package not being in place. The reduction in energy demand, along with the 0.3 percentage point cut in employer NICs, has reduced costs for business. Cambridge Econometrics estimated that the CCL/NICs package will reduce overall unit costs for business by 0.13 per cent by 2010 compared with the package not being in place.

7.33   The CCL is playing a crucial role in enabling the UK to meet its Kyoto targets. CCL rates have not been raised since its introduction. **Budget 2006 announces that, to ensure the UK continues to make progress in tackling climate change, CCL rates will increase in line with current inflation. The inflation increase will be introduced on 1 April 2007. The Government is committed to returning CCL revenue to business, discussing with business the most effective way of supporting investment in energy efficiency and the environment.**

CCL exemption for natural gas in Northern Ireland

7.34   The temporary CCL exemption for natural gas used in Northern Ireland was introduced in 2001 to encourage the development of the fledgling gas market in Northern Ireland and to encourage businesses to switch to natural gas from more polluting fuels such as coal and oil. **The exemption was due to expire on 31 March 2006 but, as the gas market in Northern Ireland remains small and the infrastructure still limited, it will be extended for a further five years until 31 March 2011,** which should encourage the market's further development.

Climate change agreements

7.35   Climate change agreements (CCAs), which allow energy-intensive firms an 80 per cent reduction on the CCL in return for the introduction of energy-saving measures, were introduced in 2001 alongside the levy. CCAs were originally forecast to save 2.5 MtC a year. Audited findings show that CCAs have already been successful – exceeding targets by an extra 1 MtC in the first target period to 2002, and 1.4 MtC in the second period to 2004. Indeed, CCAs have increased carbon savings above the level that would have been achieved if all firms paid the full CCL rate. By 2010, it is estimated that CCAs will deliver carbon savings of around 2.8 MtC per year. Regular reviews of existing CCAs by the Department for Environment, Food, and Rural Affairs (Defra) continue to ensure that the energy efficiency improvements and emissions reductions delivered by the agreements are maximised.

7.36   Building on the evidence provided by the initial round of CCAs, Budget 2004 announced that the number of energy-intensive sectors eligible to apply for them was to be extended. Following state aids approval for the extended scheme in autumn 2005, four sectors agreed CCAs with Defra in January 2006. These sectors are: British Calcium Carbonate

Federation, covering the production of calcium carbonate-based mineral products; Contract Heating Treatment Association, covering the heat treatment of metals; British Compressed Gases Association, covering the production of industrial gases; and Kaolin and Ball Clay Association, covering the production of kaolinitic clay.

7.37   State aids approval has now been received to enable the horticulture sector to sign a CCA and, consequently, the Government will remove the temporary 50 per cent CCL discount for the energy used in horticulture from 1 April 2006. A further five sectors are also expected to sign CCAs shortly covering: the production of industrial film from molten polymer; 'wet' processes such as fabric treatment and dyeing; the production of cristobalite from a silica sand source; the production of plastic sheets and meshes that are used in contact with soil to stabilise structures such as embankments or roads; and the production of potash.

Enhanced Capital   **7.38**   Alongside the CCL and CCAs, the Government has also introduced further measures
Allowances & the   to help improve energy efficiency and reduce emissions in the business sector. Since 2001, the
Carbon Trust   Government has offered 100 per cent first-year enhanced capital allowances (ECAs) which provide up-front tax relief for spending by business on designated energy-saving technologies, of which there are now more than 13,000 approved products. The Government has also increased funding for the Carbon Trust which provides businesses with advice and information on improving their energy efficiency. In 2004-05, the Carbon Trust worked with over 2,800 organisations, resulting in cost savings of £200 million for business.

7.39   As well as from the Carbon Trust, businesses can access information on energy efficiency from a number of other sources, including through Business Links, but evidence shows that many still do not know how to get the support they need. The Financial Secretary and Richard Ellis (Chair of East of England Development Agency) will co-chair a group including Regional Development Agencies, the CBI, Engineering Employers Federation, British Chambers of Commerce, the Federation of Small Businesses, and the Carbon Trust to examine how best to provide information and support to business on energy efficiency.

7.40   In February 2003, the Carbon Trust launched a scheme designed to increase the energy efficiency of small and medium-sized enterprises by offering them interest-free loans to fund capital energy-saving projects. Over 300 loans have been made to date, worth over £8 million. These have generated energy savings of about £3 million so far. The 2005 Pre-Budget Report announced an additional £35 million for the Carbon Trust to expand its loan and grant schemes.

Box 7.2 The climate change levy package

The climate change levy, climate change agreements, ECAs for energy-saving technologies and funding for the Carbon Trust have together cut carbon emissions by a total of over 28 million tonnes so far.

In each of the next five years, it is projected that the whole CCL package will deliver carbon savings of over 6 MtC a year – accounting by 2010 for 40 per cent of the UK's total carbon reductions.

Reducing emissions in the household sector

7.41   Households have an important role to play in tackling climate change as they account for over a quarter of UK energy consumption and carbon emissions. Many simple energy efficiency measures can reduce emissions and energy bills but are not taken up due to a variety of market failures. Government intervention can help to change behaviour by raising awareness of the benefits of energy efficiency measures, reducing short-term cost barriers and also sending effective signals to the marketplace.

7.42   Since 1997, the Government has introduced measures to encourage investment in energy efficiency across all parts of the household sector. In particular, the Government has taken targeted action to support households to make the most cost-effective energy efficiency improvements – such as insulation, central heating and energy-efficient lighting. These measures have also helped to reduce the number of households in fuel poverty.

Raising awareness **7.43**   A lack of information can be a barrier to households investing in cost-effective energy efficiency measures. For instance, turning down a central heating thermostat by one degree celsius can save over £35 and 80 kilograms of carbon each year. Cavity wall insulation typically saves £85-110 and 200 kilograms of carbon a year, rapidly repaying the initial outlay. The Energy Saving Trust works to raise awareness of energy efficiency in households by providing advice, training and accreditation schemes.

Energy Efficiency Commitment **7.44**   In 2002, the Government introduced the Energy Efficiency Commitment (EEC). The EEC requires energy suppliers to achieve targets for installing energy efficiency measures in the household sector, particularly among the most vulnerable. The current phase of the EEC, over 2005-08, roughly doubles the activity of the first phase; combined, these should deliver savings of nearly 1 MtC a year by 2010. A range of measures is supported under this programme including providing by 2008 over 40 million energy-efficient light bulbs, increasing the number in UK homes by over 50 per cent; and installing cavity wall insulation in 1.7 million homes. Offers under the scheme often reduce the cost to the householder of cavity wall insulation to less than £200, so it could pay for itself in two to three years.

7.45   Nevertheless the Government believes that more could be done, and more quickly. As a first step, **Budget 2006 announces that suppliers will be able to count extra work carried out in this EEC period towards their targets in the next period. As a result, British Gas, EDF, npower, PowerGen, and Scottish and Southern Energy have agreed with the Government that they will carry out between them an extra 250,000 subsidised installations of home insulation over the next two years. This will bring forward annual carbon savings of 35,000 tonnes and reduce annual household bills by around £20 million.**

Supporting local initiatives **7.46**   To support this programme, the Government believes that more innovative, locally-led ways of promoting energy efficiency could unlock consumer demand and trigger a step change in take up. As existing successful partnerships such as those in Braintree and the "Hotspots" initiative in London and Kent show, local authorities are well placed to raise local awareness and help address householders' concerns, leading to increased uptake of energy efficiency measures. **In this Budget the Government is therefore announcing £20 million over the next two years, to help local authorities and others work in partnership with energy companies to promote and incentivise energy efficiency measures to households.**

Piloting new technologies **7.47**   Energy suppliers have an important role to play in reducing energy demand and new approaches could help in this. For example, modern technology can make it easier to inform householders of the real-time costs of their energy consumption so they can see immediate benefits from reducing unnecessary energy use. New 'smart' meters and feedback devices attached to existing meters which provide this information might therefore help encourage behaviour change to reduce carbon emissions, as well as facilitating other efficiency gains in energy markets. **Budget 2006 announces £5 million to help co-finance with energy companies a pilot study in the use of 'smart' meters and associated feedback devices.**

More efficient electrical goods   **7.48**   Labelling, standards and other requirements for large household appliances have raised the share of A-rated fridges and freezers from 1 per cent in 1997 to 65 per cent in 2005, saving 0.45MtC a year by 2010 compared with 1999 and enough electricity to power 750,000 homes. Smaller consumer electronics such as TVs, DVD players and digital set-top boxes emit up to 1MtC a year when on standby, costing each household around £25 a year in wasted electricity. The Government committed last July at Gleneagles to promote an international 1-Watt Initiative to reduce these emissions, and is concerned that progress in reducing them is too slow. **Budget 2006 therefore announces a new initiative, in partnership with major retailers and the Energy Saving Trust, to introduce voluntary schemes in the retail sector which encourage the purchase of more energy efficient alternatives in consumer electronics.**

Warm Front   **7.49**   The Government's Warm Front programme provides a package of energy efficiency measures to householders in receipt of certain benefits, in order to take properties to a level of energy efficiency where there will be minimal risk of fuel poverty in the future. The scheme has already assisted over one million households since its launch in June 2000, and in the 2005 Pre-Budget Report the Government announced additional funding of £300 million to help pensioners with the cost of installing central heating in their homes. In addition to the social benefits, the programme is expected to reduce carbon emissions by 0.32 MtC a year by 2010.

Reduced VAT rates   **7.50**   Since 1997, the Government has introduced reduced VAT rates on a range of professionally-installed energy-saving materials – including insulation, draught stripping and central heating controls – which are available to all households. Reduced VAT rates and grants are also available to encourage households to adopt microgeneration technologies such as solar panels and wind turbines.

Private rented sector   **7.51**   A particular market failure exists in the private rented sector because cost savings from investing in energy efficiency are difficult for landlords to recover in increased rent. In Budget 2004, the Government took action to correct this market failure by introducing the Landlords Energy Saving Allowance (LESA) which provides an allowance of up to £1,500 for landlords who invest in cavity wall and loft insulation. Budget 2005 extended LESA to solid wall insulation. **Budget 2006 announces the extension of LESA to draught proofing and the insulation of hot water systems. The Government will also seek to improve awareness of LESA among landlords and examine a possible extension of LESA to corporate landlords.**

7.52   In the 2005 Pre-Budget Report, the Government announced that it intended to implement a Green Landlord Scheme by reforming the existing Wear and Tear Allowance and making it conditional on the energy efficiency level of the property. **The Government continues to explore how the Wear and Tear Allowance should be reformed to incentivise landlords to invest in energy efficiency, with a view to introducing the new allowance structure alongside the forthcoming Energy Performance Certificates.**

Building regulations   **7.53**   The Government will continue to drive forward improvements in the sustainability of new housing through tougher building regulations. The new Part L building regulations, which come into force on 6 April 2006, will increase the energy efficiency of new buildings by 20 per cent – and by 40 per cent overall taking into account the previous update in 2002. For householders this will mean that the fuel bills for an average three-bed semi-detached home with gas central heating built to the new 2006 building regulations will be £120 a year less than its equivalent built in 1997. These new standards (including measures for boilers announced in April 2005) will deliver a saving of 0.98 MtC per year by 2010, equivalent to the amount of carbon emitted from nearly 1 million dwellings built to current building regulations.

Code for Sustainable Homes   **7.54**   Consultation recently closed on the Government's proposed new Code for Sustainable Homes, which will set five standards for new homes to encourage more sustainable building and give householders clear information about their running costs. Following consultation, the Government will strengthen the Code to support further improvements in environmental standards. The Government will consider making energy efficiency ratings mandatory for new and existing homes, setting minimum standards of energy and water efficiency for every level of the Code and raising the lowest levels of the Code above mandatory building regulations. In addition, from 1 April 2006 all new homes funded by English Partnerships and the Housing Corporation will meet standards broadly equivalent to level three of the Code. The Government will continue to work with the housebuilding industry and environmental organisations to encourage take up of the Code and to identify barriers to achieving a higher proportion of low-carbon and zero-carbon homes.

Reducing emissions in the public sector

7.55   The public sector has an important role to play in setting an example to encourage all individuals, households and firms to improve their energy efficiency and limit their environmental impact. In March 2005, the Government published *Securing the Future: delivering the UK sustainable development strategy* which committed all government departments to produce focused action plans to reduce carbon emissions and to renew them annually.

7.56   At the local authority level, a best value energy efficiency indicator is in place which requires local authorities to address their energy consumption. In addition, the sixth round of Beacon Councils focused on sustainable energy, with seven local authorities awarded Beacon Status. In particular, Woking Borough Council has been recognised as an example of best practice and innovation in sustainable energy – see Box 7.3. To help invigorate improved energy performance, the Government is making money available for energy efficiency projects in the public sector under the 2005-06 round of the Invest to Save Budget, with 22 projects already at full bid stage. The Carbon Trust is also piloting a revolving loan fund to support energy efficiency investment by local authorities. A seminar to be held at HM Treasury later this year will bring together central and local government to encourage the further dissemination of best practice and innovation.

Box 7.3 Woking Borough Council

Woking Borough Council is the only local authority to be awarded a Queen's Award for Enterprise in recognition of its work in energy services. Over the past 10 years, Woking has made £4.9 million of energy-efficiency savings in local authority properties, and is estimated to be saving all its Council Tax payers £700,000 per year – an average of £20 per household. This has been achieved by reducing their energy consumption by 40 per cent in a decade.

In 2003, the Council set a new target to reduce their environmental footprint by 80 per cent by 2090. By 2010 they aim to purchase 100 per cent of electricity and thermal energy needs from local sustainable sources, including 20 per cent of electricity from local renewable sources.

Among its energy saving initiatives, the Council has developed:

- the UK's first sustainable energy 200 Kilowatt-electric fuel cell;
- the first private wire electricity, district heating and cooling sustainable energy station in the country; and
- the use of photovoltaic cells, which use the sun's rays to collect heat, on council-owned properties to create sustainable electricity for central heating, hot water and light.

Reducing emissions in the transport sector

7.57 Transport is the second largest source of carbon dioxide emissions in the UK, and emissions are continuing to grow. In addition, the transport sector emits high levels of air pollutants. It is therefore important to tackle the emissions from this sector to address both climate change and local air quality issues. However, this objective must be progressed alongside the need to maintain a safe, clean and efficient transport system that underpins sustainable economic growth, boosts productivity, extends mobility and helps create a more inclusive society. The Government is helping to achieve this by adopting a long-term strategy of promoting lower carbon transport including alternative fuels, improving fuel efficiency and giving economic incentives to individuals to make more sustainable transport choices.

7.58 As shown in Chart 7.2, while volatile oil prices pushed up fuel costs in 2005-06, the cost of motoring has remained broadly constant in real terms over the last decade. Household disposable income has risen steadily over the same period due to sustained economic growth, and therefore motoring costs relative to household disposable income continues to decrease. This trend is expected to continue in coming years.

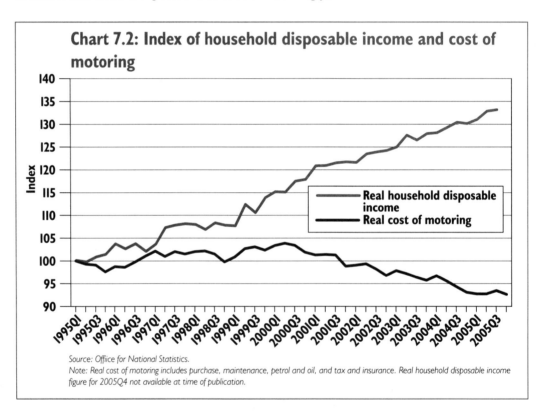

Chart 7.2: Index of household disposable income and cost of motoring

Source: Offiice for National Statistics.
Note: Real cost of motoring includes purchase, maintenance, petrol and oil, and tax and insurance. Real household disposable income figure for 2005Q4 not available at time of publication.

Fuel duty **7.59** It is the Government's policy that fuel duty rates should rise each year at least in line with inflation as the UK seeks to meet its targets of reducing polluting emissions and funding public services. At the 2005 Pre-Budget Report, with continuing market volatility, the Government announced a continuation of the freeze on main fuel duty rates. Budget 2006 announces an inflation-based increase in main fuel duties but, because of continuing oil market volatility, the changes in rates will be deferred until 1 September 2006.

Rebated oils **7.60** Maintenance of the differential between main and rebated fuel duty rates supports the Oils Strategy to tackle fraud. **The Government today announces an increase in duty of 1.25 pence per litre for rebated oils, maintaining the differential between main and rebated fuel duty rates, to take effect from 1 September in line with main fuel duty rates.** As part of the Government's continuing assessment of its strategy to tackle oils fraud, the Government will examine with those sectors that make heavy use of rebated oils the wider impact of the Oils Strategy. Further detail on tackling fraud, and changes to the Excepted Vehicles Schedule, is in Chapter 5.

EPD derogations **7.61** The UK has a number of derogations from the Energy Products Directive that enable oils for certain uses to be charged duty at a reduced rate. These derogations are due to expire at the end of 2006. While more information will be required to inform the case the UK makes to the European Commission, as indicated in the Pre-Budget Report the Government will apply for an extension of the derogations for fuel used in private air and pleasure craft navigation, and waste oils reused as fuel. The Government publishes today an initial Regulatory Impact Assessment on the effects of ending the derogation for private pleasure craft which will be used to inform the case for extension.

Sulphur-free **7.62** Sulphur-free fuels offer local air quality benefits, while helping the latest engine
fuels technologies work more efficiently. Following informal discussions with the oil industry, the Department for Transport expects to publish draft regulations shortly to ensure the widespread availability of sulphur-free diesel and sulphur-free 'super' grades of petrol. The Government is committed to allowing the industry the required lead time to bring forward the fuels, but, subject to agreement, would expect the fuel to be available on forecourts by the start of 2007. The Government today announces that it will make deregulatory changes to the Hydrocarbon Oil Duties Act 1979 to encourage the delivery of sulphur-free fuels at lower cost. These changes, which will come in later this year, will simplify the specification applicable to ultra-low sulphur diesel, which will facilitate the switch to sulphur-free.

Alternative road **7.63** Higher oil prices and the need to develop a diverse range of energy supply routes has
fuels emphasised the importance of developing alternative fuels. The Alternative Fuels Framework, published in the 2003 Pre-Budget Report, set out the Government's commitment to promoting the development of sustainable alternatives to fossil fuel, and affirmed the need for fiscal incentives to reflect environmental benefits. The framework committed the Government to a three-year rolling guarantee for biofuel and road fuel gas duty rates, offering certainty to support investment.

Biofuels **7.64** Biofuels offer significant benefits over fossil-based fuels including lower life-cycle carbon emissions, air quality improvements, diversification and security of supply. To support the development of biofuels, the Government has introduced duty differentials for both biodiesel (in 2002) and bioethanol (in 2005) of 20 pence per litre. This level of duty incentive is already guaranteed until 2007-08. The biofuels market share in the UK has increased six-fold since 2003, having now grown to 118 million litres, or 0.25 per cent of road fuels.

Renewable **7.65** In November 2005 the Government announced it would introduce a Renewable
Transport Fuel Transport Fuel Obligation (RTFO) – a long term mechanism requiring transport fuel suppliers
Obligation to ensure a set percentage of their sales are from a renewable source. The RTFO will be introduced in 2008-09, with the obligation level set at 5 per cent in 2010-11. This will deliver savings of 1 MtC by 2010.

7.66   Budget 2006 sets out further details on the RTFO. The level of obligation will be 2.5 per cent in 2008-09 and 3.75 per cent in 2009-10. This will ensure significant growth of biofuels prior to reaching the 5 per cent level in 2010-11, while recognising the time required to build production capacity and develop the necessary infrastructure to blend and supply the fuels. RTFO levels beyond 2010-11 will be set in due course, but the Government intends that the target should rise beyond 5 per cent after 2010-11, so long as infrastructural requirements and fuel and vehicle technical standards allow, and subject to the costs being acceptable to the consumer.

7.67   Budget 2006 also announces an extension of the 20 pence per litre (ppl) biofuels duty incentive until 2008-09, offering further certainty to the industry. In addition, the RTFO buy-out price – the price paid by fuel suppliers who fail to meet their obligation – for 2008-09 will be set at 15ppl. The combination of duty incentive and buy-out price is also guaranteed at 35ppl in 2009-10 but will reduce to 30ppl in 2010-11. This approach offers further certainty to encourage investment and also provides a kick start to the mechanism in the crucial first two years. The Government also expects that the emphasis will move from the duty incentive towards the buy-out price as the principal support mechanism in future years.

7.68   Further consultations on aspects of the design of the RTFO will be taken forward by Department for Transport over the next 12 months. The Government anticipates consulting on draft secondary legislation by the end of this year. Work led by the Low Carbon Vehicle Partnership will also focus on the issue of carbon and sustainability assurance, which reflects the importance the Government attaches to ensuring that biofuels are delivered in a way which maximises life-cycle carbon savings, while ensuring biofuels are sourced sustainably.

Enhanced capital   **7.69**   In October 2004, the Government published a stakeholder discussion document on a
allowance for   possible enhanced capital allowance (ECA) for the cleanest biofuels production plant, to
biofuels   support innovation and help develop the lowest-carbon biofuels production methods. In the 2005 Pre-Budget Report the Government announced that, subject to state aids approval, it would go ahead with a 100 per cent first-year allowance for biofuels plant that meet certain qualifying criteria and which make a good carbon balance inherent in the design. HM Revenue and Customs (HMRC) published a Partial Regulatory Impact Assessment alongside the Pre-Budget Report, setting out how the scheme would work.

7.70   Further discussions with stakeholders have taken place on both the detailed qualifying criteria for the scheme and how the administration would work. The Government has now applied for State aids clearance and, subject to that, envisages the scheme being in place early in 2007.

7.71   Budget 2005 also announced the start of a tendering process for a pilot project to examine the potential for using fuel duty incentives to support the use of biomass in conventional fuel production. The Government is in discussion with interested parties on the scope for such a pilot. It will report on progress in the 2006 Pre-Budget Report. The Government will also review the current definition of biodiesel in the Hydrocarbon Oil Duties Act 1979 to ensure it remains fit for purpose and enables environmentally-friendly fuels which meet fuel quality standards to receive recognition through the duty system. HMRC will take forward discussions with stakeholders in the coming months and report on progress at the Pre-Budget Report.

Road fuel gases **7.72**   The Government remains committed to offering support through duty incentives to liquefied petroleum gas (LPG) and natural gas (NG). In line with the established Alternative Fuels Framework, the Government today announces that, from 1 September 2006, duty rates on LPG will increase by the equivalent of 2.25 pence per litre, to reduce the differential with main rates by 1 penny per litre which will reflect more accurately the environmental benefits of the fuel; and that, also from 1 September, duty rates on NG will increase by the equivalent of 1.25 pence per litre, maintaining the differential with main rates. Furthermore, the Government announces that the duty differential between LPG and main road fuels will be reduced by the equivalent of 1 penny per litre each year to 2008-09, and that the duty differential between NG rates and main duty rates will be maintained each year until 2008-09, to reflect the differing environmental benefits of the two fuel types.

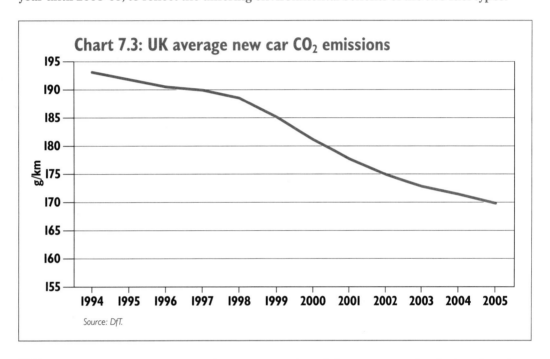

Chart 7.3: UK average new car CO_2 emissions

Source: DfT.

Lower-emission **7.73**   Average carbon emissions from new cars have fallen every year for the last decade as
vehicles Chart 7.3 shows. Innovation in car manufacturing has been vital to this, while progress is being supported both by a voluntary agreement between the European Commission and car manufacturers to reduce new car emissions, and by the measures the UK Government has taken to incentivise the purchase of less polluting vehicles. However, evidence suggests that improvement in the carbon emissions profile of private vehicles is less strong than that for company and business cars and that provision of clearer information and stronger signals to private motorists may be required.

Vehicle excise **7.74**   Fiscal incentives are one of a number of instruments that can promote improvements
duty to vehicle fuel efficiency. Vehicle excise duty (VED) for cars was reformed in 2001 and is now based on graduated carbon dioxide bands which give a clear signal to motorists to choose less polluting vehicles. New energy efficiency vehicle labels – matching the graduated VED structure – were introduced into car showrooms last year, raising consumer awareness of the potential fuel savings available from using lower emissions vehicles.

7.75   To strengthen environmental incentives, the Government announces further reforms to VED:

- a new higher band of graduated VED (band G), set at £210 for petrol cars, will be introduced for the most polluting new cars (those above 225g of carbon dioxide emissions per kilometre);

- the VED rate for the small number of cars with the very lowest carbon emissions (band A) will be reduced to £0 to encourage take-up and assist the development of the low carbon car market;

- VED rates will also be reduced for band B by £35 and C by £5, frozen for bands D and E, and increased by £25 for band F;

- rates for pre-2001 registered cars and light goods vehicles in the lower band will be frozen with the higher band increased by £5;

- the reduced rate of graduated VED for alternative fuel cars will be extended to include those cars manufactured to run on high blend bioethanol (E85); and

- In total, 50 per cent of cars will see their VED frozen or reduced. Three million cars will pay VED of £100 or less.

7.76   Motorbike VED rates and the standard rate for post-2001 light goods vehicles (LGVs) will be increased in line with inflation (with VED for LGVs rounded to the nearest £5), while Heavy Goods Vehicles (HGV) and bus VED will be frozen. All VED changes will take effect from 23 March 2006.

Vehicle emission standards   **7.77**   The European Commission is currently consulting on new 'Euro V' emissions standards for cars and small vans. The Government will consider the case for incentivising the early uptake of Euro V standards through company car tax and other instruments, ahead of the formal requirement to fit Euro V standard technology. Euro IV emissions standards for vans will become mandatory for all vans registered after 31 December 2006. The reduced rate of VED for Euro IV vans will be removed for vans registered after that date, but remain for the lifetime of vans meeting the requirements registered before that date.

7.78   As announced in the 2005 Pre-Budget Report, the Euro IV standard for HGVs and buses will become mandatory from October 2006, and from that date newly-registered HGVs and buses will no longer be eligible for a reduced pollution certificate (RPC). However, vehicles which obtain an RPC before that date will retain the benefit for the life of the vehicle, as long as they continue to meet the normal testing requirements. The scheme will also remain open to those who fit pre-October 2006 registered vehicles with the qualifying technology. The Government will continue to consider the scope for an incentive for early take-up of Euro V standards for HGVs and buses. In addition, the Government is currently reviewing the UK Air Quality Strategy and will publish a consultation shortly.

Company car tax   **7.79**   Company car tax (CCT) was reformed in 2002 and, like VED, is now based on carbon emissions, encouraging the take up of environmentally-friendlier cars. The CCT changes are making significant carbon savings, forecast to be between 0.4 and 0.9 MtC per year by 2020. The Government is publishing today the report on the second stage of the company car tax evaluation which shows that: as a result of the reforms, carbon dioxide emissions were 0.2 – 0.3 MtC lower in 2005; company cars are estimated to have carbon dioxide emissions around 15g per kilometre lower on average in 2004 than if the reform had not taken place; and around 90 per cent of company car drivers and employers providing company cars say they know about the new system. To further promote environmentally friendly vehicles, Budget 2006 announces that the threshold for the minimum percentage charge rate for calculating benefit in kind from company cars will be reduced from 140g of carbon dioxide per kilometre to 135g of carbon dioxide per kilometre for 2008-09. The Government also announces a new lower 10 per cent band for company cars with carbon dioxide emissions of 120g per kilometre or less for 2008-09. In light of the findings from the company car tax evaluation that show a rise in the number of employee car ownership schemes (ECOS), HM Revenue and Customs will review the taxation of ECOS and benefits employees derive from them, with a view to possible changes.

Capital allowances for cars 7.80   As set out in Chapter 5, the Government is giving further consideration to modernising the capital allowance regime for business cars and is publishing alongside the Budget a consultation document *Modernising tax relief for business expenditure on cars.* The proposed package contains options to incentivise the purchase of cleaner cars, including introducing a new car pool with a range of first-year allowances for cars depending on carbon dioxide emissions. This would build on the existing 100 per cent first-year allowance for cars with very low emissions, and reforms to VED and company car tax.

Company car fuel 7.81   The VAT fuel scale charge, which is a simplified scheme for taxing road fuel when business cars are used for private motoring, is being adjusted with effect from 1 May 2006 to reflect changes in fuel prices. As announced in the 2005 Pre-Budget Report, subject to obtaining a derogation from the European Commission, a new VAT fuel scale charge which will follow a carbon emissions basis is to be introduced with effect from 1 May 2007 as part of the Government's strategic approach to vehicle tax working alongside the reformed company car tax and fuel benefit charge. The Budget 2006 announces that the company car fuel benefit charge calculation figure will be maintained at £14,400 in 2006-07.

Aviation 7.82   Greenhouse gas emissions from aviation are making a significant and growing contribution to climate change. The Government recognises the importance of introducing a long-term, evidence-based strategy for tackling emissions from aviation, while noting that it is important to strike a balance between environmental, social and economic concerns. The Government believes that the best approach to tackling global aviation emissions is an international one, and that the most effective method for ensuring that aviation contributes to global climate stabilisation is to include aviation in the EU Emissions Trading Scheme (EU ETS).

7.83   The Government made advancing the inclusion of aviation in the EU ETS a priority for the UK's Presidency of the EU in 2005, with the aim of ensuring inclusion by 2008 or as soon as possible thereafter. Good progress has been made and a significant step was taken in September 2005 with the publication of the European Commission's Communication on Reducing the Climate Change Impact of Aviation[1]. A legislative proposal on aviation and the EU ETS is expected by the end of 2006. The Government will continue to work to secure further progress and recognises the need to build the evidence base further. The Government therefore announces today funding for an international scientific conference in the UK this summer that has a key focus on increasing understanding of the impact of aviation on climate change. In addition, the Government is undertaking talks with other Member States to consider how best to assist the Commission in taking forward work at European level to inform the legislative proposal.

Air passenger duty 7.84   The Government recognises that its focus on including aviation in the EU ETS should not preclude further work on other policy instruments, including APD, to tackle emissions from aviation. But decisions on APD rates need to be considered in the context of wider social and economic factors, particularly the current volatile oil market. The Government today announces a freeze in APD. However, the Government is aware that economic instruments, including APD, may provide a route through which improved environmental performance in the aviation sector can be incentivised and so will continue to explore options for developing further such measures. The Government also announces that, from 1 November, the scope of the European rate of APD will be widened to include Croatia, as an applicant country to the EU.

---

[1] Reducing the Climate Change Impact of Aviation: Communication from the Commission to the Council, the European Parliament, the European Economic and Social Committee, and the Committee of the Regions, September 2005

IMPROVING WASTE MANAGEMENT

7.85 Efficient use of resources and the effective management of waste are essential features of an environmentally sustainable economy. Since 1997, the Government has introduced a number of measures to develop more sustainable waste management practices, reduce the UK's reliance on landfill and ensure that waste producers consider the full costs of the disposal of waste when making decisions. These measures aim to ensure that the UK will meet its international obligations, including the reduction in the quantity of biodegradable municipal waste disposed to landfill sites stipulated in the EU Landfill Directive. Minimisation of waste depends on building the right incentives to enable the production cycle to take account of changing patterns of consumption. As part of the Waste Strategy Review, Defra launched a consultation on 14 February 2006 on proposals for a revised strategy and the policies for implementing it.

Landfill tax **7.86** Landfill tax applies the 'Polluter Pays' principle to encourage waste producers to seek more sustainable waste management options. In 2003, the Government took a long-term strategic view and announced that, from 2005-06, the standard rate of landfill tax covering active wastes would increase by at least £3 per tonne each year, towards a medium to long-term rate of £35 per tonne. The increases in the standard rate of landfill tax are contributing to a move away from over-reliance on landfill and provisional figures show that between 1997 and 2005, the volume of active waste disposed at landfill sites fell by almost 16 per cent, with the biggest fall occurring in the last year. **The Government confirms that the standard rate of landfill tax will increase by £3 per tonne to £21 per tonne from 1 April 2006. The lower rate, covering inactive or inert waste, will remain unchanged.**

Improving local waste management **7.87** Municipal waste accounts for 10 per cent of all waste in England. In Budget 2003, £260 million was set aside for a three-year targeted waste performance and efficiency grant for local authorities in England. £3.5 million of that has already been allocated to over 50 different schemes designed by local authorities and their partners to trial positive incentives for household waste recycling and reduction. The Landfill Allowance Trading Scheme – the world's first trading scheme for municipal waste – has now been operating for almost a year, with 23 trades recorded so far, resulting in 455,000 allowances sold for the value of £9.6 million. The planning system has also been modified to provide a more effective framework for delivering the significant expansion in new waste management facilities that will be needed to meet EU obligations and national targets. In addition, the Kelly Review, detailed in Chapter 3, is examining the scope for smarter procurement of waste infrastructure.

Recycling landfill tax revenue **7.88** Budget 2003 announced that future increases in the standard rate of landfill tax would be introduced in a way that is revenue neutral to business as a whole and to local government. The Business Resource Efficiency and Waste (BREW) Programme was launched in March 2005 to return these additional landfill tax receipts to business in England. In 2006-07, BREW will allocate £95 million to eleven programmes. These include those offering direct advice and support to businesses on resource efficiency and waste minimisation, providing longer-term market transformation; and research and development projects.

Enhanced capital allowances for waste **7.89** The Government is exploring the potential to introduce an enhanced capital allowances scheme to support new waste management facilities. The 2005 Pre-Budget Report confirmed that this work is currently focused on developing options to encourage investment in developing markets for the outputs (for example, refuse derived fuel) of new waste treatment facilities and the Government will continue to engage with stakeholders to assess the potential of this proposal.

Landfill Tax Credit Scheme

7.90   The Landfill Tax Credit Scheme (LTCS) redresses some of the environmental costs of landfill by improving the environment in the vicinity of landfill sites. Projects benefiting from LTCS funding include the reclaiming of land, improvements to local community facilities and repairs to places of worship. 2006 marks the tenth anniversary of the scheme and the Government recognises the important contribution it has made. This year, in 2006-07, the Government will increase the value of the scheme to £60 million, an increase of over £10 million. The Government also issues a challenge to the private and voluntary sector partners in the scheme to use this additional money to fund opportunities for young people to volunteer on environmental projects.

PROTECTING THE UK'S COUNTRYSIDE AND NATURAL RESOURCES

7.91   The Government is committed to ensuring that the UK's natural resources are managed prudently. In particular it aims to improve river water quality, biodiversity and land use. The Government has sought to correct market failures where commercial activity has an impact on the wider environment, and to do so in a way that balances the need to maintain economic growth with the need to encourage a sustainable approach for the long term, particularly in sectors with a significant direct impact on the economy, such as agriculture and quarrying.

Aggregates levy

7.92   The aggregates levy was introduced in 2002 to ensure that the external costs associated with the exploitation of aggregates are reflected in the price of aggregate, and to encourage the use of recycled aggregate. There continues to be strong evidence that the levy is achieving its environmental objectives, with sales of primary aggregate down and production of recycled aggregate up. The Government expects that the rates of the levy will at least keep pace with inflation over time, although it accepts that the levy is still bedding in. The Government announces today that in 2006-07 the rate of the levy will be frozen at £1.60 a tonne.

Investment in water-efficient technologies

7.93   Enhanced capital allowances to support business investment in designated water-efficient technologies were introduced in 2003 and currently cover more than 700 approved products. In 2006 the Government will add three further technology classes to the scheme. Work to define the precise performance standards for these technologies is continuing. The addition of these groups will be worth £5 million during their first full year, 2007-08.

Water pollution from agriculture

7.94   Farming practices have a significant impact on water pollution through the use of fertilisers, feed and pesticides. The Government is currently assessing possible policy options to tackle diffuse water pollution from agriculture (DWPA), and remains committed to ensuring that the costs of such pollution do not fall on water customers. The Government plans to consult on the most cost-effective options for dealing with DWPA in the second half of 2006. The industry-led voluntary initiative on measures to reduce the environmental damage caused by the agricultural use of pesticides – which has resulted in some improvements in farming practices since its introduction – has been in place since April 2001 and is due to end on 31 March 2006. The Government will review the voluntary initiative in 2006 to assess its impact and identify further improvements, while continuing to keep options for a pesticide tax or other economic instrument under review.

Land use   **7.95**   The Government's commitment to achieving 60 per cent of all new development on brownfield sites, and more efficient use of land through higher densities where appropriate, will ensure that land usage and potentially adverse environmental impacts are minimised. This has resulted in 72 per cent of all development in England being on brownfield sites in 2004, up from 56 per cent in 1997. In addition, the average density of developments has increased from 25 dwellings per hectare in 1997 to 40 dwellings per hectare in 2005. At the same time, since 1997 some 19,000 hectares of land, an area approximately the size of Liverpool, have been added to green belt designated land, with a further 12,000 hectares awaiting approval in local plans.

Table 7.1: The Government's policy objectives and Budget measures

Sustainable Development Indicator and recent trend data	Recent Government Measures

Tackling Climate Change

Targets
Joint Defra/DTI/DfT PSA – reduce greenhouse gas emissions to 12.5 per cent below 1990 levels in line with Kyoto commitment and move towards a 20 per cent reduction in carbon dioxide emissions below 1990 levels by 2010.

Progress
UK greenhouse gas emissions were 14.6 per cent below 1990 levels in 2004[1]
Carbon dioxide emissions fell by 5.6 per cent during this period.

- Climate Change Programme, DETR, November 2000.
- UK Emissions Trading Scheme, Defra, August 2001.
- Energy Efficiency Commitment, Defra, April 2002 and April 2005.
- Renewables Obligation, Defra, April 2002 and December 2003.
- Energy White Paper, DTI 2003.
- Energy Efficiency – the Government's plan for Action, Defra, April 2004.
- EU ETS Phase I began January 2005, EU ETS Phase II consultation in July 2005.
- Energy Effiency Commitment 2 introduced April 2005
- Package of fiscal measures, including climate change levy (see Table 7.2).

Air Quality

Targets
Joint Defra/DfT PSA – to improve air quality by meeting the Air Quality Strategy for seven key air pollutants between 2003 and 2010.

Progress
Provisional results for 2005 show average UK urban background levels of particulate pollution (PM10) decreased from 36 micrograms per cubic metre in 1993 to 22 micrograms in 2005. Urban ozone levels increased from 42 micrograms per cubic metre to 56 micrograms, due to the reduction in other urban pollutants which tend to suppress ozone.
The average number of days with moderate or higher air pollution decreased from 50 to 21 in urban areas and from 44 to 39 in rural areas between 1995 and 2005[2] (provisional estimates).

- Air Quality Strategy DETR January 2000 and Addendum, Defra February 2003, and Review, Defra 2004-06, Review of Air Quality Strategy due April 2006.
- Implementation of Integrated Pollution, Prevention and Control regime, Defra 2002-2007.
- Air Transport White Paper, DfT, December 2003.
- Ten Year Plan for Transport, DETR July 2000, and Future of Transport White Paper, July 2004.
- Continued support for local air quality management system.
- Negotiation and implementation of EU air quality directives and international agreements 2004-06.
- Review of the Transport Energy Grant Programmes, DfT 2004-06.
- Fiscal measures including fuel differentials for less polluting fuels (see Table 7.2).

Improving Waste Management

Targets
Defra PSA – enable at least 25 per cent of household waste to be composted or recycled in 2005-06.
Landfill Directive target to reduce the volumes of biodegradable municipal waste disposed of at landfill to 75 per cent of 1995 levels by 2010, 50 per cent by 2013, and 35 per cent by 2020.

Progress
Around 23 per cent of household waste in England was recycled or composted in 2004-05. Active waste disposed to landfill has fallen from 50.4 million tonnes in 1997-98 to 47.3 million tonnes in 2003-04.

- Waste Strategy 2000, DETR, May 2000.
- Waste Implementation Programme, Defra, 2002.
- Reform of the Waste Minimisation and recycling challenge fund.
- Landfill allowance (trading) schemes enacted by the Waste and Emissions Trading (WET) Act 2003.
- Business resource and efficiency waste programme (BREW) 2004.
- Waste Strategy review consultation published by Defra in Feb 2006.
- Landfill tax and related measures (see Table 7.2).

Regenerating the UK's towns and cities

Targets
ODPM PSA 5: 60 per cent of housing development to be on previously developed land.
ODPM PSA 1: Work with departments to help meet PSA floor targets to deliver neighbourhood renewal and tackle social inclusion.
ODPM PSA 8: Deliver cleaner, safer and greener public spaces.

Progress
In 2004, 72 per cent of new housing was on previously developed land, including conversions, increasing from around 54 per cent in 1990.[3]
Latest data shows the gap between the most deprived areas and the rest of the country has narrowed on several key indicators, including health, crime and education.
There are currently 22 Urban Regeneration Companies in the UK.

- Sustainable Communities "building the future" launched in February 2003.
- Feb 2005 Planning Policy Statement 1 placed sustainability for the first time as a core principle of the planning system.
- SR04 made available £525m a year through the Neighbourhood Renewal Fund to tackle deprivation in the most deprived areas and maintained commitment to New Deal For Communities programmes.
- SR04 announced Safer and Stronger Communities Fund providing single funding stream to improve liveability.
- National Nuisance Vehicle Strategy launched in November 2004.
- Feb 2005 English Partnerships launched pilot programme with 12 local authorities to tackle England's legacy of derelict and brownfield land, to bring 66,000 hectares of brownfield land into beneficial use.
- Budget 2005 announced the Local Enterprise Growth Initiative to increase investment and enterprise in the most deprived areas.
- Package of fiscal measures including contaminated land tax credit (see Table 7.2).

Protecting the UK's countryside and natural resources

Targets
Defra PSA – positive trends in the Government's headline indicators of sustainable development (includes wildlife, river water quality, land use).

Water Framework Directive – requires achievement of good chemical and ecological status in surface water by 2015.

Progress
- Farmland birds almost halved between 1977 and 1993. However, declines have reduced in recent years and 2004 populations were virtually unchanged from 1993.
- Woodland birds fell by about 24 per cent between 1975 and 1992. Since then, however, populations have remained broadly constant.
- In 2004 about 62 per cent of rivers in England were rated as having good chemical quality and approximately 70 per cent of English rivers were of good biological quality.
- In 2006, Sites of Special Scientific Interest land in target condition rose to 71 per cent in April 2003.

- Rural White Paper, DETR, November 2000.
- Strategy for Sustainable Farming and Food, Defra, December 2002.
- Regulations transposing the Water Framework Directive came into force 2 January 2004.
- Developing measures to promote catchment-sensitive farming (Defra-HMT consultation), June 2004.
- Defra consulting on pesticides strategy.
- England Rural Development Programme.
- Environmental Stewardship, England's new agri-environment scheme, launched March 2005.
- Aggregates levy and aggregates levy sustainability fund (see table 7.2).

---

[1] The six main greenhouse gases are: carbon dioxide, methane, nitrous oxide, hydroflurocarbons, perflourocarbons and sulphur hexafluoride.
[2] Air quality indicator for sustainable development 2005 (provisional): statistical release, Defra, 2006.
[3] Land use change in England. Residential Development to 2004 (January 2006).

Table 7.2: The environmental impacts of Budget measures

Budget measure	Environmental impact
Climate Change and Air Quality	
Climate change levy package	Climate change levy is estimated to deliver annual emissions savings of over 3.5 million tonnes of carbon (MtC) by 2010[1].
	Climate change agreements are estimated to deliver annual emissions savings of 2.8 MtC by 2010.
	Total CCL package including Carbon Trust, is estimated to deliver annual emissions savings of over 7.5 MtC a year by 2010.
Fuel duty	By deferring fuel duty revalorisation to September 2006 a small increase in carbon emissions is expected compared to a revalorisation at Budget.

Fuel duty differentials including:
– to facilitate a market switch:
  • From leaded to unleaded;
  • From low sulphur to ultra-low sulphur diesel (ULSD);
  • From low sulphur to ultra-low sulphur petrol (ULSP).
– to encourage growth in the use of more environmentally-friendly fuels:
  • Road fuel gases;
  • biodiesel (20ppl differential);
  • bioethanol (20ppl differential).
	The shift to ULSP from ordinary unleaded is estimated to have reduced emissions of nitrogen oxide by 1 per cent, carbon monoxide by 4 per cent and volatile organic compounds by 1 per cent per year[2].
	
	The shift to ULSD from ordinary diesel is estimated to have reduced emissions of particulates by 8 per cent and nitrogen oxides by up to 1 per cent per year.
	
	The road fuel gas differential has reduced emissions of particulates and nitrogen oxides, which has helped to improve local air quality.
	
	The increased use of biodiesel and bioethanol will reduce CO_2 emissions overall typically by around 50 per cent per litre of biofuel used.

Support for biofuels	The Renewable Transport Fuel Obligation (RTFO) introduced from 2008-09 is expected to save 1 MtC by 2010[3]. The enhanced capital allowance for biofuel plant could save a further 0.06 MtC by 2010[4].
Rebated fuels	Maintaining the differential with main road fuels will reduce levels of fraud, and will deliver small CO_2 and local air pollution benefits through increased use of less polluting fuels and less use of rebated fuels, which are more polluting.
Vehicle excise duty (VED)	The sharpening of environmental signals will help deliver reductions in CO_2 emissions. Numbers of vehicles in 3 lowest CO_2 emission graduated VED bands is forecast to grow significantly in the longer term in part due to VED reform.
Company car tax (CCT)	CO_2 emissions savings of reformed CCT system estimated to be 0.2 to 0.3 MtC in 2005, forecast to rise to between 0.4 and 0.9 MtC per year in the long run[5].
Company car fuel benefit charge	The number of company car drivers getting free fuel for private use has fallen by around 600,000 since 1997, partly as a result of changes to the company car tax system in April 2002 and changes to the fuel benefit rules in April 2003, helping to reduce levels of CO_2 emissions, local air pollutants and congestion[6].
VAT fuel scale charge	The reforms are expected to deliver small reduction in CO_2.
Air passenger duty (APD)	A freeze in APD will result in a small increase in carbon emissions and local air pollutants from aviation.
Landlords Energy Saving Allowance (LESA)	Small reduction of carbon emissions.
Reduced rate of VAT on professionally-installed energy saving materials and microgeneration (from 17.5% to 5%)	Small reduction of carbon emissions.
Reduced rate of VAT on domestic fuel and power (from 8% to 5%)	Estimated to increase carbon emissions by 0.2 million tonnes by 2010[7].

[1] Modeling the Initial Effects of the Climate Change Levy, Cambridge Econometrics, available at www.hmrc.gov.uk.
[2] Using NETCEN emissions models – further detail on methodology used is provided in NETCEN's January 2000 report 'UK Road Transport Emissions Projections'.
[3] Department for Transport modeling.
[4] HMRC modelling.
[5] HMRC modelling.
[6] HMRC modelling.
[7] HMRC modelling.

Table 7.2: The environmental impacts of Budget measures (continued)

Budget measure	Environmental impact
Energy Efficiency Commitment (EEC)	Phase I (2002-2005) is estimated to have reduced emissions by 0.35 MtC per year by 2005. Phase 2 (2005-2008) is expected to bring in an additional 0.62 MtC annual saving by 2008. Budget announcement could bring forward 35,000 tonnes of annual carbon savings.
Warm front (previously called the Home Energy Efficiency Scheme)	Estimated annual carbon savings of 0.32 MtC a year by 2010.
Voluntary initiative on consumer electronics	Annual emissions from household goods are estimated to be 1 MtC. An early estimate suggests savings of up to 65 per cent can be achieved at low cost to manufacturers, retailers and consumers, with 0.1-0.2 MtC potentially saved in 2010. Actual savings will depend on final agreement.
Microgeneration – £50 million to enable the installation of microgeneration technologies in 30,000 buildings	Carbon savings by 2010 around 0.01 MtC per year.
'Smart' meter pilot	An estimated 0.2 MtC could be saved in 2010 from better metering and billing.
Improving Waste Management	
Landfill tax	Provisional figures show that, between 1997 and 2005, the total quantity of waste disposed to landfill sites registered for landfill tax fell by 28 per cent, while the amount of active waste disposed to landfill fell by 16 per cent[8].
Landfill tax credit scheme (LTCS)	The LTCS has provided £630 million for projects since its introduction.
Regenerating the UK's towns and cities	
Contaminated land tax credit	Bringing forward remediation of contaminated land.
Capital allowances for flats over shops	Bringing empty space over shops back into the residential market, while reducing the pressure for new greenfield development.
Reforms to VAT on conversion and renovation	Reduced pressure on greenfield site development.
Protecting the UK's countryside and natural resources	
Aggregates levy and aggregates levy sustainability fund	An 8 per cent reduction in sales of aggregates between 2001 and 2003. Reductions in noise and vibration, dust and other emissions to air, visual intrusion, loss of amenity and damage to wildlife habitats.
Enhanced capital allowances for water efficiency technologies	More sustainable use of water by business.

[8] Data at www.uktradeinfo.com, in calendar years.

ILLUSTRATIVE LONG-TERM FISCAL PROJECTIONS

To safeguard long-term economic growth and ensure inter-generational fairness it is important that Budget decisions are consistent with the long-term sustainability of the public finances. The illustrative long-term fiscal projections presented in this annex provide an assessment of the long-term sustainability of the Government's fiscal policies over the period up to 2035-36, in line with the requirements of the *Code for fiscal stability*. The key points are:

- the UK remains well-placed to deal with potential future spending pressures due to ageing and other factors;

- given the projected profile for tax revenue and transfers current public consumption can grow at around assumed GDP growth after the medium term while meeting the Government's golden rule; and

- public sector net investment can grow more or less in line with the economy without jeopardising the sustainable investment rule.

This conclusion concurs with the findings of the 2005 *Long-term public finance report*, which provides a more detailed examination of the long-term public finances. The report finds that, on a range of assumptions and using a number of techniques, the UK's fiscal position is sustainable in the long term on the basis of current policies, and that the UK is well-placed relative to many other developed countries to face the challenges ahead. However, the Government remains vigilant to future risks and is not complacent about the long-term challenges posed by an ageing population. It will therefore continue to update and report on assessments of long-term fiscal sustainability.

A.1 The Government's fiscal policy framework, as set out in the *Code for fiscal stability*,[1] is designed to ensure transparent, long-term decision-making. Fiscal policy is set to ensure sustainable public finances, with consideration to the short, medium and long term. Long-term fiscal sustainability helps to promote long-term economic growth and ensures that financial burdens are not shifted to future generations.

Illustrative long-term fiscal projections **A.2** To assess the sustainability and inter-generational impact of fiscal policy, the Code requires the Government to publish illustrative long-term fiscal projections covering a period of at least 10 years. In practice, a 30-year horizon has been adopted. The projections published in previous Budgets showed that the UK's long-term fiscal position was relatively favourable and that the Government is in the position to meet its two fiscal rules – the golden rule and the sustainable investment rule – over the long term.

A.3 To complement and enhance the illustrative projections, the Government has published the *Long-term public finance report* each year since 2002, most recently alongside the 2005 Pre-Budget Report.[2] The 2005 report examined long-term challenges to the public finances and provided a comprehensive assessment of the sustainability of the public finances. It also updated the illustrative long-term fiscal projections in Budget 2005. The projections in this annex provide a further update, incorporating the Budget 2006 medium-term spending and revenue projections. The underlying assumptions and methodology remain broadly unchanged from previous years.

---

[1] *Code for fiscal stability*, HM Treasury, 1998.

[2] 2005 *Long-term public finance report: an analysis of fiscal sustainability*, HM Treasury, December 2005.

LONG-TERM SOCIO-ECONOMIC TRENDS

A.4   Declining fertility rates and improvements in life expectancy over past decades have led to a general ageing of the population in the UK and throughout most of the developed world. Since Budget 2005, the Government Actuary's Department (GAD) has published a new set of projections, based on the Office for National Statistics' mid-year 2004 population estimate.[3] The new population projections use the same assumption regarding the long-term fertility rate (the average number of children per woman) as the previous ('2003-based') projections, which remains at 1.74. Long-term annual net migration is assumed to be 145,000 per year, 15,000 more than previously.[4]

A.5   However, the new population projections are based on a higher life expectancy assumption than the previous projections, with life expectancy at birth assumed to be 81.4 for males and 85 for females.[5] The evolution of the understanding of mortality trends illustrates the importance of updating long-term fiscal projections and the need to assess the sustainability of the public finances on a regular basis.

A.6   Based on the latest principal projections, the UK's population will increase from nearly 60 million today to around 68 million by the mid 2030s, before continuing to grow (at a relatively slower rate) to around 70 million by 2070. The population structure is also projected to change substantially. Chart A.1 shows the wide variations between the projected change in size of different age groups, with the older age groups projected to increase substantially in absolute size over the next 30 years. According to the projections, the number of people aged 65-84 years will increase by more than 50 per cent, while the number of people aged 85 years and over will more than double. The latter trend is also projected to continue beyond 2035, with four times as many people projected to be in this age group in 2050 than there are now.

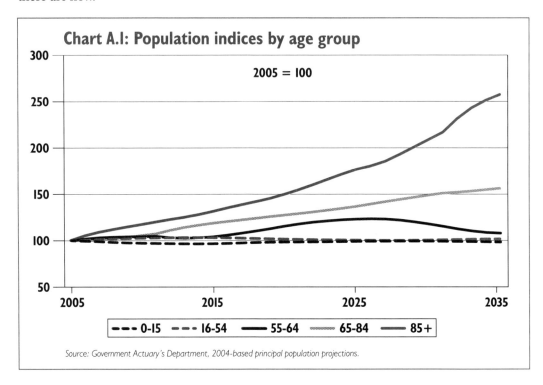

Chart A.1: Population indices by age group

2005 = 100

Legend: 0-15   16-54   55-64   65-84   85+

Source: Government Actuary's Department, 2004-based principal population projections.

---

[3] Available at www.gad.gov.uk.

[4] For a comparative table of the assumptions used in GAD population projections, see 2005 *Long-term public finance report: an analysis of fiscal sustainability*, HM Treasury, December 2005.

[5] Period life expectancy at birth in 2031. For more details of the revisions to the life expectancy assumption, see 2005 *Long-term public finance report: an analysis of fiscal sustainability*, HM Treasury, December 2005.

A.7   The composition of the population will change as a result. Whereas those aged between 16 and 64 years make up nearly two-thirds of the total population now, their share is projected to fall by around $5^1/_2$ percentage points between now and 2035. At the same time the share of people aged 65 years and over, which currently make up around 16 per cent of the total population, is projected to rise by around 8 percentage points over this period, and the share of those aged 85 years and over is projected to rise by just over 2 percentage points, from its present level of around 2 per cent. By contrast the share of children (those aged up to 15 years) in the total population is projected to fall by around $2^1/_2$ percentage points over the same period, from its current level of nearly 20 per cent.

A high degree of uncertainty   **A.8**   Any long-term projection is subject to a high degree of uncertainty.[6] To deal with this uncertainty, GAD has produced high and low variants around the principal projections. For example, the high fertility variant assumes that the average number of children per woman is 1.94, while the high longevity variant assumes life expectancy at birth in 2031 of $83^1/_2$ years for males and $86^1/_2$ years for females. The variants differ markedly from the principal projections in terms of future overall size and composition of the population, and suggest that governments should attempt to plan for a wide range of potential outcomes.[7] To this end, a cautious approach to assessing the long-term sustainability of the public finances is taken below.

Other long-term trends   **A.9**   However, demographic change is only one of a number of trends that may have a significant impact upon public finances in the future. The 2007 Comprehensive Spending Review will be informed by a detailed assessment of the long-term trends and challenges that will shape public services over the next decade.[8] This includes the intensification of cross-border economic competition; the acceleration in the pace of innovation and technological diffusion; continued global uncertainty and poverty, with ongoing threats of international terrorism and global conflict; and increasing pressures on our national resources and global climate.

METHODOLOGY AND ASSUMPTIONS

A.10   The methodology for producing the long-term fiscal projections presented in this annex determines the rate at which current public consumption can grow while the Government meets its fiscal rules. This is achieved by projecting the evolution of tax receipts, transfer payments (such as pensions) and capital consumption (depreciation) over the coming decades. Subtracting transfers and capital consumption from tax revenues provides a measure of the financial resources available for current public consumption.[9]

A.11   Up to and including 2010-11, the end of the medium-term forecast period, the long-term illustrative projections are based on the fiscal forecasts and assumptions presented in Chapter C of the Financial Statement and Budget Report (FSBR). Beyond that, the long-term projections are based on the assumption of current policy, in other words it is assumed that the Government will leave current policy unchanged in the future. This should not be interpreted as meaning that policy will not change over time but is used so that the long-term projections do not pre-judge future government policy.

---

[6] For example, a study of UK population projections cites a census from 1891 that projected the combined population stock of Australia and New Zealand in 1981 to be 94 million, five times greater than the projected outcome. See *Accuracy and uncertainty of the national population projections for the United Kingdom*, Chris Shaw, *Population trends No.77*, 1994, page 24. The study was revealed in a letter to *Royal Statistical Society News*, February 1994.

[7] For a discussion of the use of scenarios in long-term planning see 2005 *Long-term public finance report: an analysis of fiscal sustainability*, December 2005.

[8] For further details, see Chapter 6.

[9] See *Budget 2000: Prudent for a Purpose: Working for a Stronger and Fairer Britain*, HM Treasury, March 2000 for a discussion of the methodology.

Economic A.12 Table A.1 sets out the economic assumptions that underlie the long-term fiscal
assumptions projections after 2010-11. To deal with the uncertainty involved in projecting long-term
trends, particularly cautious assumptions are used. Productivity is assumed to grow by $1^3/_4$ per
cent a year from 2011-12, which is $^1/_4$ per cent lower than the neutral view of productivity
growth. This is in line with the 'lower productivity' scenario used in the 2005 *Long-term public
finance report*, reflecting a cautious approach to projecting long-term fiscal aggregates.

A.13 Annex A of Budget 2005 introduced an alternative approach to projecting gender- and
age-specific employment rates and total employment levels beyond the medium term. The
illustrative projections presented in this year's Budget use this alternative approach, the so-
called 'cohort' method, for the employment projections (see Box A.1 for more details of the
methodology). The growth rates for productivity and employment generate the growth rates
for GDP from 2011-12 onwards.

Table A.1: Real GDP growth and its components

Year	2011-12 to 2015-16	2016-17 to 2025-26	2026-27 to 2035-36
Productivity	$1^3/_4$	$1^3/_4$	$1^3/_4$
Employment	$^1/_4$	0	0
Real GDP	2	$1^3/_4$	$1^3/_4$

Source: HM Treasury.

Taxation and A.14 For the period up to and including 2010-11, the illustrative long-term fiscal
spending projections are based on the forecasts and assumptions presented in Chapter C of the FSBR.
assumptions Unless stated otherwise, high-level policy settings in 2010-11 are then assumed to continue
throughout the rest of the projection period. For example, the Government is assumed to
raise the same amount of revenue as a proportion of GDP as in 2010-11, offsetting possible
changes in tax bases by changing policy in a revenue neutral way. Tax revenues are also
assumed to be equal to total current spending from 2011-12 onwards. This implies that, by
assumption, the golden rule is met, with the current budget in balance at all times.

A.15 Current public consumption is calculated as the difference between tax revenues and
other current spending, which comprises transfers and capital consumption. Transfers
mainly consist of social security spending (e.g. Disability Living Allowance) and debt interest
payments. The latter are calculated using the projected debt stock and a long-term interest
rate, which is assumed to equal the implicit average interest rate between 2006-07 and 2010-
11. Under the assumption that the current budget is in balance, the growth of public sector
net debt reflects growth in public sector net investment. As in previous illustrative long-term
projections, the share of public sector net investment in GDP is reset at 1.8 per cent beyond
the medium term.

Box A.1: Employment projections

In previous illustrative projections, a basic assumption was made that the overall employment rate remains unchanged at the end of the medium term. Although simple and transparent, this method did not take into account the effect of ageing or the recent trend of increasing female labour market participation upon future participation rates. The 'cohort' method of projecting employment[a] attempts to capture these trends by using historical participation rates to calculate the probability that a male or female will enter or leave the labour market at a specific age. These probabilities can then be applied to existing and future participants in the labour market to build up a projected lifetime participation profile of each cohort. By applying these projections of participation rates to the latest population projections provided by the Government Actuary's Department, a long-term projection of total employment is obtained. The chart below indicates that the employment path projected using the cohort method is more stable between now and 2035 than that projected using the previous assumption of a constant employment rate.

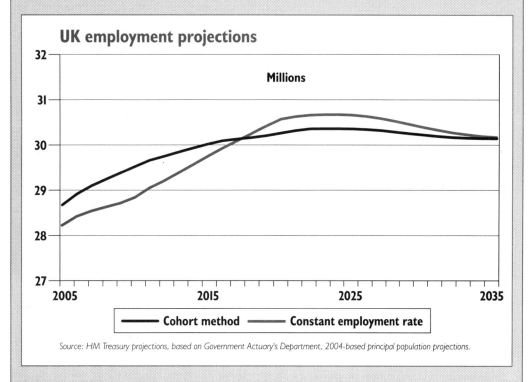

Source: HM Treasury projections, based on Government Actuary's Department, 2004-based principal population projections.

In January 2006, the Office for National Statistics published employment projections for the period 2006-2020.[b] Their findings were broadly comparable with those presented here, with a similar increase in the labour force projected to occur between now and 2020.

[a] This method has also been used by the Organisation for Economic Co-operation and Development (OECD) and European Commission in labour market projections. See *Coping with ageing: A Dynamic Approach to Quantify the Impact of Alternative Policy Options on Future Labour Supply in OECD Countries*, OECD, June 2004 and *The impact of ageing on public expenditure: projections for the EU25 Member States on pensions, health care, long-term care and unemployment transfers (2004-2050)*, European Union Economic Policy Committee, February 2006.
[b] *Labour Force Projections 2006-2020*, Office for National Statistics, January 2006.

ILLUSTRATIVE PROJECTIONS

A.16 Chart A.2 shows the projected evolution of total current spending, transfers, current consumption and net debt as a share of GDP between 2005-06 and 2035-36, given the assumptions stated above. Total current spending is projected to increase between 2005-06 and 2010-11, and then remain stable by assumption. Transfers are projected to fall from 17.6 per cent in 2005-06 to 16.1 per cent by 2035-36, while current consumption is projected to fall initially before increasing from 20.6 per cent in 2011-12 to 21.7 per cent in 2035-36. Hence current consumption can grow at around assumed GDP growth while still meeting the fiscal rules. Starting from just over 38 per cent in 2011-12, net debt is projected to remain broadly stable before rising beyond the mid 2020s, reaching 39.7 per cent by 2035-36, consistent with the sustainable investment rule. The projected changes in net debt emphasise the importance of ensuring sound public finances in the medium term to prepare for future developments.

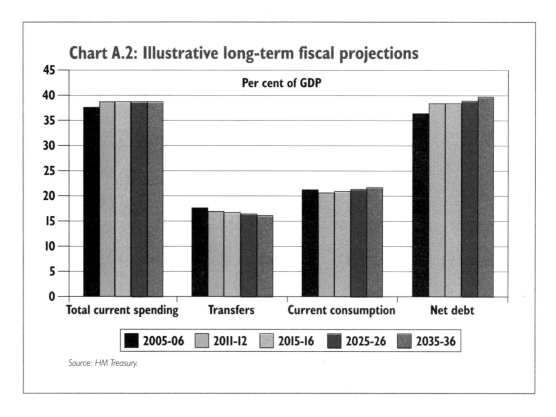

Chart A.2: Illustrative long-term fiscal projections

Source: HM Treasury.

A.17 The illustrative long-term fiscal projections presented here yield similar conclusions to those presented in the 2005 *Long-term public finance report,* which uses a broader range of techniques, assumptions and modelling approaches to assess long-term sustainability. The report demonstrates that the UK fiscal position is sustainable in the long term on the basis of current policies and that the UK is well placed relative to many other developed countries to face the challenges ahead. In addition to an overall assessment of long-term fiscal sustainability, the 2005 *Long-term public finance report* also identifies individual spending trends: health spending is likely to increase the most as a share of GDP over the coming decades, while spending on education is projected to remain relatively stable.

Sensitivity **A.18** Long-term projections of any type are inevitably subject to a high degree of **analysis** uncertainty. The outcome of any projection exercise depends on the underlying assumptions. These include population projections and assumptions regarding productivity, revenue, labour market participation and social security spending. It is important to determine the sensitivity of baseline projections to changes in the assumptions. The 2005 *Long-term public finance report* illustrates the effect of different interest rate and productivity assumptions and includes a more detailed discussion of the uncertainty surrounding long-term projections.[10]

INTERNATIONAL COMPARISONS

Population **A.19** The UK is not alone in facing an ageing population, and many countries are projected **ageing: a global** to age more rapidly than the UK. Chart A.3 shows the historical and projected evolution of the **phenomenon** demographic old-age dependency ratio between 1950 and 2035 in selected regions and countries. While the UK is projected to observe an increase in the demographic old-age dependency ratio from 24 per cent at present to around 38 per cent by 2035, a steeper increase is projected for the EU average, rising from 24 per cent to 44 per cent over this period. Japan is projected to experience a marked increase in the demographic old-age dependency ratio, reaching 57 per cent by 2035.

A.20 The ageing trend is not limited to the developed world. For example, Chart A.3 indicates that China is projected to age significantly over the next three decades, with a projected increase in the demographic old-age dependency ratio from 11 per cent to 31 per cent between now and 2035. In addition, other less-developed regions are also projected to age, albeit from a lower starting point.

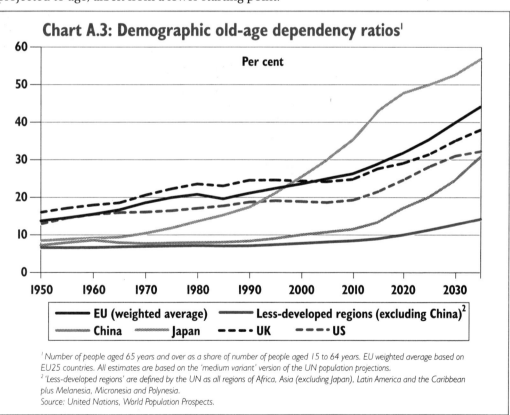

Chart A.3: Demographic old-age dependency ratios[1]

[1] Number of people aged 65 years and over as a share of number of people aged 15 to 64 years. EU weighted average based on EU25 countries. All estimates are based on the 'medium variant' version of the UN population projections.
[2] 'Less-developed regions' are defined by the UN as all regions of Africa, Asia (excluding Japan), Latin America and the Caribbean plus Melanesia, Micronesia and Polynesia.
Source: United Nations, World Population Prospects.

---

[10] The 2004 *Long-term public finance report: an analysis of fiscal sustainability*, HM Treasury, December 2004 projected spending and revenue using different employment projections, while the 2003 *Long-term public finance report: fiscal sustainability with an ageing population*, HM Treasury, December 2003, analysed the effects of different fertility, longevity and migration assumptions on spending projections.

US A.21 As can be seen from Chart A.3, the US is projected to age relatively slowly in comparison with a number of developed and developing countries. Nonetheless, fiscal imbalances are projected to arise in the US over the coming decades. The US Congressional Budget Office (CBO) regularly publishes long-term analysis covering a wide range of topics, including future social security spending. The CBO projects that spending on social security will increase from 4.2 per cent of GDP in 2005 to 6.4 per cent by 2050,[11] while spending on Medicare and Medicaid (the two principal public health care schemes) is projected to rise from just over 4 per cent of GDP in 2005 to 12.6 per cent by 2050, due to a combination of demographic and non-demographic factors.[12] In addition, the CBO also projects the evolution of the future budget position and debt based on current policies. Based on the 'intermediate-spending scenario' and the assumption that tax revenue will remain unchanged as a share of GDP after 2014, the CBO projects the deficit on the total budget to rise to around 19 per cent of GDP by 2050, with federal debt rising to over 250 per cent of GDP over the same period.[13]

EU A.22 In February 2006, the EU's Economic Policy Committee (EPC) published detailed findings on the impact of an ageing population on future spending trends.[14] It found that age-related spending is projected to rise substantially in some EU Member States if existing policies remain unchanged (see Chart A.4).[15] Across the EU as a whole, age-related spending is projected to increase to around 27 per cent of GDP by 2050. Chart A.4 indicates that projected spending pressures are not confined to the existing EU15, with many EU10 countries projected to observe increases in age-related expenditure between now and 2050.

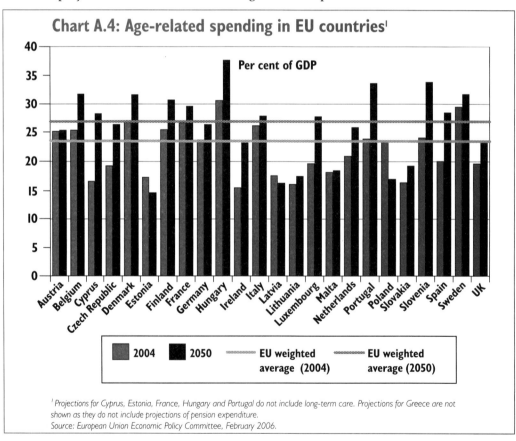

Chart A.4: Age-related spending in EU countries[1]

[1] Projections for Cyprus, Estonia, France, Hungary and Portugal do not include long-term care. Projections for Greece are not shown as they do not include projections of pension expenditure.
Source: European Union Economic Policy Committee, February 2006.

---

[11] See *The Long-Term Budget Outlook*, Congressional Budget Office, December 2005, page 4.

[12] Assuming that 'excess cost growth' will decline to one percentage point.

[13] *The Long-Term Budget Outlook*, Congressional Budget Office, December 2005, page 14.

[14] *The impact of ageing on public expenditure: projections for the EU25 Member States on pensions, health care, long-term care and unemployment transfers (2004-2050)*, European Union Economic Policy Committee, February 2006.

[15] Age-related spending comprises spending on pensions, health, long-term care, education and unemployment benefits in these projections.

A.23   There is substantial variation in the scale of future spending pressures, with age-related spending in 2050 projected to range between 15 per cent and 38 per cent of GDP among EU countries. Based on the EPC projections, age-related spending for the UK is projected to remain below the EU average throughout the projection period, reaching just over 23 per cent of GDP by 2050.[16] As can be seen from the chart, this is broadly equal to the current EU average.

Other developed **A.24**   Many other developed countries will also have to deal with the fiscal challenges that
countries arise from an ageing population. For example, recent projections published by the Japanese Ministry of Finance suggest a rise in social security benefits from $23^{1}/_{2}$ per cent of GDP in 2004 to 29 per cent of GDP in 2025.[17] Underpinning this is a particularly marked rise in medical care spending, which is projected to rise as a share of GDP over this period. A recent International Monetary Fund (IMF) report commented on the long-term fiscal challenge faced by Canada, noting a projected rise in public health care spending of almost 7 per cent of GDP between now and 2050.[18] The IMF concludes that '... fiscal sustainability would be jeopardized unless significant debt reduction is achieved ahead of the retirement of the baby boom generation and health care spending is constrained'.[19] A recent report published by the New Zealand Treasury also projects a significant increase in health spending as a share of GDP between now and 2050.[20] Similarly, the Australian Government Productivity Commission recently projected an increase in fiscal pressure (the extent to which government spending outpaces revenue growth) in Australia of 5.7 percentage points of GDP between 2003-04 and 2044-45.[21]

CONCLUSIONS

A.25   The fiscal projections presented in this annex show that the UK's public finances are broadly sustainable over the long term, confirming the detailed findings presented in the 2005 *Long-term public finance report*. Current public consumption can grow at around assumed GDP growth beyond the medium term, ensuring that resources are available to meet potential future spending pressures. The golden rule and the sustainable investment rule are both met throughout the projection period, with net debt projected to be below 40 per cent of GDP in the long run. Public sector net investment can grow more or less in line with the economy without jeopardising the sustainable investment rule. The UK is also well-placed to face future challenges relative to many other developed countries.

A.26   However, notwithstanding the use of prudent and cautious assumptions, a wide range of unforeseen developments and spending pressures could arise over the projection period. The Government will therefore continue to update and report on its assessments of long-term fiscal sustainability, both through regular publication of the Long-term public finance report alongside the Pre-Budget Report and through the illustrative long-term fiscal projections presented with each Budget, so as to ensure that all fiscal policy decisions are set within a sustainable long-term framework.

---

[16] This conclusion is similar to that reached on the basis of the projections presented in the 2005 *Long-term public finance report: an analysis of fiscal sustainability,* HM Treasury, December 2005.

[17] See *Current Japanese Fiscal Conditions and Issues to be Considered,* Ministry of Finance, Japan, 2005, page 21. Social security benefits represent the total expenditures paid under the social security system and include medical care, pensions and welfare.

[18] *Canada: 2004 Article IV Consultation-Staff Report; Staff Statement; and Public Information Notice on the Executive Board Discussion,* International Monetary Fund, March 2004, page 13.

[19] *Ibid,* page 12. The IMF reaches similar conclusions in its 2005 Report. See *Canada: 2005 Article IV Consultation-Staff Report; Staff Statement; and Public Information Notice on the Executive Board Discussion,* International Monetary Fund, March 2005.

[20] *Modelling New Zealand's Long-term Fiscal Position,* New Zealand Policy Perspectives Paper 06/01, February 2006.

[21] *Economic Implications of an Ageing Australia,* Australian Government Productivity Commission, March 2005.

Financial Statement
and Budget Report

BUDGET POLICY DECISIONS

A.1   The Economic and Fiscal Strategy Report (EFSR) explains how the measures and other decisions announced in Budget 2006 build on those already introduced to advance the Government's long-term goals. This chapter of the Financial Statement and Budget Report (FSBR) brings together in summary form all the measures and decisions announced in Budget 2006 and since Budget 2005, including in the 2005 Pre-Budget Report, that affect the Budget arithmetic, giving their estimated effect on government revenues and spending to 2008-09.[1]

A.2   The chapter sets out how the Budget 2006 measures affect the tax and benefit system and government spending. This includes a summary of the main rates and allowances for the personal tax and benefit system, the business tax system, Value Added Tax, environmental taxes, and other indirect taxes.

A.3   The appendices to this chapter provide additional information on Budget measures:

- Appendix A1 provides details of tax changes and other policy decisions which were announced in Budget 2005 or earlier, but which take effect from or after April 2006;

- Appendix A2 explains in detail how the effects of the Budget measures on government revenues are calculated; and

- Appendix A3 provides estimates of the costs to the Government of some of the main tax allowances and reliefs.

BUDGET POLICY DECISIONS

A.4   Table A1 summarises the Budget 2006 measures and their effects on government revenues and spending. These include tax measures, national insurance contributions (NICs) measures, measures that affect Annually Managed Expenditure (AME), and additions to Departmental Expenditure Limits (DEL). Measures that are financed from existing DEL provisions are not included.

---

[1] The contents of the brackets after each measure in this chapter refer to the line in Tables A1 and A2 where its costs or yield is shown. The symbol '-' indicates that the proposal has no Exchequer effect. The symbol '*' indicates that the effect is negligible, amounting to less than £3 million a year.

Table A1: Budget 2006 policy decisions

		(+ve is an Exchequer yield)		£ million
	2006-07 indexed	**2007-08 indexed**	**2008-09 indexed**	**2006-07 non-indexed**
MEETING THE PRODUCTIVITY CHALLENGE				
1 Changes to venture capital schemes	*	−15	−15	*
2 Extending the scope of R&D tax credits	0	−15	−40	0
3 Real Estate Investment Trusts	+35	+155	+130	+35
INCREASING EMPLOYMENT OPPORTUNITY FOR ALL				
4 Work Focused Interviews for lone parents	0	−20	0	0
5 Doubling skills coaching pilots for women	−5	−5	0	−5
6 Expanding the National Employer Training Programme	−10	−10	0	−10
7 Matched funding for Sector Skill Councils	−5	−5	0	−5
BUILDING A FAIRER SOCIETY				
Supporting families and communities				
8 Income tax: indexation of starting and basic rate limits	0	0	0	−570
9 Child Tax Credit: uprating child element in line with earnings until 2009-10	0	0	−200	0
10 Employer-supported childcare	−10	−20	−25	−10
11 Inheritance tax: increase of threshold	0	0	−10	0
12 Stamp duty land tax: increase of threshold	−40	−30	−30	−40
Protecting tax revenues				
13 Financial products avoidance	+125	+135	+100	+125
14 VAT: Countering Missing Trader Fraud	+100	+500	+425	+100
15 Countering CGT avoidance	0	+40	+35	0
16 Avoidance using employment related securities	+70	+65	+45	+70
17 VAT: supplies of goods under finance agreements	*	+10	+15	*
18 Rebated oils: changes to excepted vehicles schedule	0	+10	+10	0
Duties and other tax changes				
19 Alcohol duties: freeze spirits, cider and sparkling wine, revalorise beer and wine duties	−35	−30	−30	+170
20 Tobacco duties: revalorise rates	0	0	0	+25
21 VAT: reduced rate for contraceptive products	−5	−10	−10	−5
22 Further changes to oil valuation for tax purposes	+40	+80	+80	+40
23 Changes to group relief in corporation tax	−50	−50	−50	−50
24 Film tax reliefs: expanding the scope	*	−10	−10	*
25 Stamp duty land tax: ending relief for initial transfers into unit trusts	+50	+50	+40	+50
26 Removal of income tax exemption for loaned computers	+50	+100	+150	+50
27 Aligning the inheritance tax treatment for trusts	0	+15	+15	0
PROTECTING THE ENVIRONMENT				
Environment				
28 Climate change levy: revalorise from 1 April 2007	−20	−20	−20	0
29 Climate change levy: exemption of gas used in Northern Ireland	*	*	−5	*
30 Aggregates levy: freeze	−10	−10	−10	0
31 Enhanced Capital Allowances for water efficient technologies	*	−5	−5	*
32 Increasing the landfill tax credit scheme	−10	−10	−10	−10
Transport				
33 VAT: revalorise fuel scale charges	0	0	0	+10
34 Company car tax thresholds	−10	−20	+25	−10
35 Fuel duties: revalorise rates from 1 September 2006	−275	0	0	+380

Table A1: Budget 2006 policy decisions

	(+ve is an Exchequer yield)			£ million
	2006-07 indexed	**2007-08** indexed	**2008-09** indexed	**2006-07** non-indexed
36 Fuel duties: maintain differential for rebated oils from 1 September 2006	+40	+75	+80	+50
37 Fuel duties: maintain differential for biodiesel and bioethanol until 2008	*	0	+10	0
38 Fuel duties: maintain differential for road fuel gases	*	0	+5	*
39 Vehicle Excise Duties: enhancing environmental incentives	+5	+5	+5	+115
40 Other VED changes	0	+20	+35	+10
41 Air passenger duty: freeze	−10	−30	−30	0
OTHER POLICY DECISIONS				
42 Supporting further education reform	0	−55	0	0
43 Direct payments to schools	−270	−440	0	−270
44 Additional Police Community Support Officers	−100	0	0	−100
45 2012 Olympics: supporting elite athletes	−30	−35	0	−30
TOTAL POLICY DECISIONS	**−380**	**+415**	**+705**	**+115**
* negligible				
MEMO ITEMS				
Resetting of the AME margin	−90	+200		

A.5 Table A2 summarises the impact on government revenues and spending of other measures introduced since Budget 2005, including those measures announced in the 2005 Pre-Budget Report.

Table A2: Other measures announced since Budget 2005

			(+ve is an Exchequer yield)			£ million
			2006-07 indexed	**2007-08** indexed	**2008-09** indexed	**2006-07** non-indexed
MEETING THE PRODUCTIVITY CHALLENGE						
a	†	VAT: increased thresholds for cash and annual accounting schemes	*	−55	0	*
b	†	50% first year capital allowances for small enterprises	0	−60	+15	0
INCREASING EMPLOYMENT OPPORTUNITY FOR ALL						
c	†	Indexation of the Working Tax Credit	0	0	0	-300
d	†	Increase in Housing Benefit disregard	−5	−5	−5	−5
BUILDING A FAIRER SOCIETY						
e	†	Tax credits package	−100	+200	+50	−100
f	†	Reform of film tax incentives	+30	-10	+30	+30
g	†	Sale of lessors	+35	+85	+155	+35
h	†	Oil valuation for tax purposes	+40	+80	+80	+40
i	†	Tackling tax motivated incorporation	−50	+390	+530	−50
j	†	Indexation of income tax allowances	0	0	0	−870
k	†	Indexation of national insurance rates and limits	0	0	0	−550
l	†	Class 2 NICs: no increase in flat rate charge for self employed	−5	−5	−5	0
m		NICs quinquennial review of contracted-out rebates	0	−15	+55	0
n		Tax exemption for bank accounts of holocaust survivors	−5	*	*	−5
o		Stamp duty on shares: reconstruction relief	−20	−20	−20	−20
p	†	Aligning taxation of gambling machines with the Gambling Act	+25	+40	+30	+30
q	†	North Sea oil: increase in supplementary charge and first year allowance elections	+900	+2,300	+2,400	+900
r	†	Introducing Ringfence Expenditure Supplement	0	*	−5	0
s	†	Continued higher Winter Fuel Payments	−665	−680	−690	−665
t	†	Tackling pensioner fuel poverty	−150	−125	0	−150
Protecting revenues						
u	†	Financial avoidance using stock lending arrangements	+30	+30	+30	+30
v		Life assurance companies: closing avoidance opportunities	+115	+85	+85	+115
w	†	Corporate intangible assets avoidance	+90	+120	+120	+90
x	†	Prevention of abuse of corporate capital losses	+210	+300	+300	+210
y	†	Capital gains: preventing abuse of capital redemption policies	+35	+100	+75	+35
z	†	Enhancing the strategy to tackle tobacco smuggling	+50	+90	+115	+50
aa	†	Preventing income tax avoidance from transfer of assets abroad	*	+10	+30	*
PROTECTING THE ENVIRONMENT						
ab	†	Enhanced Capital Allowances for the cleanest biofuels production plant	0	−30	−20	0
ac	†	Fuel duties: freeze of main rates	−625	−630	−650	0
ad	†	Fuel duties: freeze of biofuel rates	−5	−5	−15	0
ae	†	Fuel duties: freeze of road fuel gases	−5	−5	−5	0
af	†	Exemption of oils used for electrcity generation	−5	−5	−5	−5
TOTAL POLICY DECISIONS[1]			**−80**	**+2,180**	**+2,690**	**−1,155**

* negligible.

† Announced in the 2005 Pre-Budget Report.

[1] Excludes the effects of measures taken to manage the transition arising from the move to International Accounting Standards and changes to the Income recognition rules in UK GAAP. The impact of these changes is detailed in Table A2.1.

Note: As required by the Code for Fiscal Stability, the 2005 Pre-Budget Report economic and fiscal projections were based on, and included the impact of, all Government decisions and circumstances that could be quantified with reasonable accuracy by the day the projections were finalised.

PERSONAL TAX AND SPENDING MEASURES

Income tax

Bands, rates and
personal
allowances

A.6   As announced in the 2005 Pre-Budget Report, all income tax personal allowances will be increased by statutory indexation. (j)

A.7   The starting and basic rate limits are increased with statutory indexation and there are no changes to the income tax rates. (8)

A.8   As announced in Budget 2004 the Lifetime Allowance for tax privileged pension schemes will be £1.5 million for 2006-07. The Annual Allowance will be £215,000 for 2006-07.

Table A3: Bands of taxable income 2006-07

2005-06	£ a year	2006-07	£ a year
Starting rate 10 per cent	0 – 2,090	Starting rate 10 per cent	0 – 2,150
Basic[1,2] rate 22 per cent	2,091 – 32,400	Basic[1,2] rate 22 per cent	2,151 – 33,300
Higher[2] rate 40 per cent	over 32,400	Higher[2] rate 40 per cent	over 33,300

[1] The rate of tax applicable to savings income in Section 1A ICTA 1988 remains at 20 per cent for income between the starting and basic rate limits.

[2] The rates applicable to dividends are 10 per cent for income up to the basic rate limit and 32.5 per cent above that.

Table A4: Income tax allowances 2006-07

		£ a year	
	2005-06	2006-07	Increase
Personal allowance			
age under 65	4,895	5,035	140
age 65-74	7,090	7,280	190
age 75 and over	7,220	7,420	200
Married couple's allowance[1]			
aged less than 75 and born before 6th April 1935	5,905	6,065	160
age 75 and over	5,975	6,135	160
minimum amount[2]	2,280	2,350	70
Income limit for age-related allowances	19,500	20,100	600
Blind person's allowance	1,610	1,660	50

[1] Tax relief for this allowance is restricted to 10 per cent.

[2] This is also the maximum relief for maintenance payments where at least one of the parties is born before 6 April 1935.

Effects on the Scottish Parliament's tax varying powers - statement regarding Section 76 of the Scotland Act 1998

A.9   A one penny change in the Scottish variable rate in 2006-07 could be worth approximately plus or minus £280 million, and is broadly unaffected by these changes. In the Treasury's view, an amendment to the Scottish Parliament's tax-varying powers is not required as a result of these changes.

National insurance contributions

A.10   As announced in the 2005 Pre-Budget Report, the national insurance contributions (NICs) thresholds and limits will increase in line with inflation. There will be no change to NICs rates for employers and employees, or the profit-related NICs paid by the self-employed. (k)

A.11   The flat rate of Class 2 NICs paid by the self-employed and the special rate of Class 2 for share fishermen will be frozen at 2005-06 levels which are £2.10 and £2.75 respectively. All other NICs rates for 2006-07 will increase in line with inflation: the special rate of Class 2 for volunteer development workers will be £4.20; the rate of Class 3 voluntary contributions will be £7.55. (l)

A.12   As announced on 1 March 2006, from April 2007 the reduction in total employer and employee NICs for individuals in defined benefit occupational schemes who have contracted out of the state second pension will increase from 5.1 per cent to 5.3 per cent. For individuals in defined contribution pension schemes who have contracted out, the NICs rebate below the age-related cap will increase by between 0.5 per cent and 1.9 per cent, while the cap will be reduced from 10.5 per cent to 7.4 per cent. (m)

Table A5: Class 1 national insurance contribution rates 2006-07

Earnings[1] £ per week	Employee (primary) NICs rate[2] per cent	Employer (secondary) NICs rate[3] per cent
Below £84 (LEL)	0	0
£84 to £97 (PT/ST)	0[4]	0
£97 to £645 (UEL)	11	12.8
Above £645	1	12.8

[1] The limits are defined as LEL – lower earnings limit; PT – primary threshold; ST – secondary threshold; and UEL – upper earnings limit.

[2] The contracted-out rebate for primary contributions in 2006–07 is 1.6 per cent of earnings between the LEL and UEL for contracted-out salary-related schemes (COSRS) and contracted-out money purchase schemes (COMPS).

[3] The contracted-out rebate for secondary contributions is 3.5 per cent of earnings between the LEL and UEL for COSRS and 1.0 per cent for COMPS. For COMPS, an additional age-related rebate is paid direct to the scheme following the end of the tax year. For approved personal pensions, the employee and employer pay NICs at the standard, not contracted-out rate. An age and earnings related rebate is paid direct to the personal pension provider following the end of the tax year.

[4] No NICs are actually payable but a notional primary Class 1 NIC will be deemed to have been paid in respect of earnings between LEL and PT to protect benefit entitlement.

Table A6: Self-employed national insurance contribution rates 2006-07

Annual Profits[1]	Self employed NICs	
	Class 2	Class 4
£ per year	£ per week	per cent
Below £4,465 (SEE)	0[2]	0
£4,465 to £5,035 (LPL)	£2.10	0
£5,035 to £33,540 (UPL)		8
Above £33,540		1

[1] The limits are defined as LPL – lower profits limit and UPL – upper profits limit.

[2] The self-employed may apply for exemption from paying Class 2 contributions if their earnings are less than, or expected to be less than, the level of the Small Earnings Exception (SEE).

Other personal taxes, benefits and spending measures

Tax credits **A.13**   As announced in the 2005 Pre-Budget Report, the Government will introduce a number of measures to improve the operation of tax credits, providing greater certainty for claimants, while maintaining flexibility to respond to falls in income and changes in circumstances. The disregard in tax credits for increases in income between one tax year and the next will rise from £2,500 to £25,000 from April 2006. (e)

Child Tax Credit **A.14**   As announced in the 2005 Pre-Budget Report, the child element of the Child Tax Credit will be increased by £75 to £1,765 a year from 6 April 2006, in line with earnings growth.

A.15   The Government will increase the child element of the Child Tax Credit at least in line with average earnings up to, and including, 2009-10. (9)

Working Tax **A.16**   As announced in the 2005 Pre-Budget Report, all the elements of Working Tax Credit
Credit rise in line with inflation (the increase in the RPI in the year to September 2005), as do the disabled child elements of Child Tax Credit. (c)

A.17   As announced in the 2005 Pre-Budget Report, the earnings disregard in Housing Benefit and Council Tax Benefit will rise in line with inflation to £14.90 in April 2006. (d)

Child Trust Fund **A.18**   The Government will make further payments of £250 into Child Trust Fund accounts at age 7, with children from lower-income families receiving £500. (–)

Table A7: Child and Working Tax Credits rates and thresholds

	2006-07 £ a year
Working Tax Credit	
Basic element	1,665
Couples' and lone parent element	1,640
30 hour element	680
Disabled worker element	2,225
Severe disability element	945
50+ Return to work payment (16-29 hours)	1,140
50+ Return to work payment (30+ hours)	1,705
Childcare element of the Working Tax Credit	
Maximum eligible cost for one child	£175 per week
Maximum eligible cost for two or more children	£300 per week
Per cent of eligible costs covered	80 per cent
Child Tax Credit	
Family element	545
Family element, baby addition	545
Child element	1,765
Disabled child element	2,350
Severely disabled child element	945
Income thresholds and withdrawal rates	
First income threshold	5,220
First withdrawal rate (per cent)	37 per cent
Second income threshold	50,000
Second withdrawal rate (per cent)	6.67 per cent
First threshold for those entitled to Child Tax Credit only	14,155
Income disregard	25,000

Individual Savings Accounts   **A.19**   As announced in the 2005 Pre-Budget Report, legislation was introduced with effect from 27 December 2005 enabling Credit Unions to sell products within the cash component of an ISA. (*)

Fuel poverty   **A.20**   As announced in the 2005 Pre-Budget Report, the Government will set aside £300 million over the next 3 years to assist pensioners in installing central heating systems and will continue Winter Fuel Payments to the over 60s for the duration of this Parliament. (s)(t)

Pensions tax simplification   **A.21**   Budget 2006 announces a small package of supplementary measures to ensure, with effect from 6 April 2006, the new pensions tax regime operates as intended. (*)

A.22   As announced in the 2005 Pre-Budget Report, the Government has also taken action to prevent abuse of the pension simplification rules by bringing forward legislation commencing on 6 April 2006 to prevent tax advantages being gained when Self Invested Personal Pension schemes invest in residential property, or individuals recycle pension lump sums to generate artificial levels of tax relief. (–)

IHT and pensions simplification A.23 As announced in the 2005 Pre-Budget Report, legislation will be brought forward in Finance Bill 2006 to clarify how inheritance tax will apply to choices under the new pension scheme rules which take effect from 6 April 2006. (–)

Employer-supported childcare A.24 From April 2006 the tax and national insurance exemption for employer supported childcare will be increased from £50 to £55 per wek. The qualifying conditions will remain unchanged. (10)

Employer-provided equipment A.25 The Government will remove the current exemption for employer-provided equipment from 6 April 2006. The tax exemption for mobile phones will be refocused to prevent exploitation, also with effect from 6 April 2006. (26)

VDU users: eye tests and glasses A.26 A measure will be introduced, with effect from 6 April 2006, to remove the tax charge where an employer pays for eye tests and/or corrective glasses for VDU users. (*)

Holocaust victims A.27 As announced on 19 July 2005, legislation will be introduced which will exempt from tax certain payments made in relation to UK and foreign bank and building society accounts of Holocaust victims. The exemption will cover payments made from 6 April 1996 onwards. (n)

Charity payments in benefits A.28 As announced in the 2005 Pre-Budget Report, from October 2006 charitable, voluntary and personal injury income payments will be fully disregarded when assessing eligibility for Income Support and Jobseeker's Allowance. In addition a 52-week grace period will be introduced for personal injury lump sum payments when assessing eligibility for these benefits and for working age Housing Benefit and Council Tax Benefit. (*)

Housing Benefit A.29 A package of measures will be introduced to further simplify and reduce anomalies in the Housing Benefit system, including:

- applying more regulations equally to both customers and their partners;

- implementing regulations that clarify the treatment of owner-occupiers and former owner-occupiers and their partners; and

- enabling tennants to recieve Housing Benefit on the rental portion of a shared ownership arrangement, where the tenancy is granted by an organisation other than a Housing Association or Housing Authority. (–)

Support for lone parents A.30 From April 2007, all lone parents who have been on benefit for at least a year will, at a minimum, be required to attend a Work Focused Interview every six months. (4)

Women and Work Commission A.31 In response to the Women and Work Commission Report *Shaping a Fairer Future*,[2] the Government today announces a package of measures to enhance lifelong learning opportunities for women in training and work. (5) (6) (7)

---

[2] *Shaping a Fairer Future*, Women and Work Commission, February 2006.

CHARITIES AND COMMUNITIES

Gift Aid declarations **A.32** As announced in the 2005 Pre-Budget Report, with effect from 1 November 2005, charities no longer need to send donors a written record of oral declarations, provided that the charity keeps sufficient records of declarations, available for audit by HM Revenue and Customs. (–)

Gift Aid for charity subsidiaries **A.33** As announced in the 2005 Pre-Budget Report, with effect from 1 April 2006, a measure will be introduced to enable subsidiary companies owned by one or more charities to donate their profits to parent charities using Gift Aid. (*)

Exemption for trading profits **A.34** A measure will be introduced for chargeable periods commencing on or after 22 March 2006 extending tax exemption for trades that are wholly charitable, to trades that are only partially charitable. Exemption will be available in respect of the profits of the part trade that is charitable. (*)

Social housing sinking funds **A.35** As announced in the 2005 Pre-Budget Report, the trust rate of tax on income for service charge and sinking funds which are held on trust for tenants and leaseholders in social housing will be reduced to a standard rate from 6 April 2006. (*)

Band Aid Charitable Trust **A.36** The Government will make a special payment to the Band Aid Charitable Trust, representing its existing commitment to cover the cost of the VAT collected on sales of the Live Aid DVD up to 2009-10, and an additional one-off donation of £250,000 in support of the Live 8 DVD.

2012 Olympics: elite athletes **A.37** The Government will make available up to £200 million over the next seven years to fund elite athletes, including paralympic athletes. (42)

London Olympic Games and Paralympic Games **A.38** In accordance with the Government's commitments on tax in the bid, measures will be introduced to exempt the London Organising Committee of the Olympic Games from corporation tax, with effect from 22 October 2004, and to provide powers to make tax provisions in relation to the International Olympic Committee and non-UK resident competitors and support staff. (–)

TAXES ON CHARGEABLE GAINS, INHERITANCE TAX AND STAMP TAXES

Capital gains tax   **A.39**   The capital gains tax annual exempt amount is increased in line with statutory indexation to £8,800. (*)

Inheritance tax   **A.40**   As announced in Budget 2005, the inheritance tax threshold will increase above statutory indexation to £285,000 for new tax charges arising on or after 6 April 2006, and again to £300,000 for new tax charges arising on or after 6 April 2007. Budget 2006 announces the inheritance tax threshold will continue to increase above expected statutory indexation to £312,000 in 2008-09 and £325,000 in 2009-10. (11)

Tax regime for trusts   **A.41**   A measure will be introduced, with effect from 22 March 2006, to provide that the inheritance tax exemptions which presently apply to some types of trust will only be available in certain prescribed circumstances. (27)

A.42   A package of measures will be introduced with effect from 6 April 2006, to reduce burdens on the smallest trusts and harmonise key trust-related tests and definitions for income tax and capital gains tax. (*)

Stamp duty land tax   **A.43**   From 23 March 2003 the starting threshold for stamp duty land tax will increase from £120,000 to £125,000 for residential property transactions. The starting thresholds for residential transactions in Enterprise Areas and commercial transactions remain at £150,000. (12)

SDLT: deregulatory amendments   **A.44**   A number of measures will be introduced simplifying the stamp duty land tax legislation and thereby reducing compliance burdens. Some of these measures will take effect from 12 April 2006 and others from Royal Assent. (*)

Stamps: company acquisitions and reconstructions   **A.45**   Following the announcement on 22 July 2005 a measure will be introduced, effective from the day after Royal Assent, to enable relief from stamp duty and stamp duty reserve tax in respect of certain corporate acquisitions and reconstructions to be claimed by companies registered outside the UK as well as those registered in the UK. (o)

BUSINESS TAXES AND SPENDING MEASURES

Corporation tax   **A.46**   The main rate of corporation tax will be set at 30 per cent for financial year 2007-08. As announced in the 2005 Pre-Budget report, the non-corporate distribution and starting rates of corporation tax will be replaced with a new single banding set at the existing small companies' rate of 19 per cent from 1 April 2006. (–) (i)

A.47   As announced in the 2005 Pre-Budget Report, from April 2006 the rate of first year capital allowances for small businesses' spending on plant and machinery will be increased from 40 per cent to 50 per cent for a period of one year. (b)

Group relief   **A.48**   With effect from 1 April 2006, the Government will introduce a small extension to the group relief legislation for companies which will, in some very limited circumstances, allow a UK company to claim relief for otherwise unrelievable foreign losses incurred in the European Economic Area. (23)

Demutualisation and transfers of insurance business   **A.49**   Measures will be introduced, with effect from 22 March 2006, to provide a relief from stamp duty land tax on a demutualisation and to provide reliefs from unintended tax charges in connection with transfers of insurance business generally. (–)

Apportionment rules　**A.50**　A measure was introduced, generally with effect from 1 January 2006, to permanently extend the apportionment rules for income and gains from a life assurance company's inherited estate. (–)

Life insurance policies　**A.51**　As announced on 7 October 2005, a measure was introduced with effect from that date, preserving and simplifying existing practice to ensure that unexpected tax effects do not arise for holders of qualifying life assurance policies where there is a variation in the basis on which any investment element in the policy is allocated to them by the insurer. (*)

North Sea oil taxation　**A.52**　As announced in the 2005 Pre-Budget Report, with effect from 1 January 2006, the supplementary charge is increased to 20 per cent. North Sea oil companies will be able to elect to defer 100 per cent relief for capital expenditure incurred in 2005 into the following year. (q)

A.53　As announced in the 2005 Pre-Budget Report, with effect from 1 January 2006, a Ring Fence Expenditure Supplement was introduced to uplift all expenditure by North Sea oil companies without taxable income to ensure the value of tax relief is maintained over time. This will replace and extend the current Exploration Expenditure Supplement. (r)

Oil tax pricing　**A.54**　As announced in the 2005 Pre-Budget Report, with effect from 1 July 2006, changes will be made to the way in which oil is valued for non arm's length transactions to ensure a fairer and less distortionary tax system. (h)

Nominations scheme and blended oils　**A.55**　A package of measures will be introduced, with effect from 1 July 2006, making changes to the Nominations Scheme and sales of blended oils. This will remove or refine rules that are distorting the tax system and ensure a level playing field for all North Sea oil companies. (22)

Energy Act 2004　**A.56**　Measures will be introduced, with effect from 22 March 2006, to ensure that tax provisions in sections 29 and 30 of Energy Act 2004 have the intended effect. (–)

Sale of lessors　**A.57**　As announced in the 2005 Pre-Budget Report, with effect from 5 December 2005, a package of measures was introduced to address a potential loss of tax when a lessor company that has benefited from capital allowances, changes hands. (g)

Alternative finance products　**A.58**　From 1 April 2006 for corporation tax, and 6 April 2006 for income tax, further alternative finance products, including diminishing musharaka and wakala transactions, will receive tax treatment equivalent to that of existing products. (*)

A.59　A measure will be introduced with effect from Royal Assent which will extend to all entities, including companies, the reliefs from multiple stamp duty land tax charges currently enjoyed by individuals. (*)

Accounting standards　**A.60**　As announced in the 2005 Pre-Budget Report, the Government will legislate in Finance Bill 2006 to enable most businesses affected by changes in the income recognition rules in UK GAAP to spread any extra tax charge arising in respect of periods of account ending on or after 22 June 2005 over three to six years.

A.61　As announced in the 2005 Pre-Budget Report, with effect from 1 January 2005 a measure was introduced to amend the definition of a securitisation company to exclude companies other than those with permitted activities.

Film tax relief A.62 As announced in the 2005 Pre-Budget Report, subject to state aid approval, from 1 April 2006 new incentives for filmmaking will be introduced to replace the existing reliefs. Budget 2006 also announces the minimum UK spend threshold will be set at 25 per cent. (f) (24)

Lloyds: double A.63 As announced in the 2005 Pre-Budget Report, regulations will be introduced with
taxation relief effect from accounting periods ending on or after 31 December 2006 to simplify double taxation relief for Lloyd's corporate underwriters. These regulations are being drafted in consultation with the Lloyd's market. (*)

Venture capital A.64 From 6 April 2006 the Government will introduce a new rate of 30 per cent income tax
schemes relief for investments in Venture Capital Trusts (VCTs) together with further changes to refocus the VCT scheme, Enterprise Investment Scheme and Corporate Venturing Scheme on small companies facing barriers to accessing finance. (1)

Real Estate A.65 The Government will introduce UK Real Estate Investment Trusts (UK-REITs), with
Investment effect from 1 January 2007, to improve the efficiency of the property investment market. A
Trusts conversion charge will be applied to companies electing to join the regime to ensure no overall cost to the Exchequer. (3)

Housing A.66 In parallel to the introduction of UK-REITs, legislation relating to Housing Investment
Investment Trusts is being repealed in relation to accounting periods beginning on or after the day on
Trusts which the Finance Bill is passed. (–)

R&D tax credits A.67 The Government intends to extend additional support to R&D performing companies with between 250 and 500 employees, subject to the outcome of state aid discussions with the European Commission. Detailed proposals will be published later this year. (2)

A.68 As announced in December 2005, with effect from 1 April 2006, the time limit and claims process for claiming a payable credit will be brought into line with the rules for claiming enhanced relief. In addition, minor technical changes will be made to expand the scope of the R&D tax credits, subject to state aid approval. (*)

Enterprise A.69 As announced on 5 December 2005, a measure will be introduced, effective from 1
Management September 2003, to allow intended corporation tax relief where companies grant discounted
Incentives Enterprise Management Incentive options to employees over shares that carry restrictions or conversion rights. (*)

Employee share A.70 As announced in the 2005 Pre-Budget Report, HM Revenue and Customs intends
ownership to improve further the process for administration of tax-advantaged employee share schemes. (–)

VALUE ADDED TAX

VAT registration A.71 From 1 April 2006, the VAT registration threshold will be increased from £60,000 to £61,000 and the deregistration threshold from £58,000 to £59,000. (*)

Flexible payment A.72 As announced in the 2005 Pre-Budget Report, from 1 April 2006 the turnover
options threshold up to which businesses can take advantage of the Annual Accounting Scheme will increase from £660,000 to £1.35 million. The Government has also written to the European Commission for a derogation to increase the turnover limit. (a)

Imported works of art A.73 Following a recent judgement by the European Court of Justice, the Government is amending the law concerning valuation of imported works of art. Following Royal Assent any auctioneer's fees involved will be taxed at the standard rate of VAT. (*)

Buildings and land A.74 A measure will be introduced with effect from Royal Assent to enable legislation to be enacted that will replace current VAT option to tax land and property provisions with legislation that is clearer and easier to use. (*)

Option to tax A.75 As announced in the 2005 Pre-Budget Report, a package of measures will be introduced between 2006 and 2009 to implement changes necessary to facilitate the revocation of the option to tax. (–)

Contraceptive products A.76 With effect from 1 July 2006, the Government will reduce the rate of VAT chargeable on contraceptive products to 5 per cent. The full list of goods and services subject to a reduced rate of VAT will therefore be: children's car seats, contraceptive products, domestic fuel and power, installation of energy-saving materials and heating equipment, certain residential conversions and renovations, certain non-exempt welfare activities and women's sanitary products. (21)

ENVIRONMENTAL AND TRANSPORT TAXES

Climate change levy A.77 Climate change levy (CCL) rates will increase in line with current inflation from 1 April 2007. (28)

CCL: rate for horticulture A.78 As announced in the 2005 Pre-Budget Report, the temporary 50 per cent rate of CCL for energy used in horticulture will expire after 31 March 2006 as state aid approval has now been granted for the horticulture sector to sign a climate change agreement. (–)

CCL: Northern Ireland gas exemption A.79 The exemption from CCL for natural gas in Northern Ireland will be extended for a further five years, until 31 March 2011. (29)

Reduced VAT rate for wood-fuelled boilers A.80 As announced in the 2005 Pre-Budget Report, a reduced rate of VAT of 5 per cent was introduced on 1 January 2006 for the installation of wood-fuelled boilers. (*)

Landlords Energy Saving Allowance **A.81** The Landlords Energy Saving Allowance – an allowance of up to £1500 for landlords who invest in cavity wall, loft or solid wall insulation – will be extended to draught proofing and the insulation of hot water systems. (*)

Fuel duties **A.82** The 2005 Pre-Budget Report announced a continuation of the freeze on main fuel duty rates. Budget 2006 announces an inflation-based increase for main fuel duties, but because of continuing oil market volatility the changes in rates will be deferred until 1 September 2006. (ac) (35)

Rebated oils duties **A.83** The 2005 Pre-Budget Report announced an immediate increase of 1.22 pence per litre (ppl) in the duty on rebated oils. Budget 2006 announces rebated oils duties will increase by 1.25ppl from 1 September, to maintain the differential with main fuel duty rates and support the UK Oils Strategy. (–) (36)

Energy products directive **A.84** The Government will apply for renewal of the derogations on private pleasure flying, private pleasure crafts, and waste oils. (–)

Red diesel: excepted vehicles **A.85** The excepted vehicles schedule will be revised from 1 April 2007 to clarify the vehicles permitted to use red diesel. (18)

Electricity generation **A.86** As announced in the 2005 Pre-Budget Report, with effect from 1 January 2006, rebated heavy oils used to generate electricity have been relieved from duty. (af)

Biofuels **A.87** The 2005 Pre-Budget Report announced the 20ppl duty incentive for biodiesel and bioethanol would be guaranteed until 2007-08. Budget 2006 announces the duty incentive will be further guaranteed until 2008-09. (ad) (37)

ECAs for biofuels **A.88** As announced in the 2005 Pre-Budget Report, subject to state aids approval, the Government will establish an Enhanced Capital Allowance scheme for the cleanest biofuels production plant. (ab)

Road fuel gases **A.89** The 2005 Pre-Budget Report announced a continuation in the freeze in duty rates on road fuel gases. Budget 2006 announces natural gas (NG) rates will increase by the equivalent of 1.25ppl, maintaining the differential with main rates. Liquefied petroleum gas (LPG) rates will increase by the equivalent of 2.25ppl to reduce the differential with main fuel duty by 1ppl and reflect more accurately their environmental benefits. Both changes will be deferred until 1 September 2006. (ae)

A.90 The Government today also announces the duty differential between LPG and main road fuels will be reduced by the equivalent of 1ppl each year to 2008-09, and that the duty differential between NG rates and main duty rates will be maintained each year until 2008-09, to reflect the differing environmental benefits of the two fuel types. (38)

Vehicle excise duty **A.91** The Government today announces a new higher band of Graduated VED (G) for the most polluting new cars, set at £210, and the reduction, to £0, of Band A. Bands B and C are also reduced. Bands D and E are frozen and band F is increased. (39)

A.92   Motorbike VED rates and the standard rate for light goods vehicles will be increased in line with inflation. VED for Heavy Goods Vehicles and buses will be frozen in 2006-07. The reduced rate of VED for Euro IV vans will be removed for vans registered after the date on which these emissions standards become mandatory for all new vehicles (31 December 2006), but remain for the life of existing vans meeting the requirements registered before that date. All changes to VED take effect for licences taken out from 23 March 2006. (40)

Company car tax   **A.93**   From 6 April 2008, the level of carbon dioxide emissions qualifying for the lower 15 per cent threshold of company car tax will reduce by 5 grams per kilometre (g/km) from 140 g/km to 135 g/km. In addition, a new 10 per cent band for cars with carbon dioxide emissions of 120g/km or below will be introduced. (34)

Fuel benefit rates   **A.94**   The company car fuel benefit tax charge will remain frozen at £14,400 for 2006-07. (–)

Revalorisation of fuel scale charge   **A.95**   From 1 May 2006, the VAT fuel scale charges will be increased in line with pump prices. In addition, as confirmed in the 2005 Pre-Budget Report, the fuel scale charge will be based on carbon dioxide emissions from 1 May 2007. (33)

Air passenger duty   **A.96**   The Government today announces a freeze in the rates of Air Passenger Duty. (41)

A.97   From 1 November 2006, the scope of the European rate of Air Passenger Duty will be widened to include Croatia, as an applicant country to the European Union. (*)

Landfill tax   **A.98**   As confirmed in the 2005 Pre-Budget Report, with effect from 1 April 2006, the standard rate of landfill tax will increase by £3 per tonne to £21 per tonne in 2006/07. The lower rate for inert wastes remains at £2 per tonne.

Landfill Tax Credit Scheme   **A.99**   The Government today announces the value of the Landfill Tax Credit Scheme for 2006-07 will increase to £60 million. (32)

Aggregates levy   **A.100**   The Government today announces the rate of the aggregates levy will remain frozen at £1.60 per tonne in 2006-07. (30)

Enhanced capital allowances   **A.101**   The list of designated water-efficient technologies qualifying for 100 per cent enhanced first-year capital allowances will be expanded during 2006, to include three further technology classes. (31)

Table A8a: VED bands and rates for cars registered after 1 March 2001 (graduated VED)

VED band	CO$_2$ emissions (g/km)	VED rate (£)		
		Cars using alternative fuels	Petrol car	Diesel car
A	100 and below	0	0	0
B	101 to 120	30	40	50
C	121 to 150	90	100	110
D	151 to 165	115	125	135
E	166 to 185	140	150	160
F	186 and above[1]	180	190	195
G	226 and above[2]	200	210	215

[1] Cars registered before 23 March 2006.
[2] Cars registered on or after 23 March 2006.

Table A8b: VED bands and rates for private and light goods vehicles registered before 1 March 2001 (pre-graduated VED)

Engine size	VED rate (£)
1549cc and below	110
Above 1549cc	175

OTHER INDIRECT TAXES AND DUTIES

Tobacco duties   **A.102**   From 6pm on Budget Day 2006, tobacco duty rates will rise in line with inflation to maintain the real price of tobacco. (20)

Table A9: Changes to tobacco duties

	Effect of tax[1] on typical item (increase in pence)	Unit
Cigarettes	9	packet of 20
Cigars	3	packet of 5
Hand-rolling tobacco	8	25g
Pipe tobacco	5	25g

[1] Tax refers to duty plus VAT.

Alcohol duties   **A.103**   Excise duty rates on spirits, cider and sparking wine will be frozen, while the rates on beer and wine will increase in line with inflation from midnight on 26 March 2006. (19)

Table A10: Changes to alcohol duties

	Effect of tax[1] on typical item (increase in pence)	Unit
Beer	1	Pint of beer @ 4.2% abv
Wine	1	175ml glass typical strength
Wine	4	75cl bottle typical strength
Sparkling Wine	0	75cl bottle typical strength
Spirits	0	70cl bottle @ 37.5% abv
Spirits-based RTDs	0	275ml bottle @ 5.4% abv
Cider	0	Pint of cider typical strength
Sparkling cider	0	175ml typical strength

[1] Tax refers to duty plus VAT.

Simplification of alcohol duty
A.104 A number of obsolete regulatory requirements will be removed from the alcohol legislation and others will be simplified. Changes to regulations will come into effect from 1 May 2006, and changes to primary law from Royal Assent. (*)

Betting and gaming duties
A.105 Gaming duty bands will rise in line with inflation for accounting periods starting on or after 1 April 2006. (-)

Gaming machines
A.106 Measures will be introduced to simplify some administrative aspects of amusement machine licence duty. (*)

A.107 As announced in the 2005 Pre-Budget Report, the definition of gaming machines for VAT purposes was changed from 6 December 2005. In addition a further measure will be introduced, with effect from 1 August 2006, to align the excise definition of a gaming machine with the Gambling Act and introduce new rates and licence categories. (p)

PROTECTING TAX REVENUES

Extending the disclosure regime
A.108 Further to the announcement in the 2005 Pre-Budget Report, a measure will be introduced, with effect from 1 July 2006, to update and extend the disclosure regime to the whole of income tax, corporation tax and capital gains tax.

Employment-related securities
A.109 A measure is introduced, effective from 2 December 2004, to prevent employment-related securities options being used in avoidance schemes. (16)

Life assurance companies
A.110 As announced on 29 September 2005, measures were introduced effective from that date, to prevent life assurance companies deducting payments of bonuses paid out of untaxed surplus and deferring taxation of gains from investments. (v)

Stock lending arrangements
A.111 As announced in the 2005 Pre-Budget Report, a measure was introduced, with effect from 5 December 2005, to prevent companies and others from avoiding tax on interest using schemes involving stock lending arrangements. (u)

Dividend strips
A.112 As announced on 20 January 2006, a measure was introduced, with effect from that date, to prevent avoidance of tax by financial institutions and share dealers through the purchase and sale of the rights to dividends on shares. (–)

Financial products
A.113 A package of measures will be introduced, with effect from 22 March 2006, to prevent avoidance of tax using schemes involving financial products. (13)

Corporate capital losses
A.114 As announced in the 2005 Pre-Budget Report, three targeted anti-avoidance rules were introduced, with effect from 5 December 2005, to prevent tax motivated behaviour involving the creation and use of capital losses by companies. (x)

Intangible assets
A.115 As announced in the 2005 Pre-Budget Report, measures will be introduced, with effect from 5 December 2005, to prevent unintended tax relief from arising where rights in existing intangible assets are transferred between related parties. (w)

Chargeable gains: policies of insurance etc
A.116 As announced in the 2005 Pre-Budget Report, with effect from 5 December 2005, a measure was introduced to counter tax avoidance schemes designed to generate capital losses on certain insurance policies (including capital redemption policies) and annuities. (y)

Protecting charitable tax reliefs
A.117 A package of measures will be introduced to counter abuse of charitable reliefs. With effect from 22 March 2006 new rules will prevent donors extracting value from a charity and make it easier to restrict charitable tax reliefs where a charity has incurred non-charitable expenditure. With effect from 1 April 2006 all companies will be subject to the same limit on benefits received as a result of a gift to charity. (*)

Transfer of assets abroad **A.118** As announced in the 2005 Pre-Budget Report, loopholes were closed, with effect from 5 December 2005, in the legislation that prevents UK resident individuals avoiding income tax by transferring assets to overseas trusts and companies. (aa)

IHT: avoidance **A.119** As announced in the 2005 Pre-Budget Report, a measure was introduced with effect from 5 December 2005, to counter inheritance tax avoidance that uses second-hand interests in foreign trusts and close a loophole which allows individuals to avoid paying either inheritance tax or the income tax charge on pre-owned assets. (*)

Controlled Foreign Company rules **A.120** A measure will be introduced, with effect from 22 March 2006, to bring additional treaty non-resident companies within the Controlled Foreign Companies legislation. (–)

VAT: face value vouchers **A.121** A package of targeted anti-avoidance measures will be introduced, with effect from Royal Assent, to help prevent avoidance involving face value vouchers, such as phone cards. (*)

VAT: MTIC – reverse charge **A.122** A measure will be introduced to put in place a framework for a revised mechanism for accounting for VAT on certain goods to tackle Missing Trader Intra-Community (MTIC) fraud. (14)

VAT: MTIC – enhanced powers **A.123** Measures will be introduced, with effect from Royal Assent, to confirm HM Revenue and Customs' right to evidence inspection of goods and allow HM Revenue and Customs to direct individual businesses to keep additional records, where these might assist in identifying tax loss through MTIC fraud. (*)

Supplies by finance companies **A.124** A measure will be introduced to close a loophole in the VAT treatment of goods sold, for the second time, by a finance company. The basis on which bad debt relief is claimed in connection with certain credit agreements will also be simplified. These measures take effect in relation to goods delivered under such agreements on or after 1 September 2006. (17)

Film partnerships **A.125** As announced on 10 March 2006, with effect from that date, a measure was introduced to counter a scheme which sought to provide individuals in film partnerships with a tax advantage greater than the amount invested while avoiding any taxable income at a later date. (–)

Film exit schemes **A.126** As announced on 20 December 2005, a measure was introduced, with effect from that date, to counter avoidance by individuals in partnerships where existing exits legislation is triggered without establishing a tax charge. (–)

Tackling tobacco smuggling **A.127** The Government today publishes a refreshed strategy to tackle tobacco smuggling. This includes the measures announced in the 2005 Pre-Budget Report to further restrict the availability of cigarettes and hand-rolling tobacco to smugglers, and to tackle the problem of counterfeit tobacco products. (z)

Mutual assistance **A.128** As announced in the 2005 Pre-Budget Report, legislation will be introduced in Finance Bill 2006 to extend current mutual assistance arrangements to cover the exchange of information on all taxes and assistance in the recovery of tax debts.

CGT: bed and breakfasting rules **A.129** A measure will be introduced with effect from 22 March 2006, to counter tax avoidance schemes by preventing bed and breakfasting identification rules applying to certain disposals of securities. (15)

SDLT: seeding relief **A.130** With effect from 22 March 2006 seeding relief for newly formed unit trusts will be withdrawn. (25)

ADDITIONAL SPENDING AND DEBT MANAGEMENT DECISIONS

Annually Managed Expenditure **A.131** In line with usual practice, this Budget sets the Annually Managed Expenditure (AME) margin to £1 billion in 2006-07 and £2 billion in 2007-08.

Police Community Support Officers **A.132** The Government will provide an additional £100 million to bring Police Community Support Officer recruitment to 16,000 by April 2007. This will also fund development of a new service to publish local crime and police performance data on a regulatory basis. (45)

Direct payments to schools **A.133** Budget 2006 announces additional resources of £270 million in 2006-07 and £440 million in 2007-08. This will provide further resources to support personalisation in schools in England, including a total of £585 million in direct payments to headteachers over the next two years. (43)

Further education reform **A.134** A package of measures will be introduced to support a programme of reform in further education, details will be set out in a forthcoming White Paper to be published on 27 March 2006. (44)

BUDGET POLICY DECISIONS: APPENDICES

APPENDIX A1: MEASURES ANNOUNCED IN BUDGET 2005 OR EARLIER

A1.1   This appendix sets out a number of tax, benefit and other changes which were announced in Budget 2005 or earlier and which will take effect from April 2006 or later. The revenue effects of these measures have been taken into account in previous economic and fiscal projections.

Table A1.1: Measures announced in Budget 2005 or earlier which take effect from April 2006 or later

		(+ve is an Exchequer yield)			£ million
		2006-07 indexed	**2007-08 indexed**	**2008-09 indexed**	**2006-07 non-indexed**
a	Child Tax Credit: uprate child element in line with earnings until 2007-08	–210	–450	–440	–510
b	Working Tax Credit: increase childcare element to 80%	–130	–130	–130	–130
c	Improving support to 16-19 year olds in learning	–135	–155	–220	–135
d	Extension of paid maternity leave to 9 months	0	–385	–385	0
e	ISAs: extension of higher investment limits until April 2010	–65	–150	–220	–65
f	Increase lower capital limits within means tested benefits	–15	–15	–15	–15
g	Increasing capital limits for IS/JSA from £8,000 to £16,000	–5	–5	–5	–5
h	Social Fund reform	–5	–5	–5	–5
i	Incapacity benefit: linking rules	–10	–20	–20	–10
j	Pension tax simplification	–25	–70	–165	–25
k	Abolition of hospital downrating	–65	–65	–65	–65
l	Modernising the taxation of leasing	+65	+170	+215	+65
m	Company car tax: reform of the diesel supplement	+55	+130	+200	+55
TOTAL POLICY DECISIONS		**–545**	**–1,150**	**–1,255**	**–845**

Child Tax Credit **A1.2**   As announced in Budget 2005, the child element of the Child Tax Credit will increase at least in line with average earnings up to and including 2007-08. (a)

Working Tax Credit **A1.3**   As announced in the 2004 Pre-Budget Report, from April 2006 the maximum proportion of childcare costs covered by the childcare element of the Working Tax Credit will be increased from 70 to 80 per cent. (b)

Extending financial support to 16-19s in learning **A1.4**   As announced in Budget 2005, from April 2006 Child Benefit, Child Tax Credit and Income Support will be extended to 19-year-olds completing a course of non-advanced education or training which they started before their 19th birthday, up to a limit of age 20, and Child Benefit and Child Tax Credit will be extended to unwaged trainees on work-based learning programmes arranged by the Government. (c)

Statutory Maternity Pay **A1.5**   As announced in the 2004 Pre-Budget Report, paid maternity leave will be extended from six to nine months from April 2007. (d)

Individual Saving Accounts **A1.6**   As announced in the 2004 Pre-Budget Report, the Government will extend further the existing higher ISA limits of £7,000, with a maximum of £3,000 in cash, until at least April 2010. (e)

Treatment of capital limits **AI.7** As announced in Budget 2004 and Budget 2005, from April 2006 the threshold above which savings begin to reduce eligibility for Income Support, Jobseeker's Allowance, Housing Benefit and Council Tax Benefit will be raised from £3,000 to £6,000. (f)

AI.8 As announced in Budget 2005, from April 2006 the upper capital thresholds for Income Support and Jobseeker's Allowance will be raised from £8,000 and £16,000. (g)

Social Fund **AI.9** As announced in the 2004 Pre-Budget Report, the Government will enact a package of measures to reform the Social Fund, including the abolition of the double debt rule and the lowering of the highest loan repayment rates. (h)

Linking rules **AI.10** As announced in Budget 2005, the incapacity benefits linking rules will be improved from October 2006 to better support claimants during the transition from benefits to work. (i)

Pension tax simplification **AI.11** As announced in Budget 2004 and legislated in Finance Acts 2004 and 2005, reforms will be introduced, with effect from 6 April 2006, to simplify the current pension tax regime. There will be a single universal regime for tax privileged pensions to replace the existing complex regimes. (j)

Hospital downrating **AI.12** As announced in Budget 2005, downrating of the basic state pension and some other benefits for those staying in hospital for more than 52 weeks will be abolished from April 2006. (k)

Leasing **AI.13** As announced in the 2004 Pre-Budget Report, from 1 April 2006 the taxation of leased plant and machinery will be aligned with the tax treatment of other similar forms of finance. (l)

Company car tax **AI.14** As announced in the 2004 Pre-Budget Report, from 6 April 2006, the waiver of the 3 per cent diesel supplement for diesel cars that meet Euro IV emissions standards will cease for cars registered on or after 1 January 2006. The Regulation introducing this change (SI 2005/2209) was laid before the House of Commons on 8 August 2005. (m)

APPENDIX A2: EXPLAINING THE COSTINGS

A2.1 This appendix explains how the Exchequer effects of the Budget measures are calculated. In the context of these calculations, the net Exchequer effects for measures may include amounts for taxes, national insurance contributions, social security benefits and other charges to the Exchequer, including penalties.

Calculating the costings

A2.2 The net Exchequer effect of a Budget measure is generally calculated as the difference between applying the pre-Budget and post-Budget tax and benefit regimes to the levels of total income and spending at factor cost expected after the Budget. The estimates do not therefore include any effect the tax changes themselves have on overall levels of income and spending. However, they do take account of other effects on behaviour where they are likely to have a significant and quantifiable effect on the cost or yield and any consequential changes in revenue from related taxes and benefits.

A2.3   These include estimated changes in the composition or timing of income, spending or other tax determinants. For example, the estimated yield from increasing the excise duty on spirits would include the change in the yield of VAT and other excise duties resulting from the new pattern of spending. The calculation of the expected effect of changes in duty rates on consumer demand for excise goods assumes that any change in duty is passed on in full to consumers. Where the effect of one tax change is affected by implementation of others, the measures are generally costed in the order in which they appear in Tables A1, A2 and A1.1.

A2.4   The non-indexed base columns shown in Tables A1, A2 and A1.1 show the revenue effect of changes in allowances, thresholds and rates of duty including the effect of any measures previously announced but not yet implemented from their pre-Budget level. The indexed base columns strip out the effects of inflation by increasing the allowances, thresholds and rates of duty in line with prices in this and future Budgets.

A2.5   A policy which has been previously announced but not yet implemented is also stripped out of the indexed numbers. Measures announced in this Budget are assumed to be indexed in the same way for future Budgets. The indexed base has been calculated on the assumption that:

- income tax and national insurance allowances and thresholds, and the single person, couple, lone parent and disabled worker elements of the Working Tax Credit and the capital gains tax annual exempt amount all increase in line with the Retail Price Index (RPI) to the September prior to the Budget;

- the child element of the Child Tax Credit rises in line with the annual increase in average earnings until 2008-09;

- the inheritance tax threshold rises to £285,000 in 2006-07 and £300,000 in 2007-08;

- air passenger duty, climate change levy, aggregates levy, vehicle excise duty, fuel, tobacco and alcohol duties all rise in line with the projected annual increase in the RPI to the September following the Budget; and

- VAT thresholds and gaming duty bands rise in line with the increase in the RPI to the December prior to the Budget.

A2.6   Implementation dates are assumed to be: Budget day for fuel and tobacco duties; 10 days after Budget day for alcohol duties; May for amusement machine licence duty; July for insurance premium tax; November for air passenger duty; and April for all other taxes, duties and tax credits.

A2.7   The yields of measures that close tax avoidance loopholes or tackle tax fraud represent the estimated direct Exchequer effect of the measures with the existing level of activity.

A2.8   These costings are shown on a National Accounts basis. The National Accounts basis aims to recognise tax when the tax liability accrues irrespective of when the tax is received by the Exchequer. However, some taxes are scored on a receipts basis, principally due to the difficulty in assessing the period to which the tax liability relates. Examples of such taxes are corporation tax, self-assessment income tax, inheritance tax and capital gains tax. This approach is consistent with other Government publications.

Notes on individual Budget measures

International Accounting Standards **A2.9**   As announced, the Government has brought in legislation to make the tax system compatible with International Accounting Standards (IAS), and also announced its intention to bring in legislation to spread the impact of changes to the income recognition rules in UK Generally Accepted Accounting Practice (GAAP). The Government continues to work with business to manage the impact of accounting changes. Table A2.1 details the impact on the underlying profile of tax receipts and the arrangements to manage the transition for tax purposes of the following aspects:

- changes announced in July 2005, spreading over 10 years the majority of the transitional arrangements from the move to International Accounting Standards;

- the treatment of impairment losses under the new International Accounting Standards; and

- the changes in income recognition rules in UK GAAP.

Table A2.1: Impact of the changes to accounting standards

	(+ve is an Exchequer yield)			£ million
	2006–07 indexed	2007–08 indexed	2008–09 indexed	2006–07 non-indexed
IAS: general transition – impact on corporation tax revenues	–340	–80	+50	–340
IAS: general transition – effect of transitional arrangements	+340	+80	–50	+340
IAS: treatment of impairment losses – impact on corporation tax revenues	–680	–230	0	–680
IAS: treatment of impairment losses – effect of transitional arrangements	+610	+140	–90	+610
Income recognition rules: impact on income tax revenues	+380	+40	0	+380
Income recognition rules: effect of transitional arrangements	–240	+70	+75	–240
TOTAL	**+70**	**+20**	**–15**	**+70**

Employment related securities options **A2.10**   This measure consists of anti-avoidance legislation utilising the retrospective powers introduced following the Paymaster General's statement of 2 December 2004. The revenues shown in Table A1 are additional to the amounts included in estimated receipts for 2005-06 from the remuneration-based avoidance measure announced in the 2004 Pre-Budget Report.

VAT: MTIC – reverse charge **A2.11**   As required by the *Code for fiscal stability*[3] the fiscal impact from this measure is included in the public finance projections on a cautious basis to ensure all Government decisions and circumstances are included by the day the projections are finalised.

Corporation tax **A2.12**   The estimated impact in 2006-07 is reduced from the 2005 Pre-Budget Report forecast due to changes in distribution practices by some companies as a result of the announcement.

Child Trust Fund **A2.13**   The long-run cost of Child Trust Fund age 7 payments is expected to be £240 million a year.

Sale of lessors **A2.14**   The yield is expected to increase to £225 million by 2010-11.

---

[3] *Code for fiscal stability*, HM Treasury, 1998.

Film tax reliefs **A2.15**   The yield from the replacement of current film tax reliefs announced in the 2005 Pre-Budget Report is expect to increase to £70 million by 2009-10 and then reduce gradually to around zero by 2017-18.

North sea oil taxation **A2.16**   The revenue yield from this measure has been revised since the 2005 Pre-Budget Report to take into account revised forecasting assumptions. In particular an estimated £0.75 billion in receipts previously expected to be recieved in 2006-07 was received in the latter part of 2005-06 as companies elected to defer relief for capital expenditure.

VED: environmental incentives **A2.17**   The cost to the Exchequer is expected to be £10 million over six years.

APPENDIX A3: TAX ALLOWANCES AND RELIEFS

A3.1   This appendix provides estimates of the revenue cost of some of the main tax allowances and reliefs.

A3.2   Tax reliefs can serve a number of purposes. In some cases they may be used to assist or encourage particular individuals, activities or products, and so may be an alternative to public expenditure. In this case they are often termed 'tax expenditures'. There may, for example, be a choice between giving a tax relief as an allowance or deduction against tax, or by an offsetting cash payment.

A3.3   Many allowances and reliefs can reasonably be regarded (or partly regarded) as an integral part of the tax structure – called 'structural reliefs'. Some do no more than recognise the expense incurred in obtaining income. Others reflect a more general concept of 'taxable capacity'. The personal allowances are a good example: to the extent that income tax is based on ability to pay, it does not seek to collect tax from those with the smallest incomes. However, even with structural reliefs of the latter kind, the Government has some discretion about the level at which they are set. Many other reliefs combine both structural and discretionary components. Capital allowances, for example, provide relief for depreciation at a commercial rate as well as an element of accelerated relief. It is the latter element which represents additional help provided to business by the Government and is a 'tax expenditure'.

A3.4   The loss of revenue associated with tax reliefs and allowances cannot be directly observed, and estimates have to be made. This involves calculating the amount of tax that individuals or firms would have had to pay if there were no exemptions or deductions for certain categories of income or expenditure, and comparing it with the actual amount of tax due.

A3.5   The estimates in Table A3.1 below show the total cost of each relief. The classification of reliefs as tax expenditures, structural reliefs and those elements combining both is broadbrush and the distinction between the expenditures and structural reliefs is not always straightforward. In many cases the estimated costs are extremely tentative and based on simplifying assumptions and must be treated with caution. The figures make no allowance for the fact that changes in tax reliefs may cause people to change their behaviour. This means that figures in Table A3.1 are not directly comparable with those of the main Budget measures shown earlier in this chapter.

A3.6   Estimation of behavioural effects is difficult. The sizes of behavioural changes will obviously depend on the measure examined and possible alternative behaviours. For example, removing the tax privileges of a form of saving may just lead people to switch to another tax-privileged form of saving.

A3.7 The estimated costs of reliefs and allowances given in Table A3.1 are costed separately and cannot be added up to give a meaningful total. The combined yield of withdrawing two related allowances could differ significantly from the sum of individual costs. Similarly the sum of the costs of component parts of reliefs may differ from the total shown.

A3.8 The Government regularly publishes estimates of tax expenditures and reliefs. Largely because of the difficulties of estimation, the published tables are not comprehensive but do cover the major reliefs and allowances. The figures are shown on a full-year accruals basis unless otherwise specified and only reliefs with an estimated annual costs of at least £50 million are shown. The costs of minor tax reliefs can be found on the HM Revenue and Customs websites. More details on individual tax allowances and reliefs can be found in the HM Treasury publication, *Tax ready reckoner and tax reliefs*, published alongside the 2005 Pre-Budget Report.

Table A3.1: Estimated costs of principal tax expenditures and structural reliefs

	£ million	
	2004-05	**2005-06**
TAX EXPENDITURES		
Income tax		
Relief for:		
Approved pension schemes	12,300	13,700
Share Incentive Plan	260	320
Approved savings-related share schemes	110	130
Enterprise Management Incentives	50	60
Approved Company Share Option Plans	100	120
Personal Equity Plans	450	450
Individual Savings Accounts	1,175	1,300
Venture Capital Trusts	220	315
Enterprise Investment Scheme	170	140
Professional subscriptions	75	90
Rent a room	90	90
Exemption of:		
First £30,000 of payments on termination of employment	1,000	1,000
Interest on National Savings Certificates including index-linked certificates	120	100
Premium Bond prizes	150	170
Income of charities	890	1,020
Foreign service allowance paid to Crown servants abroad	95	85
First £8,000 of reimbursed relocation packages provided by employers	300	300
Life assurance premiums (for contracts made prior to 14 March 1984)	55	55
Tax credits:		
Child Tax Credit	3,300	3,600
Working Tax Credit	1,100	1,000
Corporation tax		
R&D tax credits	480	510
Income tax and corporation tax		
Small budget film tax relief	350	340
Large budget film tax relief	170	220
National insurance contributions		
Relief for:		
Share Incentive Plan	180	210
Approved savings-related share schemes	80	90
Employer contributions to approved pension schemes	6,700	7,400
Capital gains tax		
Exemption of gains arising on disposal of only or main residence	13,000	12,500

Table A3.1: Estimated costs of principal tax expenditures and structural reliefs

	£ million	
	2004-05	2005-06
Inheritance tax		
Relief for:		
Agricultural property	215	225
Business property	180	200
Exemption of transfers to charities on death	385	425
Value added tax		
Zero-rating of:		
Food	10,200	10,600
Construction of new dwellings (includes refunds to DIY builders)	6,400	6,550
Domestic passenger transport	2,150	2,250
International passenger transport (UK portion)	100	100
Books, newspapers and magazines	1,550	1,550
Children's clothing	1,150	1,200
Water and sewerage services	1,050	1,050
Drugs and supplies on prescription	1,300	1,350
Supplies to charities	200	200
Ships and aircraft above a certain size	600	600
Vehicles and other supplies to disabled people	400	400
Reduced rate for:		
Domestic fuel and power	2,000	2,000
Certain residential conversions and renovations	150	150
Energy-saving materials	50	50
Women's sanitary products	50	50

STRUCTURAL RELIEFS

	2004-05	2005-06
Income tax		
Personal allowance	36,700	38,200
Corporation tax		
Life companies reduced rate of corporation tax on policy holders' fraction of profit	750	950
Income tax and corporation tax		
Double taxation relief	8,000	8,000
National insurance contributions		
Contracted-out rebate occupational schemes:		
Rebates deducted at source by employers	7,200	7,400
Rebates paid by the Contributions Agency direct to the scheme	200	200
Personal and stakeholder pensions	2,400	2,200

Table A3.1: Estimated costs of principal tax expenditures and structural reliefs

	£ million	
	2004-05	2005-06
Value added tax		
Refunds to:		
Northern Ireland Government bodies of VAT incurred on non-business purchases under the Section 99 refund scheme	300	300
Local Authority-type bodies of VAT incurred on non-business purchases under the Section 33 refund scheme (includes national museums and galleries under the Section 33A refund scheme)	6,650	7,550
Central Government, Health Authorities and NHS Trusts of VAT incurred on contracted-out services under the Section 41(3) refund scheme	3,700	3,900
RELIEFS WITH TAX EXPENDITURE AND STRUCTURAL COMPONENTS		
Income tax		
Age-related allowances	2,200	2,300
Reduced rate for savings	170	200
Exemption of:		
British Government securities where owner not ordinarily resident in the UK	970	970
Child Benefit (including one parent benefit)	1,060	1,090
Long-term incapacity benefit	610	610
Industrial disablement benefits	50	50
Attendance allowance	100	100
Disability living allowance	320	330
War disablement benefits	90	100
War widow's pension	70	70
Corporation tax		
Small companies' reduced corporation tax rate	3,530	3,860
Starting rate of corporation tax	410	460
Exemption for gains on substantial shareholdings	260	260
Income tax and corporation tax		
Capital allowances	17,700	18,100
Of which:		
First year allowances for SMEs	370	450
Enhanced capital allowances for energy saving technology	180	170
Capital gains tax		
Indexation allowance and rebasing to March 1982	290	270
Taper relief	3,500	4,500
Exemption of:		
Annual exempt amount (half of the individual's exemption for trustees)	1,550	1,850
Gains accrued but unrealised at death	650	700

Table A3.1: Estimated costs of principal tax expenditures and structural reliefs

	£ million	
	2004-05	**2005-06**
Petroleum revenue tax		
Uplift on qualifying expenditure	160	70
Oil allowance	560	820
Safeguard: a protection for return on capital cost	130	40
Tariff receipts allowance	40	40
Exemption for gas sold to British Gas under pre-July 1975 contracts	60	90
Inheritance tax		
Nil rate band for chargeable transfers not exceeding the threshold	9,400	10,000
Exemption of transfers on death to surviving spouses	1,600	1,800
Stamp duty land tax		
Exemption of transfers of land and property where the consideration does not exceed the £60,000 threshold in 2004-05 and the £120,000 threshold in 2005-06 and non-residential land and property where the consideration does not exceed the £150,000 threshold	170	530
Exemption of all residential transfers in designated disadvantaged wards where the consideration exceeds £60,000 in 2004-05, £120,000 in 2005-06 but does not exceed £150,000, and exemption of all non-residential transfers in designated disadvantaged wards in 2004-05	1,000	240
Transfers to charities	60	120
Group relief	770	1,730
Transfers to registered social landlords	60	60
National insurance contributions		
Reduced contributions for self-employed not attributable to reduced benefit eligibility (constant cost basis)	1,700	1,900
Value added tax		
Exemption of:		
Rent on domestic dwellings	2,850	2,950
Supplies of commercial property	150	150
Private education	300	300
Health services	800	850
Postal services	500	500
Burial and cremation	100	100
Finance and insurance	3,650	3,900
Betting and gaming and lottery duties	1,200	1,250
Small traders below the turnover limit for VAT registration	300	300
Vehicle Excise Duty		
Exemption for disabled motorists	140	140

B THE ECONOMY

Overall economic developments since the 2005 Pre-Budget Report have been as forecast. In 2005, the UK economy was affected by sustained rises in oil prices, weak euro area demand and a subdued housing market. In previous decades these factors would have risked being accompanied by recession. By contrast, the Government's macroeconomic framework has continued to deliver unprecedented macroeconomic stability with low inflation, and GDP now having grown for 54 consecutive quarters. Economic growth has gradually increased momentum through the latter stages of 2005 and into 2006, and the outlook is for growth to pick up to above-trend rates.

G7 economic developments have also been in line with Pre-Budget Report expectations. World growth has remained strong, due partly to the underlying momentum of some emerging economies, particularly in Asia. Oil prices have remained high. The composition of global growth, with strong growth in Asia and other emerging markets contrasting with relative weakness in Europe, accounts for some of the recent undershoot of UK export market growth relative to that of world trade. Financial conditions remain benign, with long-term interest rates remaining historically low despite some gradual increases in rates at shorter-term maturities.

UK GDP growth has firmed compared with early 2005, but remains slightly below trend. Despite the ongoing dampening effects of higher oil prices, still subdued average earnings growth, and households continuing to consolidate their finances, private consumption growth has picked up through the course of 2005. Business investment growth has remained modest according to latest estimates, as firms have continued to adopt a cautious approach to stepping up capital spending despite healthy profitability. As the economy adjusts to higher oil prices, both consumption and investment are expected to strengthen.

With the Government's macroeconomic framework continuing to deliver domestic stability, the UK economy remains well placed for a further pick-up in growth to above-trend rates by early 2007. Overall, the Budget forecast is as set out in the 2005 Pre-Budget Report:

- GDP is forecast to grow by 2 to $2\frac{1}{2}$ per cent in 2006, rising to above-trend rates of $2\frac{3}{4}$ to $3\frac{1}{4}$ per cent in both 2007 and 2008. The Treasury's trend growth judgement is unchanged, so the output gap is still expected to close in 2008-09;

- CPI inflation is expected to remain close to target as inflation expectations remain firmly anchored. The ongoing effects of higher energy prices exert slightly more upward pressure this year than previously expected, but have only a temporary effect on inflation.

Global risks will continue to have a key bearing on UK economic prospects, and challenging judgements will continue to be faced in setting monetary and fiscal policy.

INTRODUCTION[1,2]

B.1   This chapter discusses recent economic developments and provides updated forecasts for the UK and world economies in the period to 2008. It begins with an overview of developments and prospects in the world economy. It then outlines the Government's latest assessment of the UK economy, followed by a more detailed discussion of sectoral issues and risks.

THE WORLD ECONOMY

Overview

B.2   Developments in the global economy have been broadly as forecast in the 2005 Pre-Budget Report. World output growth in 2005 was driven by emerging Asia, particularly China, as well as by continued robust growth in the US.

B.3   World growth has contributed to the sustained increase in the level of oil prices. Oil prices have remained high since the autumn, whilst at the same time world growth is now estimated to have been slightly stronger than expected, largely reflecting the strength of underlying momentum in Asia.

B.4   World trade growth has remained robust, despite having moderated compared with the four-year high reached in 2004. The importance of world trade growth to the growing prosperity of the global economy underlines the need to avoid protectionist responses to the competitive pressures brought to bear by the expansion and increasing integration of emerging markets into the global economy.

Table B1: The world economy

	Percentage changes on a year earlier unless otherwise stated			
		Forecast		
	2005	**2006**	**2007**	**2008**
Major 7 countries[1]:				
Real GDP	$2\frac{1}{2}$	$2\frac{1}{2}$	$2\frac{1}{2}$	$2\frac{1}{2}$
Consumer price inflation[2]	$2\frac{1}{2}$	$2\frac{1}{2}$	$2\frac{1}{4}$	$2\frac{1}{2}$
Euro area: Real GDP	$1\frac{1}{2}$	$1\frac{3}{4}$	2	2
World GDP	$4\frac{1}{2}$	$4\frac{1}{2}$	$4\frac{1}{2}$	$4\frac{1}{2}$
World trade in goods and services	7	$7\frac{3}{4}$	7	$6\frac{3}{4}$
UK export markets[3]	$6\frac{1}{4}$	$7\frac{1}{4}$	$6\frac{1}{4}$	6

[1] *G7: US, Japan, Germany, UK, France, Italy and Canada.*

[2] *Per cent, Q4.*

[3] *Other countries' imports of UK goods and services weighted according to their importance in UK exports.*

---

[1] The UK forecast is consistent with output, income and expenditure data to the fourth quarter of 2005 released by the Office for National Statistics (ONS) on 24 February 2006. This release also contained revisions to earlier quarters of 2005 which the Treasury has carried through to other national accounts series that the ONS has not yet revised, in particular sectoral saving and borrowing. A fully consistent national accounts dataset for 2005 will be published by the ONS on 29 March 2006. A detailed set of charts and tables relating to the economic forecast is available on the Treasury's internet site (http://www.hm-treasury.gov.uk) and copies can be obtained on request from the Treasury's Public Enquiry Unit (020 7270 4558).

[2] The forecast is based on the assumption that the exchange rate moves in line with an uncovered interest parity condition, consistent with the interest rates underlying the economic forecast.

B.5   Oil prices have doubled over the past two years, alongside rises in other energy and some non-fuel commodity prices, and been accompanied by continued strong growth in world GDP. This supports the view that the escalation in oil prices over the recent past, in contrast to that of the 1970s or 1980s, has reflected strong demand which has created a tight market in which supply-side factors have had a disproportionate impact on prices. Nevertheless, such high oil and energy prices are likely to have undermined GDP growth by denting disposable incomes, profits and confidence to some extent, although the impact has varied depending on country-specific factors, including underlying momentum and energy intensity.

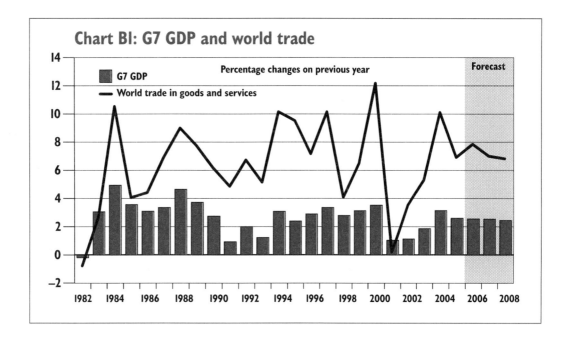

Chart B1: G7 GDP and world trade

B.6   In spite of these sharp and sustained rises in oil prices, as well as marked growth in other industrial input prices, world inflation has remained relatively low. Moreover, the pick-up in headline inflation has not fed through to comparable increases in core inflation, which has remained relatively low and stable to date. Three key factors are thought to be holding down inflationary pressures and expectations: the credibility of central banks and monetary authorities anchoring inflectionary expectations; the downward pressure on traded goods prices stemming from the increasing integration of China, India and other emerging economies into the global economy; and the increase in the mobility of labour, particularly in Europe and wider Asia, holding down wage pressures.

B.7   Long-term interest rates have been stable or even declined, contrary to what may have been expected on the basis of expectations of future short-term interest rates and term risk premia, rising short-term rates, particularly in the US, and high energy and non-oil commodity prices contributing to inflationary pressures. However, in the event current account imbalances and high levels of liquidity in the global economy, with the tendency of some Central Banks, particularly in Asia, to accumulate foreign assets, have fed into strong demand for US bonds and tended to hold down yields. This may mean that investors are driving down risk premia and perhaps under-pricing risk. Low long-term interest rates may have contributed to the run-up in asset prices in some sectors and economies, tending to add to current account imbalances.

B.8   G7 GDP is expected to grow in line with the Pre-Budget Report forecast, with growth at 2¹/₂ per cent in 2006. The weaker growth in the US at the end of 2005 is expected to be largely offset by a rebound in early 2006, but underlying growth is still expected to moderate somewhat during 2006 and 2007. Slower US growth is expected to coincide with a more established and robust recovery in Japan, together with signs that confidence and sentiment are improving in the euro area, which should feed through to strengthening activity.

B.9   The risks to the outlook remain as identified in the Pre-Budget Report. Further sustained rises in oil prices could undermine confidence and lead to weaker than expected GDP growth. Furthermore, the persistence of global imbalances in an increasingly integrated world economy raises the risk of an abrupt reaction in financial markets, for example in exchange rates or bond yields. It is possible that low long-term bond yields may reflect the under-pricing of risk. There is also the continued threat of global competitive pressures giving rise to protectionist policy responses, and the ongoing possibility that inappropriate timing of monetary or fiscal policy adjustment could undermine fragile recoveries in some economies. On the upside, growth disparities are already narrowing, and with conditions supportive of growth there is potential for faster growth in activity in the US, Asia and the euro area. Moreover, the underlying momentum of the world economy has proved stronger than expected over the recent past.

G7 activity

B.10   The US economy has grown at a robust pace over the past three years since its recovery began in early 2003, averaging 4 per cent annualised growth between mid-2003 and late 2005, above estimated potential rates and thus reducing the negative output gap built up during the 2001 downturn.

B.11   US domestic demand growth maintained considerable strength in the third quarter of 2005, despite the disruption caused by the hurricanes to regional production, the labour market, confidence and energy prices. Growth weakened in late 2005 due to a range of temporary factors, and it is expected to show a marked rebound in the first quarter of 2006. Whilst private consumption growth is expected to moderate from the strength of the past couple of years, business investment should sustain domestic demand growth over the forecast horizon. Similarly, as import growth begins to moderate, partly in line with consumption, and the export sector recovers, reflecting lagged response to past dollar depreciation and possible benefit from firmer overseas demand, the current account deficit should begin to narrow, albeit slowly.

B.12   Stronger growth in the euro area emerged in the second half of 2005, due to robust export performance, stronger industrial production and a rise in business sentiment that stimulated some recovery in investment expenditure. However, because of the more muted performance in the first half of the year, growth in 2005 as a whole slowed and significantly lagged that of the G7 and other advanced economies. In addition, lower than expected official GDP growth statistics for the fourth quarter of 2005 highlight the underlying fragility of the recovery. Domestic demand growth slowed in 2005 due to weak private consumption growth affected by persistently high unemployment, restrained wage growth and marked energy price rises. A moderate recovery is expected throughout 2006 as investment expenditure gathers pace and export demand continues to grow, reflecting robust world trade growth and further gains in competitiveness.

B.13   Performance in the euro area as a whole masks significant cross country variations both in terms of strength and sectoral orientation. Weaker economic growth from the major euro area economies, particularly Germany and Italy, has been offset by more robust growth in Spain and some of the smaller Member States. Growth in Germany has been driven by strong export performance, while France has been more reliant on domestic demand.

Box B1: Global imbalances

Imbalances in trade and financial flows have increased over the past five years. The US current account deficit hit a new high in 2005, exceeding 6 per cent of GDP, or $760 billion. By contrast, the Japanese current account surplus exceeded $150 billion, China and other high growth East Asian economies generated a surplus of $210 billion, and Russia and all Middle Eastern countries traded a surplus of $320 billion. Together the surpluses of these three groupings were equivalent to more than 80 per cent of the US deficit over the past two years.

Much attention has focused on the financing of the US trade position through official purchases of US assets, especially US bonds, by Asian Central Banks. China and Japan have together amassed $930 billion of US Treasury securities and continue to increase their reserve holdings at a rate of $2 billion a month. Nevertheless, in 2004 purchases of official assets

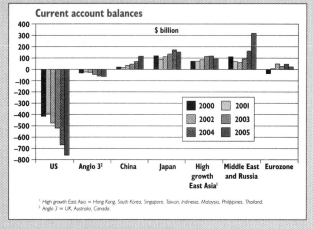

represented only about a quarter of all overseas purchases of US assets, whilst purchases of non-official (private sector) assets accounted for the remainder.

In addition, there is evidence that the profits generated by higher oil revenues are also supporting the accommodative financing environment as oil exporters seek overseas investment opportunities.

Typically, the financing requirements of a large and persistent current account deficit tend to put upward pressure on nominal and real interest rates. However, yields on US long-term bonds have remained low, despite the Federal Reserve increasing the Federal Funds rate by 200 basis points during 2005. This largely reflects strong global demand for bonds at least partly associated with global imbalances, and the relatively favourable investment opportunities and low inflation expectations in the US, encouraging private domestic and foreign investors to hold US assets. As long as private (domestic and foreign) and official sectors are willing to buy US assets, the external deficits can be maintained with a stable currency.

However, a US deficit of more than 6 per cent of GDP, with the counterpart of high saving and current account surpluses in other key economies, limits the capacity of the global economy to adjust to macroeconomic shocks, and makes the dollar more vulnerable. A quick reversal in the financing environment may leave the US exposed to a disorderly adjustment of its balance of payments position, via interest rates, the exchange rate and equity markets, with global economic ramifications. An orderly rebalancing of the global economy will require key players to adopt domestic economic policies that are supportive of more sustainable growth, trade and financial flows. G7 policy makers have committed to adopting domestic policies that will contribute to more balanced domestic and therefore global growth.

Box B2: Government policy on EMU

The Government's policy on membership of the single currency was set out by the Chancellor in his statement to Parliament in October 1997. In principle, the Government is in favour of UK membership; in practice, the economic conditions must be right. The determining factor is the national economic interest and whether, on the basis of an assessment of the five economic tests, the economic case for joining is clear and unambiguous. An assessment of the five economic tests was published in June 2003. This concluded that: *"since 1997, the UK has made real progress towards meeting the five economic tests. But, on balance, though the potential benefits of increased investment, trade, a boost to financial services, growth and jobs are clear, we cannot at this point in time conclude that there is sustainable and durable convergence or sufficient flexibility to cope with any potential difficulties within the euro area."*

The Chancellor's statement to the House of Commons on 9 June 2003 on UK membership of the European single currency set out a reform agenda of concrete and practical steps to address the policy requirements identified by the assessment. The Budget reports on proress including:

- the introduction in December 2003 of a symmetric inflation target as measured by the Consumer Price Index (CPI). CPI inflation has been within 1 percentage point of its target since its inception;

- reforms to address both supply and demand in the housing market through implementing a programme of change to increase supply and responsiveness of the housing market as recommended in the Barker review and action taken in response to the Miles review on the mortgage market, described further in Chapter 3; and

- reforms at national, regional and local level to enhance the flexibility of labour, capital and product markets in the UK. Chapters 3 and 4 provide further detail.

As part of the policy of 'prepare and decide', the Government coordinates appropriate euro preparations across the UK economy. The Government also supports business in dealing with the euro as a foreign currency. Further information is available on the Treasury's euro website www.euro.gov.uk.

On the Stability and Growth Pact, the Government continues to emphasise the need for a prudent interpretation of the Pact as described in Budget 2005. The reforms to the Pact agreed in March 2005 rightly place a greater focus on the avoidance of pro-cyclical policies, and on achieving low debt levels and thereby enhancing the long-term sustainability of public finances, with the flexibility for low debt countries such as the UK to invest in the provision of much needed public services. The Government continues to work closely with Member States and EU institutions as the success of the reforms will depend on how they are implemented. It is also essential to recognise the importance of national frameworks and national ownership of fiscal policy.

In his statement to the House of Commons on 9 June 2003, the Chancellor committed the Government to an annual review of progress. The Government does not propose a euro assessment to be initiated at the time of this Budget. The Treasury will again review the situation at Budget time next year as required by the Chancellor's June 2003 statement.

B.14 Japan's economic recovery has continued, with above-trend growth since 2003. In contrast to previous upturns, growth has been supported by strong contributions from domestic demand, improving prospects for the sustainability of the present recovery. The considerable monetary stimulus of recent years, and the restructuring of the corporate and financial sectors, have translated into greater profitability, renewed consumer optimism and improving labour market prospects. The recovery is forecast to continue in 2006, as the elimination of lingering deflationary pressures results in real interest rates coming down, providing further support to growth. Some moderation is expected in 2007, as accommodative monetary policy unwinds further and export market growth begins to moderate.

Emerging markets and developing economies

B.15   Emerging market economies are growing strongly, helped by continued strength in global demand, and a virtuous circle of improved fundamentals and a positive financing environment. Favourable financing conditions are reflected in the premium on emerging market bonds falling below 200 basis points3 for the first time in February 2006, driven by improved economic fundamentals, less exposed debt positions and the continuing 'search for yield' in financial markets.

B.16   Asia continues to be the fastest growing region, with developing Asia4 recording growth of just under 8 per cent in 2005, and with growth expected to be around 8 per cent in 2006. China continues to lead the region's growth, with strong domestic demand compensating for a declining contribution from net exports to deliver expected growth of 91/2 per cent this year, following almost 10 per cent in 2005. India, the region's other major emerging market economy, may be seeing the beginning of its own sustained period of rapid growth, with around 8 per cent expected in 2006, following broad-based growth of around 71/4 per cent in 2005.

B.17   Rapid global growth has kept commodity prices high, benefiting key commodity exporters in Latin America and Africa. Growth in Latin America is forecast at just over 4 per cent this year, the third consecutive year of growth at or above this rate, and the first time this has happened since the early 1970s. Africa is expected to see growth of $5^{1}/_{2}$ per cent in 2006, its highest growth rate since 1974, delivering the fourth consecutive year of growth above 4 per cent, the strongest run of growth since the early 1960s.

B.18   Rising oil prices have benefited oil exporters, improving their trade performance significantly and raising GDP growth. In 2005 the average current account surplus in the Middle East exceeded 15 per cent of GDP, whilst members of OPEC and Russia had an average current account surplus of 23 per cent of GDP. Domestic and regional equity markets, particularly those in the Middle East, have shown strong and broadly based growth, and many oil exporters have taken the opportunity to reduce public sector debt, strengthening their long-term fiscal position. In addition, oil producers have been exporting large quantities of capital. Rising demand from oil producers as they recycle revenues will also increase demand for imports and contribute to world trade growth.

World trade

B.19   World trade has continued to grow solidly, in line with the overall strength of the world economy, but also reflecting the increasing integration of emerging economies into the global economy and of production systems across regions. Expectations of strengthening domestic demand in the major emerging economies, particularly China, should contribute to sustained trade growth over the next few years. However, the competitive challenge presented by the expansion and integration of major emerging economy exporters has encouraged protectionist sentiment, particularly in the EU and the US. With trade being a significant source of global prosperity, these challenges need to be met through flexibility and efficient allocation of resources, rather than through erecting damaging trade barriers.

---

[3] As measured by the Goldman Sachs Emerging Market Bond Index (EMBI).

[4] Developing Asia consists of all East and South Asia except Japan, the Koreas, Taiwan, Hong Kong, and Singapore.

B.20 World trade growth has been largely driven by Asia, with the Asia-Pacific region contributing around 40 per cent to world trade growth over the past three years, in contrast to around 15 per cent from each of the US, the euro area and the rest of Europe. Asia accounts for just 15 per cent of UK export markets, whereas the euro area, which is growing more slowly, accounts for around half of the UK's export markets. In 2006 UK export market growth is expected to strengthen as world trade growth remains robust and the composition shifts in the UK's favour, with some pick-up in demand from the euro area, and higher US import growth as strong imports in late 2005 feed through to 2006.

Box B3: The importance of trade to world growth

World trade growth is a key source of rising global prosperity. Free trade:

- enables consumers and businesses to engage in transactions with wider markets, increasing choice and opportunities;
- increases transparency and competition, and therefore efficiency and productivity; and
- promotes more rapid assimilation of technological innovations into world-wide production processes.

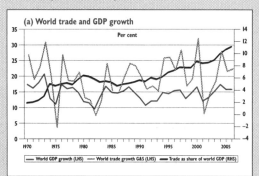
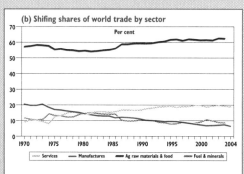

World trade has made an increasingly important contribution to world output growth in recent decades, with trade accounting for almost 30 per cent of world GDP in 2005, almost three times its share in 1970[a]. Manufactures account for the majority of cross-border trade, at around 60 per cent of the total, a share that has remained fairly stable over the past three and a half decades. However, services have increased significantly as a proportion of world trade, doubling from around 10 per cent in 1970 to around 20 per cent in 2004. Moreover, the impediments to trade in services are declining quickly, due to advances in communications and information technology, and gradual withdrawal of protectionism in some service industries.

The importance of free trade in raising growth and living standards means that adopting protectionist policies in the face of competitive pressures constrains growth and long-term opportunities. A more beneficial and resource-efficient strategy is to move further towards an open and fair multi-lateral trading system, and to adopt domestic policies that enhance flexibility and facilitate the movement of resources between sectors[b].

Results from studies of the gains from full trade liberalisation vary depending on the assumptions used, but the World Bank estimates that full liberalisation of agriculture and industrial trade over the next five years could yield gains of $290 billion a year by 2015. That would reduce the number of people living on no more than $1 a day by 32 million, or 5 per cent, by 2015. Progress towards a successful outcome in the multi-lateral World Trade Organisation negotiations is critical to the pursuit of an open and fair world trading system, the continuation of robust and sustainable world growth, and the raising of living standards. A multi-lateral trading system is more efficient and more transparent than an increasing array of bilateral and regional trade agreements.

[a] Based on IMF September 2005 WEO data; GDP and world trade at current prices.
[b] See *Long-term global economic challenges and opportunities for the UK*, HM Treasury, December 2004.

Oil and commodity prices

B.21   Oil prices have increased sharply since the beginning of 2004, though in real terms they have remained below historic peaks. The price of Brent crude oil, the European standard, rose from a low of $10 a barrel in 1999 to a peak of over $67 a barrel in September 2005. Prices declined from this peak towards the end of 2005, but have risen again in early 2006 to average $62 a barrel for the year to date, compared to an average of $55 a barrel during 2005.

B.22   Rapid growth in the demand for oil, particularly from emerging market economies, and limited investment, have been primary causes of low levels of spare capacity and rising oil prices since 2004. In this environment, supply disruptions and uncertainties have had a magnified impact on price. An imbalance between the demand and supply of different grades of crude in a constrained refining environment has also contributed to pressure on prices. The further increase in prices in early 2006 has been driven by strong demand, further supply disruptions (in Iraq, Nigeria and Russia) and an increase in perceptions of geo-political supply risk.

B.23   Higher nominal oil prices are expected to be sustained into the medium term. G8 Finance Ministers continue to take global action to address high and volatile oil prices and their impacts.

B.24   In the past, such rapid rises in oil prices have had a significant impact on global economic growth. Four key factors have served to mitigate some of the potentially adverse impact of the recent oil price increases: first, high oil prices have stemmed largely from strong world demand; second, more stable macroeconomic frameworks, in particular greater credibility of monetary policy and authorities, have limited the pass-through to core inflation and anchored inflationary expectations, reducing the need for a more marked monetary tightening; third, the pass-through has also been limited by greater competition in the world economy maintaining pressure on margins and wage rates; and fourth, the energy intensity of production is lower than in the past.

B.25   Non-fuel commodity prices have also been rising due to increased global demand, reflecting the strength of world output, as well as supply constraints for some commodities in key producing regions. Whilst non-fuel commodity prices have risen by 17 per cent over the past year, industrial input prices have risen by 24 per cent and metal prices have risen by over 30 per cent. Metals that are extensively used in manufacturing and industrial output, such as copper, iron and steel, have seen even stronger price increases.

G7 inflation

B.26   G7 headline inflation picked up during 2005, reflecting the escalation of energy costs, and particularly oil prices, in the autumn. The rise in G7 inflation from mid-2005 primarily reflected developments in US inflation. Headline inflation in other G7 economies also rose, but it did so to a lesser degree than in the US. In Japan, deflation gradually subsided during 2005 with a return to positive rates of inflation towards the end of the year, although underlying price pressures remain weak.

B.27   In the G7 economies, headline inflation has risen broadly in accordance with energy prices, whereas core inflation has remained very stable. This reflects the limited pass-through of energy price increases to other goods and services, and hence from headline inflation to core inflation. The credibility of monetary frameworks has been a key factor contributing to the limited pass-through by anchoring inflation expectations at low rates.

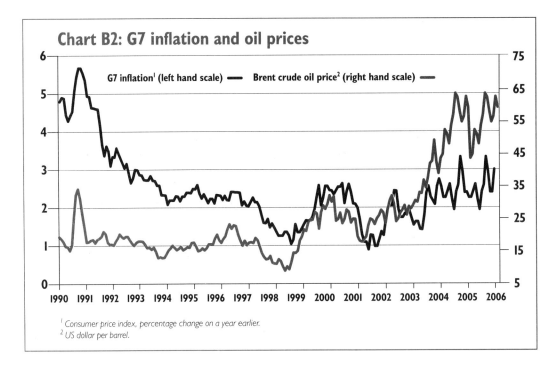

Chart B2: G7 inflation and oil prices

G7 inflation[1] (left hand scale) ——   Brent crude oil price[2] (right hand scale) ——

[1] Consumer price index, percentage change on a year earlier.
[2] US dollar per barrel.

Forecast issues and risks

B.28   Whilst there are some upside risks relating to a stronger recovery in the US in early 2006, more persistent strength in Japan than projected or a quicker recovery in the euro area, there are also some downside risks to the current projections and the strength of the world and G7 economies. These risks remain broadly similar to those at the time of the 2005 Pre-Budget Report – the persistence of global imbalances, high and volatile oil and energy prices, inflationary pressures necessitating more marked monetary tightening, and the possibility of increasingly protectionist trade policies.

B.29   The improved growth prospects in Japan and the euro area are positive developments in terms of narrowing current account imbalances over the medium term, and the stability of core inflation has allowed monetary policy to be adjusted at a gradual pace with short rates at relatively modest levels. As the euro area and Japan join the US in removing monetary stimulus, it is possible that the world economy will begin to face a somewhat tighter financial environment, though high levels of liquidity, particularly in Asia, are likely partly to offset the tightening in monetary conditions at the short end by holding down longer-term interest rates. Nevertheless, there is a risk that if the market begins to lose confidence in US economic prospects and its capacity to finance its outstanding liabilities associated with the current account and fiscal deficits, agents will demand higher rates of return over the medium term, and longer-term interest rates will rise. However, unless high levels of global liquidity are adjusted simultaneously, the saving surplus will seek alternative investment opportunities, holding down yields elsewhere.

B.30   Policy makers continue to strive for a successful outcome to the Doha multilateral trade negotiations to ensure further progress towards an open, fair and transparent world trading system, and hence growing global prosperity, though this is no guarantee that unilateral barriers to trade will not be created.

UK ECONOMY

Overview of recent developments

B.31   The UK economy was resilient in the face of a number of challenges in 2005. After strong growth at above-trend rates in late 2003 and through the first half of 2004, GDP decelerated from mid-2004 and has since grown at below-trend rates in the face of sustained higher oil prices, weak demand growth in the euro area, and a slowing housing market.

B.32   In previous decades, such factors would have risked being accompanied by recession. By contrast, the Government's macroeconomic framework has continued to deliver an unprecedented period of sustained and stable economic growth with low inflation. UK GDP has now expanded for 54 consecutive quarters. On the basis of quarterly national accounts data, this is the longest unbroken expansion since records began 50 years ago. Moreover, the current economic expansion has persisted for well over twice the duration of the previous period of unbroken growth.

B.33   Overall developments since the 2005 Pre-Budget Report have been as forecast. GDP rose by 0.6 per cent in the final quarter of 2005, remaining a little below trend although slightly stronger than in the second and third quarters and significantly above growth at the start of last year. Growth in the final quarter was underpinned by rising private and government consumption, alongside a small positive contribution from net trade, while investment fell back.

B.34   Growth in non-oil GVA, which is the basis for the Government's output gap estimates, has followed a similar profile to that of total GDP although it has been a little smoother: total GDP has been affected by variations in oil production over the past 18 months. Non-oil GVA grew fractionally faster than total GDP in the third quarter of last year and at the same, below-trend rate as GDP in the final quarter.

B.35   In 2005 as a whole, UK GDP is currently estimated to have risen by $1^3/_4$ per cent, consistent with the 2005 Pre-Budget Report forecast. UK GDP growth last year was above growth in the euro area as a whole for the tenth consecutive year, with UK growth, on average, only behind that of North America amongst G7 economies since 1997.

B.36   The economy has undergone a degree of rebalancing in recent years. The ratio of nominal private consumption to GDP has trended downwards significantly since its peak in 2001 despite a run of relatively strong real consumption growth, part of which helped to shield the UK economy between 2001 and 2003 from some of the negative effects of the sharpest slowdown in the world economy for around 30 years. More recently real private consumption growth has moderated from around $3^1/_2$ per cent in 2004 as a whole to around $1^1/_2$ per cent in the year to the second half of 2005. Consumer spending grew at the same rate as GDP in 2005 as a whole, whereas growth in total investment and to a lesser extent government consumption exceeded GDP growth, and net exports made a neutral contribution. Whole economy investment rose by $3^1/_4$ per cent last year, weaker than growth in 2004, but stronger than for the three previous years.

B.37   Against a backdrop of above-trend UK GDP growth, the Monetary Policy Committee (MPC) of the Bank of England pre-emptively increased interest rates on five occasions between November 2003 and August 2004. This followed a pre-emptive series of rate cuts during the global downturn between 2001 and 2003. The MPC subsequently reduced repo rates by 25 basis points on 4 August 2005, with rates remaining unchanged since then. The expansionary impact of fiscal policy has moderated since 2002-03.

B.38   CPI inflation rose above target in the second half of 2005, peaking in September, primarily on account of the direct and indirect effects of oil price rises. However, CPI inflation declined in the final quarter to just below target by the end of the year, and stood at target in February 2006, despite high oil prices and wider energy costs still putting some residual upward pressure on inflation in recent months.

B.39   Revisions to the national accounts made subsequent to the 2005 Pre-Budget Report have relieved some of the tension between the recorded path of GDP growth since early 2004 and other indicators of activity and demand. The slowdown in output growth from mid-2004 is now less pronounced than previously estimated. However, it is still relatively marked given other economic developments at that time, and over more recent quarters the official estimates of output have continued to suggest somewhat weaker growth than private sector business survey indicators of manufacturing and service sectors.

B.40   Latest labour market data also now look to be more consistent with below-trend growth, in contrast to much of 2005 when employment and unemployment indicators had remained significantly more buoyant than might have been expected on the basis of measured output growth. Having remained broadly stable for the first three quarters of 2005, the employment rate has subsequently fallen back by 0.4 percentage points to 74.5 per cent in late 2005 and early 2006, while the unemployment rate rose by $^1/_4$ percentage point to around 5 per cent over the same period. Moreover, average earnings growth has continued to track down. However, it is unclear thus far to what degree the labour market has undergone an underlying softening and to what extent some of the recent weakening may be temporary and erratic.

B.41   Recent data therefore appear broadly consistent with the view that sustained high oil prices and consumers' caution over their finances, with house price inflation subdued and muted growth in average earnings, have continued to dampen UK GDP growth. Nevertheless uncertainties continue to surround the precise extent to which the economy has been operating below trend over the recent past.

Trend growth and the output gap

B.42   The Treasury's neutral estimate of the economy's trend rate of growth of output for Budget 2006 remains at $2^3/_4$ per cent a year to the end of 2006, slowing to $2^1/_2$ per cent thereafter due to the demographic effects of post-War baby-boom women reaching retirement age and depressing the growth rate of the working-age population. This is unchanged from the 2005 Pre-Budget Report.

B.43   Table B2 presents historical estimates of trend output growth and its decomposition for the first half of the current cycle and for the previous cycle, together with the forward-looking assumptions for trend growth based on projections of its components for the current phase of the cycle and beyond. These also remain unchanged from the Pre-Budget Report. Over the first half of the current economic cycle, between the on-trend points in 1997 and 2001, trend productivity growth, measured on an output per hour worked basis, was 2.6 per cent a year, compared with around 2 per cent over the previous two economic cycles as discussed further in Chapter 3.

B.44   Consistent with past practice, projections of the public finances are based upon the lower end of the economic forecast ranges, which are anchored around the deliberately cautious assumption of annual trend output growth $\frac{1}{4}$ percentage point lower than the neutral view – see Box C2. For Budget 2006 this cautious assumption for the trend growth rate has been audited by the NAO under the rolling review process,[5] as was proposed in the 2005 Pre-Budget Report.

B.45   Chart B3 shows the estimated output gap profile over the past and the forecast going forward. With only marginal upward revisions to output growth, the output gap profile over the recent past remains very similar to that at the time of the Pre-Budget Report. The negative output gap at the end of last year is now estimated at $-1\frac{1}{4}$ per cent, slightly narrower than forecast at the time of the Pre-Budget Report, reflecting the small revisions to the data for previous quarters.

Table B2: Contributions to trend output growth[1]

	Estimated trend rates of growth, per cent per annum					
	Trend output per hour worked[2,3]		Trend average hours worked[3]	Trend employment rate[3]	Population of working age[4]	Trend output
	Underlying	Actual				
	(1)	(2)	(3)	(4)	(5)	(6)
1986Q2 to 1997H1	2.22	2.04	−0.11	0.36	0.24	**2.55**
Over the recent past						
1997H1 to 2001Q3						
Budget 2002	2.14	1.96	−0.37	0.36	0.66	**2.63**
Budget 2003	2.35	2.14	−0.47	0.43	0.50	**2.61**
PBR 2003 and Budget 2004	2.65	2.44	−0.47	0.42	0.54	**2.94**
PBR 2004 and Budget 2005	2.70	2.50	−0.43	0.41	0.58	**3.06**
PBR 2005	2.79	2.59	−0.44	0.42	0.58	**3.15**
Budget 2006	2.79	2.59	−0.44	0.42	0.58	**3.15**
Projection[5]						
2001Q4 to 2006Q4						
Budget 2002	2.10	2.00	−0.1	0.2	0.6	**$2\frac{3}{4}$**
Budget/PBR 2003, Budget/						
PBR 2004 and Budget 2005	2.35	2.25	−0.1	0.2	0.5	**$2\frac{3}{4}$**
PBR 2005	2.25	2.15	−0.2	0.2	0.6	**$2\frac{3}{4}$**
Budget 2006[6]	2.25	2.15	−0.2	0.2	0.6	**$2\frac{3}{4}$**
2006Q4 onwards						
PBR 2004 and Budget 2005	2.35	2.25	−0.1	0.2	0.3	**$2\frac{1}{2}$**
PBR 2005	2.25	2.15	−0.2	0.2	0.4	**$2\frac{1}{2}$**
Budget 2006[6]	2.25	2.15	−0.2	0.2	0.4	**$2\frac{1}{2}$**

[1] Treasury analysis based on judgement that 1986Q2, 1997H1 and 2001Q3 were on-trend points of the output cycle. Figures independently rounded. Trend output growth is estimated as growth of non-oil gross value added between on-trend points for the past, and by projecting components going forward.
Columns (2) + (3) + (4) + (5) = (6).
Full data definitions and sources are set out in Annex A of 'Trend Growth: Recent Developments and Prospects', HM Treasury, April 2002.
[2] The underlying trend rate is the actual trend rate adjusted for changes in the employment rate, i.e. assuming the employment rate had remained constant.
Column (1) = column (2) + (1-a).column (4), where a is the ratio of new to average worker productivity levels. The figuring is consistent with this ratio being of the order of 50 per cent, informed by econometric evidence and LFS data on relative entry wages.
[3] The decomposition makes allowance for employment and hours worked lagging output. Employment is assumed to lag output by around three quarters, so that on-trend points for employment come three quarters after on-trend points for output, an assumption which can be supported by econometric evidence. Hours are easier to adjust than employment, and the decomposition assumes that hours lag output by just one quarter, though this lag is hard to support by econometric evidence. Hours worked and the employment rate are measured on a working-age basis.
[4] UK resident household basis.
[5] Neutral case assumptions for trend from 2001Q3.
[6] Underlying trend assumptions around which the mid-points of the GDP forecast growth ranges from 2006Q1 are anchored.

[5] See Box 2.1 and NAO Audit of Assumptions for Budget 2006.

B.46   The Pre-Budget Report noted a number of uncertainties surrounding the output gap estimates over the recent past. To a large extent, these uncertainties remain. Below trend output growth coupled with robust employment growth since mid-2004, implies that the widening of the output gap has been accompanied by weaker productivity growth, according to the latest national accounts and labour market data. However, with the labour market showing signs of some easing in the last quarter of 2005, it is possible that the observed weak productivity growth may – at least in part – be attributable to labour hoarding during the period of weak demand.

B.47   The fall in the employment rate since the third quarter of 2005, following the slight rise over the previous year, together with the latest national accounts data, implies a marked pick-up in productivity growth in the final quarter, resulting in some rebalancing in the drivers of the output gap from productivity to employment. But as previously discussed, the apparent labour market softening in the final quarter could be temporary and erratic, which means that the assessment of previous labour hoarding unravelling towards the end of the year remains tentative.

B.48   Although the suggested softening of the labour market has gone some way towards reconciling output and labour market indicators, the extent of the measured cyclical slowdown in productivity continues to puzzle many commentators. There is still some difficulty reconciling strong output growth in the first half of 2004 and the subsequent slowing of growth with evidence from private sector business surveys.

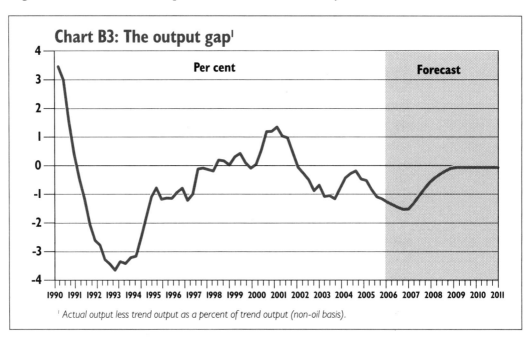

Chart B3: The output gap[1]

[1] Actual output less trend output as a percent of trend output (non-oil basis).

B.49   Indicators of capacity utilisation in manufacturing continue to support the assessment of a widening output gap since mid-2004, though not to the extent implied by the latest national accounts data. The BCC measure of utilisation in the service sector picked up at the end of 2005 following weakness in the first three quarters of 2005. Business survey indicators of recruitment difficulties show that firms in the services sector were finding it slightly more difficult to find suitable labour at the end of 2005, while the picture for manufacturing is more mixed.

B50   However, average earnings growth was fairly weak in 2005 as a whole, and fell further in the final quarter, with the whole economy rate excluding bonuses down to around $3^{3}/_{4}$ per cent in recent months, compared to about $4^{1}/_{2}$ per cent in late 2004. This lends support to the view that a significant negative output gap remains. CPI inflation has slowed back to target, though developments in oil prices mean that CPI inflation is a less clear indicator of overall capacity pressures than normal.

B.51   Overall, national accounts and labour market data point to a sizable negative output gap in 2005, widening slightly through the year. While there appears to be a consensus amongst external forecasters that the UK is currently operating with a negative output gap, there is some uncertainty regarding the exact magnitude of that gap, and its quarterly path. Different methodological approaches to determining the economy's cyclical position tend to result in somewhat different conclusions[6].

Box B4: Older workers

The labour market activity rate of older workers, aged 50 and above, has risen by around $3^{1}/_{2}$ percentage points over the past decade. By contrast, over the same period, the activity rate of those aged between 16 and 49 has fallen by around $1^{1}/_{2}$ percentage points. As a result, the contribution of people over 50 to the working-age activity rate has risen from around $14^{1}/_{2}$ per cent in 1992 to 18 per cent last year.

For the individual, remaining active in the labour market for longer can raise financial standards of living during retirement. It can also increase social inclusion and improve health.

Higher activity rates have important implications for the UK economy as a whole. The rising trend in participation among older people, all else equal, raises the economy's trend rate of growth, because rising activity rates broadly translate into increases in the employment rate component of trend output growth. Changes in the participation rate of older workers could also affect the productivity and average hours components of trend output growth.

Despite some cyclical influences, activity rate rises amongst older workers over the past decade have mostly been driven by structural factors, including an ageing population, less gender discrimination and other social and economic changes.

Going forward, there are a number of factors which are likely to raise the activity rate of older workers further. The State Pension Age will be equalised by 2020 at 65. Although some female workers may already have started adapting to this change, the experience of New Zealand – which underwent a similar policy change between 1992 and 2000 – points to further upward effects on participation. Moreover, age discrimination legislation will come into effect from October 2006; and the proportion of people aged 50 or over in the population is forecast to hit almost 50 per cent by 2024. This means that the participation behaviour of older workers will become an increasingly important factor in whole economy performance.

---

[6] See *Evidence on the UK Economic Cycle*, HM Treasury, July 2005

Summary of prospects

B.52   Sound macroeconomic fundamentals continue to support growth and stability in the UK, helping the economy to remain far more resilient to challenges and shocks than it has in the past. As a result of the domestic macroeconomic stability that the Government's policies have delivered, the UK is well placed for a resumption of above-trend growth as the effects of current dampening influences on activity abate. However, uncertainties about the effects of high oil prices and current levels of household and corporate debt pose particular risks to the outlook, both downside and upside.

Table B3: Summary of forecast[1]

| | | | Forecast | |
	2005	2006	2007	2008
GDP growth (per cent)	$1\frac{3}{4}$	2 to $2\frac{1}{2}$	$2\frac{3}{4}$ to $3\frac{1}{4}$	$2\frac{3}{4}$ to $3\frac{1}{4}$
CPI inflation (per cent, Q4)	$2\frac{1}{4}$	2	2	2

[1] See footnote to table B9 for explanation of forecast ranges.

B.53   Overall, the economic forecast is unchanged from the 2005 Pre-Budget Report. Following growth of $1\frac{3}{4}$ per cent in 2005, UK GDP is expected to grow by between 2 and $2\frac{1}{2}$ per cent this year, still slightly below trend rates. This reflects a number of factors. Private consumption growth is expected to be further restrained by continued household appetite for saving, weak growth in labour incomes, and the residual effects of higher energy prices. Companies are likely to remain cautious about stepping up business investment in the face of high oil prices, further below-trend growth in the near term, and high levels of capital gearing.

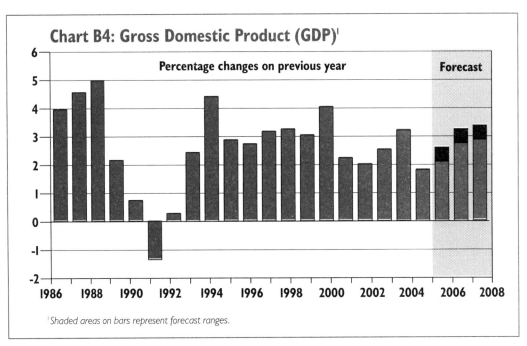

Chart B4: Gross Domestic Product (GDP)[1]

Percentage changes on previous year

[1] Shaded areas on bars represent forecast ranges.

B.54   However, the economy has already shown signs of gradually increasing momentum through the latter stages of 2005 and into 2006. The Government's macroeconomic framework has continued to deliver unprecedented stability, with inflation at target, despite the effects of higher oil prices, and GDP growth remaining above rates seen when the economy has faced shocks in past decades. So the economy remains well placed to see a renewed period of above-trend growth from 2007 and beyond as factors temporarily subduing growth over the recent past abate.

B.55   With the effects on spending of previous oil price rises and the recent adjustment in the household saving ratio receding, private consumption growth should firm a little further in 2007 and 2008, although rising at rates well below recent peaks and growth in the economy as a whole. With adjustment to higher oil prices working through and corporate fundamentals generally supportive, companies should be well placed to undertake firmer growth in investment spending as demand accelerates in 2007. As a result, GDP growth is forecast to be above trend rates at between $2^3/_4$ and $3^1/_4$ per cent in both 2007 and 2008, with spare capacity being absorbed and the output gap closing in 2008-09, unchanged from the 2005 Pre-Budget Report judgement.

B.56   The 2006 Budget forecast implies further rebalancing of GDP growth going forward, with business investment accelerating and outpacing private consumption from the end of 2006. Private consumption growth is expected to be in line with GDP growth this year, but to fall short of it thereafter. Net exports are forecast to make a neutral contribution to GDP growth, in contrast to the negative contribution in the years preceding 2005.

B.57   CPI inflation is expected to remain close to target, as inflation expectations remain firmly anchored, and energy prices exert slightly more upward pressure on inflation in 2006 than expected at the time of the Pre-Budget Report.

UK DEVELOPMENTS AND PROSPECTS IN DETAIL

Demand

B.58   The share of nominal consumption expenditure in UK GDP stabilised in 2005, having drifted down in each of the previous four years largely on the back of strong price competition in retail and other consumer markets.

B.59   Real private consumption rose by around $1^3/_4$ per cent in 2005. The slowing in private consumption growth compared with much of the recent past accords with the pattern of Budget and Pre-Budget Report forecasts since 2004, although the magnitude of that slowdown, on the basis of latest estimates, is somewhat greater than had been forecast.

B.60   Consumer spending growth picked up in the second half of 2005. However, this was from a weak base and growth remains below its long-run average. There are a number of factors that have continued to impinge on underlying household expenditure growth. Latest data, including data revisions introduced since the Pre-Budget Report, now show households increased saving in 2005, with the saving ratio estimated at around $5^1/_4$ per cent for the year as a whole, compared with $4^1/_2$ per cent in 2004. This is consistent with households undertaking some adjustment to their financial positions following strong borrowing and build up of debt over recent years. Additionally, with the labour market softening a little, there may have been some increase in the precautionary motive for saving. Moreover, average earnings growth has remained subdued and below most forecasters' prior expectations for 2005, although growth in non-labour components of household income boosted growth in nominal disposable income compared to 2004. Nevertheless, growth in real disposable income and consumption has been squeezed by higher than expected inflation through much of last year, largely reflecting the ongoing effects of oil-related rises in energy prices.

B.61   Most recent evidence is consistent with consumer spending growth gathering gradual momentum through the past year, although still below rates prevailing prior to the recent slowdown. Retail sales growth has clearly picked up from its trough, with sales in recent months averaging over $2^1/_2$ per cent up on a year earlier. Consumer confidence also appears to have firmed of late.

B.62   The Budget forecast for private consumption growth in 2006 is slightly higher than in the Pre-Budget Report, on account of the level effects arising from stronger than expected growth in the fourth quarter of 2005. Spending in 2006 is expected to continue being affected by higher energy prices and households' efforts to readjust their financial positions in response to high levels of borrowing over previous years. As these factors abate, private consumption growth should pick up from 2007, although remaining well below the peaks reached earlier this decade.

B.63   Latest official business investment estimates suggest private sector capital expenditure grew at only modest rates from the end of 2004 and through 2005. Ostensibly, this is consistent with the recent behaviour in a number of factors that are commonly perceived to have a strong influence on business investment. Subdued domestic demand and slower export market growth for much of the past year are likely to have discouraged firms from expanding capital budgets. High oil prices are likely to have been a further factor underpinning companies' reluctance to invest. Capital gearing remains high, despite having declined a little since its 2003 peak, and may have also acted as a constraint on business investment growth. In addition, it has been suggested that some companies may have been undertaking further adjustment in the face of still high pension fund deficits, though it is not clear that this has been materially holding back investment: profits, after taking into account pension fund payments, remain relatively high.

B.64   Nonetheless, there are grounds for thinking that business investment may have been somewhat stronger over the recent past than presently suggested by the official data. In particular, corporate profitability has been strong throughout the past two or so years; and business investment data are prone to relatively large revisions. So it is possible that later estimates may present a firmer picture of private capital spending than currently prevails. One important source of revisions arises from methodological and measurement advances. For example, as discussed in Box B6, the Office for National Statistics has recently published details of improvements to the way in which computer software investment is measured, suggesting that firms' own account in-house software investment has been significantly under-estimated in the UK.

B.65   Business investment growth is expected to remain at only modest rates over the near term, in response to still subdued growth of private consumption and companies' desire to reduce still high levels of capital gearing. However, with the corporate sector carrying substantial reserves of liquidity, and a historically low cost of capital contributing to a supportive financial environment, the foundations remain in place for a stronger pick-up in business investment to emerge later in 2006 and into 2007 and 2008. Business investment is projected to rise by between 1 to $1\frac{1}{2}$ per cent this year – close to growth in 2005 – rising to $4\frac{1}{2}$ to $5\frac{1}{4}$ per cent in 2007 and to $4\frac{1}{2}$ to $5\frac{1}{4}$ per cent in 2008.

B.66   Government investment is estimated to have risen by $18\frac{1}{2}$ per cent in 2005, continuing the strong growth of recent years. It is forecast to rise robustly again this year and next, in line with the Government's spending plans.

B.67   Interpretation of trade data was complicated in 2005 by the discovery of new Missing Trader fraud, which affects the figures for both imports and exports but not net trade. At face value, UK goods and services export volumes rose at their fastest rate for five years in 2005, up by $5\frac{1}{4}$ per cent on 2004. However, excluding Missing Trader activity, underlying export growth last year was more subdued, at just under 3 per cent. Chapter 5 sets out steps to strengthen the Government's strategy for combating the fraud.

B.68   Goods and services import growth also moderated last year, easing from a four-year high of $6\frac{3}{4}$ per cent in 2004 to around $4\frac{3}{4}$ per cent in 2005. Excluding Missing Trader activity, import volumes grew by just $2\frac{1}{2}$ per cent in 2005. This is broadly consistent with the slowdown in UK domestic demand growth since around mid-2004. As a result, the contribution from net trade to UK GDP growth last year was broadly neutral, in contrast to the run of negative contributions since 1997, with the exception of 2000.

B.69 Total export volume growth in 2006 is forecast to be about the same as last year, though this masks an underlying firming as UK export market growth picks up on the back of stronger demand from the euro area. (Missing Trader activity is assumed to make a zero contribution to growth in trade volumes). With export growth expected to be a little above that of imports over the forecast horizon, net trade is forecast to make a broadly neutral contribution to GDP growth throughout.

Table B4: Contributions to GDP growth[1,2]

| | Percentage points, unless otherwise stated | | | |
| | | Forecast | | |
	2005	**2006**	**2007**	**2008**
GDP growth, per cent	$1\frac{3}{4}$	$2\frac{1}{4}$	3	3
Main components:				
Private consumption	$1\frac{1}{4}$	$1\frac{1}{2}$	$1\frac{3}{4}$	2
Business investment	$\frac{1}{4}$	0	$\frac{1}{2}$	$\frac{1}{2}$
Government	$\frac{3}{4}$	$\frac{3}{4}$	$\frac{3}{4}$	$\frac{3}{4}$
Change in inventories	$-\frac{1}{4}$	0	0	0
Net trade	0	0	0	0

[1] Components may not sum to total due to rounding and omission of private residential investment, transfer costs of land and existing buildings and the statistical discrepancy.
[2] Based on central case. For the purpose of public finance projections, forecasts are based on the bottom of the forecast GDP range.

B.70 The Budget forecast shows further rebalancing of GDP growth going forward, with business investment accelerating and outpacing real private consumption from the end of 2006. Private consumption is expected to grow in line with GDP this year, but then to undershoot it as the economy moves to above-trend rates of growth in 2007 and 2008. Net exports are forecast to make a neutral contribution to GDP growth, in contrast to the negative contribution in the years preceding 2005.

Output

B.71 Manufacturing output was subdued through much of 2005 and declined by around 1 per cent for the year as a whole, following on from the strongest growth in the sector for four years in 2004. Manufacturing output growth has been held back by a number of factors over the recent past: continued weak growth in the euro area over much of 2005 restrained external demand for UK manufactured output, while high oil prices caused a sharp rise in producer input prices, squeezing margins and impinging on corporate confidence. At the same time, subdued growth in private consumption and business investment have acted to depress demand for manufacturing output.

B.72 Private sector business survey evidence on manufacturing activity has been mixed in recent months, but points to some gradual strengthening in output growth, already evident in the most recent data. Manufacturing output is forecast to rise by $\frac{1}{2}$ to 1 per cent this year, slightly less than in the Pre-Budget Report forecast, reflecting data revisions, and to rise by $1\frac{3}{4}$ to $2\frac{1}{4}$ per cent in 2007 and 2008 with stronger whole economy GDP growth.

B.73 Service sector output rose by just over $2\frac{1}{2}$ per cent in 2005, down from $3\frac{1}{2}$ per cent in 2004, reflecting lower growth in demand for both household and business services and a sharp fall in service sector export growth: last year was a particularly subdued year for services exports, which rose by just 1 per cent compared with 2004. This partly reflects the impact of the 7 July London terrorist attacks on tourism in the third quarter, but also more generalised weakness in external demand for service sector output. Private sector business survey evidence has, however, suggested a marked pick-up in demand for service sector output in early 2006, with the CIPS report on services showing the Activity Index at its highest for nearly two years in February.

Inflation

B.74   CPI inflation has fallen back since the time of the 2005 Pre-Budget Report, and by more than most commentators expected. CPI inflation rose through the summer to peak at $2\frac{1}{2}$ per cent in September, principally reflecting higher oil prices feeding through to the energy prices faced by households. Since then CPI inflation has fallen, edging down to fractionally below target in both December and January, before returning to target in February. This is despite high oil prices and wider energy costs still exerting residual upward pressure on inflation, and provides evidence of inflation expectations remaining firmly anchored, reflecting the credibility of the Government's monetary policy framework.

B.75   The increases in both oil and gas prices mean that energy prices are currently contributing 0.6 percentage points to CPI inflation. In particular, wholesale gas prices have risen significantly in the past six months, spiking sharply upwards on a number of occasions due to supply concerns. The recently announced increases in domestic gas prices from most major UK suppliers indicate that these increases in costs are beginning to be passed through to consumers. Reflecting this, energy prices are expected to continue to make a significant contribution to CPI inflation in the coming months, before easing off later in the year as the effects of last year's increase in oil prices falls out of the annual rate.

B.76   Both RPI and RPIX inflation have remained broadly where they were last autumn. RPI inflation stood at 2.4 per cent in February while RPIX inflation – the previous basis for the Government's inflation target – was a little lower at 2.3 per cent. The wedge between RPIX inflation and CPI inflation fell to zero in September, partly as a result of the slowdown in house price inflation, for the first time since the inception of the CPI. Subsequently, it has widened a little, although it has remained narrow relative to the wedge that prevailed between the two inflation rates for much of 2003 and 2004.

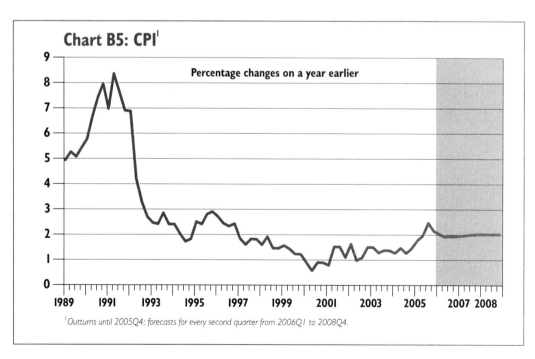

Chart B5: CPI[1]

Percentage changes on a year earlier

[1] Outturns until 2005Q4; forecasts for every second quarter from 2006Q1 to 2008Q4.

B.77 House price inflation appears to have firmed a little compared with much of the period through late 2004 and the first half of 2005. Both the Halifax and Nationwide have reported moderate three-month on three-month rates of house price inflation in recent months which are a little stronger than rates prevailing a year earlier. Moreover, annual rates of house price inflation look to have recently been running at around a range of 4 to 5 per cent, significantly below the rates of well in excess of 20 per cent that prevailed from autumn 2002 through to summer 2003.

Box B5: Globalisation and inflation

The integration of low cost emerging markets into the global economy in recent years has important implications for both global commodity prices and UK consumer prices. China alone now accounts for 6 per cent of world trade, and emerging Asia as a whole accounts for around 20 per cent, and its share is growing. This growth in global trade flows has had a significant effect on global demand. In the past 10 years alone, Chinese demand for oil has doubled, and primary non-oil commodity prices have risen significantly over the past few years. However, there is little indication so far that the commodity price increases have had any overall sustained influence on core consumer price pressures in the UK. In part this is because the effect on prices will not be all one way. The increased participation of developing economies in international trade has resulted in a sharp increase in the supply of cheap goods and services, and is also likely to have provided a boost to competitive pressures in all developed countries.

This has served to lower UK inflationary pressures, through the direct effect of cheaper non-oil import prices and downward pressure on domestic production costs. The first of these effects is illustrated in the chart, which shows that over the recent past the prices of (non-oil) imported goods and services have consistently grown at a slower rate than overall prices

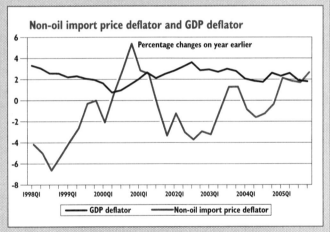

in the economy. Moreover, the effects of increased competition from emerging markets can also have an effect on the dynamics of wage settlements – the correlation between wages increases and price inflation has decreased throughout developed economies over the past decade. Looking forward, the potential for an extended period of expansion in developing economies such as China implies that the duration of the disinflationary impact owing to globalisation is likely to be lengthy. Moreover, it also suggests that current and future wage settlements in the UK may be increasingly influenced by global competitive pressures.

B.78 Recent evidence is therefore consistent with the view that to date the UK housing market has undergone a smooth realignment, without a prolonged period of declining prices as experienced in the economic cycle of the 1980s and 1990s.

B.79 CPI inflation is expected to move marginally below target in coming months. However, CPI inflation is forecast to be back around its 2 per cent target by the end of 2006, as previous rises in oil and wholesale gas prices continue to feed though to household utility bills. Energy price increases are now expected to exert slightly more upward pressure on inflation this year than expected at the time of the Pre-Budget Report. Beyond 2006, CPI inflation is projected to remain close to target as inflation expectations remain firmly anchored.

The household sector

Table B5: Household sector[1] expenditure and income

| | Percentage changes on previous year unless otherwise stated | | | |
| | | Forecast | | |
	2005	2006	2007	2008
Household consumption[2]	$1\frac{3}{4}$	2 to $2\frac{1}{2}$	$2\frac{1}{4}$ to $2\frac{3}{4}$	$2\frac{1}{2}$ to 3
Real household disposable income	$2\frac{1}{4}$	$2\frac{1}{2}$ to $2\frac{3}{4}$	2 to $2\frac{1}{2}$	$2\frac{1}{4}$ to $2\frac{3}{4}$
Saving ratio[3] (level, per cent)	$5\frac{1}{4}$	$5\frac{3}{4}$	$5\frac{1}{2}$	$5\frac{1}{2}$

[1] Including non-profit institutions serving households.

[2] Chained volume measure.

[3] Total household resources less consumption expenditure as a percent of total resources, where total resources comprise households' disposable income plus the increase in their net equity in pension funds.

B.80 The share of nominal consumption expenditure in UK GDP remained flat in 2005, having drifted down in each of the previous four years largely on the back of strong price competition in retail and other consumer markets.

B.81 Revisions to real private consumption since the 2005 Pre-Budget Report indicate a slightly more even profile for growth through 2004 and weaker outturns in the first half of 2005 than previously estimated. For 2005 as a whole, private consumption growth was just $1\frac{3}{4}$ per cent. However, this entailed particularly subdued growth in the first half of the year with quarterly private consumption growth picking up through the course of the year: in the fourth quarter it had reached 0.7 per cent, from a first quarter outturn of virtually zero.

B.82 In contrast to generally downward revisions to real private consumption, real household disposable income growth last year is now estimated to have been stronger than expected at the time of the 2005 Pre-Budget Report, partly reflecting data revisions.

B.83 Despite the gradual acceleration of private consumption throughout 2005, stronger nominal household income growth did not fully feed through into higher consumption growth. Indeed, the household saving ratio is estimated to have risen from $4\frac{1}{2}$ per cent in 2004 to around $5\frac{1}{4}$ per cent in 2005. It would appear that there have been several factors which have limited the expansion of private consumption. Sustained increases in oil prices have led to rising energy bills and dampened real income and consumption growth. Alongside a rise in unemployment in recent months, households have continued to adjust to high levels of personal debt by exercising more caution over their finances. This has been evidenced by, for example, substantially more moderate growth of unsecured credit, which has been rising at its slowest rate in around 12 years in recent months. All these factors have therefore kept real private consumption growth well below its average of the past eight years and accounted for most of the slowdown in UK GDP growth between 2004 and 2005.

B.84 The pattern of monthly retail sales volumes has been uneven in recent months. Nonetheless, three-month on three-month growth in retail sales has clearly picked up from its trough in early 2005. In the three months to February, retail sales volumes stood around 0.5 per cent up on the previous three months and $2\frac{3}{4}$ per cent higher than a year earlier.

B.85 Consumer confidence has picked up a little from the lows seen towards the end of 2005. Although seasonal factors associated with the effects of promotional activity on major purchases may have artificially buoyed overall confidence at the start of this year, there also appears to have been a modest underlying improvement in sentiment. In particular, consumers' expectations of the performance of the economy over the next year have increased since late 2005 and now lie close to their long-run average, while households' perceptions of both their current and future financial situation have also firmed a little since late 2005.

B.86 The outlook for private consumption is little changed compared with the Pre-Budget Report. Despite more robust consumer activity in the final quarter of 2005, real private consumption growth is expected to remain relatively moderate as households continue to adjust to still rising energy bills and high levels of debt, and as labour income growth remains sluggish. Underpinned by continued domestic macroeconomic stability, private consumption growth is forecast to pick up slightly as these dampening influences abate, while continuing to grow somewhat slower than real GDP over the forecast horizon. Private consumption is forecast to rise by 2 to $2\frac{1}{2}$ per cent this year and to fall short of GDP growth thereafter, growing by $2\frac{1}{4}$ to $2\frac{3}{4}$ per cent in 2007 and $2\frac{1}{2}$ to 3 per cent in 2008. The saving ratio is expected to rise again in 2006, and then to remain at levels just above its average over recent years.

Companies and investment

B.87 Over the recent past, the corporate sector has faced a low cost of capital, non-manufacturing profitability has been strong, and corporate cash flow has been healthy. Private non-financial corporations have now been net lenders in every quarter since the start of 2002, with their surplus building to an estimated 2 per cent of GDP in 2005. Yet business investment, on the basis of latest estimates, grew modestly in 2005, rising by $1\frac{1}{2}$ per cent on the previous year, and compared with growth of $3\frac{1}{4}$ per cent in 2004 – its strongest for four years.

B.88 Business investment data are prone to large revisions, and accounting conventions mean that the data do not include spending that many businesses would view as investment. In particular, as discussed in Box B6, current UK national accounts practices mean that much of companies' own account, or in-house, software spending is excluded from measurement. Intangible investment, like product innovation and increasing employees' human capital is also excluded, partly reflecting the obvious obstacles to accurately measuring these factors. Moreover, as the UK and other developed economies continue to shift to producing higher value-added manufactured goods and services, the nature of investment will also change.

B.89 The changing structure and strong performance of the UK economy reflects firms' ability to respond to global challenges, new business processes and changing consumer tastes. Service sector output now accounts for 73 per cent of total output and 80 per cent of jobs, up from only 55 per cent and 68 per cent respectively two decades ago. Within this broad category, financial services, education, creative industries and health now contribute 25 per cent of total output and 32 per cent of jobs. These changes to the structure of the economy will likely affect the way in which business investment is viewed and recorded.

B.90 Not only is the nature of business investment changing, the relative price of investment goods has also been falling in recent years. Capital goods prices declined in eight of the past nine years, making it possible for companies to increase real investment by holding capital budgets unchanged from year to year. Such factors could partly help to explain why the recorded nominal business investment to GDP ratio is currently low by historical standards.

B.91 However, there are a number of reasons why real business investment growth may have been subdued over the recent past, with companies reluctant to pursue expansive investment strategies. Cyclical factors are likely to have contributed: subdued private consumption growth alongside weak growth in key UK exports over much of 2005 will have tended to discourage companies from raising physical capacity. High oil prices have also probably contributed to the recent reluctance to step up capital expenditure.

B.92 Capital gearing, which remains high by historical standards, albeit down on its 2003 peak, is likely to have been another influence on corporate investment; and steps taken by companies to reduce pension fund deficits have also been cited by some as a factor constraining capital expenditure. Some evidence points to companies having long-run balance sheet (capital gearing) targets, so when gearing is driven above desired long-run levels, adjustments to profits (costs and prices), dividends, net equity issuance and/or investment may be made to rein in gearing.

B.93 Defined benefit pension liabilities are very similar to long-term debt. Nevertheless, there is no clear evidence for the UK that increased pension contributions have significantly affected business investment in aggregate. This does not preclude the possibility of increased stock of net pension liabilities being a factor impacting on investment spending. However, companies are still in possession of significant cash holdings. The UK corporate sector has increased its holdings of currency and deposits by about two thirds, or around £200 billion, over the past three years, mainly with overseas monetary and financial institutions. So the evidence does not suggest, at least at an aggregate level, that cash constraints are preventing companies from investing or paying down pension fund deficits at the present time.

Table B6: Gross fixed capital formation

| | Percentage changes on previous year | | | |
| | | Forecast | | |
	2005	**2006**	**2007**	**2008**
Whole economy[1]	$3\frac{1}{4}$	$1\frac{3}{4}$ to 2	4 to $4\frac{1}{2}$	4 to $4\frac{1}{2}$
of which:				
Business[2,3]	$1\frac{1}{2}$	1 to $1\frac{1}{2}$	$4\frac{1}{2}$ to $5\frac{1}{4}$	$4\frac{1}{2}$ to $5\frac{1}{4}$
Private dwellings[3]	$-\frac{1}{2}$	0 to $\frac{1}{4}$	$2\frac{3}{4}$ to $3\frac{1}{4}$	3 to $3\frac{1}{2}$
General government[3]	$18\frac{1}{2}$	$8\frac{1}{2}$	7	5

[1] Includes costs associated with the transfer of ownership of land and existing buildings.

[2] Private sector and public corporations' non-residential investment. Includes investment under the Private Finance Initiative.

[3] Excludes purchases less sales of land and existing buildings.

B.94 Nonetheless, other indicators point to rather more robust business investment spending growth than current official statistics suggest. In particular, corporate profitability has been sustained at healthy rates while the cost of capital has been kept historically low due to a combination of low inflation, domestic macroeconomic stability and strong global liquidity. There have been marked divergences between sectors in recent quarters, with relatively robust growth in large parts of the service sector being offset by weakness in other, smaller sectors like construction and manufacturing. However, recent official outturns are not particularly out of line with private business survey evidence on company intentions with respect to capital spending.

B.95 Business investment growth is expected to remain muted in the near term. However, with corporate fundamentals relatively sound, liquidity high and the cost of capital historically low, within the context of sustained domestic macroeconomic stability, the corporate sector should be relatively well placed to undertake somewhat stronger business investment growth as domestic demand growth picks up and stronger underlying export growth becomes established. The projections for business investment growth remain cautious relative to rates reached in the late 1990s and in previous economic cycles, in accordance with the greater stability of investment growth through the post-2000 global downturn, and the element of downside surprise over the past few years.

Box B6: Business investment – revisions and measurement issues

Investment figures tend to get revised substantially over time as, for example, new and more comprehensive data become available and improvements to statistical methodologies are introduced. On average, estimates of both whole economy and business investment growth have been revised up over recent years. For example, the provisional estimate of business investment growth in the year to the first quarter of 2002 was –1.1 per cent, but latest estimates suggest growth was positive, at 2 per cent.

As the UK and other developed economies continue to shift to producing higher value-added manufactured goods and services, the nature of investment will change. The boundaries between manufacturing and services are also likely to become increasingly blurred. Likewise, it may become less clear whether what is classed as investment in the national accounts is consistent with firms' definitions of investment. For example, expenditure on R&D, organisational change, training and some elements of branding and software investment are all currently recorded as current expenditure in the national accounts, whereas firms might reasonably consider them investments aimed at raising future capacity and efficiency.

These developments present significant measurement challenges for national statistical offices. However, progress is being made. For example, the Office for National Statistics has recently published details of improvements to the way in which computer software investment is measured. These revisions have important implications for understanding the economy, suggesting that firms' own-account, in-house software investment has been significantly under-estimated in the UK. Existing estimates suggest that total software investment was £8 billion in 2003, whereas revised estimates suggest a figure of around £21 billion. Software investment is now thought to have accounted for around 12 per cent of UK investment in 2003, and 1.9 per cent of GDP, suggesting that UK software investment is similar to that in the US as a percent of GDP.

These estimates are experimental and will not be incorporated into the national accounts until summer 2007. In addition, as highlighted above, other revisions are also likely to be made to the investment data between now and then. However, all else equal:

- the increase in own account software investment of £10.5 billion will add around 1 per cent to the level of GDP;
- the effect on GDP growth may be up to 0.1 percentage points a year; and
- the investment to GDP ratio will be higher, rising from 16 per cent in 2003 on current estimates to around 17 per cent.

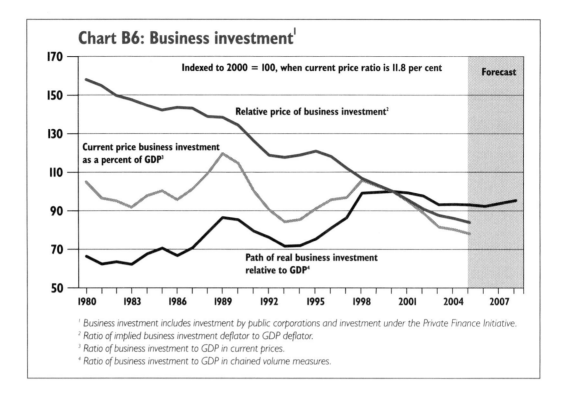

Chart B6: Business investment¹

Indexed to 2000 = 100, when current price ratio is 11.8 per cent

Forecast

Relative price of business investment²

Current price business investment as a percent of GDP³

Path of real business investment relative to GDP⁴

¹ Business investment includes investment by public corporations and investment under the Private Finance Initiative.
² Ratio of implied business investment deflator to GDP deflator.
³ Ratio of business investment to GDP in current prices.
⁴ Ratio of business investment to GDP in chained volume measures.

B.96 Government investment is expected to continue to grow strongly, consistent with the Government's aim to deliver world-class public services through sustained investment matched by far-reaching reform. Whole economy investment is expected slightly to outpace business investment in 2006, before this is reversed as business investment growth strengthens.

Trade and the balance of payments

B.97 Volumes of goods and services exports rose by around 5¼ per cent in 2005, up on the 4½ per cent growth recorded in 2004. However, trade figures over the recent past have been distorted by Missing Trader activity, which boosts both measured exports and imports – measured net exports are largely unaffected. As a result, the underlying growth of exports over the past year has been much more subdued than headline figures suggest. Excluding Missing Trader activity, exports of goods and services are estimated to have risen by just under 3 per cent last year, compared with growth of around 5¼ per cent in 2004.

B.98 A number of factors have held back export growth in recent quarters. For much of 2005, still subdued GDP growth, and in particular import demand, in the euro area – which accounts for around half of UK export markets – hampered underlying growth of UK exports. At the same time, oil exports fell last year, in spite of sustained high oil prices, reflecting both short-term disruptions to production and long-term structural factors related to the underlying depletion of North Sea oil reserves.

B.99 Last year exports of UK services are estimated to have risen by just 1 per cent compared with 2004, the weakest growth for 13 years. Some of this likely reflects the short-term effects on tourism following the 7 July terrorist atrocities in central London. However, demand for UK service sector exports may have also experienced more generalised weakness as a result of muted growth in some key export markets through much of 2005.

B.100 Import growth fell back in 2005 on the back of the weaker expansion in domestic demand although, broadly consistent with the pattern of GDP growth, it picked up a little between the beginning and the end of the year. Goods and services import volumes rose by around 4³/₄ per cent in 2005, down from 6³/₄ per cent in 2004. So net trade made a more or less neutral contribution to GDP growth last year, following a run of significant negative contributions since 1997, with the exception of 2000.

B.101 The sterling exchange rate index remains close to the level prevailing at the time of the 2005 Pre-Budget Report.

B.102 The overall UK current deficit widened sharply in the third quarter of 2005, reflecting a larger trade deficit, largely due to the accounting treatment of insurance claims associated with Hurricane Katrina, and a sharp decline in the UK's surplus on overseas income. However, quarterly current account data can be erratic, and over 2005 as a whole the current deficit is estimated to have averaged around 2¹/₄ per cent of GDP, as expected in the Pre-Budget Report.

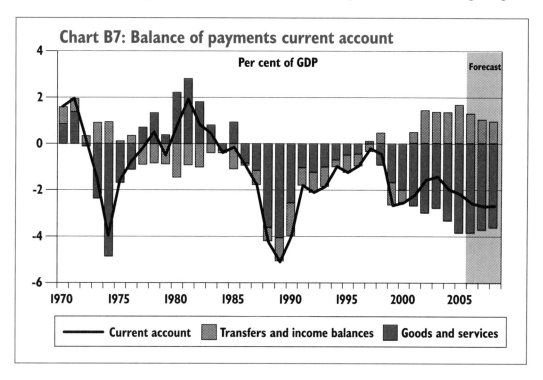

Chart B7: Balance of payments current account

B.103 The UK is estimated to have continued to run another record surplus on overseas income earnings in 2005, at around 2³/₄ per cent of GDP. UK income earnings have been maintained at record levels in recent quarters by a number of factors. Sustained rises in oil prices have tended to boost UK oil companies earnings from overseas by more than they have increased foreign oil companies returns on their UK subsidiaries, as a result the UK's continued position as a net overseas oil investor. More generally, rates of return earned on UK investments overseas have historically tended to be above those foreign investors have been able to earn on their investments in the UK, and this continues to remain the case.

Box B7: Foreign Direct Investment

The **UK** has traditionally been a large source and recipient of Foreign Direct Investment (FDI), holding the highest stock of inward FDI as a percent of GDP in the G7 (see chart).

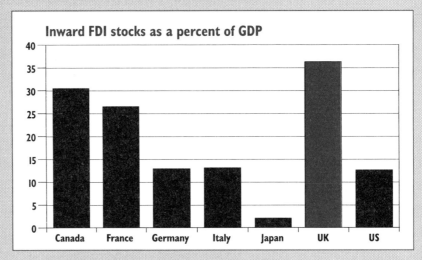

Inward FDI stocks as a percent of GDP

Following the global downturn in cross-border investment earlier this decade, FDI inflows to the UK picked up significantly in 2004 and 2005. International comparisons suggest that in 2005 the UK topped the global FDI inflow table for the first time since 1977, attracting around half of all inflows to Europe[a]. Almost half of the inflows to the UK in 2005 can be accounted for by the restructuring of Shell Transport and Trading Company plc and Royal Dutch Petroleum Company into Royal Dutch Shell, highlighting the volatile nature of international investment flows. However, even leaving aside this transaction, the UK still received more inward investment in 2005 than the second biggest recipient, the US.

FDI can be an important source of new ideas, management techniques and production methods. As such, FDI can lead to improvements in productivity directly – for example, through its impact on the productivity of firms which have been involved in cross-border mergers and acquisitions – and indirectly, through spillovers – for example, the diffusion of knowledge and techniques throughout the economy. Studies have found that foreign-owned multinationals are more productive than both British owned multinationals and domestic firms. There are also a significant number of jobs linked to FDI projects in the UK. Figures show a rise in inward investment projects of 31 per cent in 2004-05 compared with the previous financial year, with more than 39,000 jobs linked to these new projects[b].

Unprecedented macroeconomic stability and sustained growth since 1997, as well as the introduction of microeconomic reforms aimed at increasing the flexibility of the UK's product and labour markets, are likely to have contributed to the attractiveness of the UK as a destination for international investment. This is reflected in business surveys, which have shown the UK rising up rankings of investor confidence in recent years[c] and maintaining its attractiveness to investors in the face of increasing competition from emerging markets like India and China[d].

[a] UNCTAD press release PR/2006/002, 23 January 2006.
[b] *UK inward investment 2004/05*, Report by UK Trade and Investment.
[c] A.T. Kearney's 2004 FDI Confidence Index showed the UK rising from seventh to fourth place.
[d] See Ernst and Young's European Attractiveness Surveys 2004 and 2005.

B.104　Total export growth in 2006 is forecast to be about the same as last year. However, this masks a firming in underlying export growth excluding fraudulent Missing Trader activity as UK export market growth picks up this year, partly on the back of stronger demand from the euro area. The forecast assumes that export and import volumes grow in line with underlying trade, ie excluding Missing Trader activity. This amounts to making the neutral assumption that Missing Trader activity stays flat at its 2005 level in each year of the forecast. Steps to strengthen the Government's strategy for combating the fraud are set out in Chapter 5, and in so far as Missing Trader activity changes from its 2005 level, then both export and import forecasts would be affected, but not the forecast for net trade. With export growth expected to be a little above that of imports over the forecast horizon, despite some assumed further loss of export market share, net trade is forecast to make a broadly neutral contribution to GDP growth throughout.

B.105　With the trade deficit expected to remain broadly flat, and the income surplus expected to ease back somewhat from last years record level, the current deficit is projected to widen in 2006 and then remain stable over the forecast horizon at around $2^3/_4$ per cent of GDP.

Table B7: Trade in goods and services

| | Percentage changes on previous year | | | | | £ billion |
| | Volumes | | Prices[1] | | | Goods and services balance |
	Exports	Imports	Exports	Imports	Terms of trade[2]	
2005	$5^1/_4$	$4^3/_4$	$1^3/_4$	$3^3/_4$	$-1^3/_4$	-47
Forecast						
2006	5 to $5^1/_2$	$4^1/_4$ to $4^3/_4$	$1^1/_4$	$1^3/_4$	$-^1/_2$	$-49^1/_4$
2007	$4^3/_4$ to $5^1/_4$	$4^1/_2$ to 5	$^3/_4$	$^3/_4$	$^1/_4$	$-50^1/_4$
2008	$4^3/_4$ to $5^1/_4$	$4^1/_2$ to 5	$^1/_2$	$^1/_2$	0	$-51^3/_4$

[1] Average value indices.

[2] Ratio of export to import prices.

Independent forecasts

B.106　Some outside forecasts have edged up a little in recent months. The latest average of independent forecasts for GDP growth in 2006 is 2.2 per cent, at the centre of the Budget forecast range of 2 to $2^1/_2$ per cent.

B.107　For 2007, the latest independent average for GDP growth stands at 2.4 per cent, below the Budget range of $2^3/_4$ to $3^1/_4$ per cent, although a number of prominent outside forecasts come within the range, and the average is depressed by one extreme outlier. Outside forecasts for 2008 currently average 2.7 per cent, at the lower end of the Budget range of $2^3/_4$ to $3^1/_4$ per cent.

B.108　Despite the latest estimates for growth in 2005 being lower than forecast in last year's Budget, the Treasury has continued to maintain a good forecast performance in recent years. Since 1997, Treasury forecasts for GDP growth have on average been more accurate than those of almost all prominent external forecasters, as well as showing improvement on the Treasury's own previous track record.

Table B8: Budget and independent[1] forecasts

	Percentage changes on a year earlier unless otherwise stated					
	2006			2007		
	March	Independent		March	Independent	
	Budget	Average	Range	Budget	Average	Range
Gross domestic product	2 to 2½	2.2	1.4 to 2.8	2¾ to 3¼	2.4	0.1 to 2.9
CPI (Q4)	2	1.9	1.4 to 2.4	2	2.0	1.6 to 2.8
Current account (£ billion)	−32¾	−28.4	−45.7 to −18.7	−36½	29.3	−45.2 to −15

[1] 'Forecasts for the UK Economy: A Comparison of Independent Forecasts', March 2006.

Forecast risks

B.109 The set of risks surrounding the Budget 2006 economic outlook is similar to those surrounding the 2005 Pre-Budget Report forecast. However, the balance of risks has shifted a little, with domestic risks having receded while global uncertainties have increased somewhat. Globalisation means that the UK economy shares ever increasingly in the risks affecting the world economy, and that domestic risks are harder to differentiate.

B.110 Uncertainty continues to surround the current output gap estimate given ongoing uncertainty as to whether the latest vintage of ONS data is correctly approximating the degree to which the economy has been growing below trend over the recent past. To the extent that the economy has been growing more (less) quickly than implied by existing data, then that would mean less (more) scope for above-trend growth over the forecast horizon.

B.111 The forecast for private consumption continues to be surrounded by both upside and downside risks. Further unexpected weakness of average earnings growth would tend to undermine household expenditure, although the boost to employment from weakening labour costs would tend at least partly to offset this effect. Related downside risks to consumption growth also come from the current uncertainties about the extent to which the recent increase in unemployment may prove temporary and erratic. In so far as it might tend to encourage higher precautionary saving, it would inhibit spending. Independent forecasters expect a marginal strengthening of employment growth next year.

B.112 Private consumption growth also poses the potential for upside surprises relative to the Budget forecast. With increasing evidence that the housing market has undergone a smooth realignment with some modest recent firming in house prices, and with consumer confidence having firmed, household spending could accelerate more sharply than envisaged.

B.113 Business investment growth could also surprise on the upside, as has previously been recognised in recent Pre-Budget and Budget Reports, despite the weakness in capital spending indicated by latest official estimates for 2005 and the uncertainties surrounding the effects capital gearing and pension fund deficits are presently having on investment.

Table B9: Summary of economic prospects[1]

	Percentage changes on a year earlier unless otherwise stated					
					Average errors from past forecasts[5]	
			Forecast[2,3,4]			
	2005	**2006**	**2007**	**2008**	**2006**	**2007**
Output at constant market prices						
Gross domestic product (GDP)	$1\frac{3}{4}$	2 to $2\frac{1}{2}$	$2\frac{3}{4}$ to $3\frac{1}{4}$	$2\frac{3}{4}$ to $3\frac{1}{4}$	$\frac{3}{4}$	$\frac{1}{2}$
Manufacturing output	-1	$\frac{1}{2}$ to 1	$1\frac{3}{4}$ to $2\frac{1}{4}$	$1\frac{3}{4}$ to $2\frac{1}{4}$	$1\frac{1}{4}$	2
Expenditure components of GDP at constant market prices[6]						
Domestic demand	$1\frac{3}{4}$	2 to $2\frac{1}{4}$	$2\frac{3}{4}$ to $3\frac{1}{4}$	$2\frac{3}{4}$ to $3\frac{1}{4}$	$\frac{3}{4}$	$\frac{3}{4}$
Household consumption[7]	$1\frac{3}{4}$	2 to $2\frac{1}{2}$	$2\frac{1}{4}$ to $2\frac{3}{4}$	$2\frac{1}{2}$ to 3	$\frac{3}{4}$	1
General government consumption	2	$2\frac{1}{2}$	$2\frac{1}{2}$	$2\frac{1}{2}$	1	$1\frac{1}{4}$
Fixed investment	$3\frac{1}{4}$	$1\frac{3}{4}$ to 2	4 to $4\frac{1}{2}$	4 to $4\frac{1}{2}$	$2\frac{1}{2}$	$2\frac{1}{4}$
Change in inventories[8]	$-\frac{1}{4}$	$-\frac{1}{4}$ to 0	0 to $\frac{1}{4}$	0	$\frac{1}{4}$	$\frac{1}{4}$
Exports of goods and services	$5\frac{1}{4}$	5 to $5\frac{1}{2}$	$4\frac{3}{4}$ to $5\frac{1}{4}$	$4\frac{3}{4}$ to $5\frac{1}{4}$	$1\frac{3}{4}$	$3\frac{1}{4}$
Imports of goods and services	$4\frac{3}{4}$	$4\frac{1}{4}$ to $4\frac{3}{4}$	$4\frac{1}{2}$ to 5	$4\frac{1}{2}$ to 5	$2\frac{1}{4}$	$2\frac{1}{2}$
Balance of payments current account						
£ billion	$-26\frac{3}{4}$	$-32\frac{3}{4}$	$-36\frac{1}{2}$	$-38\frac{1}{4}$	$7\frac{1}{4}$	8
per cent of GDP	$-2\frac{1}{4}$	$-2\frac{1}{2}$	$-2\frac{3}{4}$	$-2\frac{3}{4}$	$\frac{1}{2}$	$\frac{3}{4}$
Inflation						
CPI (Q4)	$2\frac{1}{4}$	2	2	2	–	–
Producer output prices (Q4)[9]	$2\frac{1}{2}$	$1\frac{3}{4}$	2	2	1	$1\frac{1}{2}$
GDP deflator at market prices	$2\frac{1}{4}$	$2\frac{1}{4}$	$2\frac{1}{2}$	$2\frac{3}{4}$	$\frac{1}{2}$	$\frac{1}{2}$
Money GDP at market prices						
£ billion	$1211\frac{1}{4}$	1266 to 1269	1334 to 1345	1409 to 1428	9	9
percentage change	4	$4\frac{1}{2}$ to $4\frac{3}{4}$	$5\frac{1}{2}$ to 6	$5\frac{1}{2}$ to $6\frac{1}{4}$	$\frac{3}{4}$	$\frac{3}{4}$

[1] The forecast is consistent with output, income and expenditure data for the fourth quarter of 2005, released by the Office for National Statistics on 24 February 2006. See also footnote 1 on the first page of this chapter.

[2] All growth rates in tables throughout this chapter are rounded to the nearest $\frac{1}{4}$ percentage point.

[3] As in previous Budget and Pre-Budget Reports, the economic forecast is presented in terms of forecast ranges, based on alternative assumptions about the supply-side performance of the economy. The mid-points of the forecast ranges are anchored around the neutral assumption for the trend rate of output growth of $2\frac{3}{4}$ per cent to the end of 2006 and $2\frac{1}{2}$ per cent thereafter. The figures at the lower end of the ranges are consistent with the deliberately cautious assumption of trend growth used as the basis for projecting the public finances which is $\frac{1}{4}$ percentage point below the neutral assumption.

[4] The size of the growth ranges for GDP components may differ from those for total GDP growth because of rounding and the assumed invariance of the levels of public spending within the forecast ranges.

[5] Average absolute errors for current year and year-ahead projections made in spring forecasts over the past 10 years. The average errors for the current account are calculated as a percent of GDP, with £ billion figures calculated by scaling the errors by forecast money GDP in 2006 and 2007.

[6] Further detail on the expenditure components of GDP is given in Table B10.

[7] Includes households and non-profit institutions serving households.

[8] Contribution to GDP growth, percentage points.

[9] Excluding excise duties.

Table B10: Gross domestic product and its components

	Household consumption[1]	General government consumption[2]	Fixed investment[2]	Change in inventories	Domestic demand[2]	Exports of goods and services	Total final expenditure	Less imports of goods and services	*Plus* statistical discrepancy[3]	GDP at market prices
	£ billion chained volume measures at market prices, seasonally adjusted									
2005	749.9	232.1	187.5	2.7	1171.9	306.0	1477.9	348.9	0.3	1129.2
2006	765.6 to 767.9	237.7	190.8 to 191.4	1.1 to 1.9	1195.3 to 1198.9	321.6 to 322.5	1516.8 to 1521.4	364.1 to 365.2	0.3	1153.0 to 1156.5
2007	783.6 to 789.8	243.9	198.6 to 200.2	1.8 to 3.8	1227.9 to 1237.7	337.0 to 339.7	1564.9 to 1577.4	380.4 to 383.5	0.3	1184.7 to 1194.2
2008	803.9 to 814.3	250.1	206.7 to 209.3	1.9 to 5.1	1262.5 to 1278.8	353.1 to 357.6	1615.6 to 1636.4	397.4 to 402.5	0.3	1218.5 to 1234.2
2005 1st half	372.8	115.1	92.6	1.7	582.2	150.8	733.0	171.4	0.1	561.7
2005 2nd half	377.1	117.0	94.9	1.0	589.7	155.2	744.9	177.5	0.1	567.5
2006 1st half	380.8 to 381.5	118.2	94.8 to 95.0	0.8 to 1.0	594.7 to 595.7	158.9 to 159.2	753.6 to 755.0	180.3 to 180.6	0.1	573.4 to 574.5
2006 2nd half	384.7 to 386.4	119.5	96.0 to 96.4	0.3 to 0.8	600.6 to 603.2	162.6 to 163.3	763.2 to 766.5	183.8 to 184.6	0.1	579.6 to 582.0
2007 1st half	389.3 to 391.9	121.2	98.2 to 98.9	0.5 to 1.3	609.1 to 613.2	166.5 to 167.7	775.7 to 780.9	188.0 to 189.2	0.1	587.8 to 591.8
2007 2nd half	394.3 to 397.9	122.7	100.4 to 101.3	1.3 to 2.5	618.8 to 624.5	170.5 to 172.0	789.3 to 796.5	192.5 to 194.2	0.1	596.9 to 602.4
2008 1st half	399.5 to 404.2	124.3	102.4 to 103.6	1.0 to 2.5	627.3 to 634.6	174.5 to 176.6	801.9 to 811.2	196.7 to 198.9	0.1	605.3 to 612.4
2008 2nd half	404.4 to 410.1	125.7	104.2 to 105.7	0.8 to 2.6	635.2 to 644.2	178.5 to 181.1	813.7 to 825.2	200.7 to 203.6	0.1	613.1 to 621.8
	Percentage changes on previous year[4,5]									
2005	1¾	2	3¼	-¼	1¾	5¼	2½	4¾	0	1¾
2006	2 to 2½	2½	1¾ to 2	-¼ to 0	2 to 2¼	5 to 5½	2¾ to 3	4¼ to 4¾	0	2 to 2½
2007	2¼ to 2¾	2½	4 to 4½	0 to ¼	2¾ to 3¼	4¾ to 5¼	3¼ to 3¾	4½ to 5	0	2¾ to 3¼
2008	2½ to 3	2½	4 to 4½	0	2¾ to 3¼	4¾ to 5¼	3¼ to 3¾	4½ to 5	0	2¾ to 3¼

[1] Includes households and non-profit institutions serving households.
[2] Also includes acquisitions less disposals of valuables.
[3] Expenditure adjustment.
[4] For change in inventories and the statistical discrepancy, changes are expressed as a percent of GDP.
[5] Growth ranges for GDP components do not necessarily sum to the ½ percentage point ranges for GDP growth because of rounding and the assumed invariance of the levels of public spending within the forecast ranges.

C THE PUBLIC FINANCES

> The Budget 2006 projections for the public finances are broadly in line with the 2005 Pre-Budget Report and show that the Government is meeting its strict fiscal rules:
>
> - the current budget since the start of the current economic cycle in 1997-98 shows an annual average surplus up to 2008-09 of 0.1 per cent of GDP, showing the Government is meeting the golden rule on the basis of cautious assumptions. The average annual current surplus from 2008-09 to the end of the forecast period is about 0.7 per cent of GDP; and
>
> - public sector net debt is projected to be low and stable over the forecast period stabilising at around 38½ per cent of GDP, below the 40 per cent ceiling set in the sustainable investment rule.

INTRODUCTION

C.1   Chapter 2 describes the Government's fiscal policy framework and shows how the projections of the public finances are consistent with meeting the fiscal rules. This chapter explains the latest outturns and the fiscal projections in more detail. It includes:

- five-year projections of the current budget and public sector net debt, the key aggregates for assessing performance against the golden rule and the sustainable investment rule, respectively;

- projections of public sector net borrowing, the fiscal aggregate relevant to assessing the impact of fiscal policy on the economy;

- projections of the cyclically-adjusted fiscal balances; and

- detailed analyses of the outlook for government receipts and expenditure.

C.2   The fiscal projections continue to be based on deliberately cautious key assumptions audited by the National Audit Office (NAO).

MEETING THE FISCAL RULES

C.3   Table C1 shows five-year projections for the current budget and public sector net debt, the key aggregates for assessing performance against the golden rule and the sustainable investment rule respectively. Outturns and projections of other important measures of the public finances, including net borrowing and cyclically-adjusted fiscal balances, are also shown.

Table C1: Summary of public sector finances

	Per cent of GDP							
	Outturns		Estimate	Projections				
	2003-04	2004-05	2005-06	2006-07	2007-08	2008-09	2009-10	2010-11
Fairness and prudence								
Surplus on current budget	-1.9	-1.6	-0.9	-0.6	0.1	0.5	0.7	0.8
Average surplus since 1997-1998	0.5	0.2	0.1	0.0	0.0	0.1	0.1	0.2
Cyclically-adjusted surplus on current budget	-1.4	-1.3	-0.3	0.4	0.7	0.7	0.7	0.8
Long-term sustainability								
Public sector net debt[1]	33.2	35.0	36.4	37.5	38.1	38.3	38.4	38.4
Core debt[1]	32.8	34.3	35.2	35.4	35.5	35.7	35.9	36.0
Net worth[2]	28.5	29.0	26.0	24.8	23.3	22.9	22.9	22.8
Primary balance	-1.6	-1.7	-1.3	-1.1	-0.5	-0.1	0.1	0.1
Economic impact								
Net investment	1.3	1.8	2.1	2.2	2.3	2.3	2.3	2.3
Public sector net borrowing (PSNB)	3.2	3.4	3.0	2.8	2.2	1.7	1.6	1.5
Cyclically-adjusted PSNB	2.7	3.0	2.4	1.9	1.6	1.6	1.6	1.5
Financing								
Central government net cash requirement	3.5	3.3	3.2	3.2	2.6	2.1	2.1	1.8
Public sector net cash requirement	3.5	3.3	3.0	2.9	2.4	1.8	1.8	1.5
European commitments								
Treaty deficit[3]	3.1	3.3	3.2	3.0	2.4	1.9	1.7	1.6
Cyclically-adjusted Treaty deficit[3]	2.6	2.9	2.5	2.0	1.8	1.7	1.7	1.7
Treaty debt ratio[4]	39.5	40.8	42.6	43.9	44.5	44.5	44.5	44.5
Memo: Output gap	-0.6	-0.4	-1.2	-1.4	-0.7	-0.1	0.0	0.0

[1] Debt at end March; GDP centred on end March.

[2] Estimate at end December; GDP centred on end December.

[3] General government net borrowing on a Maastricht basis.

[4] General government gross debt measures on a Maastricht basis.

The golden rule   **C.4**   The projections show that the Government is meeting the golden rule, on the basis of cautious assumptions, with an average annual surplus on the current budget over this economic cycle of around 0.1 per cent of GDP. On this basis, and based on cautious assumptions, the Government is meeting the golden rule and there is a margin against the golden rule of £16 billion in this cycle, including the Annually Managed Expenditure (AME) margin. The cyclically-adjusted surplus, which allows underlying or structural trends in the public finances to be seen more clearly by removing the estimated effects of the economic cycle, shows a small deficit in 2005-06, but a surplus of 0.4 per cent of GDP in 2006-07 and higher surpluses from 2007-08 onwards.

C.5   The economy is projected to return to trend in 2008-09. With the economy assumed to be on trend from then on, the projections show, based on cautious assumptions, that the average surplus over the period 2008-09 to 2010-11 is 0.7 per cent of GDP. At this early stage, and based on cautious assumptions, the Government will therefore continue to meet the golden rule after the end of this cycle.

The sustainable   **C.6**   The sustainable investment rule is also met over the economic cycle. In 1996-97, **investment rule**   public sector net debt stood at 44 per cent of GDP. The tough decisions on taxation and expenditure taken by the Government, including the decision to use the proceeds from the auction of spectrum licenses to repay debt, reduced debt to around 30 per cent of GDP by the end of 2001-02. It is now projected to grow slowly, as the Government borrows modestly to fund increased investment in public services, reaching around 38½ per cent of GDP by the end of the economic cycle, and stabilising at that level for the remainder of the forecasting period. The projections for core debt, which exclude the estimated impact of the economic cycle, rise 36 per cent of GDP. This is consistent with the fiscal rules, and with the key objective of intergenerational fairness that underpins the fiscal framework.

Net worth   **C.7**   Net worth is the approximate stock counterpart of the current budget. Modest falls in net worth are expected for the remainder of the projection period from the high level of 29 per cent of GDP in 2004-05. At present, net worth is not used as a key indicator of the public finances, mainly as a result of the difficulties involved in accurately measuring many government assets and liabilities.

C.8   Chart C1 shows public sector net debt and net worth as a per cent of GDP from 1992-93 to 2010-11.

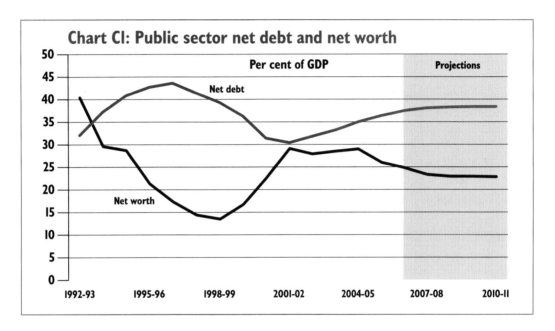

Net investment   **C.9**   As a result of decisions taken in the 2004 Spending Review public sector net investment is projected to rise from 1.1 per cent of GDP in 2002-03 to $2^1/_4$ per cent from 2006-07 onwards. This increase is sustainable and fully consistent with the Government's long-term approach and the fiscal rules, since net debt is being held at a stable and prudent level, below 40 per cent of GDP.

Net borrowing   **C.10**   Public sector net borrowing is expected to fall in every year of the forecast period from 3.4 per cent of GDP in 2004-05 to 3.0 per cent in 2005-06, and then to a level of $1^1/_2$ per cent of GDP by 2010-11.

Financing   **C.11**   The central government net cash requirement was 3.3 per cent of GDP in 2004-05. It is projected to be around 3.2 per cent in 2005-06, and falls to 1.8 per cent of GDP by 2010-11, mirroring the profile of net borrowing.

European commitments   **C.12**   Table C1 shows the Treaty measures of debt and deficit used for the purposes of the Excessive Deficit Procedure - Article 104 of the Treaty. The public finance projections set out in Budget 2006, which show the Government is meeting its fiscal rules over the cycle, maintaining low debt and sustainable public finances, combined with sustainable increases in public investment, are fully consistent with a prudent interpretation of the Pact. The projections meet the EU Treaty reference value for general government gross debt (60 per cent of GDP) by a considerable margin. In addition, the cyclically-adjusted level of general government net borrowing is 2.5 per cent of GDP in 2005-06 and is at 2 per cent of GDP or below from 2006-07 onwards.

CHANGES TO THE FISCAL BALANCES

C.13   Table C2 compares the latest estimates for the main fiscal balances with those in Budget 2005 and in the 2005 Pre-Budget Report.

Table C2: Fiscal balances compared with Budget 2005 and the 2005 Pre-Budget Report

	Outturn[1]	Estimate[2]	Projections				
	2004-05	2005-06	2006-07	2007-08	2008-09	2009-10	2010-11
Surplus on current budget (£ billion)							
Budget 2005	-16.1	-5.7	1	4	9	12	
Effect of revisions and forecasting changes	-3.8	-4.2	-6 1/2	-6 1/2	-5	-3 1/2	
Effect of discretionary changes	0.0	-0.8	2	2 1/2	2 1/2	2	
PBR 2005	-19.9	-10.6	-4	0	7	11	13
Effect of revisions and forecasting changes	0.9	-0.8	-2 1/2	1/2	0	-1	-1 1/2
Effect of discretionary changes	0.0	0.0	- 1/2	1/2	1	1/2	1/2
Budget 2006	**-19.0**	**-11.4**	**-7**	**1**	**7**	**10**	**12**
Net borrowing (£ billion)							
Budget 2005	34.4	31.9	29	27	24	22	
Changes to current budget	3.8	4.9	5	4	2 1/2	1 1/2	
Changes to net investment	0.6	0.1	0	0	0	0	
PBR 2005	38.8	37.0	34	31	26	23	22
Changes to current budget	-0.9	0.8	3	-1	- 1/2	1/2	1
Changes to net investment	1.7	-0.6	- 1/2	- 1/2	0	0	0
Budget 2006	**39.7**	**37.1**	**36**	**30**	**25**	**24**	**23**
Cyclically-adjusted surplus on current budget (per cent of GDP)							
Budget 2005	-0.8	-0.3	0.1	0.3	0.6	0.8	
PBR 2005	-1.3	-0.1	0.7	0.7	0.7	0.7	0.8
Budget 2006	**-1.3**	**-0.3**	**0.4**	**0.7**	**0.7**	**0.7**	**0.8**
Cyclically-adjusted net borrowing (per cent of GDP)							
Budget 2005	2.4	2.4	2.2	2.0	1.6	1.5	
PBR 2005	2.9	2.2	1.6	1.6	1.6	1.5	1.4
Budget 2006	**3.0**	**2.4**	**1.9**	**1.6**	**1.6**	**1.6**	**1.5**
Net debt (per cent of GDP)							
Budget 2005	34.4	35.5	36.2	36.8	37.1	37.1	
PBR 2005	34.7	36.5	37.4	37.9	38.2	38.2	38.2
Budget 2006	**35.0**	**36.4**	**37.5**	**38.1**	**38.3**	**38.4**	**38.4**

[1] The 2004-05 figures were estimates in Budget 2005.
[2] The 2005-06 figures were projections in Budget 2005.

Changes between Budget 2005 and the 2005 Pre-Budget Report

C.14   In the 2005 Pre-Budget Report, the current budget was revised down by £3 3/4 billion in 2004-05 and by around £5 billion a year in 2005-06 and 2006-07. The revisions were smaller in subsequent years and the current balance returned to surplus in 2007-08.

C.15   These revisions were mainly due to a combination of higher expenditure and lower receipts in 2004-05 and to lower projections of receipts, especially non-North sea corporation tax and VAT for 2005-06 onwards. However, these shortfalls were lower than would have been expected given changes in the level of money GDP and its components, partly because of higher receipts from North Sea taxes and partly because of the strong performance of the financial sector, which was not affected by slower economic growth in the same way as the rest of the economy.

C.16 Discretionary changes, including a further addition to the special reserve to meet the cost of military operations in Iraq and the UK's other international obligations, led to a further reduction in the current budget in 2005-06. For 2006-07 onwards, discretionary changes led to improvements in the current budget as changes to the North Sea oil taxation regime and further measures to combat tax fraud and avoidance more than offset extra spending on winter fuel payments for pensioners.

Changes between the 2005 Pre-Budget Report and Budget 2006

C.17 The Budget 2006 projections are broadly in line with those in the Pre-Budget Report, locking in the Government's prudent stance. The estimated outturn for the public sector current balance for 2005-06 is a deficit of £11.4 billion, compared with a deficit of £10.6 billion in the Pre-Budget Report, and the deficit is also higher in 2006-07. In later years there are only small changes in the current balance which returns to surplus in 2007-08.

C.18 The reclassification of the BBC as part of central government has no impact on overall public sector balances, but has led to higher projections of both receipts and expenditure than in the Pre-Budget Report. Other than this, overall receipts in 2005-06 are slightly above the Pre-Budget report projections, but current expenditure is now slightly higher, leading to the slightly larger deficit on the current balance. The expenditure increase in 2005-06 is broadly offset by reductions in subsequent years and the higher deficit on the current balance in 2006-07 arises from lower receipts projections, largely because of changes to economic determinants affecting North Sea tax revenues. There are only small forecasting changes to overall receipts in subsequent years.

C.19 Although public sector net investment in 2005-06 is projected to show growth of 24 per cent on 2004-05, the estimated outturn is now expected to be about £$\frac{1}{2}$ billion lower in 2005-06 than expected in the Pre-Budget Report. This largely offsets the change to the current balance and public sector net borrowing in 2005-06 is £37.1 billion, only very slightly higher than in the Pre-Budget Report. Net investment is also expected to be slightly lower than projected in the Pre-Budget Report in 2006-07 and 2007-08, and the path of public sector net borrowing is broadly in line with the Pre-Budget Report.

C.20 Discretionary changes include a commitment to increase the child element of the Child Tax Credit in line with average earnings to the end of this parliament, the introduction of Real Estate Investment Trusts, measures to modernise the tax system and to tackle tax fraud and avoidance, as well as other budget policy decisions. They also include resetting the AME margin.

FORECAST DIFFERENCES AND RISKS

C.21 The fiscal balances represent the difference between two large aggregates of expenditure and receipts, and forecasts are inevitably subject to wide margins of uncertainty. Over the past ten years, the average absolute difference between year-ahead forecasts of net borrowing and subsequent outturns has been around 1 per cent of GDP. This difference tends to grow as the forecast horizon lengthens. A full account of differences between the projections made in Budget 2003 and Budget 2004, and the subsequent outturns were provided in the *End of year fiscal report*, published alongside the 2005 Pre-Budget Report.

C.22 Overall, the economic forecast is unchanged from the 2005 Pre-Budget Report. Following growth of $1^3/_4$ per cent in 2005, UK GDP is expected to grow by between 2 and $2^1/_2$ per cent this year, still slightly below trend rates, reflecting a number of temporary factors. Private consumption growth is expected to be restrained by continued household appetite for saving, subdued growth in labour incomes, and the residual effects of higher energy prices. In the corporate sector, higher oil prices and high levels of gearing are likely to restrain the growth of business investment this year.

C.23   The set of risks surrounding the Budget 2006 economic outlook is similar to those surrounding the 2005 Pre-Budget Report forecast. The balance of risks has shifted a little, with domestic risks having receded while global uncertainties have increased somewhat. Globalisation means that the UK economy shares increasingly in the risks affecting the world economy and means that domestic risks are harder to differenciate.

C.24   The forecast for private consumption continues to be surrounded by both upside and downside risks. Further unexpected weakness of average earnings growth would tend to undermine household expenditure, although the boost to employment from weakening labour costs would tend at least partly to offset this affect.

C.25   A second important source of potential errors results from misjudging the position of the economy in relation to trend output. To minimise this risk, the robustness of the projections is tested against an alternative scenario in which the level of trend output is assumed to be one percentage point lower than in the central case. Chart C2 illustrates the Budget projection for this cautious case.

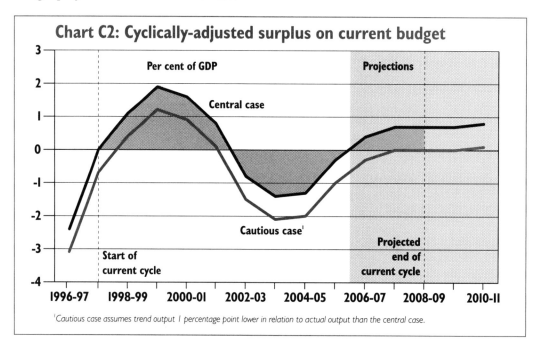

C.26   The Government has used the cautious case and cautious, audited assumptions to build a safety margin against unexpected events. This was combined with the decision to consolidate the public finances when the economy was above trend, which resulted in low debt. This has allowed the Government to safeguard the increase in investment in priority public services, allow the automatic stabilisers to work in full during the period of global economic uncertainty in the early part of the decade and meet in full the UK's international commitments, while continuing to meet the fiscal rules.

ASSUMPTIONS

C.27   The fiscal projections are based on the following assumptions:

- the economy follows the path described in Chapter B. In the interests of caution, the fiscal projections continue to be based on the deliberately prudent and cautious assumption of trend output growth of $2\frac{1}{2}$ per cent up to 2006-07, $\frac{1}{4}$ percentage point lower than the Government's neutral view. The Government's neutral view of trend output is reduced to $2\frac{1}{2}$ per cent between

2007-08 and 2010-11, and so, to maintain a cautious approach, an assumption of $2^1/_4$ per cent is used in the public finances projections, still a $^1/_4$ percentage point lower than the Government's neutral view;

- there are no tax or spending policy changes beyond those announced in or before this Budget, and the indexation of rates and allowances. Consistent with the *Code for fiscal stability*, the forecast does not take account of measures proposed in this Budget for consultation or other proposals where final decisions have yet to be taken, such as further extensions to maternity and paternity leave and the replacement of the current system of incapacity benefits;

- firm Departmental Expenditure Limits (DEL) as set out in the 2004 Spending Review up to 2007-08, but adjusted for the impact of policy decisions and reclassifications;

- total AME programmes to 2007-08 have been reviewed. The total has been adjusted for reclassification changes and for the cost of spending measures in this Budget. In accordance with normal practice the Government has decided to reset the AME margin to £1 billion in 2006-07 and to £2 billion in 2007-08;

- as is normal, the Treasury is setting out its assumption for public sector current expenditure for the period beyond the current Spending Review. Public sector current expenditure is forecast to grow by 2.0 per cent in real terms in 2008-09 and by 1.9 per cent in 2009-10 and 2010-11. This means that, on average, public sector current expenditure is forecast to grow by $2^1/_4$ per cent a year in real terms over the forecast period 2006-07 to 2010-11; and

- net investment is assumed to remain at $2^1/_4$ per cent of GDP in 2008-09 and subsequent years.

Table C3: Economic assumptions for the public finance projections

			Percentage changes on previous year				
	Outturn	Estimate			Projections		
	2004-05	2005-06	2006-07	2007-08	2008-09	2009-10	2010-11
Output (GDP)	2 3/4	1 3/4	2 1/4	3	2 3/4	2 1/4	2 1/4
Prices							
CPI	1 1/2	2	2	2	2	2	2
GDP deflator	2 1/4	2	2 1/2	2 3/4	2 3/4	2 3/4	2 3/4
RPI[1] (September)	3	2 3/4	2 3/4	3	3	2 3/4	2 3/4
Rossi[2] (September)	1 1/4	2	2 1/4	2 1/4	2 1/4	2 1/4	2 1/4
Money GDP[3] (£ billion)	1,178	1,224	1,281	1,353	1,428	1,499	1,573

[1] Used for revalorising excise duties in current year and uprating income tax allowances and bands and certain social security benefits in the following year.

[2] RPI excluding housing costs, used for uprating certain social security benefits.

[3] Not seasonally adjusted.

C.28   The forecasts for different inflation indices are based on the conventional assumptions about the interrelationships between them. But, as in Chapter B notes, these relationships can change over time and are kept under review.

C.29   The key assumptions underlying the fiscal projections are audited by the National Audit Office (NAO) under the three-year rolling review process. Details of the audited assumptions are given in Box C1.

Box C1: Key assumptions audited by the NAO[a]

- **Dating of the cycle[e]** — The end date of the previous economic cycle was in the first half of 1997.

- **Privatisation proceeds[f]** — Credit is taken only for proceeds from sales that have been announced.

- **Trend GDP growth[f]** — 2½ per cent a year to 2006 and 2¼ per cent in subsequent years.

- **UK claimant unemployment[d]** — Rising slowly to 0.97 million in 2007-08, from recent levels of 0.91 million.

- **Interest rates[f]** — 3-month market rates change in line with market expectations (as of 10 March).

- **Equity prices[b]** — FTSE All-share index rises from 3004 (close 10 March) in line with money GDP.

- **VAT[b,c,e]** — The VAT gap will rise by 0.5 percentage points per year from a level that is at least as high as the estimated outturn for the current year.

- **Consistency of price indices[b]** — Projections of price indices used to project the public finances are consistent with CPI.

- **Composition of GDP[c]** — Shares of labour income and profits in national income are broadly constant in the medium term.

- **Funding[c]** — Funding assumptions used to project debt interest are consistent with the forecast level of government borrowing and with financing policy.

- **Oil prices[e]** — $57.4 a barrel in 2006, the average of independent forecasts, and then constant in real terms.

- **Tobacco[f]** — The underlying market share of smuggled cigarettes will be set at least at the latest published outturn. For Budget 2006, a share of 16 per cent is used for 2006-07 onwards.

---

[a] For details of all NAO audits before the 2003 Pre-Budget Report, see Budget 2003, 9 April 2003 (HC500).

[b] Audit of Assumptions for the 2003 Pre-Budget Report, 10 December 2003 (HC35).

[c] Audit of Assumptions for the Budget 2004, 17 March 2004 (HC434).

[d] Audit of Assumptions for the Budget 2005, 16 March 2005 (HC452).

[e] Audit of Assumptions for the 2005 Pre-Budget Report, 5 December 2005 (HC707).

[f] Audit of Assumptions for the Budget 2006, 22 March 2006 (HC937).

The audited assumptions

C.30 For this Budget, the Comptroller and Auditor General has audited the assumption for underlying trend growth used for the purpose of projecting the public finances, which is set a ¼ percentage point below the Government's neutral view. The review concluded that over the past four years the assumption has been reasonable and cautious, though other assumptions could have been adopted that would have introduced a greater degree of caution. Looking forward, the review concluded that the assumption currently remains reasonable and cautious but recommended that, because of the uncertainties involved in estimating trend growth rates, the Treasury kept its estimate under review.

C.31 The assumption for forecasting revenue from duty on tobacco, that the illicit market share is set at least at the latest published outturn level, would normally be due for review under the three-year rolling review. However, firm data for the illicit market share is currently only available for the first year of the rolling review period so that it is not possible to reach a conclusion for the three-year period as a whole. The Comptroller and Auditor General has therefore reviewed the evidence for 2003-04, concluding that the assumption had added caution to the fiscal projections in that year, and reviewed the issues that have arisen in producing an estimate for 2004-05. The Comptroller and Auditor General recommended areas of further analysis that HM Revenue and Customs (HMRC) will undertake over the next year and will be invited to conduct a full review at Budget 2007.

C.32 The Comptroller and Auditor General reviewed the yield from the Budget 2003 direct taxation compliance package and found that the projections of yield were reasonable and the method adopted to make adjustments to the projections in the light of outturn evidence was a helpful one to ensure caution.

C.33 The Comptroller and Auditor General also audited the conventions on short-term interest rates and privatisation proceeds. He concluded that the interest rate assumption methodology that three-month forward interest rates will be based on market expectations, was a reasonable one and incorporates an element of caution through the risk premium embodied in the forward rates. Over the past three years interest rate projections had been higher than outturn more often than not, and so been cautious to this extent, on the basis that higher interest rates have a negative impact on the public finances. The review concluded that the convention on privatisation proceeds had led to no systematic forecasting errors over the review period and that for the future it remains reasonable and is based on being cautious. In view of potentially large future privatisation receipts, close attention should be paid to the profile of receipts included in the fiscal projections.

C.34 Consistent with the *Code for fiscal stability*, the forecast does not take into account impact of the finance leases on public sector net debt, as the impact cannot be accurately estimated. The Office for National Statistics (ONS) is undertaking a programme of work to quantify the impact of these finance leases and is planning to issue the first estimates in mid-2006.

Box C2: Trend growth and caution in the public finances

Since 1997 the **NAO** has audited key assumptions underlying the public finance projections to ensure that they are consistent with the principles of transparency and responsibility. The key source of caution in the fiscal projections is the trend growth assumption, which has been audited by the **NAO** alongside Budget 2006.

The cautious trend growth assumption holds the annual growth of real non-oil **GVA** to a $\frac{1}{4}$ percentage point below the Government's neutral view of growth. As a result, the rate of economic growth used to forecast the public finances is at the bottom end of the projection range for **GDP** growth, as shown in the table below. Once the output gap has been closed in 2008-09, output - for the purposes of the public finance projections - grows at the trend rate of $2\frac{1}{4}$ per cent.

Table GDP growth (per cent)

	2005-06	2006-07	2007-08	2008-09	2009-10	2010-11
Neutral[1]	$1\frac{3}{4}$	$2\frac{1}{4}$ to $2\frac{3}{4}$	3 to $3\frac{1}{2}$	$2\frac{3}{4}$ to $3\frac{1}{4}$	$2\frac{1}{4}$ to $2\frac{3}{4}$	$2\frac{1}{4}$ to $2\frac{3}{4}$
For public finances	$1\frac{3}{4}$	$2\frac{1}{4}$	3	$2\frac{3}{4}$	$2\frac{1}{4}$	$2\frac{1}{4}$

[1] *The neutral GDP growth forecast is the same as that in Table 2.2 and B3. In this Table it is presented for financial years, but in Table 2.2 and B3 it is presented for calendar years. See footnote to table B9 for explanation of forecast ranges.*

With lower growth in each year of the five-year projection period, the level of money **GDP** becomes progressively more cautious. The **NAO**-audited assumption on the composition of **GDP** – that labour income and profits receive broadly constant shares of GDP - ensures that the impact of the cautious trend growth rate feeds through equally to wages and salaries, the key determinant of income tax, and corporate profits, the key determinant of corporation tax. The **NAO**-audited equity price assumption, that the stock market rises in line with nominal **GDP**, ensures that equity prices, too, are constrained by the cautious trend growth assumption.

In the projections in Budget 2006, money **GDP** is around £19 billion lower in the public finance projection than the neutral view by 2010-11, with a direct feed-through in terms of lower wages and salaries and lower non-North Sea profits. In terms of the Budget receipts forecast, the effect of using the cautious trend growth assumption rather than the neutral view is to reduce the level of tax receipts in 2010-11 by between £6 billion and £8 billion.

FISCAL AGGREGATES

C.35 Tables C4 and C5 provide more detail on the projections for the current and capital budgets.

Table C4: Current and capital budgets

	Outturn	Estimate	Projections				
	2004-05	2005-06	2006-07	2007-08	2008-09	2009-10	2010-11
Current budget							
Current receipts	451.3	486.1	516	553	585	615	645
Current expenditure	455.4	481.9	507	534	559	585	612
Depreciation	15.0	15.6	17	18	19	20	21
Surplus on current budget	**-19.0**	**-11.4**	**-7**	**1**	**7**	**10**	**12**
Capital budget							
Gross investment	41.9	47.9	52	55	57	60	63
Less asset sales	-6.3	-6.6	-7	-7	-7	-7	-7
Less depreciation	-15.0	-15.6	-17	-18	-19	-20	-21
Net investment	20.7	25.7	29	31	32	34	36
Net borrowing	**39.7**	**37.1**	**36**	**30**	**25**	**24**	**23**
Public sector net debt - end year	**419.8**	**455.8**	**493**	**530**	**560**	**590**	**619**
Memos:							
Treaty deficit[1]	38.5	38.6	38	32	27	26	26
Treaty debt[2]	480.4	520.9	563	602	635	668	700

£billion

[1] General government net borrowing on a Maastricht basis.
[2] General government gross debt on a Maastricht basis.

Table C5: Current and capital budgets

	Outturn	Estimate	Projections				
	2004-05	2005-06	2006-07	2007-08	2008-09	2009-10	2010-11
Current budget							
Current receipts	38.3	39.7	40.3	40.9	41.0	41.0	41.0
Current expenditure	38.7	39.4	39.6	39.5	39.2	39.0	38.9
Depreciation	1.3	1.3	1.3	1.3	1.3	1.3	1.3
Surplus on current budget	**-1.6**	**-0.9**	**-0.6**	**0.1**	**0.5**	**0.7**	**0.8**
Capital budget							
Gross investment	3.6	3.9	4.1	4.1	4.0	4.0	4.0
Less asset sales	-0.5	-0.5	-0.5	-0.5	-0.5	-0.4	-0.4
Less depreciation	-1.3	-1.3	-1.3	-1.3	-1.3	-1.3	-1.3
Net investment	1.8	2.1	2.2	2.3	2.3	2.3	2.3
Net borrowing	**3.4**	**3.0**	**2.8**	**2.2**	**1.7**	**1.6**	**1.5**
Public sector net debt - end year	**35.0**	**36.4**	**37.5**	**38.1**	**38.3**	**38.4**	**38.4**
Memos:							
Treaty deficit[1]	3.3	3.2	3.0	2.4	1.9	1.7	1.6
Treaty debt ratio[2]	40.8	42.6	43.9	44.5	44.5	44.5	44.5

Per cent of GDP

[1] General government net borrowing on a Maastricht basis.
[2] General government gross debt on a Maastricht basis.

C.36 Following a deficit of 3 per cent of GDP in 1996-97, current budget surpluses of more than 2 per cent were recorded in 1999-00 and 2000-01. These surpluses allowed the Government to use fiscal policy to support monetary policy during the economic slowdown in 2001 and 2002, and as a result the current budget moved into deficit. The current budget is expected to remain in deficit until 2006-07 and then move back into surplus in 2007-08, with increasingly larger surpluses in later years, reaching 0.7 per cent of GDP in 2010-11.

C.37   The current budget surplus is equal to public sector current receipts minus public sector current expenditure and depreciation. The reasons for changes in receipts and current expenditure are explained in later sections.

C.38   Table C4 also shows that net investment is projected to increase from £21 billion in 2004-05 to £31 billion in 2007-08, as the Government seeks to rectify historical under-investment in public infrastructure. These increases are sustainable and fully consistent with the Government's long-term approach and the fiscal rules, as debt is being held at 38.4 per cent of GDP or less throughout the projection period, within the 40 per cent limit set by the sustainable investment rule.

RECEIPTS

C.39   This section looks in detail at the projections for public sector tax receipts. It begins by looking at the main determinants of changes in the overall projections since the 2005 Pre-Budget Report, before looking in detail at changes in the projections of individual tax receipts. Finally, it provides updated forecasts for the tax-GDP ratios.

Changes in total receipts since the 2005 Pre-Budget Report

C.40   Table C6 provides a detailed breakdown of the main factors that have led to the changes in the overall projections since the 2005 Pre-Budget Report.

Table C6: Changes in current receipts since the 2005 Pre-Budget Report

	£ billion					
	Estimate	Projections				
	2005-06	2006-07	2007-08	2008-09	2009-10	2010-11
Effect on receipts of non-discretionary changes in:						
Assumptions audited by the NAO	0	1	2	1 1/2	1 1/2	1 1/2
Other economic determinants	0	-2	- 1/2	0	0	0
Other forecasting changes	3	1/2	1	1 1/2	1/2	1/2
Total before discretionary changes[1]	**3**	**0**	**2 1/2**	**3**	**2 1/2**	**2**
Discretionary changes[2]	0	0	1	1	1	1/2
Total change[1]	**3**	**0**	**3 1/2**	**4 1/2**	**3 1/2**	**2 1/2**

[1] Total may not sum due to rounding.
[2] Includes measures announced since the 2005 Pre-Budget Report.

Economic determinants audited by the NAO
    C.41   Changes in economic determinants audited by the NAO increase current receipts by £1 billion in 2006-07 and by around £1½ to £2 billion thereafter. The main effect is from a higher projection for equity prices. The climb in the UK stock market since the Pre-Budget Report has raised the starting point for the equity price assumption, by around 8 per cent. Higher equity prices boost capital and stamp taxes and receipts of corporation tax paid by life assurance companies. There is also a smaller effect from higher dollar oil prices, which are $1.40 a barrel higher in 2006 than in the Pre-Budget Report. This increases North Sea revenues.

Other economic **C.42** Other economic determinants reduce current receipts by £1³/₄ billion in 2006-07
determinants relative to the 2005 Pre-Budget Report but have little overall effect on receipts thereafter. Recent labour market developments mean that growth in the wage and salary bill is likely to be more modest than previously anticipated during 2006-07. There is also likely to be a marked effect on North Sea revenues in 2006-07 from lower than expected oil production and higher than anticipated capital expenditure. From 2007-08, these factors have little impact on North Sea revenues, while there are positive impacts on receipts from non-North Sea corporation tax determinants and from equity volumes on stamp duty and capital gains tax.

Fiscal forecasting **C.43** There are a number of other forecasting changes. The ONS reclassification of the BBC
changes to the central government sector from the public corporations sector means TV licences are now included as receipts and boosts the level of current receipts throughout the forecast. The change is however fiscally neutral. Other factors include the impact of recent outturn data, not explained by economic factors, the impact of the smoking ban in enclosed workplaces and the lower projections for VAT refunds and council tax which are broadly fiscally neutral.

Tax-by-tax analysis

C.44 Table C7 shows the changes to the projections of individual taxes since Budget 2005 and the 2005 Pre-Budget Report for 2005-06 and 2006-07. Table C8 contains updated projections for the main components of public sector receipts for 2004-05, 2005-06 and 2006-07.

Table C7: Changes in current receipts by tax since Budget 2005 and the 2005 Pre-Budget Report

	£ billion			
	Budget 2005		**PBR 2005**	
	2005-06	**2006-07**	**2005-06**	**2006-07**
Income tax (gross of tax credits)	-2.1	-3.6	0.1	-0.7
Income tax credits	-0.7	-1.0	-0.1	-0.3
National insurance contributions	2.8	2.4	1.2	0.8
Non-North Sea corporation tax[1]	-3.1	-4.0	0.2	0.1
North Sea revenues	2.6	3.3	0.6	-1.5
Capital taxes[2]	-0.3	0.3	0.0	0.3
Stamp duty	1.2	1.7	0.7	0.8
Value added tax	-2.7	-3.6	-0.7	-0.8
Excise duties[3]	-1.8	-2.5	-0.8	-0.8
Other taxes and royalties[4]	0.9	-0.5	-0.5	-1.7
Net taxes and national insurance contributions	**-3.1**	**-7.5**	**0.7**	**-3.8**
Other receipts and accounting adjustments	2.5	3.6	2.4	3.6
Current receipts	**-0.6**	**-4.0**	**3.1**	**-0.2**

[1] National accounts measure: gross of enhanced and payable tax credits.
[2] Capital gains tax and inheritance tax.
[3] Fuel, alcohol and tobacco duties.
[4] Includes business rates, council tax and money paid into the National Lottery Distribution Fund, as well as other central government taxes.

Table C8: Current receipts

	£ billion		
	Outturn 2004-05	Estimate 2005-06	Projection 2006-07
HM Revenue and Customs			
Income tax (gross of tax credits)	127.2	136.0	144.0
Income tax credits	-4.3	-4.7	-4.6
National insurance contributions	78.1	85.4	89.6
Value added tax	73.0	73.7	76.5
Corporation tax[1]	34.1	42.7	49.0
Corporation tax credits[2]	-0.5	-0.5	-0.6
Petroleum revenue tax	1.3	2.0	1.9
Fuel duties	23.3	23.5	24.0
Capital gains tax	2.3	2.9	3.8
Inheritance tax	2.9	3.2	3.6
Stamp duties	9.0	10.9	12.2
Tobacco duties	8.1	8.0	8.0
Spirits duties	2.4	2.3	2.3
Wine duties	2.2	2.3	2.4
Beer and cider duties	3.3	3.3	3.4
Betting and gaming duties	1.4	1.4	1.4
Air passenger duty	0.9	0.9	1.0
Insurance premium tax	2.4	2.3	2.4
Landfill tax	0.7	0.7	0.8
Climate change levy	0.8	0.7	0.7
Aggregates levy	0.3	0.3	0.3
Customs duties and levies	2.2	2.2	2.2
Total HMRC	**371.1**	**399.8**	**424.4**
Vehicle excise duties	4.7	5.0	5.1
Business rates	18.7	20.3	21.4
Council tax[3]	20.1	21.0	22.0
Other taxes and royalties[4]	11.7	12.8	13.6
Net taxes and national insurance contributions[5]	**426.5**	**458.7**	**486.5**
Accruals adjustments on taxes	1.4	2.3	2.3
Less own resources contribution to European Union (EU) budget	-4.1	-4.3	-4.2
Less PC corporation tax payments	-0.1	-0.1	-0.1
Tax credits adjustment[6]	0.5	0.6	0.6
Interest and dividends	5.5	5.3	5.7
Other receipts[7]	21.6	23.5	25.6
Current receipts	**451.3**	**486.1**	**516.4**
Memo:			
North Sea revenues[8]	5.2	9.7	10.2

[1] National accounts measure: gross of enhanced and payable tax credits.

[2] Includes enhanced company tax credits.

[3] Council tax increases are determined annually by local authorities, not by the Government. As in previous years, council tax figures are projections based on stylised assumptions and are not Government forecasts.

[4] Includes VAT refunds and money paid into the National Lottery Distribution Fund.

[5] Includes VAT and 'traditional own resources' contributions to EU budget.

[6] Tax credits which are scored as negative tax in the calculation of NTNIC but expenditure in the national accounts.

[7] Includes gross operating surplus and rent; net of oil royalties and business rate payments by Local Authorities.

[8] Consists of North Sea corporation tax, petroleum revenue tax and royalties.

Income tax and national insurance contributions
C.45 Income tax and National Insurance Contributions (NICs) in 2005-06 are expected to be around £1.2 billion above the 2005 Pre-Budget Report projection. The rise is primarily in NICs, in part reflecting lower personal pension rebates. There has also been a reallocation of receipts from income tax to NICs since the 2005 Pre-Budget Report. Self-assessment receipts are likely to be close to the level assumed in the 2005 Pre-Budget Report forecast, although more of the receipts scored in January rather than February compared with last year.

C.46 Pay-As-You-Earn (PAYE) and NICs receipts from wages and salaries are lower than anticipated in the 2005 Pre-Budget Report, reflecting recent average earnings and employment data. However, the impact from whole economy labour market developments on PAYE and NICs receipts has been partly offset by continued high receipts from the financial sector, which has a larger proportion of taxpayers who pay some of their income at the higher rate than elsewhere in the economy. Recent outturns suggest bonus growth in the financial sector is having a substantial impact on receipts growth.

C.47 In line with recent trends in labour market data, the growth in the wage and salary bill in 2006-07 is expected to be below the 2005 Pre-Budget Report projection, and leads to lower income tax in 2006-07. As in 2005-06, and consistent with the forecast for non-North Sea corporation tax, buoyant activity in the financial sector during 2006 is expected to boost income tax and NICs and provide a partial offset to the weaker growth in overall wages and salaries.

Non-North Sea corporation tax
C.48 Non-North Sea corporation tax receipts are estimated to grow by 16 per cent in 2005-06, slightly higher than expected in the 2005 Pre-Budget Report, with the January instalment payments particularly strong. Robust growth in receipts from financial sector companies has offset much weaker growth from industrial and commercial companies, where profits have been affected by higher input costs resulting from the rise in oil prices.

C.49 Growth in non-North Sea corporation tax is expected to remain buoyant in 2006-07, before gradually easing to a more moderate growth rate, broadly in line with the economy as a whole. A combination of sharply higher equity prices on a year earlier, strong commercial profit figures for many financial firms and a pickup in merger and acquisition activity all suggest that corporation tax receipts from the financial sector should remain robust in 2006-07. Thereafter, financial company profits are expected to grow in line with their long-run trend. Receipts from industrial and commercial companies should also be boosted through 2006 and 2007 as the economy picks up momentum. Relative to the 2005 Pre-Budget Report, higher equity prices are expected to increase receipts growth from life assurance companies and the more modest revival expected in business investment in the Budget forecast is likely to mean less capital allowances to be offset against tax.

North Sea revenues
C.50 North Sea revenues have grown significantly in 2005-06. This has resulted from a combination of higher oil and gas prices, the impact of the Budget 2005 measure to change payment dates for corporation tax instalments for North Sea companies and from the measure announced in the 2005 Pre-Budget Report to allow companies to defer 100 per cent first year capital allowances from 2005 to 2006. As anticipated in the 2005 Pre-Budget Report, the growth in North Sea revenues during 2005-06 was back-end loaded into the final months of the financial year. North Sea companies paid their first two quarterly instalments on their 2005 accounts in July and October. The Budget 2005 measure meant that both remaining instalments were due before the end of 2005-06 (rather than partly in April 2006 as in the previous system). In addition, the rise in the oil price over last summer meant that their first two instalment payments would not have fully taken on the implications for profits of the higher oil price, further boosting their instalment payments in January 2006. There were also additional payments relating to the 2005 Pre-Budget Report measure on deferring capital allowances. This added around £0.6 billion to receipts in 2005-06. The 2005 Pre-Budget Report had assumed that all the relevant receipts from this change would score in 2006-07. As a result of the earlier scoring, there will be a compensating reduction in receipts in 2006-07.

C.51   The projections for North Sea revenues use the NAO-audited assumption on oil prices. In line with the average of independent forecasts, oil prices are expected to average $57.4 a barrel in 2006, compared with an assumption of $56 a barrel in the 2005 Pre-Budget Report. They are then assumed to be constant in real terms. However, in 2006-07 the impact on North Sea revenues of the slightly higher oil price is more than offset by changes in assumptions on production and capital expenditure levels. Oil and gas production is expected to show a modest temporary drop in 2006 based on a survey of North Sea producers, compared with the small rise assumed in the 2005 Pre-Budget Report. Furthermore North Sea companies have raised their capital expenditure levels. With 100 per cent relief on all expenditure, this will have an immediate impact on receipts. From 2007-08 onwards, production returns to levels only slightly below those in the 2005 Pre-Budget Report projections and North Sea revenues are broadly unchanged from the 2005 Pre-Budget Report levels.

Capital gains tax and inheritance tax   C.52   Receipts from capital gains tax are forecast to record growth of around 25 per cent in 2005-06. This reflects the rise in the equity market in 2004-05 and continuing effects from the disposal of business assets following the maturing of the business asset taper in 2002-03. Higher equity prices will push up receipts of capital gains tax and inheritance tax by around £$\frac{1}{2}$ billion in total compared with the 2005 Pre-Budget Report, although tax payment lags mean most of this effect will only be observed from 2007-08 onwards.

Stamp duties   C.53   Stamp duties are expected to be £0.7 billion above the 2005 Pre-Budget Report projection in 2005-06, reflecting strong growth in both duties on shares and on land and property. Stamp tax on land and property has benefited from the continued upturn in housing market activity in the final part of 2005, reflected in the pick up in property transactions. In addition, receipts have also been boosted by robust growth in the commercial property market. Higher than expected equity prices and transactions have boosted stamp duty on shares with the starting point for the equity price assumption around 8 per cent higher than in the 2005 Pre-Budget Report. The higher equity price projection results in higher stamp duty on shares throughout the projection period.

VAT receipts   C.54   Growth in VAT receipts over the past year has been subdued and relative to the 2005 Pre-Budget Report projection, receipts are expected to be £0.7 billion lower in 2005-06. Growth has been affected by a combination of weak consumer spending growth, which accounts for around two-thirds of the total VAT tax base, the composition of consumer spending and further losses from fraudulent attacks on the system, in particular Missing Trader Intra-Community (MTIC) fraud. Real private consumption growth was subdued in 2005, while the slowdown was most pronounced in spending on consumer durables. This led to a decline in the proportion of spending subject to the standard rate of VAT. Year-on-year growth in VAT receipts has improved from the first half of 2005-06, but not by as much as expected in the 2005 Pre-Budget Report projection. Consumer spending growth has picked up moderately but remains below its long-run average.

C.55   The VAT forecast is partly determined by the NAO-audited assumption on VAT, whereby the VAT gap (the difference between the theoretical liability to VAT and VAT receipts as a percentage of the theoretical liability) is assumed to increase by 0.5 percentage points per year from at least the estimated outturn for the current year, before adjustments for the impact of the VAT compliance strategy. However, the forecast for 2006-07 assumes that the pre-strategy VAT gap rises by more than 0.5 percentage points. This largely reflects recent growth in MTIC fraud. As set out in Chapter 5, a series of measures have been introduced to protect VAT revenues and complement those introduced as part of the VAT Compliance Strategy. At the 2005 Pre-Budget Report the Government re-affirmed its commitment to tackling MTIC fraud. HMRC have since taken a number of steps to strengthen their operational response to the fraud and the Government is introducing a series of legislative changes to support this. This will increase VAT receipts, particularly from 2007-08 onwards. Growth in VAT receipts should also be boosted by the expected gradual strengthening in the economy

Excise duties **C.56** Receipts of fuel duties have continued to be affected by the impact of oil market volatility and related high pump prices, and the effect of that on demand for fuel. This lowers revenues because fuel duties are charged on a per litre basis. With oil prices remaining around $60 a barrel, above the level assumed in the 2005 Pre-Budget Report, fuel duty revenues are expected to be £0.3 billion lower in 2005-06 than in the 2005 Pre-Budget Report projection. The decision to delay the revalorisation of fuel duties until September 2006 will further reduce revenues in 2006-07. The 2005 Pre-Budget Report had assumed, in line with convention, that fuel duties would rise in line with inflation on the day of the Budget.

C.57 The weakness in overall consumer spending in 2005 is likely to have been a factor in the sluggish growth in alcohol duty and the small drop in tobacco receipts expected in 2005-06. The 2005 Pre-Budget Report had assumed some acceleration in the year-on-year growth in both alcohol and tobacco receipts in the final part of the financial year. The tobacco forecast includes an estimate of the impact of the smoking ban on consumption in enclosed workplaces. This reduces receipts by around £0.5 billion a year from 2007-08.

Council tax **C.58** Council tax increases are determined annually by local authorities, not by the Government. The council tax figures for 2007-08 onwards are based on stylised assumptions and are not government forecasts. The methodology used to derive these assumptions is the same as in Budget 2005. The projected increase in 2006-07 is based on the latest available estimates released by the Chartered Institute for Public Finance and Accountancy (CIPFA) and the increases for later years on the arithmetic average of national council tax increases since their introduction. The increase in 2006-07 is lower than that assumed in the 2005 Pre-Budget Report with council tax expected to be £0.7 billion lower. Since changes to council tax are broadly balanced by changes to locally-financed expenditure, they have little material impact on the current balance or net borrowing.

Other taxes and **C.59** The main changes to the projection for other taxes and receipts are due to the **receipts** decision taken by the ONS and announced on 20 January 2006 that TV licences should no longer be regarded as a service charge, and the consequent reclassification of the BBC and S4C to the central government sector from the public corporations sector. Although this change is fiscally neutral for the public sector, it adds to both receipts and expenditure totals. The forecast for 2007-08 is based on an increase of RPI on the 2006-07 forecast and does not represent the Government's view on the level of the TV licence fee to apply from April 2007.

C.60 HM Treasury has decided to continue to follow Organisation for Economic Co-operation and Development (OECD) Revenue Statistics guidelines, which treat such licence receipts as a service charge, in respect of TV licence receipts following OECD guidelines allows the tax-GDP ratio to be more easily compared internationally. These receipts are not included in net taxes and social security contributions, but are included in other receipts.

C.61 Other receipts are also higher than in the 2005 Pre-Budget Report because of higher accruals adjustment, particularly from NICs, and higher interest and dividend receipts. The Budget forecast does not include the impact from the Pension Protection Fund (PPF) either on receipts or expenditure. The PPF is funded by an annual levy, but given that payments from the PPF to pension schemes are expected to be similar over time to the levy charged, the introduction of the PPF is expected to be fiscally neutral.

Tax-GDP ratio

C.62   Table C9 shows projections of receipts from major taxes as a per cent of GDP, and Table C10 sets out current and previous projections of the overall tax-GDP ratio, based on net taxes and national insurance contributions. Chart C3 shows the tax-GDP ratio from 1980-81 to 2010-11.

C.63   The tax-GDP ratio is expected to rise from 36.2 per cent in 2004-05 to 37.5 per cent in 2005-06. Growth in receipts in 2005-06 has been stronger than would have been expected given the cyclical developments in the economy, primarily because of stronger growth in the financial sector and higher receipts of North Sea taxes. With net taxes and national insurance contributions £0.7 billion higher in 2005-06 than in the 2005 Pre-Budget Report, the tax-GDP ratio is 0.1 per cent higher than expected.

C.64   From 2006-07 onwards, the rise in the tax-GDP ratio is driven by rises in the income tax and corporation tax to GDP ratios. The rise in income tax largely arises from the normal fiscal forecasting convention on tax allowances and fiscal drag. The buoyant growth in non-North Sea corporation tax is expected to persist into 2006-07, but is expected to stabilise at 3.4 per cent of GDP from 2007-08 onwards. The small rise in the tax-GDP ratio relative to the 2005 Pre-Budget Report projections reflects mainly a lower nominal GDP level.

Table C9: Current receipts as a proportion of GDP

	Per cent of GDP						
	Outturn	Estimate	Projections				
	2004-05	2005-06	2006-07	2007-08	2008-09	2009-10	2010-11
Income tax (gross of tax credits)	10.8	11.1	11.2	11.4	11.5	11.7	11.8
National insurance contributions	6.6	7.0	7.0	7.0	7.0	7.1	7.1
Non-North Sea corporation tax[1]	2.6	2.9	3.2	3.4	3.4	3.4	3.4
Tax credits[2]	-0.4	-0.4	-0.4	-0.4	-0.3	-0.3	-0.3
North Sea revenues[3]	0.4	0.8	0.8	1.0	1.0	0.9	0.8
Value added tax	6.2	6.0	6.0	6.0	5.9	5.9	5.8
Excise duties[4]	3.3	3.2	3.1	3.1	3.0	3.0	2.9
Other taxes and royalties[5]	6.6	6.9	7.1	7.1	7.1	7.1	7.2
Net taxes and national insurance contributions[6]	**36.2**	**37.5**	**38.0**	**38.5**	**38.7**	**38.7**	**38.7**
Accruals adjustments on taxes	0.1	0.2	0.2	0.2	0.2	0.2	0.1
Less EU transfers	-0.4	-0.3	-0.3	-0.3	-0.3	-0.3	-0.3
Other receipts[7]	2.3	2.4	2.5	2.5	2.5	2.5	2.5
Current receipts	**38.3**	**39.7**	**40.3**	**40.9**	**41.0**	**41.0**	**41.0**

[1] National accounts measure, gross of enhanced and payable tax credits.
[2] Tax credits scored as negative tax in net taxes and national insurance contributions.
[3] Includes oil royalties, petroleum revenue tax and North Sea corporation tax.
[4] Fuel, alcohol and tobacco duties.
[5] Includes council tax and money paid into the National Lottery Distribution Fund, as well as other central government taxes.
[6] Includes VAT and 'own resources' contributions to EU budget. Cash basis.
[7] Mainly gross operating surplus and rent, excluding oil royalties.

Table C10: Net taxes and national insurance contributions[1]

	Outturn[2]	Estimate[3]	Per cent of GDP				
				Projections			
	2004-05	2005-06	2006-07	2007-08	2008-09	2009-10	2010-11
Budget 2005	36.3	37.3	37.9	38.3	38.5	38.5	
PBR 2005	36.3	37.4	38.2	38.5	38.5	38.6	38.6
Budget 2006	36.2	37.5	38.0	38.5	38.7	38.7	38.7

[1] Cash basis. Uses OECD definition of tax credits scored as negative tax.

[2] The 2004-05 figures were estimates in Budget 2005.

[3] The 2005-06 figures were projections in Budget 2005.

C.65   Chart C3 shows the tax-GDP ratio from 1980-81 to 2010-11.

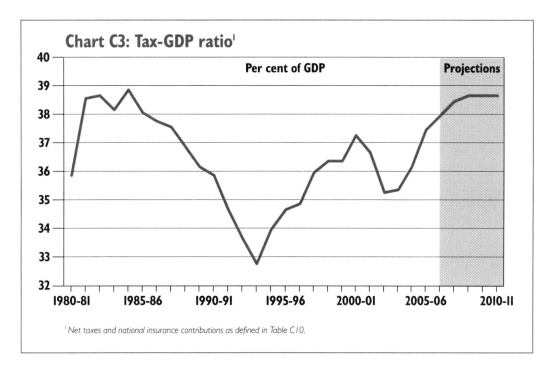

Chart C3: Tax-GDP ratio[1]

[1] Net taxes and national insurance contributions as defined in Table C10.

PUBLIC EXPENDITURE

C.66   This section looks in detail at the projections for public expenditure. The spending projections cover the whole of the public sector, using the national accounts aggregate Total Managed Expenditure (TME).

C.67   For fiscal aggregates purposes, TME is split into national accounts components covering public sector current expenditure, public sector net investment and depreciation. For budgeting and other purposes, TME is split into DEL – firm three-year limits for departments' programme expenditure, and AME – expenditure that is not easily subject to firm multi-year limits. Departments have separate resource budgets, for current expenditure and capital budgets.

Changes in TME since 2005 Pre-Budget Report

C.68   The reclassification of the BBC to central government, (see Other taxes and receipts in the tax-by-tax analysis section) adds about £2½ billion a year to current expenditure and to current receipts. After allowing for this reclassification, TME in 2005-06 is expected to be around £½ billion higher than in the 2005 Pre-Budget Report, but is around £½ billion lower in both 2006-07 and 2007-08.

C.69   Discretionary changes to TME are set out in Chapter A and include the education package in 2006-07 and 2007-08 and continued indexation of the child element of the Child Tax Credit in line with earnings in 2008-09 and 2009-10.

C.70   Public sector current expenditure increases by around £1½ billion in 2005-06, and after allowing for discretionary changes this is offset by reductions in 2006-07 and 2007-08 combined. Public sector net investment is lower by around £½ billion each year from 2005-06 to 2007-08. The changes to spending components are discussed in more detail below.

C.71   The reclassification by ONS of the BBC to central government impacts on both receipts and expenditure. Certain commercial trading subsidiaries of the BBC remain in the public corporations sector as they continue to meet the definition of a market body. Before the reclassification the BBC's production and other current operating expenses were offset by income from the licence fee to form part of the public corporation gross operating surplus, which benefits the receipts side of the public sector finances. After reclassification, the current spending of the BBC is included in public sector current expenditure. The licence fee still benefits the receipts side of the public finances and hence the surplus on the current budget is not affected. The treatment of BBC capital spending in TME is unaffected although most of it now scores as a central government contribution to capital expenditure rather than that of a public corporation.

Table C11: Total Managed Expenditure 2004-05 to 2007-08

	£ billion			
	Outturn	Estimate	Projections	
	2004-05	2005-06	2006-07	2007-08
Departmental Expenditure Limits				
Resource Budget	257.2	277.6	294.5	309.7
Capital Budget	33.6	37.4	42.5	45.6
Less depreciation	-8.3	-11.9	-11.8	-11.5
Total Departmental Expenditure Limits	**282.5**	**303.0**	**325.2**	**343.8**
Annually Managed Expenditure				
Social security benefits[1]	121.5	127.4	131.5	138.3
Tax credits[1]	15.0	15.4	15.6	15.1
Net public service pensions[2]	1.1	0.3	0.4	0.3
National Lottery	1.8	1.9	1.7	1.5
BBC domestic services	2.9	3.1	3.3	3.4
Other departmental expenditure	2.9	4.3	3.6	3.2
Net expenditure transfers to EU institutions[3]	4.8	4.4	5.4	6.5
Locally-financed expenditure[4]	24.3	26.6	27.7	29.3
Central government gross debt interest	24.0	25.7	26.3	28.0
Public corporations' own-financed capital expenditure	2.2	2.8	2.9	2.9
AME margin	0.0	0.0	1.0	2.0
Accounting adjustments[5]	8.0	8.2	7.7	8.5
Annually Managed Expenditure	**208.5**	**220.2**	**227.1**	**238.9**
Total Managed Expenditure	**491.0**	**523.2**	**552.3**	**582.8**
of which:				
Public sector current expenditure	455.4	481.9	506.7	534.2
Public sector net investment	20.7	25.7	28.8	30.9
Public sector depreciation	15.0	15.6	16.8	17.7

[1] For 2004-05 to 2006-07, child allowances in Income Support and Jobseekers' Allowance, which, from 2003-04, are paid as part of the Child Tax Credit, have been included in the tax credits line and excluded from the social security benefits line. This is in order to give figures on a consistent definition over the forecast period.

[2] Net public service pensions expenditure is reported on a national accounts basis

[3] AME spending component only. Total net payments to EU institutions also include receipts scored in DEL, VAT based contributions which score as negative receipts and some payments which have no effect on the UK public sector in the national accounts. Latest estimates for total net payments, which exclude the UK's contribution to the cost of EU aid to non-Member States (which is attributed to the aid programme), and the UK's net contribution to the EU Budget, which includes this aid, are (in £ billion):

	2004-05	2005-06	2006-07	2007-08
Net payments to EU institutions	3.2	3.9	1.3	4.8
Net contribution to EU Budget	2.6	3.3	0.6	4.2

[4] This expenditure is mainly financed by council tax revenues. See footnote to table C8 for an explanation of how the council tax projections are derived.

[5] Excludes depreciation.

C.72   Chart C4 shows TME as a per cent of GDP from 1971-71 to 2007-08.

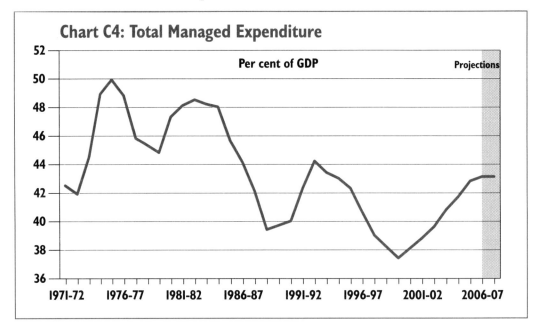

Chart C4: Total Managed Expenditure

Table C12: Changes to Total Managed Expenditure since the 2005 Pre-Budget Report

	£ billion			
	Outturn	**Estimate**	**Projections**	
	2004-05	**2005-06**	**2006-07**	**2007-08**
Departmental Expenditure Limits				
Resource Budget	-9.0	-9.4	-10.5	-11.0
Capital Budget	8.2	8.3	10.5	10.3
Less depreciation	0.0	-0.2	0.3	0.3
Total Departmental Expenditure Limits	**-0.8**	**-1.3**	**0.4**	**-0.3**
Annually Managed Expenditure				
Social security benefits	0.2	0.2	-0.2	0.0
Tax credits	-0.3	0.0	0.9	0.5
Net public service pensions	0.0	-0.4	-0.1	-0.3
National Lottery	0.0	0.2	0.1	0.1
BBC domestic services	2.9	3.1	3.3	3.4
Other departmental expenditure	0.0	-0.5	-0.1	-0.1
Net expenditure transfers to EU institutions	-0.1	0.3	-0.5	0.0
Locally-financed expenditure	-1.5	-0.4	-0.4	-0.3
Central government gross debt interest	0.0	0.1	-0.1	-0.1
Public corporations' own-financed capital expenditure	-0.3	0.0	0.2	0.2
AME margin	0.0	0.0	-0.1	0.2
Accounting adjustments	3.4	2.1	-1.3	-1.0
Annually Managed Expenditure	**4.5**	**4.6**	**1.8**	**2.4**
Total Managed Expenditure	**3.7**	**3.2**	**2.2**	**2.1**
of which:				
Public sector current expenditure	1.9	4.0	2.5	2.2
Public sector net investment	1.7	-0.6	-0.6	-0.3
Public sector depreciation	0.1	-0.1	0.2	0.2

DEL and AME analysis

C.73   Table C11 sets out projected spending on DEL and the main components of AME to the end of the 2004 Spending Review period in 2007-08. Table C12 shows changes since the 2005 Pre-Budget Report.

DEL   **C.74**   Changes to the budgeting presentation of public expenditure are largely a result of budgeting regime changes announced in the 2005 Pre-Budget Report. These changes have no impact on national accounts definitions, and so have no impact on the definitions of current expenditure for the purposes of the fiscal rules. Other changes include discretionary measures announced in Budget 2006, as set out in Chapter A, and allocations from the reserves. The main changes are:

- the movement of spending on capital grants into capital budgets, so that the budgeting presentation aligns better with the fiscal framework. This reduces the resource budget and increases the capital budget in all years, and by £10 billion by 2007-08. This has no impact on total public sector current expenditure, the relevant measure of public spending for assessing performance against the golden rule;

- the movement of structural funds and other general income from the European Union (EU) into DEL, allowing departments to offset this income against their budgets. Resource and capital DEL budgets are restated to take account of this income, reducing them in all years and by around £4 billion on resource and £0.5 billion on capital by 2007-08;

- the movement of spending under the Common Agricultural Policy (CAP) from the Department for the Environment, Food and Rural Affairs (DEFRA) AME budget into DEL, along with the associated income from the EU. This has no net effect on DEFRA's DEL totals, with the exception of small differences due to the timing of payments and provisions for disallowance. The CAP line in the budgeting presentation of TME is removed as redundant;

- the movement of payments to National Health Service (NHS) Trusts to cover their depreciation costs from outside budgets into the Department of Health's resource DEL, bringing the treatment of Trust depreciation further into line with the budgeting treatment of depreciation for central government and obviating the need for its inclusion in the accounting adjustments; as well as other reprofiling of the Department of Health's resource budget over the 2004 Spending Review period, partly to reflect the forecast return to surplus in the NHS;

- the movement of Direct School Grant from local government DEL to the Department for Education and Skills (DfES) in 2006-07 and 2007-08, increasing DfES resource DEL by £28 billion in those years; and

- setting aside provision from within existing public spending plans to help meet the costs of Iraq, Afghanistan and our other international commitments, with funding allocated to the Special Reserve line.

C.75   The detailed allocations of DELs are shown in Table C13. In line with previous practice, resource and capital DEL for 2005-06 includes an allowance for shortfall reflecting likely underspends against departmental provision. Excepting the impact of reclassifications and other budgeting changes, estimated outturn for resource DEL is broadly as forecast in the 2005 Pre-Budget Report, while slippage in capital programmes in the Department of Health and DfES mean estimated outturn for capital DEL is lower than forecast.

AME **C.76**   The main economic assumptions underpinning the AME projections are set out in Box C1 and Table C3. In particular it is assumed that the UK claimant count unemployment rises slowly to 0.97 million in 2007-08, from recent levels of 0.91 million. The AME total is also affected by the BBC change and by reclassifications described above.

C.77   Compared to the 2005 Pre-Budget Report projections, social security expenditure is forecast to be slightly higher in 2005-06, slightly lower in 2006-07 and unchanged in 2007-08. The effects of changes in economic determinants are broadly offset by changes in take up rates and average amounts claimed.

C.78   Forecasts for expenditure on the Child and Working Tax Credits are higher than in the 2005 Pre-Budget Report. This reflects the effects of changes in the economic determinants underlying the forecast, which have increased projected expenditure, and the latest administrative data, including on the overall numbers families that are in and out of work, which has also increased forecast spending.

C.79   Net public service pensions figures are shown on the transactions basis used in national accounts and consist of cash expenditure on pensions less cash income. On this basis, net pensions expenditure is slightly lower than was expected in the 2005 Pre-Budget Report, largely because of higher income to and lower expenditure by the Principal Civil Service Pension Scheme.

C.80   National lottery expenditure numbers increase slightly relative to the 2005 Pre-Budget report reflecting the latest assumption of draw downs by the distributing bodies, including draw down of extra proceeds from Olympic Lottery games.

C.81   Following the reclassification of the BBC to central government, the current and capital spending of the BBC home broadcasting service (the BBC excluding the World Service and its commercial subsidiaries) are shown aggregated into a separate AME line called BBC domestic services. The forecast for 2007-08 is based on an increase of RPI on the 2006-07 forecast and does not represent the Government's view on the level of the TV licence fee to apply from April 2007.

C.82   Other departmental expenditure in 2005-06 is lower than in the 2005 Pre-Budget Report forecast, largely because of lower capital spending.

C.83   The reclassifications and accounting changes described at the beginning of this section affect the scoring of several of the components making up the UK's net contributions to the EU. Some of the spending and receipts components are now in DEL rather than AME and the net expenditure transactions line in AME includes just the components remaining in AME, the GNI based contribution less the UK abatement. The components now in DEL have a broadly neutral effect on TME. Relative to the 2005 Pre-Budget Report, net expenditure transactions are slightly higher in 2005-06 but lower in 2006-07.

C.84   Figures on overall net payments to the EU institutions and the UK's net contribution to the EU budget are included in a footnote to Table C11. On 17 December 2005, Heads of State and Government of all Member States of the European Union agreed the multi-annual financial framework for the European Communities budget for 2007-13. This agreement has only a limited impact on overall net payments in the period covered by Table C11.

C.85 Changes to Local Authority Self-Financed Expenditure (LASFE) reflect the revision to the forecasting assumption made for increases to council tax, and changes to the forecasts of other local authority income. Council tax increases are determined annually by local authorities, not by the Government and the council tax figures for 2007-08 onwards are based on stylised assumptions and are not Government forecasts. The council tax increase in 2006-07 is lower than that assumed in the 2005 Pre-Budget Report leading to lower LASFE. Since changes to LASFE are broadly balanced by changes to council tax and other income, they have little material impact on the current balance or net borrowing.

C.86 Central government debt interest payments for 2005-06 are broadly in line with the 2005 Pre-Budget Report projections.

C.87 The changes to public corporations' own-financed capital expenditure mainly reflect reclassifications. The ONS decision to reclassify London and Continental Railways as part of the public sector adds to capital expenditure and leads to increased spending in 2005-06, 2006-07 and 2007-08, relative to the 2005 Pre-Budget Report. The BBC's capital expenditure is now included in the BBC domestic services line.

Table C13: Departmental Expenditure Limits - resource and capital budgets

	£ billion			
	Outturn	Estimate	Plans	
	2004-05	2005-06	2006-07	2007-08
Resource Budget				
Education and Skills	23.0	24.6	53.4	56.7
Health	69.2	76.9	82.0	89.1
of which : NHS	66.9	74.7	80.0	87.1
Transport	5.3	5.7	6.9	6.7
Office of the Deputy Prime Minister	3.5	3.3	3.5	3.7
Local Government	43.3	46.1	22.5	23.3
Home Office	12.0	12.7	13.1	13.6
Departments for Constitutional Affairs	3.3	3.7	3.9	4.0
Law Officers' Departments	0.6	0.6	0.7	0.7
Defence	31.3	33.3	32.6	32.8
Foreign and Commonwealth Office	1.7	2.0	1.8	1.7
International Development	3.8	4.4	5.0	5.3
Trade and Industry	4.3	5.5	5.6	5.8
Environment, Food and Rural Affairs	2.8	3.0	3.0	3.1
Culture, Media and Sport	1.3	1.4	1.5	1.6
Work and Pensions	7.8	7.9	7.8	7.7
Scotland[1]	19.3	20.8	22.2	23.4
Wales[1]	10.3	11.5	11.7	12.4
Northern Ireland Executive[1]	6.3	6.8	7.1	7.6
Northern Ireland Office	1.2	1.0	1.2	1.1
Chancellor's Departments	4.9	5.0	5.1	5.1
Cabinet Office	2.0	2.1	2.0	2.2
Invest to Save Budget	0.0	0.0	0.0	0.0
Reserve	0.0	0.0	0.9	2.1
Unallocated special reserve[2]	0.0	0.0	0.8	0.0
Allowance for shortfall	0.0	-1.0	0.0	0.0
Total Resource Budget DEL	**257.2**	**277.6**	**294.5**	**309.7**
Capital Budget				
Education and Skills	4.9	5.8	6.2	7.0
Health	2.7	3.0	5.3	6.3
of which : NHS	2.6	2.9	5.2	6.2
Transport	6.0	6.6	7.4	6.7
Office of the Deputy Prime Minister	5.1	5.6	5.7	6.2
Local Government	0.3	0.4	0.2	0.2
Home Office	1.1	1.1	1.2	1.3
Departments for Constitutional Affairs	0.2	0.2	0.1	0.1
Law Officers' Departments	0.0	0.0	0.0	0.0
Defence	6.8	6.8	6.9	7.5
Foreign and Commonwealth Office	0.1	0.2	0.2	0.1
International Development	0.0	0.0	0.0	0.0
Trade and Industry	0.8	1.3	1.2	1.1
Environment, Food and Rural Affairs	0.5	0.7	0.8	0.8
Culture, Media and Sport	0.1	0.3	0.3	0.2
Work and Pensions	0.3	0.4	0.2	0.1
Scotland[1]	2.2	2.4	2.9	3.1
Wales[1]	1.1	1.3	1.4	1.6
Northern Ireland Executive[1]	0.8	1.0	0.9	1.0
Northern Ireland Office	0.1	0.1	0.1	0.1
Chancellor's Departments	0.4	0.4	0.3	0.3
Cabinet Office	0.2	0.3	0.3	0.3
Invest to Save Budget	0.0	0.0	0.0	0.0
Reserve	0.0	0.0	0.8	1.5
Allowance for shortfall	0.0	-0.3	0.0	0.0
Total Capital Budget DEL	**33.6**	**37.4**	**42.5**	**45.6**
Depreciation	**-8.3**	**-11.9**	**-11.8**	**-11.5**
Total Departmental Expenditure Limits	**282.5**	**303.0**	**325.2**	**343.8**
Total education spending	**63.7**	**68.4**	**73.3**	**78.0**

[1] For Scotland, Wales and Northern Ireland, the split between resource and capital budgets is indicative and reflects the consequentials of the application of the Barnett formula to planned changes in UK departments' spending.

[2] This represents provision for the costs of military operations in Iraq and Afghanistan, as well as the UK's other international obligations.

C.88 The main accounting adjustments, which reconcile the DEL and AME measures of spending with the national accounts measure, are shown in Table C14. Changes to the accounting adjustments since the last forecast are mainly due to:

- the classification changes outlined above, particularly those affecting EU contributions;

- lower VAT refunds which reduce both receipts and expenditure; and

- changes to the adjustments for non-cash items in resource budgets as a result of changes in the composition of departmental spending.

Table C14: Accounting adjustments

| | £ billion | | | |
| | Outturn | Estimate | Projections | |
	2004-05	2005-06	2006-07	2007-08
Central government programmes	0.9	0.8	0.8	0.8
VAT refunds	9.6	10.5	11.4	12.2
Central government non-trading capital consumption	5.7	5.9	6.6	7.0
Non-cash items in resource budgets and not in TME	-8.9	-10.6	-12.1	-14.3
Expenditure financed by revenue receipts	0.1	0.2	0.1	0.1
Local authorities	3.6	4.0	4.8	5.4
General government consolidation	-4.5	-4.5	-4.5	-4.5
Public corporations	0.6	0.5	0.6	0.6
Financial transactions	0.4	0.5	0.7	0.8
Other accounting adjustments	0.6	0.7	-0.7	0.5
Total accounting adjustments	**8.0**	**8.2**	**7.7**	**8.5**

C.89 Table C15 shows public sector capital expenditure from 2004-05 to 2007-08.

Table C15: Public sector capital expenditure

| | £ billion | | | |
| | Outturn | Estimate | Projections | |
	2004-05	2005-06	2006-07	2007-08
Capital Budget DEL	33.6	37.4	42.5	45.6
Locally-financed expenditure	0.8	1.8	2.0	2.1
National Lottery	1.1	1.0	1.0	0.9
Public corporations' own-financed capital expenditure	2.2	2.8	2.9	2.9
Other capital spending in AME	-2.1	-1.8	-2.9	-3.2
AME margin	0.0	0.0	0.1	0.2
Accounting adjustments	0.1	0.1	0.1	0.1
Public sector gross investment[1]	**35.6**	**41.3**	**45.6**	**48.6**
Less depreciation	15.0	15.6	16.8	17.7
Public sector net investment	**20.7**	**25.7**	**28.8**	**30.9**
Proceeds from the sale of fixed assets[2]	6.3	6.6	6.6	6.6

[1] This and previous lines are all net of sales of fixed assets.
[2] Projections of total receipts from the sale of fixed assets by public sector.

C.90   Table C16 shows estimated receipts from loans and sales of assets from 2004-05 to 2007-08. The figures for sales of financial assets include proceeds in the final quarter of 2005-06 of £0.3 billion from the sale of part of the Government's shareholding in QinetiQ (formerly the Defence Evaluation and Research Agency). The table only covers general government and so does not include the sale by BNFL of its Westinghouse subsidiary, which the company expects to finalise in the next six months. The proceeds from the sale are included in the public corporations column of Table C20 (public sector net cash requirement). It is anticipated that there will be a public sector neutral transfer of the proceeds to central government.

Table C16: Loans and sales of assets

	£ billion			
	Outturn	Estimate	Projections	
	2004-05	2005-06	2006-07	2007-08
Sales of fixed assets				
Central government	1.1	1.4	1.4	1.4
Local authorities	5.2	5.2	5.2	5.2
Total sales of fixed assets	**6.3**	**6.6**	**6.6**	**6.6**
Total loans and sales of financial assets	**-2.1**	**-2.5**	**-3.2**	**-3.6**
Total loans and sales of assets	**4.1**	**4.1**	**3.4**	**3.0**

PRIVATE FINANCE INITIATIVE

C.91   Under the Private Finance Initiative (PFI) the public sector contracts to purchase services on a long-term basis so as to take advantage of private sector management skills incentivised by having private finance at risk. The private sector has always been involved in the building and maintenance of public infrastructure, but PFI ensures that contractors are bound into long-term maintenance contracts and shoulder responsibility for the quality of the work they do. With PFI, the public sector defines what is required to meet public needs and ensures delivery of the outputs through the contract. Consequently, the private sector can be harnessed to deliver investment in better quality public services whilst frontline services are retained within the public sector. The Government's position on PFI is set out in the document *PFI: Strengthening Long Term Partnerships* published alongside the Budget.

C.92   The Government only uses PFI where it is appropriate and where it expects it to deliver value for money. This is based on an assessment of the lifetime costs of both providing and maintaining the underlying asset, and of the running costs of delivering the required level of service. In assessing where PFI is appropriate, the Government's approach is based on its commitment to efficiency, equity and accountability, and on the Prime Minister's principles of public service reform. PFI is only used where it can meet these requirements, and where the value for money it offers is not at the expense of the terms and conditions of staff. The Government is committed to securing the best value for its investment programme by ensuring that there is no inherent bias in favour of one procurement option over another.

C.93   Table C17 shows a breakdown by department of the estimated capital investment in public services resulting from signed PFI contracts. Table C18 shows the estimated total capital value of contracts that are at preferred bidder stage and are expected to reach financial close within the next three years. Under PFI, the public sector contracts for services, including the availability and management of facilities, and not assets. Capital investment is only one of the activities undertaken by the private sector in order to supply these services. The figures in Tables C17 and C18 report the capital value of projects in order to show investment on a basis comparable with conventional capital procurement.

C.94   Table C19 shows a forecast of the estimated payments for services flowing from signed PFI projects. Actual expenditure will depend on the details of the payment mechanism for each contract. Payments may be lower than those estimated as a result of deductions that can be applied if the supplier fails to meet required performance standards. Variances may also occur as a result of agreed changes to the service requirements that are made during the course of the contract, or because of contractual arrangements that trigger compensation on termination. The fact that capital investment only represents one element of the overall contract means that the figures presented in this table should not be taken to be directly comparable with a public sector debt liability.

Table C17: Departmental estimate of capital spending by the private sector (signed deals)[1,2,3]

	£ million		
	Projections		
	2005-06	**2006-07**	**2007-08**
Education and Skills[4]	491	372	158
Health	943	784	621
Transport[5]	1497	1390	1085
Office of the Deputy Prime Minister	84	63	34
Home Office	61	10	0
Constitutional Affairs	25	10	0
Defence	501	375	357
Foreign and Commonwealth Office	5	5	5
Trade and Industry	6	2	0
Environment, Food and Rural Affairs	67	58	37
Culture, Media and Sport	45	26	0
Work and Pensions	51	46	55
Scotland	277	213	62
Wales	22	0	0
Northern Ireland Executive	39	27	33
Chancellor's Departments	13	5	2
Total	**4127**	**3386**	**2449**

[1] Investment in assets scored on the public sector balance sheet also score as public sector net investment.

[2] PFI activity in local authority projects is included under the sponsoring central government department.

[3] Figures do not include PFI projects undertaken by public corporations.

[4] Excludes private finance activity in educational institutions classified to the private sector.

[5] Includes estimates of the capital expenditure for the London Underground Limited Public Private Partnership PFI contracts in the years that investments are expected to take place.

Table C18: Estimated aggregated capital value of projects at preferred bidder stage[1,2]

	£ million	
	Projections	
	2005-06	2006-07
Education and Skills	313	303
Health	64	4819
Transport	52	95
Office of the Deputy Prime Minister	207	315
Home Office	0	30
Defence	0	4269
Environment, Food and Rural Affairs	55	334
Culture, Media and Sport	22	0
Scotland	0	405
Wales	61	0
Northern Ireland Executive	31	148
Total	**805**	**10718**

[1] Figures based on Departmental returns.

[2] These figures are the total capital value of projects; the actual annual capital spending figures will be lower, as capital spending on large projects is typically spread over several years.

Table C19: Estimated payments under PFI contracts - March 2005 (signed deals)[1]

	£ billion		
	Projections		
2005-06	5.9	2018-19	4.9
2006-07	6.5	2019-20	4.9
2007-08	6.7	2020-21	5.0
2008-09	6.9	2021-22	4.6
2009-10	7.3	2022-23	4.6
2010-11	7.4	2023-24	4.5
2011-12	7.6	2024-25	4.5
2012-13	7.6	2025-26	4.4
2013-14	7.7	2026-27	4.1
2014-15	7.6	2027-28	3.8
2015-16	7.7	2028-29	3.4
2016-17	7.8	2029-30	3.1
2017-18	7.1	2030-31	2.7

[1] The figures between 2005-06 and 2017-18 include estimated payments for the LUL PPP contract. These contracts contain periodic reviews each 7.5 years and therefore the service payments are not fixed after 2009-10.

FINANCING REQUIREMENT

C.95   Table C20 presents projections of the net cash requirement by sector, giving details of financial transactions that do not affect net borrowing (the change in the sector's net financial indebtedness) but do not affect its financing requirement.

Table C20: Public sector net cash requirement

	£ billion							
	2005-06				**2006-07**			
	General government		Public	Public	General government		Public	Public
	Central government	Local authorities	corporations	sector	Central government	Local authorities	corporations	sector
Net borrowing	**36.9**	**1.8**	**-1.4**	**37.1**	**35.9**	**1.9**	**-2.0**	**35.8**
Financial transactions								
Net lending to private sector and abroad	2.5	0.1	-1.0	1.6	3.1	0.1	-0.6	2.6
Cash expenditure on company securities	-0.3	0.2	0.0	-0.1	0.1	0.0	-2.9	-2.8
Accounts receivable/payable	-0.7	0.0	0.5	-0.2	2.7	0.0	-0.6	2.1
Adjustment for interest on gilts	-2.9	0.0	0.0	-2.9	-0.6	0.0	0.0	-0.6
Miscellaneous financial transactions	0.0	1.4	0.0	1.4	-2.4	0.0	2.4	0.0
Own account net cash requirement	35.4	3.5	-1.9	37.0	38.8	2.0	-3.7	37.1
Net lending within the public sector	5.2	-5.1	-0.1	0.0	2.4	-2.0	-0.4	0.0
Net cash requirement[1]	**40.6**	**-1.6**	**-2.0**	**37.0**	**41.2**	**0.0**	**-4.1**	**37.1**

[1] Market and overseas borrowing for local government and public corporation sectors.

C.96   Table C21 updates the financing arithmetic for both 2005-06 and 2006-07 in line with the updated fiscal forecasts. The central government net cash requirement (CGNCR) for 2005-06 is now forecast to be £40.6 billion, a decrease of £2.7 billion from the 2005 Pre-Budget Report forecast of £43.3 billion.

C.97   The forecast for the CGNCR for 2006-07 is £41.2 billion. Gross gilt redemptions are £29.9 billion and National Savings & Investments' net contribution to financing is estimated to be £3.0 billion. This means that the net financing requirement for 2006-07 is forecast to be £65.0 billion. The Debt Management Office (DMO) will aim to meet the net financing requirement by:

- gross gilts issuance of £63.0 billion;

- an increase in the Treasury bill stock of £2.0 billion by end March 2007; and

- a planned reduction in short-term financing of £3.1 billion (which reduces the financing requirement in 2006-07).

C.98   The gilt market experienced low and sometimes volatile yields at the longest maturities during 2005-06. These unusual conditions may continue next year. Therefore, to help both the DMO and the gilt market more generally to deal with a potentially challenging environment in 2006-07, the DMO's remit contains temporary changes intended to allow greater responsiveness in gilt issuance by the DMO during 2006-07 whilst retaining the Government's firm commitment to transparency and predictability in debt management policy. The key changes to the remit next year are that:

- the £63.0 billion of gross gilt issuance will be made up of: (i) a £53.0 billion 'core' issuance programme pre-allocated by maturity and type of gilt at Budget; and (ii) a £10.0 billion 'unallocated' gilt issuance programme to be allocated between maturity and type of gilt each quarter during 2006-07;

- the first £2.5 billion of the 'unallocated' £10.0 billion of gilt issuance will be allocated at Budget to long-dated conventional gilts in the first quarter of 2006-07; and

- the remaining £7.5 billion will be allocated between maturity and type of gilt by DMO during the last three quarters of 2006-07 (broadly £2.5 billion per quarter).

C.99 Full details of the DMO's financing remit including further information on the structure of gilts issuance and the gilt auction calendar for 2006-07 can be found in the *Debt and Reserves Management Report 2006-07* which is published alongside the Budget and is available on HM Treasury's website.

Table C21: Financing requirement forecast

£ billion	April 2005 Revised Remit[1]	2005-06 December 2005 Pre-Budget Report	March 2006 Budget	2006-07 March 2006 Budget
Central government net cash requirement	40.2	43.3	40.6	41.2
Gilt redemptions	14.6	14.6	14.6	29.9
Financing for the Official Reserves	0.0	0.0	0.0	0.0
Buy-backs	0.0	0.0	0.1	0.0
Planned short-term financing adjustment[2]	-2.7	-2.5	-2.5	-3.1
Gross Financing Requirement	52.1	55.4	52.8	68.0
less				
Assumed net contribution from National Savings and Investments	3.5	4.2	4.8	3.0
Net Financing Requirement	48.6	51.2	48.0	65.0
Financed by:				
1. Debt issuance by the Debt Management Office				
(a) Treasury bills	**-2.5**	**-1.1**	**-1.2**	**2.0**
(b) Gilts	**51.1**	**52.3**	**52.3**	**63.0**
2. Other planned changes in short-term debt[3]				
Change in Ways & Means	0.0	0.0	0.0	0.0
3. Unanticipated changes in short-term cash position[4]	0.0	0.0	3.1	0.0
Total financing	48.6	51.2	51.1	65.0
Short-term debt levels at end of financial year				
Treasury bill stock in market hands	18.0	19.2	19.1	21.1
Ways & Means	13.4	13.4	13.4	13.4
DMO net cash position	0.2	0.2	3.3	0.2

[1] Budget 2005 financing arithmetic was revised on 20 April 2005 to reflect outturn data for 2004-05.

[2] To accommodate changes to the current year's financing requirement resulting from: (i) publication of the previous year's outturn CGNCR and / or (ii) carry over of unanticipated changes to the cash position from the previous year.

[3] Total planned changes to short-term debt are the sum of: (i) the planned short-term financing adjustment; (ii) Treasury bill sales; and (iii) changes to the level of the Ways & Means advance.

[4] A negative (positive) number indicates an addition to (reduction in) the financing requirement for the following financial year.

C.100 Table C22 below sets out the split of gilt issuance between maturity and type of gilt. Table C22 will be updated and published each quarter to show how the unallocated tranche of financing is being allocated quarter-by-quarter throughout the year and shows the allocation of the initial tranche of the unallocated gilt issuance programme referred to above.

Table C22: Gilt issuance split 2006-2007

£ billion			Quarter 1	Quarter 1
			Additional gilt issuance allocation	Updated financing programme
Planned gilt sales		63.0		
Pre-allocated gilt issuance		53.0		
Of which minimum:				
Conventional	Short	10.0		10.0
	Medium	10.0		10.0
	Long	17.0	2.5	19.5
Index-linked		16.0		16.0
Total pre-allocated gilt issuance		**53.0**	**2.5**	**55.5**
Gilt issuance to be allocated		**10.0**		**7.5**

ANALYSIS BY SUBSECTOR AND ECONOMIC CATEGORY

C.101   Table C23 shows a breakdown of general government transactions by economic category for 2004-05 to 2007-08. Table C24 shows a more detailed breakdown for public sector transactions by sub-sector and economic category for 2004-05, 2005-06 and 2006-07.

C.102   The allocation of public sector transactions between sub-sectors has changed since the 2005 Pre-Budget Report, largely because of better data on the split of TME. This has the effect of substantially increasing central government net borrowing, and hence the cash requirement, and reducing local authority counterparts.

Table C23: General Government transactions by economic category

	£ billion			
	Outturn	Estimate	Projections	
	2004-05	2005-06	2006-07	2007-08
Current receipts				
Taxes on income and wealth	161.2	180.5	195.6	214.5
Taxes on production and imports	154.5	160.8	168.0	176.5
Other current taxes	27.2	27.9	29.3	28.4
Taxes on capital	2.9	3.2	3.6	3.9
Compulsory social contributions	80.2	86.6	90.6	95.9
Gross operating surplus	10.9	11.5	12.7	13.5
Rent and other current transfers	2.1	1.9	2.0	2.0
Interest and dividends from private sector and abroad	4.2	4.6	4.9	5.3
Interest and dividends from public sector	4.4	4.0	4.1	4.3
Total current receipts	**447.7**	**481.1**	**510.8**	**544.2**
Current expenditure				
Current expenditure on goods and services	254.0	271.6	286.5	302.8
Subsidies	6.5	6.2	6.6	6.6
Net social benefits	137.6	143.5	147.4	153.0
Net current grants abroad	-0.6	-4.7	-3.8	-4.7
Other current grants	33.0	38.7	41.9	45.7
Interest and dividends paid	24.4	26.3	26.7	28.4
AME margin	0.0	0.0	0.9	1.8
Total current expenditure	**454.9**	**481.4**	**506.3**	**533.7**
Depreciation	10.9	11.5	12.7	13.5
Surplus on current budget	**-18.1**	**-11.9**	**-8.3**	**-3.0**
Capital expenditure				
Gross domestic fixed capital formation	22.1	24.9	28.4	31.2
Less depreciation	-10.9	-11.5	-12.7	-13.5
Increase in inventories	0.0	0.2	0.1	0.1
Capital grants (net) within public sector	-0.2	0.5	0.6	0.5
Capital grants to private sector	10.7	13.7	14.3	14.3
Capital grants from private sector	-1.2	-1.1	-1.2	-1.1
AME margin	0.0	0.0	0.1	0.2
Net investment	**20.5**	**26.7**	**29.6**	**31.7**
Net borrowing[1]	**38.6**	**38.6**	**37.8**	**34.7**
of which:				
Central government net borrowing	38.2	36.8	35.9	32.7
Local authority net borrowing	0.4	1.8	1.9	2.0
Gross debt (Maastricht basis)				
Central government	427.6	467.5	509.3	548.2
Local government	52.9	53.4	53.4	53.4

[1] *Although this is based on the ESA95 definition of general government net borrowing (GGNB), the projections are identical to GGNB calculated on a Maastricht definition.*

Table C24: Public sector transactions by sub-sector and economic category

	£ billion			
	2004-05			
	General government			
	Central government	**Local authorities**	**Public corporations**	**Public sector**
Current receipts				
Taxes on income and wealth	161.2	0.0	-0.1	161.1
Taxes on production and imports	154.3	0.2	0.0	154.5
Other current taxes	7.7	19.4	0.0	27.2
Taxes on capital	2.9	0.0	0.0	2.9
Compulsory social contributions	80.2	0.0	0.0	80.2
Gross operating surplus	5.7	5.2	6.9	17.8
Rent and other current transfers	2.1	0.0	0.0	2.1
Interest and dividends from private sector and abroad	3.2	1.0	1.3	5.5
Interest and dividends from public sector	3.7	0.8	-4.4	0.0
Total current receipts	**421.0**	**26.7**	**3.6**	**451.3**
Current expenditure				
Current expenditure on goods and services	153.8	100.2	0.0	254.0
Subsidies	4.8	1.7	0.0	6.5
Net social benefits	123.2	14.4	0.0	137.6
Net current grants abroad	-0.6	0.0	0.0	-0.6
Current grants (net) within public sector	94.2	-94.2	0.0	0.0
Other current grants	32.9	0.0	0.0	33.0
Interest and dividends paid	24.0	0.4	0.5	24.9
AME margin	0.0	0.0	0.0	0.0
Total current expenditure	**432.3**	**22.6**	**0.5**	**455.4**
Depreciation	5.7	5.2	4.1	15.0
Surplus on current budget	**-16.9**	**-1.2**	**-0.9**	**-19.0**
Capital expenditure				
Gross domestic fixed capital formation	8.9	13.2	3.8	25.9
Less depreciation	-5.7	-5.2	-4.1	-15.0
Increase in inventories	0.0	0.0	-0.1	0.0
Capital grants (net) within public sector	8.7	-8.9	0.2	0.0
Capital grants to private sector	9.6	1.1	0.3	11.0
Capital grants from private sector	-0.3	-0.9	0.0	-1.2
AME margin	0.0	0.0	0.0	0.0
Net investment	**21.3**	**-0.7**	**0.1**	**20.7**
Net borrowing	**38.2**	**0.4**	**1.1**	**39.7**

Table C24: Public sector transactions by sub-sector and economic category

	£ billion			
	2005-06			
	General government		Public	Public
	Central government	Local authorities	corporations	sector
Current receipts				
Taxes on income and wealth	180.5	0.0	-0.1	180.4
Taxes on production and imports	160.6	0.2	0.0	160.8
Other current taxes	7.9	20.1	0.0	27.9
Taxes on capital	3.2	0.0	0.0	3.2
Compulsory social contributions	86.6	0.0	0.0	86.6
Gross operating surplus	5.9	5.6	8.4	19.9
Rent and other current transfers	1.9	0.0	0.0	1.9
Interest and dividends from private sector and abroad	3.3	1.2	0.7	5.3
Interest and dividends from public sector	3.3	0.7	-4.0	0.0
Total current receipts	**453.2**	**27.9**	**5.0**	**486.1**
Current expenditure				
Current expenditure on goods and services	164.8	106.8	0.0	271.6
Subsidies	4.4	1.8	0.0	6.2
Net social benefits	128.1	15.4	0.0	143.4
Net current grants abroad	-4.7	0.0	0.0	-4.7
Current grants (net) within public sector	100.1	-100.1	0.0	0.0
Other current grants	38.7	0.0	0.0	38.7
Interest and dividends paid	25.8	0.4	0.4	26.7
AME margin	0.0	0.0	0.0	0.0
Total current expenditure	**457.2**	**24.3**	**0.4**	**481.9**
Depreciation	5.9	5.6	4.1	15.6
Surplus on current budget	**-9.9**	**-2.1**	**0.5**	**-11.5**
Capital expenditure				
Gross domestic fixed capital formation	12.3	12.6	3.3	28.2
Less depreciation	-5.9	-5.6	-4.1	-15.6
Increase in inventories	0.2	0.0	0.0	0.2
Capital grants (net) within public sector	9.3	-8.8	-0.5	0.0
Capital grants to private sector	11.4	2.3	0.3	14.0
Capital grants from private sector	-0.3	-0.8	0.0	-1.1
AME margin	0.0	0.0	0.0	0.0
Net investment	**26.9**	**-0.3**	**-1.0**	**25.7**
Net borrowing	**36.9**	**1.8**	**-1.4**	**37.1**

Table C24: Public sector transactions by sub-sector and economic category

	£ billion			
	2006-07			
	General government			
	Central government	Local authorities	Public corporations	Public sector
Current receipts				
Taxes on income and wealth	195.6	0.0	-0.1	195.5
Taxes on production and imports	167.7	0.2	0.0	168.0
Other current taxes	8.2	21.1	0.0	29.3
Taxes on capital	3.6	0.0	0.0	3.6
Compulsory social contributions	90.6	0.0	0.0	90.6
Gross operating surplus	6.6	6.2	9.1	21.8
Rent and other current transfers	2.0	0.0	0.0	2.0
Interest and dividends from private sector and abroad	3.5	1.4	0.8	5.7
Interest and dividends from public sector	3.2	1.0	-4.1	0.0
Total current receipts	**480.9**	**29.8**	**5.7**	**516.4**
Current expenditure				
Current expenditure on goods and services	175.2	111.3	0.0	286.5
Subsidies	4.7	1.9	0.0	6.6
Net social benefits	131.5	16.0	0.0	147.4
Net current grants abroad	-3.8	0.0	0.0	-3.8
Current grants (net) within public sector	104.0	-104.0	0.0	0.0
Other current grants	41.9	0.0	0.0	41.9
Interest and dividends paid	26.3	0.4	0.4	27.2
AME margin	0.9	0.0	0.0	0.9
Total current expenditure	**480.6**	**25.6**	**0.4**	**506.7**
Depreciation	6.6	6.2	4.1	16.8
Surplus on current budget	**-6.3**	**-2.0**	**1.1**	**-7.0**
Capital expenditure				
Gross domestic fixed capital formation	14.7	13.7	3.5	31.9
Less depreciation	-6.6	-6.2	-4.1	-16.8
Increase in inventories	0.1	0.0	0.0	0.1
Capital grants (net) within public sector	9.9	-9.3	-0.6	0.0
Capital grants to private sector	11.8	2.5	0.3	14.6
Capital grants from private sector	-0.3	-0.9	0.0	-1.2
AME margin	0.1	0.0	0.0	0.1
Net investment	**29.8**	**-0.2**	**-0.8**	**28.8**
Net borrowing	**35.9**	**1.9**	**-2.0**	**35.8**

Table C25: Historical series of public sector balances, receipts and debt.

	Per cent of GDP								
	Public sector current budget	Cyclically adjusted surplus on current budget	Public sector net borrowing	Cyclically adjusted public sector net borrowing	Public sector net cash requirement	Net taxes and national insurance contributions	Public sector current receipts	Public sector net debt[1]	Public sector net worth[2]
1970-71	6.7		-0.6		1.2		43.3		
1971-72	4.2		1.1		1.4		41.4		
1972-73	2.0	2.5	2.8	2.3	3.6		39.0		
1973-74	0.3	-0.8	4.9	6.0	5.9		39.6		
1974-75	-1.1	-2.6	6.6	8.1	9.0		42.3	52.1	
1975-76	-1.6	-1.8	7.0	7.2	9.3		42.9	53.8	
1976-77	-1.2	-0.7	5.5	5.0	6.4		43.3	52.3	
1977-78	-1.4	-1.2	4.3	4.1	3.7		41.5	49.0	
1978-79	-2.6	-2.4	5.0	4.8	5.2	33.5	40.2	47.1	
1979-80	-1.9	-1.8	4.1	4.0	4.7	33.9	40.7	43.9	
1980-81	-3.0	-1.6	4.9	3.4	5.2	35.9	42.4	46.0	
1981-82	-1.4	2.5	2.3	-1.5	3.3	38.6	45.8	46.2	
1982-83	-1.5	2.8	3.0	-1.3	3.2	38.7	45.5	44.8	
1983-84	-2.0	1.7	3.8	0.1	3.2	38.2	44.4	45.1	
1984-85	-2.2	0.9	3.7	0.7	3.1	38.9	44.3	45.3	
1985-86	-1.2	0.6	2.4	0.6	1.6	38.1	43.2	43.5	
1986-87	-1.4	-1.2	2.1	1.9	0.9	37.8	42.0	41.0	
1987-88	-0.3	-1.6	1.0	2.3	-0.7	37.6	41.1	36.8	74.3
1988-89	1.7	-1.0	-1.3	1.3	-3.0	36.9	40.7	30.5	79.3
1989-90	1.4	-1.4	-0.2	2.6	-1.3	36.2	39.9	27.7	71.2
1990-91	0.4	-1.2	1.0	2.6	-0.1	35.9	38.9	26.2	60.6
1991-92	-2.0	-1.5	3.8	3.3	2.3	34.7	38.5	27.4	53.3
1992-93	-5.6	-3.6	7.6	5.6	5.9	33.7	36.6	32.0	40.4
1993-94	-6.2	-4.1	7.8	5.6	7.1	32.8	35.6	37.2	29.6
1994-95	-4.8	-3.5	6.3	4.9	5.3	34.0	36.7	40.8	28.7
1995-96	-3.4	-2.7	4.8	4.0	4.3	34.7	37.6	42.7	21.3
1996-97	-2.8	-2.3	3.5	3.1	2.9	34.8	37.0	43.6	17.3
1997-98	-0.2	0.0	0.8	0.7	0.2	36.0	38.1	41.4	14.4
1998-99	1.2	1.1	-0.4	-0.3	-0.7	36.4	38.6	39.3	13.5
1999-00	2.2	1.9	-1.7	-1.4	-0.9	36.4	38.9	36.3	16.7
2000-01	2.2	1.6	-1.6	-1.0	-3.8	37.2	39.6	31.4	22.5
2001-02	1.0	0.8	0.0	0.3	0.4	36.7	38.7	30.4	29.1
2002-03	-1.2	-0.8	2.4	2.0	2.4	35.3	37.3	31.8	27.9
2003-04	-1.9	-1.4	3.2	2.7	3.5	35.4	37.6	33.2	28.5
2004-05	-1.6	-1.3	3.4	3.0	3.3	36.2	38.3	35.0	29.1

[1] At end-March; GDP centred on end-March.

[2] At end-December; GDP centred on end-December.

Table C26: Historical series of government expenditure.

	£ billion (2004-05 prices)				Per cent of GDP			
	Public sector current expenditure	Public sector net investment	Public sector gross investment[1]	Total Managed Expenditure	Public sector current expenditure	Public sector net investment	Public sector gross investment[1]	Total Managed Expenditure
1970-71	172.7	32.4	53.1	225.8	32.6	6.1	10.0	42.7
1971-72	181.6	28.7	50.0	231.6	33.3	5.3	9.2	42.5
1972-73	189.0	27.5	49.8	238.8	33.1	4.8	8.7	41.9
1973-74	207.8	30.9	55.9	263.7	35.1	5.2	9.4	44.5
1974-75	229.9	32.7	59.5	289.4	38.8	5.5	10.0	48.9
1975-76	234.9	32.1	59.0	293.9	39.9	5.5	10.0	49.9
1976-77	242.1	26.3	54.2	296.3	39.9	4.3	8.9	48.8
1977-78	238.7	17.9	45.8	284.5	38.4	2.9	7.4	45.8
1978-79	245.8	15.5	44.1	289.9	38.4	2.4	6.9	45.3
1979-80	252.0	14.4	43.4	295.4	38.2	2.2	6.6	44.8
1980-81	259.4	11.6	40.9	300.3	40.8	1.8	6.4	47.3
1981-82	271.0	5.9	35.0	306.1	42.6	0.9	5.5	48.1
1982-83	276.8	9.7	38.0	314.8	42.7	1.5	5.9	48.5
1983-84	285.4	12.0	40.1	325.5	42.3	1.8	5.9	48.2
1984-85	293.6	10.6	37.3	330.9	42.6	1.5	5.4	48.0
1985-86	293.5	8.9	32.7	326.2	41.0	1.2	4.6	45.6
1986-87	298.0	5.3	29.5	327.5	40.1	0.7	4.0	44.1
1987-88	301.5	5.2	27.5	329.0	38.6	0.7	3.5	42.1
1988-89	294.3	2.9	25.9	320.2	36.2	0.4	3.2	39.4
1989-90	296.3	9.9	33.1	329.4	35.7	1.2	4.0	39.7
1990-91	298.1	11.9	32.1	330.3	36.1	1.4	3.9	40.0
1991-92	315.7	15.1	32.2	348.0	38.4	1.8	3.9	42.3
1992-93	331.5	16.5	32.6	364.1	40.2	2.0	3.9	44.2
1993-94	341.3	13.3	29.2	370.5	40.0	1.6	3.4	43.4
1994-95	352.0	12.9	29.4	381.5	39.7	1.5	3.3	43.0
1995-96	357.6	12.5	29.1	386.7	39.1	1.4	3.2	42.3
1996-97	358.1	6.9	21.6	379.7	38.3	0.7	2.3	40.6
1997-98	356.4	6.2	20.5	376.9	36.9	0.6	2.1	39.0
1998-99	358.8	7.5	21.2	379.9	36.1	0.8	2.1	38.2
1999-00	366.3	5.4	19.2	385.5	35.5	0.5	1.9	37.4
2000-01	385.7	6.3	20.3	406.0	36.2	0.6	1.9	38.1
2001-02	396.0	11.1	25.3	421.4	36.5	1.0	2.3	38.8
2002-03	414.2	12.7	27.5	441.6	37.3	1.1	2.5	39.8
2003-04	437.9	14.8	29.4	467.3	38.4	1.3	2.6	41.0
2004-05	455.4	20.7	35.6	491.0	38.7	1.8	3.0	41.7

[1] Net of sales of fixed assets.

CONVENTIONS USED IN PRESENTING THE PUBLIC FINANCES

FORMAT FOR THE PUBLIC FINANCES

The June 1998 Economic and Fiscal Strategy Report (EFSR), set out a new format for presenting the public finances that corresponded more closely to the two fiscal rules. The three principal measures are:

- the surplus on current budget (relevant to the golden rule);
- public sector net borrowing; and
- the public sector net debt ratio (relevant to the sustainable investment rule).

These measures are based on the national accounts and are consistent with the European System of Accounts 1995 (ESA95). Estimates and forecasts of the public sector net cash requirement (formerly called the public sector borrowing requirement) are still shown in the FSBR, but they are given less prominence.

The fiscal rules are similar to the criteria for deficits and debt laid down in the EU Treaty but there are important definitional differences:

- UK fiscal rules cover the whole public sector, whereas the Treaty deficit and debt only includes general (i.e. central and local) government;
- the fiscal rules apply over the whole economic cycle, not year to year;
- the current budget excludes capital spending, which is included in the Treaty deficit measure; and
- the UK debt measure is net of liquid assets, whereas the Treaty measure uses gross debt.

From February 2000 the Treaty deficit moved to being reported on an ESA95 basis.

NATIONAL ACCOUNTS

The national accounts record most transactions, including most taxes (although not corporation tax, self-assessment income tax and some other HMRC taxes which, because of practical difficulties, are scored on a cash basis) on an accruals basis, and impute the value of some transactions where no money changes hands (for example, non-trading capital consumption).

Full details of the sources for each table are included in Budget 2006 technical annex: data sources, available on the Treasury's internet site and on request from the Treasury's Public Enquiry Unit (020 72704558).

The outturn figures are based on series published in the monthly Public Sector Finance release (last published on 20 March 2006).

The principal measures drawn from the national accounts are described below.

FISCAL AGGREGATES

The current budget (formerly known as the current balance) measures the balance of current account revenue over current expenditure (including depreciation). The definition of the current budget presented in this chapter is very similar to the national accounts concept of net saving. It differs only in that it includes taxes on capital (mainly inheritance tax) in current rather than capital receipts. The current budget is used to measure progress against the golden rule. The actual measure is the average surplus on the current budget expressed as a ratio to GDP over the economic cycle.

Public sector net borrowing (formerly known as the financial deficit in the UK national accounts) is the balance between expenditure and income in the consolidated current and capital accounts. It differs from the public sector net cash requirement in that it is measured on an accruals basis and because certain fiscal transactions (notably net lending and net acquisition of other financial assets, which affect the level of borrowing but not the public sector's net financial indebtedness) are excluded from public sector net borrowing but included in the public sector net cash requirement.

Public sector net debt is approximately the stock analogue of the public sector net cash requirement. It measures the public sector's financial liabilities to the private sector and abroad, net of short-term financial assets such as bank deposits and foreign exchange reserves.

General government gross debt, the Treaty debt ratio, is the measure of debt used in the European Union's Excessive Deficit Procedure. As a general government measure, it excludes the debt of public corporations. It measures general government's total financial liabilities before netting off short-term financial assets.

Public sector net worth represents the public sector's overall net balance sheet position. It is equal to the sum of the public sector's financial and non-financial assets less its total financial liabilities. The estimates of tangible assets are subject to wide margins of error, because they depend on broad assumptions, for example about asset lives, which may not be appropriate in all cases. The introduction of resource accounting for central government departments will lead in time to an improvement in data quality, as audited information compiled from detailed asset registers becomes available.

PUBLIC SECTOR RECEIPTS

Net taxes and national insurance contributions (NTNIC) is a measure of net cash payments made to the UK government and differs in several respects from the national accounts measure of total public sector current receipts (PSCR). A reconciliation between the two aggregates is given in the lower half of Table C8. The main adjustments are:

- accruals adjustments, mainly on income tax, national insurance contributions and VAT, are added to change the basis of figures from cash to national accounts accruals;

- payments of customs duties and agricultural and sugar levies that are collected by the government, but then paid to the EU, are subtracted as they do not score as government receipts in the national accounts. These receipts make up the traditional own resources element of net payments to the EU;

- tax paid by public corporations is also subtracted, as it has no impact on overall public sector receipts;

- an adjustment is made for tax credits. In NTNIC, all tax credits are scored as negative tax to the extent that they are less than or equal to the tax liability of the household, and as public expenditure where they exceed the liability, in line with OECD Revenue Statistics guidelines. Although the ONS have adopted this treatment for the Working Tax Credit and Child Tax Credit, which were introduced in April 2003, they have continued to treat the Working Families' Tax Credit (WFTC), the Disabled Person's Tax Credit (DPTC) and enhanced and payable company tax credits entirely as public expenditure in the national accounts. Those parts of WFTC, DPTC and company tax credits that offset tax liability in NTNIC are added back into current receipts in Table C8;

- a similar adjustment is made for TV licences, which the ONS treat as tax receipts in the national accounts. They score as non-tax receipts in NTNIC, in line with OECD Revenue Statistics guidelines;

- interest and other non-tax receipts, which are excluded from NTNIC, are added. This excludes oil royalties, as they are already included in NTNIC, even though the national accounts treat them as non-tax receipts; and

- business rates paid by local authorities are included in the calculation of NTNIC but not PSCR. These are therefore deducted from NTNIC before arriving at PSCR.

TOTAL MANAGED EXPENDITURE

Public expenditure is measured across the whole of the public sector using the aggregate Total Managed Expenditure (TME). TME is the sum of public sector current expenditure, public sector net investment and public sector depreciation. These aggregates are based on national accounts definitions defined under ESA95.

Public sector current expenditure is the sum of expenditure on pay and related costs, plus spending on goods and services, and current grants made to the private sector. Current expenditure is net of receipts from sales of goods and services.

Public sector capital expenditure is shown in Table C15. It includes:

- gross domestic fixed capital formation (i.e. expenditure on fixed assets such as schools and hospitals, roads, computers, plant and machinery and intangible assets) net of receipts from sales of fixed assets (e.g. council houses and surplus land);

- grants in support of capital expenditure in the private sector; and

- the value of the physical increase in stocks (for central government, primarily agricultural commodity stocks).

Public sector net investment in Table C1 nets off depreciation of the public sector's stock of fixed assets.

Public sector depreciation is the annual charge that is made in relation to the reduction in value of the public sector's capital assets over a particular financial year.

For budgeting purposes, TME is further split into DEL and AME:

Departmental Expenditure Limits (DEL) are firm three-year spending limits for departments. In general DEL will cover all running costs and all programme expenditure except spending that is included in departmental AME due to it not being reasonably subject to close control over the three-year period. DEL has distinct resource and capital budgets, as shown in Table C13.

Annually Managed Expenditure (AME) is spending that cannot be reasonably subject to firm multi-year limits. AME components are shown in Table C11 and are defined as follows.

Social security benefits in AME expenditure covers contributory, non-contributory and income-related benefits for children, people of working age and pensioners. Broadly, benefits are paid in respect of retirement, unemployment, or disability, caring responsibilities and bereavement, as well as housing costs for all groups with effect from Budget 2004. Some expenditure on housing-related benefits is, however, covered by the locally financed expenditure category.

Tax credits for individuals scored as expenditure includes spending on the Working Families' Tax Credit (WFTC) and Disabled Person's Tax Credit (DPTC) and that element of the Working Tax Credit and the Child Tax Credit that is classified as public expenditure under national accounts definitions.

Net public service pensions expenditure is reported on a national accounts basis and represents the difference between the cash paid out during the year and any contributions received for the main unfunded public service pension schemes.

National Lottery expenditures relate to the distribution of the money received from the National Lottery for good causes. Funds are drawn down by distributing bodies and directed towards Lottery funded projects.

BBC domestic services includes the current and capital spending of the BBC home broadcasting service (that is the BBC excluding the World Service and its commercial subsidiaries).

Other departmental expenditure aggregates all other expenditure made by departments that is not separately identified in the AME table.

Net expenditure transfers to EU institutions include the AME spending component of the UK's contribution to the EU, comprising the Gross National Income (GNI) based contribution less the UK abatement. The other components of UK net payments to EU institutions are either included in DEL, or in public sector current receipts (VAT based contribution). Some contributions, such as CAP expenditure and receipts, have no impact on public sector fiscal aggregates as they score as direct transactions between the EU and farmers in national accounts.

Locally financed expenditure consists of local authority self-financed expenditure (LASFE) and Scottish spending financed by local taxation (non-domestic rates and, if and when levied, the Scottish variable rate of income tax). LASFE is the difference between total local authority expenditure, including most gross debt but net of capital receipts, and central government support to local authorities (i.e. Aggregate External Finance (AEF), specific grants and credit approvals).

Central government debt interest is shown gross, only interest paid within the public sector is netted off. All other receipts of interest and dividends are included in current receipts. The capital uplift on index-linked gilts is also scored here as interest at the time it accrues as is the amortisation of discounts on gilts at issue.

Public corporations' own-financed capital expenditure. This is the amount of capital expenditure by public corporations that is not financed by general government.

AME margin is an unallocated margin on total AME spending and is included as a measure of caution against AME expenditure exceeding its forecast levels.

The accounting adjustments reconcile the DEL and AME framework of departmental budgets to the national accounts measure of TME, and are shown in Table C14:

Tax credits adds in spending on individuals' tax credits which is scored as negative tax in net taxes and national insurance contributions but as public expenditure in national accounts. As explained in the public sector current receipts section this mainly includes elements of company tax credits and WFTC and DPTC, which were replaced by new tax credits in 2003-04.

Other central government programmes covers various items which relate to central government programme expenditure and where budgeting and national accounts treatment differ, for example the depreciation costs of NHS Trusts and tax credits for companies.

VAT refunds adds back refunds obtained by central government departments, local authorities and certain public corporations. DEL and AME programme expenditure are measured net of these refunds, while TME is recorded with VAT paid.

Central government non-trading capital consumption (i.e. depreciation) as measured by the ONS for national accounts is added.

Non-cash items in resource budgets and not in TME includes cost of capital charge, write-offs, notional audit fee, take-up, movements in the value, and release of provisions, the subsidy and bad debt element of student loans, and movement in stocks.

Expenditure financed by revenue receipts adds in certain receipts which are deducted from departmental budgets but which are not treated as negative expenditure in TME.

Local authorities adds in local authority depreciation and subsidies paid to local authority trading bodies, and deducts capital grants from local authorities to public corporations, local authority receipts of investment grants from private sector developers and certain license fees collected by local authorities.

General government consolidation adjusts for the fact that payments of certain taxes, grants and interest that are within the public sector do not score in TME, as TME is a consolidated public sector concept.

Public corporations adds receipts from public corporations of interest, dividends and equity withdrawals that are netted-off in budgets, interest paid by public corporations to the private sector and abroad (as property income paid by the public sector to the rest of the economy is in TME, but not in departmental budgets) and deducts the profit or loss of the Forestry Enterprise.

Financial transactions deducts net lending, acquisition of securities and profit or loss on sale of financial assets.

Other accounting adjustments deducts depreciation and impairments in AME and the cost of over 75 TV licences in AME social security as these represent payments within central government, from DWP to BBC. An adjustment is also made to reconcile to actual and expected national accounts outturn.

LIST OF ABBREVIATIONS

ADB	African Development Bank
AEF	Aggregate External Finance
AfDF	African Development Fund
AFPRB	Armed Forces Pay Review Body
AHC	After housing costs
AIDS	Acquired Immunodeficiency Syndrome
AMC	Advanced Market Commitment
AME	Annually Managed Expenditure
AMLD	Amusement machine licence duty
APD	Air passenger duty
APR	Annual Percentage Rates
ASP	Alternatively secured pension
BCC	British Chamber of Commerce
BHC	Before housing costs
BNFL	British Nuclear Fuels Plc
BP	British Petroleum
BRC	Better Regulation Commission
BRE	Better Regulation Executive
BREW	Business Resource Efficiency and Waste
BRTF	Better Regulation Task Force
CAP	Common Agricultural Policy
CBI	Confederation of British Industry
CBO	US Congressional Budget Office
CC	Competition Commission
CCAs	Climate change agreements
CCL	Climate change levy
CCPR	Climate Change Programme Review
CCS	Carbon capture and storage
CEO	Chief Executive Officer
CGNCR	Central government net cash requirement
CIPFA	Chartered Institute of Public Finance and Accountancy
CIPS	Chartered Institute of Purchasing and Supply
CMPO	Centre for Market and Public Organisation
CO2	Carbon dioxide
COMPS	Contracted out money purchase schemes
COSRS	Contracted out salary related schemes
CoVE	Centres of Vocational Excellence
CPI	Consumer Prices Index
CSR	Comprehensive Spending Review
CTC	Child Tax Credit
CVS	Corporate Venturing Scheme
DAC	Development Assistance Committee
DEFRA	Department for Environment, Food and Rural Affairs
DEL	Departmental Expenditure Limit
DfES	Department for Education and Skills
DfID	Department for International Development
DfT	Department for Transport
DH	Department of Health

DMO	Debt Management Office
DPTC	Disabled Person's Tax Credit
DTI	Department of Trade and Industry
DVLA	Driver and Vehicle Licensing Agency
DWP	Department for Work and Pensions
DWPA	Diffuse water pollution from agriculture
EC	European Communities
ECA	Enhanced Capital Allowance
ECF	Enterprise Capital Fund
EEA	European Economic Area
EEC	Energy Efficiency Commitment
EFSR	Economic and Fiscal Strategy Report
EIS	Enterprise Investment Scheme
EMBI	Emerging Market Bond Index
EMDA	East Midlands Development Agency
EPC	Economic Policy Committee
ERA	Employment Retention and Advancement
ERP	Energy Research Partnership
ESA95	European System of Accounts 1995
EU	European Union
EU ETS	EU Emissions Trading Scheme
FDI	Foreign direct investment
FE	Further Education
FJR	Fortnightly Job Review
FRS	Financial Reporting Standard
FSA	Financial Services Authority
FSBR	Financial Statement and Budget Report
FSMA	Financial Services and Markets Act
FTI	Fast Track Initiative
G7	A group of seven major industrial nations (comprising: Canada, France, Germany, Italy, Japan, UK and US).
G8	A group of eight major industrial nations (comprising: Canada, France, Germany, Italy, Japan, UK ,US and Russia).
GAAP	Generally Accepted Accounting Practices
GAD	Government Actuary's Department
GCSE	General Certificate of Secondary Education
GDP	Gross Domestic Product
GGNB	General government net borrowing
G/KM	Grams per kilometer
GLA	Greater London Authority
GNI	Gross National Income
GO	Government Offices
GP	General Practitioner
GVA	Gross Value Added
HGV	Heavy Goods Vehicles
HIPC	Heavily Indebted Poor Countries
HIT	Housing investment trusts
HIV	Human immunodeficiency virus
HMRC	Her Majesty's Revenue and Customs

HMT	Her Majesty's Treasury
IAS	International Accounting Standards
ICT	Information and Communications Technology
IDA	International Development Association
IEA	International Energy Agency
IFF	International Finance Facility
IFFIm	International Finance Facility for Immunisation
IFS	Institute for Fiscal Studies
ILO	International Labour Organisation
IMF	International Monetary Fund
IOC	International Olympic Committee
IP	Intellectual property
IPA	Initial Performance Assessment
IPCC	Intergovernmental Panel on Climate Change
IS	Income Support
ISA	Individual Savings Account
ISB	Invest to Save Budget
ITSW	International Trade Single Window
IWC	In Work Credit
JSA	Jobseeker's Allowance
LAA	Local Area Agreements
LABGI	Local Authority Business Growth Incentive
LASFE	Local authority self-financed expenditure
LATS	Landfill Allowance Trading Scheme
LBRO	Local Business Regulation Office
LDA	London Development Agency
LEGI	Local Enterprise Growth Initiative
LEL	Lower earnings limit
LESA	Landlords' Energy Saving Allowance
LFS	Labour Force Survey
LHA	Local Housing Allowance
LPG	Liquified petroleum gas
LPL	Lower profits limit
LTCS	Landfill Tax Credit Scheme
LSC	Learning and Skills Council
MDGs	Millennium Development Goals
MDRs	Marginal deduction rates
MDRI	Multilateral Debt Relief Initiative
MIG	Minimum Income Guarantee
MoD	Ministry of Defence
MORI	Market and Opinion Research International
MPC	Monetary Policy Committee
MtC	Million tonnes of carbon
MTIC	Missing Trader Intra-Community
NAO	National Audit Office
NCIS	National Criminal Intelligence Service
NDDP	New Deal for disabled people
NDLP	New Deal for lone parents

NDLP+	New Deal Plus for lone parents
NDP	New Deal for partners
NDYP	New Deal for young people
NEP	National Employment Panel
NEET	Not in education, employment or training
NG	Natural gas
NHS	National Health Service
NICs	National Insurance Contributions
NIESR	National Institute of Economic and Social Research
NTNIC	Net taxes and national insurance contributions
NVQ	National Vocational Qualification
NWDA	North West Development Agency
ODA	Overseas Development Assistance
ODPM	Office of the Deputy Prime Minister
OECD	Organisation for Economic Cooperation and Development
OFCOM	Office of Communications
OFGEM	Office of Gas and Electricity Markets
OFT	Office of Fair Trading
OGC	Office of Government Commerce
ONE	One North East
ONS	Office of National Statistics
OPEC	Organisation of Petroleum Exporting Countries
PAC	Public Accounts Committee
PAYE	Pay as you earn
PCSO	Police Community Support Officers
PCT	Primary Care Trust
PEP	Personal Equity Plan
PFI	Private Finance Initiative
PGS	Planning-gain Supplement
PPF	Pension Protection Fund
PPS3	Planning Policy Statement for Housing
PRA	Panel for Regulatory Accountability
PRB	Panel Review Body
PRGF	Poverty Reduction and Growth Facility
PSA	Public Service Agreement
PSCR	Public sector current receipts
PSNB	Public sector net borrowing
PSPC	Public Sector Pay Committee
PSNI	Public sector net investment
PSPC	Public Sector Pay Committee
PT	Primary threshold
QC	Queen's Counsel
QR	Quality-Related
R&D	Research and Development
RAE	Research Assessment Exercise
RDA	Regional Development Agency
REACH	Registration Evaluation and Authorisation of Chemicals
REITs	Real Estate Investment Trusts

RES	Regional Economic Strategies
RPC	Reduced pollution certificate
RPI	Retail Prices Index
RPIX	Retail Prices Index excluding mortgage interest payments
RTFO	Renewable Transport Fuels Obligation
S2P	State Second Pension
SBS	Small Business Service
SBRI	Small Business Research Initiative
SCS	Senior Civil Service
SEE	Small Earnings Exception
SEEDA	South East England Development Agency
SEEN	Schools Enterprise Education Network
SERPS	State Earnings Related Pension Scheme
SFLG	Small Firms Loan Guarantee
SHA	Strategic Health Authority
SI	Statutory Instrument
SIVA	Simplified import VAT accounting
SME	Small and medium-sized enterprise
SSG	School Standards Grant
SSRB	Senior Salaries Review Body
ST	Secondary threshold
STEM	Science Technology Engineering and Mathematics
TB	Tuberculosis
TIF	Transport Innovation Fund
TME	Total Managed Expenditure
TMO	Tenant Management Organisations
UEL	Upper earnings limit
UKTI	UK Trade and Investment
UN	United Nations
UNCTAD	United Nations Conference on Trade and Development
UPL	Upper profits limit
VAT	Value Added Tax
VCT	Venture Capital Trust
VDU	Visual Display Unit
VED	Vehicle excise duty
VI	Voluntary initiative
W&TA	Wear and Tear Allowance
WASD	Working Age Statistical Database
WCC	Women and Work Commission
WEO	World Economic Outlook
WFI	Work Focused Interview
WFTC	Working Families' Tax Credit
WTC	Working Tax Credit
WTO	World Trade Organisation
YF	Yorkshire Forward

LIST OF TABLES

Economic and Fiscal Strategy Report

Financial Statement and Budget Report

LIST OF CHARTS

Economic and Fiscal Strategy Report

Financial Statement and Budget Report

Cover photography:
www.third-avenue.co.uk (four images)
Mauro Fermariello/Science Photo Library
www.johnbirdshall.co.uk (two images)
Colin Edwards/Photofusion
Janine Wiedel Photolibrary/Alamy
Alan Edwards/British Gymnastics Association
Gertjan Hooijer/Istock photo.com
Peter Skinner/Science Photo Library

**Printed in the UK by The Stationery Office Limited
on behalf of the Controller of Her Majesty's Stationery Office
ID 186072   03/06**